# THE WEST GERMAN ECONOMY

# THE WEST GERMAN ECONOMY

ERIC OWEN SMITH

ST. MARTIN'S PRESS
New York

© 1983 E. Owen Smith
All rights reserved. For information write:
St. Martin's Press, Inc., 175 Fifth Avenue, New York, N.Y. 10010
Printed in Great Britain
First published in the United States of America in 1983

Library of Congress Cataloging in Publication Data

Owen Smith, E.
    The West German economy.

    1. Germany (West)--Economic conditions. I. Title.
HC286.5.093    1983        330.943'0878      83-8630
ISBN 0-312-86290-3

CONTENTS

*Contents*

# Contents

DIAGRAMS, FIGURES AND TABLES

To June, Daniel and Rebecca

PREFACE

The West German economy is studied by undergraduates
reading the final year European Economics option at
Loughborough University. When I started to teach the
course it soon became apparent that there was no comprehensive and up-to-date English text dealing with
the various aspects of one of the world's most important economies. The origins of this book therefore
lie in what became a constant need to present and
analyse data on both macro and micro economic trends
in the German economy. (Other material appeared in
the chapter on West Germany in *Trade Unions in the
Developed Economies*, a volume edited by the present
writer and published by Croom Helm in 1981.)

Several colleagues kindly commented on the drafts
of various parts of the book. In most cases they are
specialists in a particular field of their discipline,
rather than in West German affairs. However, they
were all able, by virtue of their expertise, to make
several incisive comments. It is therefore a pleasure
to formally record my gratitude, in the order in which
the relevant material appears in this book, to: Joyce
Ellis, Shaun Stewart, Peter Maunder, Peter Dawkins,
John Piper, Tony Westaway, Sue Charles, Max Hall,
Peter Lawrence, Brian Tew and Dennis Swann. In addition, a Federal government official and a senior
manager in a West German bank kindly supplied some
valuable material. An anonymous referee also made
some very useful comments. I am, of course, responsible for any remaining errors.

Also at Loughborough University, Graham Gerrard
and Max Hunt of the Computer Centre gave me valuable
advice on the use of computing facilities. Diagrams
originally supplied by the University's AVS Unit for
research papers have been re-used in this book, while
Mary Morley and Mike Hopkins of the University Library
obtained extremely useful material and detailed

references.

In addition, I am very grateful to the British Academy, the German Academic Exchange Service and the SSRC/DFG for financing study visits to the Federal Republic. Various members of staff at Mannheim and Freiburg Universities - particularly Professors Gaugler, Herberg and Külp - were very considerate hosts during these visits. The British Embassy in Bonn arranged fruitful visits to a number of organisations. It would be invidious to select any one of the many friendly representatives of these organisations for a special word of thanks. Suffice it to say that without exception I was received in a courteous and most helpful manner. It must again be emphasised, however, that I am solely responsible for the contents of this book.

Mrs Gloria Brentnall again provided expert secretarial skills. As this was also the first joint-venture in camera-ready techniques, I am particularly grateful for her indefatigable attempts to realise the desired location of diagrams, figures and tables.

As in the past, I would like to thank my wife and family for their support. Indeed, I would like to dedicate this book to June, Daniel and Rebecca.

Eric Owen Smith

# THE WEST GERMAN ECONOMY

Chapter One

INTRODUCTION

## SOME GENERAL CONSIDERATIONS

The purpose of this opening chapter is not only to
make some general introductory observations, but also
to emphasise the themes to be analysed in the rest of
the book.
This book traces the main macro- and micro-
economic trends and developments in West Germany
during the period 1950-1980. Where possible policy
implications for the 1980s are indicated. The book
also contains an analysis of the economic conditions
and recovery after the Second World War.
Readers of an English survey of this nature will
either require a fairly general treatment of the
topic as a whole, or will want to use parts of the
book as a starting point for an in-depth investigation of a particular issue. Hence the references
selected, full details of which appear in the Bibliography, are confined where possible to publications in English. Two further criteria for the
selection of references have been employed. First,
the need to guide the reader to sources which either
contain detailed references, or which, secondly,
place differing emphases and interpretations on
policy-making. At the same time, one must not lose
sight of the requirements of the more general reader.
With this in mind, the number of references is
minimised and the contemporary method of bracketing
them within the text is employed. In addition, each
chapter is designed to be as self-contained as
possible, while the contents of each chapter are
listed by section at the beginning of the book. It
will also be seen from the contents that there is an
introduction and conclusion to each of the chapters.
Some key statistical sources are mentioned in
the text and fuller details are again to be found in

1

the Bibliography.  It is also hoped that the sources
quoted at the foot of the various tables and diagrams
may be useful to the reader who is beginning a highly
detailed search.  Full details of the location of
these tables and diagrams appear at the beginning of
the book.
 For the most part, the present theoretical dis-
putations in Economics have been avoided.  This is
not only due to the lack of space, but also to the
need to present a straightforward appraisal of what
has actually happened in the West German economy during the period under review.  In particular, when it
comes to the role played by the social market
economy, the reader is presented with the model and
left to judge from the evidence.  This is because
there is already sufficient dogma at both ends of the
political spectrum as to how the model operated in
practice.
 Another important set of policy changes was
almost certain to occur while the book was entering
its final form.  One refers here to the instability,
and eventual collapse, of the Federal SPD/FDP
coalition.  But the policy problems for the 1980s
outlined in this book will not change in character.
For this reason actual data for 1981 and predictions
for the rest of the decade have been included where
possible.
 Chapters 1 to 3 inclusive are somewhat general
in character.  This is because they serve a dual
introductory purpose.  First, they are intended to
introduce the reader to the features of the West
German economy explored in depth later in the book.
Second, they are intended to set the period 1950-
1980 in a broader historical context, particularly in
terms of the nature of the post-Second World War
economic recovery.
 The detailed analysis of the West German economy
during the period 1950-1980 therefore commences in
Chapters 4 and 5.  Both of these chapters mainly
concentrate on the macro-economic aspects of the
review period.  In Chapter 4, economic trends are
reviewed, while in Chapter 5 economic policies are
examined.  This enables the writer to then concentrate on the various micro-economic aspects which
appear later in the book.  The topics covered in the
later chapters are the labour market (Chapter 6),
ownership and control (Chapter 7), banking (Chapter
8) and the industrial sector (Chapter 9).  Regional
policy is discussed in Chapter 6, while banking and
anti-trust policies are analysed in Chapters 8 and 9
respectively.

There are, however, a number of features of the
German Economy which must be emphasised.  These
features are therefore analysed in the next section.

THE GERMAN ECONOMY IN PERSPECTIVE

Six features are abolutely crucial to an understand-
ing of the German economy:

1. Changing frontiers.
2. Hyper-inflation and currency reforms.
3. A high rate of technical advance in
   industries with a high export potential.
4. A legal framework which was conducive to
   a high degree of business concentration,
   and thus the derivation of large economies
   of scale.
5. A banking sector geared to active participation in the industrial sector.
6. Active involvement by the State in economic
   and social affairs.

Since these variables have been discontinuous in
nature they operated recurrently but not necessarily
concurrently.  That is why the long-term development
of the German economy could be described (by para-
phrasing Mann, p.16) as a 'restless oscillation
between extremes'.  The convulsions and changes in
the German nation's political, social and economic
life have influenced the evolution of her institutions (Stingl, p.199).  In two centuries (1780-
1980) the German nation developed from a large
geographical area of 1,789 territories into 38 states
after the Napoleonic wars, then into one and ultimately two major economic powers.  Although decentralised decision-making in economic policy was to
continue to play a role, the initial political and
cultural complexity of Germany gradually disappeared
during the early 19th century (Schöller, p.5).
German unification proceeded more rapidly, though
not completely, under Bismarck.  Complete national
unity was established under Hitler.  After the
Second World War the nation was split again.  The
economic fluctuations which accompanied these wide-
ranging political changes were effectively even more
condensed.  In terms of the above six variations,
German economic development spans only one century.
During this century, there have been three
phases (four if one includes the early Nazi era) of
dramatic economic growth.  In the first period

(1871-1913) an hitherto tardy process of industrialisation was so transformed that Germany became the
leading industrial state on the continent.  This
achievement was in spite of inflation, a badly
bungled currency reform and company collapses in the
early 1870s (Henderson, pp.162 and 170).  It was
1876 before industrial output recovered to 1872
levels, but total German industrial production over-
took that of France in the 1870s, caught up with
Britain about 1900 and surpassed her substantially by
1910.  Indeed, by 1910 the German economy was second
only to that of the United States in terms of industrial production (Mann, p.335; Stolper, pp.34-35).
She came to challenge Britain's supremacy in the
markets of the world.  Britain's international share
in the output of manufactured goods decreased while
Germany's relative share increased.  Some observers
were 'alarmed' at this invasion of what during the
19th century had become Britain's traditional markets
(Henderson, p.173).
    Secondly, the Golden Twenties (1924-1929) saw a
remarkable recovery of the German economy.  When compared to the preceding inflation and the subsequent
Great Depression, there is little wonder that this
period is seen in retrospect as 'golden'.  Thirdly,
there was the so-called 'Economic Miracle' of 1949-
1960.  Here again there was bound to be an element of
contrast to the immediate post-1945 period, rather
like the early Hitler period after the Great Depression.  Almost any economic system and policy
would have been successful in resusitating the economy somewhat.
    As already implied, during this century Germany
has also known economic chaos, collapse and depression.  Again three periods can be isolated:
1914-1923, 1930-1932 and 1945-1948.  At the end of
these periods industrial production stood at about
half of that achieved at the end of the previous
booms (Mendershausen, p.6).
    Today, the Federal Republic of Germany - that
part of the German nation on whose economy this book
is based - has achieved living standards which are
among the world's highest, inflation rates which are
consistently among the world's lowest and exports
which are again impressively successful.  To ignore
the long-term fluctuations in economic development
would be, however, to ignore a fundamental feature of
German economic life.  It is the degree of collapse
and turbulence followed by Pheonix-like, spectacular
recoveries which represent the most significant aspects of long-term economic development.  (Post-

Second World War cyclical fluctuations are also relevant and these will be investigated below.) Since this book is principally concerned with the period 1950-1980, only one period of recovery is strictly relevant. However, the nature of that recovery cannot be fully understood unless various aspects of the preceding collapse are appreciated. In order to gain this sense of perspective, therefore, this book commences with overviews of both the 1945-1948 collapse and the 1949-1960 reovery. Where possible brief reference to parallels in economic development will be made. Many of these themes will then be applied to the period 1950-1980.

Chapter Two

ECONOMIC POLICY DURING THE ALLIED OCCUPATION

INTRODUCTION

German economic development reached a nadir during
this period. Frontier changes, another currency
collapse, economic dislocation, food, fuel and housing shortages, were all consequences of a total war
which this time, in its latter stages, had been
fought on German soil. Even the position at the end
of the First World War hardly bears comparison. This
time there was to be a somewhat different approach to
reparations, but initially the so-called Morgenthau
Plan (1944) contained proposals to re-convert Germany
to an agricultural economy (Henning, pp.187-188;
Knapp, p.417; Stolper, p.210). This plan was later
modified in 1946 so that a very broadly defined group
of industries with a military potential were prohibited. Along with other restrictions on output levels
this would put Germany back to 55 per cent of the
industrial production attained in 1938 - in other
words back to 1931! (Henning, p.189; OEEC, p.9).
Industrial plant was to be dismantled and taken as
reparation payments. Moreover, ownership and influence in industry were to be deconcentrated. Not only
were such fundamental reforms inherently unworkable,
but the gradual transition from enemy to western ally
meant that West Germany would have to be a powerful
economic partner and showpiece of western capitalism.

FRONTIER CHANGES

Just as on the formation of the Second and Third
Reichs (1871 and 1933), and after the First World
War, there were, once again, highly significant frontier changes. Territorial losses immediately following the Second World War amounted to 25 per cent of

the area of the Third Reich. The area of Greater
Germany formed since 1937 disappeared: Sudentland was
returned to Czechoslovakia; Austria regained her
independence; Luxembourg was allowed to join the
Benelux customs union; France took back Alsace and
Lorraine and again obtained effective sovereignty
over the Saar; in addition, Poland was given land up
to the Oder/Neisse line to compensate for the loss of
its eastern territories to the Russians (Mellor,
pp.131-134). Hence the Upper Silesian coal, zinc and
lead deposits were returned to Poland. German
nationals living in the eastern areas of the former
Reich were expelled. Moreover, the Russian zone of
occupation was to become the German Democratic Republic, and the area occupied by the British,
American and French the Federal Republic of Germany.
This latter area covered 48 per cent of the pre-war
Reich. In area it was 246,000 km², including Berlin,
compared to a Weimar Republic's area of 470,000; the
consequential reductions in population after each war
were 43 and 10 per cent respectively (Henning, pp.52
and 184; Mendershausen, p.25). But the population of
West Germany (44 million in 1946) was rapidly aug-
mented by a large influx of destitute expellees from
the former eastern areas of the Third Reich and
refugees from the eastern zone. By 1965 there were
to be over 14 million expellees and refugees in what
by then was the Federal Republic, a figure which
represented over 22 per cent of the population
(Mellor, p.189).

Those refugees who arrived in the west during
this early post-war period increased the strain on
the already extremely scarce food, housing, fuel and
transport resources. For these reasons, the refugees
followed the drift of the populations of the bigger
cities to the countryside. Two-thirds of the refugees initially settled in areas which possessed only
a quarter of the industrial capacity of the economy.
This tendency was particularly significant in the
chiefly agricultural Schleswig-Holstein where the
influx of refugees and homeless persons caused a rise
of 70 per cent in the local population. Nationally,
daily calorie intake in 1946 had on average fallen to
1,451 per person from 3,113 in 1936. By 1947 and
1948 agricultural production had fallen to 72 per
cent of its 1939 level. Even with strict rationing
only 60 per cent of food requirements could be met
from domestic sources (Grosser, p.83; Henning, p.191).
Food intake therefore reached average levels below
the subsistence standard (Manchester, p.682). There
was some hoarding and, as one would expect, the

situation in rural areas was not as acute as in the
cities. There was a grotesque spectacle of masses of
people trekking into the countryside in order to
barter for food. Hunger strikes took place in 1947
and a general strike was also demanded, although this
demand was successfully opposed by Hans Böckler, the
chairman of the re-emerged trade union federation.
Because of Allied bombing, the same kind of
shortages obtained in both housing and transport.
Bombing, it should be emphasised, did *not* have the
same effect on industry, as will shortly be shown.
In the last phases of the war, the whole German
transport system - rail, road and inland waterways -
had been systematically destroyed. The economy therefore disintegrated into a series of local and regional
sub-economies. There had already been housing shortages both during the Golden Twenties and the Nazi era
(Guillebaud, 1971, p.16, and 1939, p.146). But these
shortages were vastly exacerbated by the Second World
War. In the larger cities two-thirds of the housing
stock lay in ruins. The influx of refugees exacerbated the situation so that every third family did
not possess a dwelling.
  The energy crisis resulted mainly from a shortage of coal. Indeed, this was the principal shortage
which constrained economic activity in general. It
was caused in part by the compulsory exports, made at
below world prices, which were required by the Allies.
Clearly, the shortages in transport and the under-
nourished labour force in the industrial areas were
further constraints. Moreover, 17 per cent of
Germany's coal producing capacity had been lost to
Poland. The Saar had again become closely integrated
into the French economy. In the particularly bad
1946-47 winter deaths per 1,000 of the population
were 10 per cent higher than in the following years
(Henning, p.192).


INFLATION AND CURRENCY REFORM

All these shortages contributed to the collapse of
the currency. Another contributory factor lay in the
attempts of the Allies to maintain the wage and price
control first imposed by the Nazis in 1936. Food,
clothing and energy shortages resulted in a black
market in which prices were approximately between 20
and 100 times the legal prices. In these circumstances, the Reichsmark tended to lose its function
as a means of exchange, and confidence in the
currency was undermined (Stolper, p.238). Barter

became widespread - especially against Allied ciga-
rettes. Monetary imbalance, in contrast to the
Weimar inflation, was reduced by these and other
factors, since the black market either absorbed the
excess money supply where illegal prices were higher
than legal ones, or reduced the velocity of circulation where money substitutes were used. The
velocity of circulation during the Weimar inflation
had displayed a considerable rise. Hence, the
Weimar inflation was *open* while the post-1945 one was
*supressed*. From 1945 to 1948 there was no central
bank in Germany, and, of course, the whole country
was occupied. The Reichsbank of the early 1920s was
a mere tool of hard pressed governments which borrowed to maintain themselves in power and, finally,
to finance the passive resistance in the Ruhr by
giving social security benefits to strikers protest-
ing against the French occupation (MBR, p.24;
Mendershausen, p.34). In 1923 the German mark was
traded against other currencies on international and
German markets, its international exchange rate
against the dollar eventually reaching 4.2 trillion
(= $4.2 \times 10^{12}$). After 1945 there were no quotations
for the Reichsmark on the international markets and
all trading against foreign currencies ceased
(Backer, p.91). The German currency and economy were
therefore largely isolated from the outside world
after the Second World War. Both inflations were, of
course, economic and social disasters: for example,
the retail price index increased by 244 per cent in
1920, 65 per cent in 1921, 2,420 per cent in 1922 and
over 1.8 billion (= $1.8 \times 10^9$) per cent in 1923
(Henning, p.66).

Because the policy implications of the Weimar
and post-Nazi inflations are of crucial relevance to
post-Second World War central banking and national
debt policy, a slight digression is in order at this
stage.

Increases in both the money supply and national
debt were, in the last analysis, historically attributable to monetary and fiscal policies (Bresciani-
Turroni, p.400; but also see Laursen and Pedersen,
pp.78 and 123). Because the constituent states of
the Second Reich and the early Weimar Republic
reserved the power to raise taxes until 1920, the
Reich government sought to finance the First World
War by borrowing and in effect obliging the Reichsbank to increase the money supply (Flink, p.37;
Hardach, pp.11 and 18). In total, the war debt
reached RM 164 billion. Later, the astronomic
increase of the money supply during the hyper-

inflation was attributable to the Weimar government's
method of financing the budgetary deficits - to pay
for the war and the recovery - and the balance of
payments deficits arising from reparation payments.
Both deficits were financed through the Reichsbank,
again by discounting treasury bills at the Reichsbank
and obtaining the equivalent amount in banknotes or
claims upon the Reichsbank. In the few months before
the currency collapsed, 300 paper mills and 150 printing works with 2,000 presses worked night and day to
produce bank notes (Stolper, p.100). The national
debt on 15 November 1923 stood at 191.5 quintillion
marks (= 191.5 x $10^{18}$, see Henning, p.70). Moreover,
the Reichsbank later became a totally subservient tool
of the Nazi government. From 1935 to 1945 the German
currency in circulation increased from RM 5 billion to
RM 50 billion and bank deposits from RM 30 billion to
RM 150 billion. Without taking the war damage and
war-connected claims of RM 350 billion into account,
government debt had risen from RM 15 billion to
RM 400 billion. Yet Germany's national real wealth
decreased by one-third between 1935 and 1945.

Returning to the period 1945-48, it is apparent
that the complete collapse of confidence in the
currency, and the breakdown of public finance, meant
monetary and fiscal reforms were essential conditions
for recovery. Under the system of decentralised
public finance established by the Allies, powers to
implement expenditure programmes and control tax
revenue were placed mainly in the hands of the
state (*Länder*) governments (Shonfield, p.268;
Wallich, pp.158-159). Such a move effectively put
the fiscal clock back to the days of the Second Reich,
when Bismarck had tried in vain to establish independent sources of tax revenue for the central government. The decentralising influence of the Allies was
also evident in central bank reform (Reuss, p.51).
During 1947 and 1948 the Allies in the western zones
established a system of central banks in each of the
Länder to replace the branches of the former Reichsbank. The Bank deutscher Länder (Frankfurt) was
added to this decentralised system in March 1948.
The Allies gave the Bank deutscher Länder, predecessor of the Deutsche Bundesbank, considerable legal
autonomy and a substantial degree of operational
independence from the later-established Federal
Government (Hardach, p.153).

A contraction of the money supply and the re-
organisation of public and private debt were now
required. On 20/21 June 1948 a new currency
(*Deutsche Mark* - DM) was introduced. A per capita

allocation of DM 40 for RM 40 was made, followed by
a further 1:1 exchange for DM 20 two months later
(Henning, p.200; Stolper, p.243). Goods immediately
appeared in the shops, which indicated the extent of
the black market problem. The remaining RM in circulation as cash were eventually exchanged at the rate
of DM 6.5 : RM 100. Bank accounts were subjected
to a complex formula - holders of both money savings
and public debt lost heavily (Grosser, pp.97-98).
The 'equalisation of burdens' was left to the West
German authorities (see Chapter 5). As after the
Weimar inflation, the owners of real assets were the
gainers (Mann, p.589). Laursen and Pedersen (p.124)
would add that during the Weimar inflation employment
levels and productivity gains were high. But as they
also argue (p.15) Germany was left in ruins for three
years until the western Allies agreed on the drastic
1948 Currency Reform. In all these senses, the
reduction of the volume of money was draconian and
lacking in social equity. Only a military dictator-
ship could have imposed such a politically unpopular
measure (Wallich, pp.371-372). Factor incomes were
transposed at the rate of 1:1. In order to provide a
cash flow to meet factor payments, businessmen were
allowed DM 60 per employee at a rate of RM 10 : DM 1;
public sector authorities received an allowance equal
to one or two month's revenue and their old funds
were written off. In Autumn 1949 the exchange rate
of the DM against the dollar was devalued to
DM 4.20 = US$ 1.
    But the fragile nature of the monetary and fiscal
recovery during the period of re-adjustment should not
be underestimated. In spite of a 50 per cent increase
in output during the last half of 1948, recovery was
by no means assured. Money supply, credit and prices
all seemed to be getting out of hand. For monetary
and fiscal policy, therefore, the latter half of 1948
meant another unsuccessful struggle against inflationary pressure. The initial DM quotas allowed to individuals, private companies and the public sector -
when added to the new DM generated by the DM 6.5 :
RM 100 conversions - proved to be on the high side.
Central bank money was added to the already highly
liquid reserves of the banks. An unexpectedly rapid
expansion of credit was the consequence. Bank credit
rose from almost zero at the time of the reform to
DM 5.2 billion in December 1948. Moreover, the con-
version of old balances provided an additional
stimulus. Initial tightness in money supply
(DM 6 billion ten days after the reform) induced
holders to convert RM. Finally, the second

instalment of the DM 1:1 per capita allowance became
due in August. Hence by December the money supply
had more than doubled to reach DM 14.3 billion
(Wallich, Table 10, pp.74-75).

Price and tax reforms accompanied the currency
reform. The tax rates introduced by the Allies in
1946 were reduced. Incomes saved and invested were
exempted from tax altogether and this step was to play
an unexpectedly important role in the financing of the
recovery. However, prices of all but essential foodstuffs and materials were freed in July 1948. This
amounted to a freeing of 90 per cent of all prices
(Stolper, p.261). Allied price control had proved
fairly effective in restraining legal price increases.
Moreover, wage control had been even more effective
than price control. However, following the freeing
of prices, their level began to adjust to the changes
in relative costs which had occurred since the Nazi
controls were imposed in 1936, and continued under the
Allies. This brought about a rise in prices. There
was a general strike on 12 November 1948 as a protest
against the rate of inflation (Stolper, p.262). There
were also demands for another price freeze.

Union militancy was somewhat circumscribed, however. This was because the unions were reluctant to
undermine the recovery; they had in any case been
improverished by the currency reform; unemployment was
rising; finally price control on basic necessities
restrained living costs relative to raw material
prices - the former rose 14 per cent in the second
half of 1948, the latter by 21 per cent (Wallich,
p.75). Nevertheless, wage controls were lifted in
November 1948, although the unions continued to display wage restraint. It will be necessary to return
to the fiscal and monetary policies used to dampen the
inflationary pressure generated in the latter half of
1948 in the next chapter.


BUSINESS CONCENTRATION AND THE ROLE OF THE STATE

Controversy surrounding anti-trust law and banking was
increased not simply by the fact that Germany was a
defeated and occupied nation, but also by disagree-
ments among the Allies. There were four closely
related issues: reparations, the dismantling of
industrial capacity, the deconcentration of ownership
(taken to include decartelisation) and internal
German demands for the nationalisation of the means
of production. These debates were of utmost significance, since German industrial capacity remained

largely *intact*.

It must be emphasised that bomb damage to industry, as opposed to transport and housing, was *relatively negligible*. Germany's productive capacity was certainly in disarray, but her post-war industrial potential was roughly equivalent to that which had existed in 1938. Wartime destruction had simply cancelled out the additions to capacity (Dyas and Thanheiser, p.43). However, reconstruction during the war, with technically more advanced capital equipment where necessary, meant that Germany had a more superior industrial capacity after the war than before hostilities had commenced (Vogl, p.4). Generally speaking, bomber raids obliterated housing and commercial premises in city centres but left the industrial capacity on the outskirts intact (Manchester, pp.522 and 525; Mellor, p.142). Destruction of plant was only 10 per cent for metallurgy; 10-15 per cent chemicals; 15-20 per cent engineering; 20 per cent textiles (Grosser, p.91). The Ruhr was strangled ultimately by the daily output of 30,000 tons of finished goods which could not be transported away. But that was as late as January and February 1945 (Manchester, p.527). Hence in this respect the reader must carefully distinguish between the mythology and the economic reality of the condition of Germany's post-war industrial base.

Once Germany had finally been occupied, there was thus a great deal to be decided in terms of the future ownership of industry and output levels. This was particularly true in the British zone for it contained the Ruhr district where most of the coal and steel producing capacity was situated - the so-called Montan industries. In 1945, the big industrial monopolies such as *IG Farben* and Krupp were confiscated; ownership of coal and steel was passed to British military trusteeship. The British ultimately introduced twenty-four iron and steel producing companies in 1947 (Anthes, p.87). The immense concerns which had owned this capacity, along with the *IG Farben* chemical combine whose headquarters were situated in Frankfurt, were mainly the product of the Weimar period of industrial concentration. Many of their owners and managers had actively supported the rise of the Nazis. For the first few years following Germany's defeat, therefore, the trade unions (who had opposed National Socialism) were involved in the restructuring of German industry, especially in the British zone. However, a British industrialist who had signed an agreement in the Ruhr in 1939 and a former official of the

American bank whose credit promoted the growth of the massive *Vereinigte Stahlwerke* were included in the Allied military governments (Grosser, pp.40-41). Trade union bargaining power was, in fact, rather narrowly circumscribed until the Allied imposed currency reform in 1948. Initially, trade unions were allowed to organise only at plant and local levels. By 1947, however, there was a zonal federation in the British zone. This induced the Americans, and later the French, to allow inter-zonal organisation (Owen Smith, 1981, pp.179-184).

There were no coherent themes in Allied policy, at least until the East/West conflict emerged. Reparations exacted by the French and Russians, particularly the latter, were significantly higher than those imposed by Britain and the USA. Both France and Russia had been invaded and looted by the Germans. In the case of France, the amount received was in no sense the equivalent of the damage caused during the German occupation (Manchester, p.769). In the case of Russia the zonal imposition of well over 50 billion marks reparation payments undermined the relative competitiveness of East Germany compared to the western sectors (Mann, p.849). On the other hand, the USA began by being a more enthusiastic dismantler than the UK, although a change in US policy later left the British to determine the extent to which dismantling should continue (Wallich, p.349). All countries which had been at war with Germany also seized German-owned assets in their own country. Germany was also required to make reparation payments to Israel and meet the occupation costs of the Allies. Even after dismantling came to an end, certain German industries were still subject to limitations and prohibitions. Germany's aerospace and nuclear industries were not to re-emerge for many years after the Second World War as a result.

Proposals for the future of the Ruhr industry ranged from the creation of a separate political entity to French proposals that it should be 'internationalised', in order to reduce any future German threat to world peace. The Russians too wanted to exert some control over the future of the Ruhr. As the Cold War developed and as West Germany came to be treated as an ally by the western powers, an International Control Authority was established to control industry in north west Germany. Its task was to distribute among western European countries the products of the coal, iron and steel industries in these areas. But the Germans themselves put forward policies similar to those advocated after the First World

War.  For example, German trade union demands for
economic democracy and socialisation after the Second
World War echoed those of the post-First World War
period.  Another similiarity was that there was an
even larger majority of German political opinion
which was anti-capitalist and there was widespread
support for public ownership (Anthes, p.80; Horn,
p.6; Mann, p.827).  British support for such measures
had to be qualified as a result of American opposition
(Manchester, p.681; Wallich, pp.348-349).  German
nationalisation proposals were continually turned
down.

At Potsdam in 1945 it was decided that the
Russians should receive US$ 10 billion in reparations,
most of which would be taken in the form of dismantled industrial plant from their own relatively
rural zone.  Berlin's industries were dismantled with
ruthless thoroughness by the Russians in the two
months in which they had the city to themselves.
Losses from the war and dismantling left Berlin in
July 1945 with perhaps no more than 20 per cent of
its pre-war industrial capacity.  In addition, Russia
was to receive a quarter of all proposed dismantling
which was to take place in the western zones - 15 per
cent of which was to be exchanged for Russian food
and raw materials.  By 1953 Russia had taken DM 50
billion from her own zone, but when dismantling (and
therefore reparations) ceased in the western zone in
1950 the total for this area had reached only DM 5
billion.  Generally speaking the Russians were disappointed with the results of dismantling and attempting to re-built the equipment on their own soil.
They came to prefer using local labour and leaving
the plant in its original location - thus taking
current production flows as well as the capital
stock for reparation payments.  This latter step was
reminiscent of the post-First World War situation.

Moreover, the deterioration in relations between East and West (with the USSR and the USA as the
main protagonists), along with mounting opposition to
dismantling plans on the part of German trade unions
in the West, caused a dramatic modification of original plans for reparations among the western powers.
The union protests were directed against the indiscriminate proposals to include non-military capacity.
In spite of appeals for calm from their leaders, rank
and file militancy and demonstrations were provoked,
particularly at the Salzgitter iron and steel complex, even though the wisdom of the Nazi investment
decision to establish this steel plant on the low-
grade ore field was later to be questioned.  The

clear trend in the western zones was thus from zeal-
ous implementation of the dismantling programme to
one of its complete abandonment in 1950. Nevertheless, early Allied dismantling policy cost the firm
of Krupp more physical assets than the Second World
War air raids (Manchester, p.686). However, the
skills of 100,000 Krupp employees remained intact.
The French, who had not been invited to Potsdam, took
what their predominantly rural zone had to offer.
The British decided not to remove the Volkswagen works
which, like Salzgitter, had been established by the
Nazis ironically close to what was to become the
East/West German border.

There remains the vexed policy question of
deconcentration. The Potsdam Agreement defined this
as the need to break up all forms of syndicates,
trusts, cartels or any excessive concentration of
economic power. Here again the USA led the way in
the West, this time with their received theory of
trust-busting. But the whole process of deconcentration was a complex financial and legal operation.
It was decided finally to deconcentrate *IG Farben*,
the coal, iron and steel (*Montan*) industries, and the
three big banks. *IG Farben* was ultimately divided
into three: BASF (*Badische Anilan-und Sodafabrik*),
Bayer and Höchst. A large part of the Montan
industry was in the hands of Germany's industrial
families. The twelve large companies which
accounted for 90 per cent of steel output and more
than half of coal production were split up into 28
independent concerns. *Vereinigte Stahlwerke* was
broken up into thirteen of these undertakings.
Efforts to deconcentrate the three major commerical
banks were to be even less effective than in the
Montan industry. They were permitted to operate only
on a decentralised basis and this generated thirty-
three regional banks. Within four years (1952), they
re-merged so as to be organised within each of the
three western zones. Five years later the process of
amalgamation continued and they became national
institutions once again. Figure 2.1 demonstrates how
the largest of the private sector banks re-emerged.
It is significant that this process extended into the
period of economic recovery about to be discussed in
the next chapter. But since historically German
industry had been highly concentrated, it is perhaps
little wonder that it was impossible for the USA to
create the Bonn Republic in her own anti-trust image.
Probably for similar reasons de-cartelisation was
pursued with less vigour by the Allies. In short,
Germany has her own culture and economic history, not

least when it comes to the finance and structure of industry.

Figure 2.1:  The Re-emergence of the Deutsche Bank

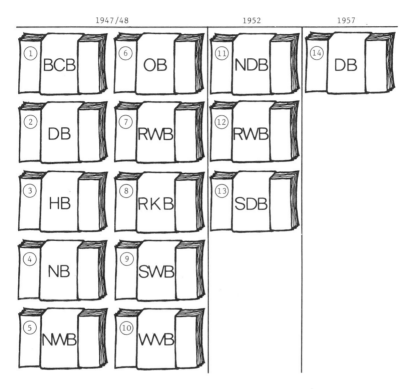

| 1947/48 | 1952 |
|---|---|
| 1  Bayerische Creditbank | 11  Norddeutsche Bank |
| 2  Disconto Bank | 12  Rheinisch-Westfälische Bank |
| 3  Hessische Bank | 13  Süddeutsche Bank |
| 4  Norddeutsche Bank in Hamburg | |
| 5  Nordwestbank | |
| 6  Oberrheinische Bank | |
| 7  Rheinisch-Westfälische Bank | |
| 8  Rheinische Kreditbank | 1957 |
| 9  Südwestbank | |
| 10  Württembergische Vereinsbank | 14  Deutsche Bank |

Source:  Deutsche Bank, *1870-1970: 100 Years of the Deutsche Bank* (undated), p.34.

Chapter Three

THE RECOVERY, 1949-1960

INTRODUCTION

Just as the last period represented a record industrial low in German economic development, this period
unambiguously differs from preceding and subsequent
periods of economic expansion. Average annual economic growth, in real terms, was more than double that
achieved in 1871-1913 (Giersch, p.14). Excluding the
Saar, industrial production in the Weimar Republic
doubled in the five-year period 1923-28, whereas in
the area which was to become the Bonn Republic it
increased by a factor of 3.5 between 1947 and 1952;
a similar relative picture emerges if one takes the
periods 1924-29 and 1948-53, when the respective
factors were 1.5 and 2.5. In both 1924 and 1948
industrial production stood at half the volume of
that achieved in 1938 (OEEC, p.9). The annual average increase in real gross national income (GNRP)
during the period 1950-1960 was 7.6 per cent; in per
capita terms it was 6.5 per cent. This compared with
2.6 per cent and 2.2 per cent in the UK, and 4.4 per
cent and 3.5 per cent in France. Only Japan (1952-
1960) achieved higher rates: 9.0 per cent and 7.8
per cent respectively (Giersch, p.15). In the case
of West Germany, motor vehicles, mechanical, electrical and chemical engineering showed large increases
in output, productivity and exports. There was even
unfounded optimism (see the next chapter) that
cyclical fluctuations had been modified. This was
because the length of the relatively minor cycles
around a gradual downward (but still highly positive)
trend in economic growth was four to five years compared to between seven and ten years in the Second
Reich (*ibid.*; p.19; Henning, pp.194-195).
    This process of recovery can be accounted for,
even though the roles played by good management and

good luck are difficult to disentangle. To use the
term 'miracle' to describe the degree of revival is
therefore misleading. In this book attention is
focused on economic explanations. More nebulous generalisations about the personal characteristics of
the German nation - for example, a capacity to maintain a steady and diligent rate of work for long
periods - will not be analysed. As interesting as
this would prove, it would be necessary, for example,
to distinguish between diligence and working in better
organised ways. In any case, a great many circumstances and events beyond German control contributed
to the recovery. West German industry enjoyed conditions which were highly propitious to economic
growth. To seek a mono-causal explanation would
therefore be fallacious.

It will be shown in this and other chapters that
business concentration and government economic intervention - both at a macro and micro level - played
crucial roles in stimulating export-led economic
growth in an area of the former Third Reich which was
industrially well-endowed. In this way the role of
the social market economy in practice may be clarified. It will also be necessary to show that a
further stimulus to demand was provided by the Korean
War boom. Moreover, foreign aid was channelled into
the balance of payments and investment, the level of
which was relatively high by international standards
due to tax incentives. The integration of refugees
was another policy issue; there was also the supply-
side consideration that the refugees contributed both
a quantitative and a qualitative dimension to the
labour market. Before turning to all these factors,
however, it is necessary to establish what theory lay
behind the recovery. In order to do this, a short
survey of the principles of the social market economy
follows.


THE SOCIAL MARKET ECONOMY

Although this phrase was coined by Professor Müller-
Armack, he has acknowledged (p.325) that his theory
was inspired by the 'Freiburg School' of economists.
During the Nazi era this school represented a kind of
intellectual resistance movement, a stand which required a great deal of personal courage and independent thinking (Wallich, p.114). Its two leading members were Professors Eucken and Böhm (Marburg, p.88).
Müller-Armack became the adviser of Professor Erhard
who, as the Allied appointed Director of Economic

Affairs and later as the first Federal Minister of
Economics, attempted to implement the policy rec-
ommendations arising from the model. Moreover, as
shown in Chapter 5, two of Erhard's successors -
Professor Schiller and Count Lambsdorff - were to be
equally ardent advocates of the system (Hallett,
pp.17-18; Lambsdorf, p.418). Both the theory and
the practice of the social market economy are therefore important.

On the theory side, it is necessary to emphasise
four fundamental principles. The first is the definition of competition employed in the model; the
second is the appropriate role for state intervention; the third is the place for anti-cyclical
measures; while the fourth principle is concerned
with the ethical and political aspects of neo-
liberalism (Denton, p.41).

In defining competition, the Freiburg School
conceived of two *pure* economic orders: the market or
the centrally-controlled forms. Competition could
only exist in the market economy, and anything which
constrained competition was detrimental to society.
Competition was the most promising means of achieving prosperity. Since there was a trend to monopol-
isation, state intervention would be necessary as a
corrective: 'even a market economy requires a framework within which to operate, and the creation of
this framework is the responsibility of the state'
(Hallett, p.19). With respect to stabilisation
policy - the third principle - the initial search by
the Freiburg School was for a built-in stabiliser.
This was to be achieved by the strict control of the
supply of money, which would eliminate cyclical fluctuations by means of signals to investors provided by
an efficiently operating price mechanism. Schiller
later found it necessary to incorporate Keynesian-
type fiscal policies - as will be seen in Chapter 5.
Finally, although Müller-Armack (p.329) denied that
the social market economy was a *Weltanschauung* like
classical liberalism or socialism, he contended that
the system provided a greater chance for personal
responsibility and individual freedom. Erhard
(p.186) undoubtedly had this in mind when he stressed
the close link between economic and social policy.
In his view individuals would not develop energy,
effort and enterprise if an all-embracing social
policy undermined incentive. Indeed, the more successful economic policy can be made, the fewer the
social policy measures which would be necessary.
Efficient production and personal freedom are the
keystones of a socially-balanced order (Watrin, p.419).

According to the Freiburg hypothesis, open
markets could be achieved by the removal of protec-
tive tariffs and State-controls on private industry,
the reduction of quasi-monopolistic privileges
granted by the State, and the banning of restrictive
practices and so on. Inequalities in income could
be modified by means of a progressive tax system,
but high marginal rates should be avoided so that the
incentive to take risks is not undermined. The first
federal chancellor (Konrad Adenauer - p.165) gave
perhaps an operationally significant test when he
defined the social market economy as a renunciation
of planning and the direction of production, labour
or sales. It was a comprehensive economic policy
combining monetary, trade, tariff, tax, investment
and social policies as well as other measures designed to ensure the welfare of the population as a
whole, including provision for the needy. The distinction in this latter definition is perhaps between
the amount of economic intervention under the Nazis
and that deemed necessary in mature capitalist economies - in this case an economy where a former level
of maturity had to be rapidly re-gained. What is
beyond doubt is that Adenauer's definition is a useful indication of the comprehensive approach adopted
by German economic policy-makers - 'a positive
attempt to mould all the elements of economic policy
into a single concept' (Denton, p.41). It demonstrates that neo-liberals did not advocate a *laissez-
faire* system.

As valuable as Adenauer's definition may be,
however, it is perhaps true to say that he delegated
economic policy-making to Erhard (Hartrich, p.159).
Thus, when Erhard received the 1949 report on restrictive business legislation from some members of the
Freiburg School, he made it clear that he viewed
monopoly power exercised by large companies with the
same repugnance as State intervention which restricted competion (Marburg, p.90). As things developed,
the Federal government, and particularly Erhard, had
little sympathy for economic planning in the French
sense, although in practice his ministry was inter-
ventionist. Both Adenauer and Erhard were opposed
to the left wing of their party (the Christian Democratic Union - CDU) which had joined in the general
advocacy of nationalisation after Germany's defeat.
This controversy resembled the liberalism v. socialism debate after the First World War (Watrin, p.406).
Indeed, Adenauer successfully associated nationalisation with the Social Democrats (SPD) before the
first federal elections in 1949. The early freeing

of markets from controls reflected Erhard's purism
when he was still Director of Economic Affairs in the
British and American zones. Christian Democrats only
supported this measure when it proved to be elector-
ally popular at the 1949 elections and even so their
majority was a narrow one. Neither was there any
great enthusiasm for the social market economy in
Britain and the USA (Hutchinson, p.436). By 1959,
however, the SPD had joined the CDU in accepting its
basic tenets. Shortly afterwards the trade unions
acknowledged the new order.
      Having reviewed the pure theory and policy impli-
cations of the social market economy, it is now possible to proceed to an analysis of the two aspects of
the model which seem to be at odds with the realities
of the West German economic recovery, that is the
policies on business concentration and government
economic intervention.


BUSINESS CONCENTRATION

Erhard was unable to convince the powerful right wing
of his party of the need to substitute competition
for concentration: he was fighting against the German
need for order, organisation and security in the large
industries. Such a situation derived from the two
conflicting views on the role of cartels and business
concentration. Affirmative claims as to the stabilising role of cartels (that is their ability to pro-
tect member-firms from ruinous competition) were
countered by analysts who insisted that the main aim
of cartel policy was to maximise the profits of members. Such critics held that the stability introduced by cartels was a stability of prices only -
output and employment levels would be varied according to trading conditions (Marburg, p.87). The economic welfare implications of such a system had
ultimately led to the foundation of the Freiburg
School during the 1930s and 1940s. Erhard's neo-
liberal views coincided more with organisations of
small independent businessmen, of which there are a
large number in West Germany, than with the views
held by the Federation of German Industry (*ibid.*,
pp.98-99). Further confusion to the debate on concentration had been caused by the Allies linking
decartelisation and deconcentration. In Germany there
had been a sharp distinction between, on the one hand,
cartels, which undertook co-ordination activities for
independently owned firms, and, on the other hand,
trusts which merged financial control. Decartel-

isation was *ultimately* emphasised more by the Allies
than deconcentration of financial control. Powers
over deconcentration were, however, maintained under
a directive issued by the Allies in 1949. In 1951 it
was indicated that these powers would be relinquished
when satisfactory legislation had been enacted. By
1954 the Allies had relinquished such powers and the
Federal government agreed to place legal restrictions
on the general restraint of competition. Moreover,
coal and steel had become subject to the special rules
of the European Coal and Steel Community.

In 1952 the Federal government submitted a draft
Bill to both Houses. But Erhard's restrictive practices policy ran into stubborn opposition from industry and was the subject of acrimonious political
debate. The Bill was withdrawn and a working party
consisting of representatives from the Ministries of
Economics and Justice, as well as the Federation of
German Industry, was established. The ensuing debate
evolved around whether there should be outright prohibition of agreements restraining trade and of
cartels, or safeguards against abuse of market power
by such organisations. As will be seen in Chapter 9,
it was 1957 before the Act against Restraints on
Competition reached the statute book. The prohibition of both vertical and horizontal agreements was
attenuated by exceptions. A further striking feature
of the Act was its mildness in relation to mergers
and dominant firms. Provisions establishing both a
supervisory Cartel Office, and enabling the Minister
of Economics to override the Office, reappeared in
the 1957 Act. (This was a direct development of the
inter-war period legislation - Gordon, pp.112-115 and
Appendix A; Marburg, p.83.)

But the actual business environment within which
the major industrial companies formulated their
strategies is not adequately described as free
market competition (Dyas and Thanheiser, p.48). For
example, each of the three successors of *IG Farben*
achieved a bigger turnover than the parent body had
ever reached. The re-emergence of the big banks has
already been mentioned (Diagram 2.1). Krupp emerged
from an Allied prison in 1951 as a national idol and
immediately started to re-build his empire. Mergers
reduced the number of companies in the Montan industry. A new firm (Grundig) along with two old firms
(Siemens and AEG) dominated the electronic and electronic engineering industries. There was a dramatic
growth in the number of companies employing more than
1,000 employees. Before the Second World War most of
these industries had been traditionally located in

the area now covered by West Germany.

Just as the Allies failed, in this sense, to
change the long-term course of German economic history, so too did the social market reformers. Particularly relevant here is the direct link between
industry and the banks, a link which reduces the role
of the stock exchange. This has meant that the creation of wealth is more important than its manipu-
lation. With the founding of the Second Reich at the
end of the Franco-Prussian War, the forerunners of
today's Big Three banks were given the task of providing investment for industrialisation. Despite the
profound changes which have occurred during the
course of the last 110 years, this banking function
has not changed. Its close involvement with industry
makes West Germany's banking system unique in the
Western world. This outstanding feature enables the
Big Three in particular to dominate the country's
stock exchanges, both as stockbrokers and investors.
They act as investment advisers and at the same time
own investment trusts. Moreover, they manage portfolios on behalf of the public. They therefore vote
on their own behalf and on behalf of their customers
(by virtue of the shares deposited at their banks for
safe-keeping). In short, their industrial influence
is extensive. It is because of this unusual uni-
veral aspect of German banking that the topic receives
so much emphasis in this book.


GOVERNMENT ECONOMIC INTERVENTION

Extreme interpretation of the doctrine of the social
market economy also underestimate the amount of
government intervention. As controller, redistributor
and probably also as economic manager the role of the
State was larger in the Bonn Republic of the early
1950s than in the Weimar Republic (Mendershausen,
p.71). Not least important here was Erhard's Ministry
of Economics. As Shonfield (pp.275 and 293) points
out, there was no need for this Ministry to be involved in the French-type of economic planning. In
the German case guide-lines were provided by the past;
there was no need for a German Monnet to invent them.
Erhard's interest was not in the market as an institution, but as a process. Corrective measures were
unhesitatingly taken. As will shortly be seen, the
incredible degree of economic balance achieved in the
early years of the new Republic was in no small
measure due to tax policy, government expenditure,
strategically-directed subsidies and, to a lesser

extent, a brief suspension of trade liberalisation
when import controls were re-introduced during the
Korean crisis.  Important exceptions to the social
market economy rule were and are to be found in housing, energy and transport policies (Owen Smith, 1979).
To what extent did fiscal and monetary policies
during the recovery correspond to social market
principles?  It was seen above how output in 1948,
which had stood at half of that achieved in 1938,
expanded by 50 per cent in the second half of the
year but prices also rose rapidly.  However, prices
had only resumed the role of a meaningful economic
indicator after the Currency Reform and the lifting
of the price freeze, also half way through 1948.
Hence when output in 1949 rose by 23 per cent but
prices fell the policy problem changed because unemployment rose rapidly.  By the end of the first
quarter of 1950 it reached 2 million or 12.2 per
cent (Wallich, Table 11, pp.80-81).  High unemployment was a serious political threat - it had facili-
tated Hitler's rise to power.  Total employment had
in fact hardly declined;  the growth in unemployment
was due to a growth in the labour force, mainly
through refugees.  Nevertheless, in the fifteen
months from January 1949 to March 1950 bank credit
increased by DM 8 billion, and the central bank became occupied with the worsening balance of payments
position.  But if it is doubtful that monetary policy
strictly observed the social market economy code,
fiscal policy seemed undoubtedly to breach it.  In
the ten quarters following the Currency Reform (July
1948 to December 1950) the combined budget of the
Federal and Länder Governments was in surplus on only
one occasion - the first quarter of 1950.  There were
thus deficits in 1948 when price inflation was a
problem, followed by a surplus when unemployment was
a problem, followed by a substantial DM 1 billion
deficit in the second quarter of 1950 when the balance of payments deteriorated so badly that foreign
currency reserves were completely exhausted.  An
important contributory factor to this enlarged deficit
was the 25 per cent reduction in personal income tax
rates enacted in April 1950 but made retroactive to
January 1950 (*Annual Report*, US High Commission,
1950).
Imports had risen more rapidly than exports as
a result of import liberalisation.  The external
imbalance grew worse as a result of panic purchases
of raw materials at the beginning of the Korean War
in June 1950.  Moreover, the reflationary expenditure programmes and tax cuts, which had been

eventually decided upon during the winter of 1950,
started to take effect at the same time as the out-
break of the Korean War. However, there was an
international increase in output and this was reflected in West Germany by rapid increases in output
and exports. The post-Korea boom drew German industry back into world markets at such prices that they
were able to re-equip large sectors of run-down
plant. Notably, the rise in exports was not initially sufficient to cover the rise in imports and
the drain on foreign exchange continued. As a result
import controls were re-introduced and the FRG took
up special credits with the European Payments Union
(Horn, p.13; Stolper, pp.266 and 274). Imports of
food - in spite of the influx of refugees - were not
responsible: German average daily calorific intake
still stood significantly below pre-war levels. Raw
material prices also began to fall after the Korean
peak. It was 1952 before export surpluses emerged.
Thus West Germany became independent of foreign aid
(see below) in the year that the Marshall Plan came
to an end (Knapp, p.424).

The real question to ask is whether German exporters would have made such inroads if scarce
resources in the United States and British economies
had not been switched to rearmament. There is a two-
part answer. First, the remarkable balance attained
with the underdeveloped, raw material supply countries
- with which Germany had prior to the Second World
War been in deficit - cannot be attributed to liberalisation. This improved trading position was due
more to the growing demand in these countries for
German capital goods. For example, Krupp saw the
underdeveloped countries of the early 1950s as the
trading partners of tomorrow. Since Krupp no longer
depended on armament production, as early as 1953 he
was emerging as Britain's most serious competitor as
an exporter of constructional machinery to the underdeveloped areas of the world. By 1956 he had a two-
year backlog of orders and backed by US$ 20 million
from German banks he explored the untapped markets
of the world (Manchester, pp.804-805). It was West
Germany's concentration on the export of capital
goods - with their high income elasticity and continually improving terms of trade - that gave her
recovery such rapid momentum in a world of rising
demand among industrial as well as underdeveloped
economies (Giersch, p.14). By 1952 50 per cent of
her exports came from the capital goods sector. A
further 17.8 per cent were provided by iron, steel
and chemicals (Wallich, p.217). Export credit,

insurance and tax rebates, were used in order to
bolster exports. In addition, the Federal Republic
had bilateral trade arrangements with South American
and East European countries.
The second reason for this export-led recovery
was an undervalued exchange rate. Once the Currency
Reform, combined with foreign aid and good harvests,
had increased the supply of food, both the time devoted to searching for food and absenteeism fell. The
Currency Reform also increased the domestic demand
for consumer goods of all kinds and most employers
increased the length of the working week rather than
providing extra employment. Output per head therefore increased substantially but the improvement in
productivity was very much less in terms of output
per man-hour (Stewart, p.3). Although German expansion prior to the Korean War had been based on increasing sales to the home market, particularly consumer goods, the competitive position of German exporters was increased by the September 1949 devaluation of the DM. At first sight it may appear that
the 20.6 per cent devaluation of the DM against the
dollar, when compared to the 30.5 per cent for most
other currencies, would fail to give such a fillip.
But West Germany had considerable unused capacity and
labour reserves. As export demand rose during the
Korean boom, unit costs fell and profits rose dramatically. This enabled German manufacturers to
self-finance an enormous investment programme.
Hence, an elastic labour supply and high rates of
capital formation on the supply side, and the pull of
export demand on the demand side, produced a high
rate of economic growth (Hennings, p.28).
In terms of capital investment, market forces
were mitigated by fiscal policy. Shipbuilding and
construction had the right to deduct loans from taxable profits. Tax exemptions for retained earnings,
together with tax aids for exporters, were also introduced between 1949 and 1951. Specially accelerated
depreciation allowances were introduced to relieve
bottlenecks in coal-steel and electricity in 1952.
Profits and depreciation allowances ('omnipotent tax
privileges' - Wallich, p.166) became the main source
of investment funds during the early years of the
recovery.
Income inequality was generally more marked in
1950 than in 1928 and 1913 - something which Wallich
(p.46) suggests was probably an essential condition
for recovery. Savings and investment, and therefore
economic growth, Wallich contends, would probably
have been lower if there had not been a high degree

of income inequality. (Capital investment was, it appears, higher than in the Weimar Republic - Mendershausen, p.48.) There were two mitigating factors in the degree of income inequality, one being the course of real wage rates and the other being a process of fiscal redistribution. Real wages rose 63 per cent between 1950 and 1960, but labour's share in the national income - adjusted for increases in the size of the employed labour force - decreased from 71 per cent to 65 per cent, thus reflecting the high degree of money wage restraint practised by German trade unions during this period (BMA, Table 1.5; Stolper, p.321). On the other hand, the extent of income redistribution through the fiscal process was greater in the Bonn Republic than in the Weimar Republic (Mendershausen, p.80; Wallich, p.50). But this redistribution covered only the barest needs of war victims, refugees and the old (Wallich, p.47). Hence, when the recipients of these transfer payments are excluded, and if it is borne in mind that many of the lowest paid would be secondary workers, the lower 50 per cent of income recipients received 16 per cent of national income in 1950 (compared to 23.2 per cent in 1928), while the top one per cent received 14.6 per cent compared to 12.9 per cent (*ibid.*, p.47). Of much more significance in terms of capital investment, however, is the probability that, for two reasons, the concentration at the top was probably understated (*ibid.*, p.48). First, in 1950 there were large corporate profits but few dividends and, therefore, a lower level of taxable income. Second, taxable income was also reduced by the widespread practice of charging personal expenditures for travel, entertainment, motor cars, and even housing to business expenses. In short, the tax system during the period of reconstruction was consciously shaped as a driving force for capital accumulation (Horn, p.11).

Moreover, about one-quarter of total gross capital investment emanated from public funds (Wallich, p.169). Housing, not surprisingly in view of what has been said about the acute housing shortage, represented the core of public investment. During the Weimar and the Nazi periods the highest output of housing per year had been in the order of 300,000. This had not been sufficient to meet the shortages which existed at these times. War damage and the influx of refugees had increased the housing difficiency to about 4 million units by 1954 (Mendershausen, p.53). Yet during the years 1949 to 1951 nearly 1 million additional dwellings were completed; by 1953 and 1954 annual output had increased to well over 500,000 per

annum, a point to be taken up later in this book
(Diagram 8.1). What must be emphasised here is that
house building in 1951 absorbed 30 per cent of net
fixed investment, as against 21 per cent for the
years 1925-28. About one half of total construction
costs was provided out of public funds until 1953
(Wallich, pp.172-173). In the case of better quality
housing, tax privileges and low-interest loans were
available (Stolper, p.311). Indeed, these subsidies
were to become a controversial issue in later years -
as will be shown in Chapter 5. Tax concessions also
encouraged companies to make interest-free housing
loans to their labour forces (Wallich, p.161).
Generally, housing expenditure was used to finance
private housing or housing co-operatives (*ibid.*,
p.171). Yet the fact remains that housing represented the core of public investment, even though the
bulk of new housing was of the low cost variety
(*Sozialer Wohnungsbau*). Rent per square metre was
specified and the return to the landlord allowable in
the cost calculations was fixed (*ibid.*, p.172).

OTHER CONTRIBUTORY FACTORS TO THE RECOVERY

Foreign aid played a significant role in relieving
the economic plight of post-Second World War Germany,
as well as expediting the recovery. In absolute magnitude, post-Second World War *aid* from the USA considerably exceeded the post-First World War long-term
*loans*: on a net basis the former (1946-53) amounted
to US$ 3.6 billion, compared to US$ 1.7 billion in
the latter case (1924-28) (Mendershausen, p.105).
The total aid received by Germany from the three
western Allied governments amounted to roughly
US$ 4.4 billion, including $800 million (£1 = $4.03)
from the UK and $15 million from France (Wallich,
p.355). The GARIOA (Government and Relief in Occupied Areas) operation, which accounted for very
roughly half of total foreign aid, was essentially an
emergency programme directed towards the relief of
starvation and not towards the reconstruction of the
economy. It was replaced in 1948 by the ERP (European Recovery Programme or, more popularly, 'Marshall
Aid'). As Knapp points out (p.430): 'The inclusion
of West Germany in the ERP had profound effects on
the entire economic and political development of post-
war Germany.' Horn (p.11) is even more specific as
far as the subject-matter of this chapter is concerned: 'Marshall Plan aid played a crucial role in
the successful recovery of the German economy during

the critical period from 1948 to the Korea crisis.'
     Together with the currency reform and the lift-
ing of price and distribution controls, then, the
Marshall Plan sparked off the revival of Germany's
industrial output.  As a direct contribution to total
resources, the aid as such was not a decisive factor.
But indirectly the aid had two impacts.  First, the
ERP aid was also largely in the form of foodstuffs,
and this prevented starvation and relieved the balance
of payments because precious foreign exchange could be
used to purchase raw materials for industry.  Second,
when the physical goods supplied in the form of aid
were sold to German consumers, a DM counterpart fund
was generated.  It was this fund which was used for
capital investment in the process of reconstruction.
In terms of investment generation, the role of the
counterpart funds was surprisingly small.  Wallich
(p.366) estimates a total expenditure of DM 5 billion,
of which DM 3.5 billion was invested.  In both supply-
ing foreign aid and generating counterpart funds, however, the Allies were, in turn, generating important
qualitative rather than quantitative effects.  Counterpart funds played a strategic role in German investment; apart from Investment Assistance funds, counterpart investment was probably the most carefully planned
of all capital expenditures (Wallich, p.175): it was
channelled into the sectors where economic bottlenecks
existed and for which the limited capital market could
not make funds available (Horn, p.11; Knapp, p.424).
     Assistance in supplying foreign exchange for im-
ports, which was so decisive in the resolution of West
Germany's balance of payments problems, reached an
absolute peak of US$ 1.026 billion in 1948 (64 per cent
of the total value of imports) then fell to 43 per cent,
18 per cent and 12 per cent in 1949, 1950 respectively
(Henning, p.209; Wallich, p.357).  This inflow of aid
began, as did the recovery generally, while the constitution of the future Bonn Republic was still being
discussed.  Germany also had no defence spending commitments during the recovery and this released resources for the export industries.  It is true that up
to 1950 the absence of a defence burden was balanced
by the costs of occupation that West Germany was required to bear;  but after 1950 the gradual expansion
of her own defence forces was offset by a reduction in
occupation costs, so that in real terms defence expenditure of both types remained at the 1950 level
(Denton, p.51).  Thus, as the national product rose in
the 1950s, the proportion going to defence fell from
5 per cent in 1950 to 2.7 per cent in 1958.  Moreover,
the contributions to West Germany's invisible exports,

made by Allied forces stationed on German soil, improved her balance of payments situation (Wallich,
p.361). This contrasted to the drain on Britain's
foreign exchange caused by her overseas military
commitments.

The refugees (including expellees) who flooded
into the western parts of Germany after the Second
World War became a major contributory factor to the
recovery. Although on the demand-side they initially
proved to be an added burden during the trough of
1945-48, they became a valuable supply-side benefit
in terms of the effort, quantity and quality which
they contributed to the labour market during the recovery - as will be shown in more depth below. Managerial and technical skills among the immigrants were
valuable in transplanting the electrical, optical and
ceramics industries from east to west (Mendershausen,
p.46). After 1953, refugees from East Germany included skilled craftsmen, doctors, technicians and
scientists (Stolper, p.338). Their numbers were so
high that they compensated for the population losses
during two world wars and the Great Depression.

It should be added that changing frontiers again
became relevant on 1 January 1957 when the Saar was
again politically united with Germany. The canalis-
ation of the Mosel river was an agreed condition.
The integration of the Saar proceeded smoothly during
a period when coal output was becoming more of a
liability than an asset in the sense that shortages
gave way to overproduction (Grosser, pp.479-480).


CONCLUSION

To summarise, then, the newly-founded Bonn Republic
possessed an advantageous industrial base. In
addition, she possessed an elastic supply of factors,
plus a distribution of income and a tax system which
favoured profits and investments. It was lucky for
Germany that she received American aid and was able
to participate in a world-wide boom. Finally, it can
be noted that West Germany reached full employment
levels between 1960 and 1966, but thereafter the
economy became more susceptible to international
monetary speculation and cyclical economic activity.
It is to these economic contrasts that the analysis
now turns.

Chapter Four

ECONOMIC TRENDS

INTRODUCTION

During the three decades covered in this chapter,
economic growth rates in West Germany declined and,
after 1966, fluctuations in economic activity became
more serious. Throughout the 1950s and the 1960s,
and to a lesser extent during the 1970s, the strategy
of economic growth was based on a dynamic export
sector (Vollmer, pp.576-577). By the end of the
1970s, although the West German economy remained the
strongest in Europe, structural re-adjustment was
necessary. These structural problems arose from the
high level of domestic costs, increased international
competition and a rapid growth of the labour force.
In short, the West German economy had not adapted to
the cost conditions and relative factor prices which
are appropriate to a highly industrialised economy
well-endowed with both human and physical capital
(Hennings, p.85; Vollmer, pp.577 and 587). Also at
the end of the 1970s, real interest rates were high
and there were large current account and budget
deficits. The challenge thus facing economic policy-
makers was to try to induce the re-emergence of
export-led growth.
        In this chapter the macro-economic trends cul-
minating in the structural problems just mentioned
are examined. Basically, this will necessitate an
analysis of various aspects of national output and
income, employment and price levels, and measures of
efficiency. The balance of payments will also be
discussed. This will provide a backcloth for the
examination of economic policy problems and prescriptions which follows in the next chapter.

NATIONAL OUTPUT AND INCOME

Economic Growth
Table 4.1 demonstrates how the annual averages of
four indicators of real economic growth (real national
income, industrial production, real gross capital formation and productivity) all followed a marked downward trend during the three decades under review.

Table 4.1:  Average Annual Percentage Changes in Real
Economic Growth Indicators

|  | GNRP | Industrial production | Real gross capital formation | Productivity |
|---|---|---|---|---|
|  | (1) | (2) | (3) | (4) |
| 1951–1960 | +8.0 | +9.6 | +10.9 | +5.8 |
| 1961–1970 | +4.7 | +5.4 | +7.6 | +4.5 |
| 1971–1980 | +2.9 | +2.2 | +3.1 | +3.2 |
| (1981 | −0.3 | −1.8 | −3.3 | +0.6) |

Notes:
(a) All cols 1951–1960 excl. Saarland and West Berlin.
(b) Col. (1) National Income concepts are discussed below –
Table 4.5.
(c) Cols (1), (3) and (4) 1951–1960 at 1962 prices; 1961–1970
and 1971–1980 at 1970 prices.
(d) Col. (2) 1970=100.
(e) Col. (3) defined as gross investment in machinery and
equipment excl. construction.
(f) Col. (4) defined as GDRP per economically active person.
(g) 1981: Data provisional; Col. (2) 1976=100; Col. (3) includes construction.

Sources:  Calculated from Dresdner Bank, *Statische
Reihen*, pp.1-2; IdDW, Tables 8, 12 and 43; BMA,
Table 1.1.

As was pointed out in Chapter 3 economic growth rates
during the 1950s were bound to be higher because of
reconstruction and the various other factors which
were highly propitious to economic growth.  Capital
investment, it will be recalled, generally forged
ahead pulling employment, industrial production and
productivity in its wake.  The only exception was
1957.  Once the growth in the labour force came to an

end in the 1960s, something to be explored later,
there was a decline in growth rates. Put another
way, with the achievement of full employment, the
economy ran up against a supply ceiling (Vollmer,
p.577). Further, capital investment actually decreased on the previous year in 1966 and 1967. In
the 1970s, falls in the labour force until 1977 and
average annual capital investment in 1971-75, caused
a further slow-down in growth rates. Significantly,
by the 1970s the rise in industrial production had
fallen below the growth rate of real national income.
    In Table 4.2, and its accompanying note, the
annual average growth rates in the components of real
national income are traced.

Table 4.2:  Annual Average Percentage Changes of Real
National Income and its Components

| | GNRP | Exports of goods and services | Gross fixed capital formation | | Private consumption |
|---|---|---|---|---|---|
| | | | Machinery and Equipment | Construc- tion | |
| 1951-1960 | +8.0 | +16.7 | +10.9 | +9.3 | +7.8 |
| 1961-1970 | +4.7 | +7.8 | +7.6 | +3.5 | +5.0 |
| 1971-1980 | +2.9 | +6.1 | +3.1 | +1.8 | +3.1 |

Notes:
(a) 1951-1960 excl. Saarland and West Berlin.
(b) In real terms, approximately 56 per cent of GNRP in 1980
was private consumption, 18 per cent public consumption, 24 per
cent gross capital formation and the net contribution from
foreign trade (exports of goods and services - imports of goods
and services) was approximately 2 per cent of GNRP - BMA,
Tables 1.2a and 1.2b.  Over 80 per cent of gross capital formation is undertaken by the private sector - IdDW, Table 13.
(National income concepts are discussed in Table 4.5 below.)

Sources:   See Table 4.1.


Again, the downward trend is readily discernible, and
once more the basic causal factors were discovered in
Chapter 3.  In the 1950s, the enormous fillip to exports given by an increasingly undervalued exchange
rate contrasts to experience in the 1970s.  The consumption and construction booms of the 1950s are also

reflected in Table 4.2. These too, perhaps inevitably, came to an end by the 1970s.
But a slow-down in growth rates must not, of course, be confused with current nominal levels of domestic income. In this latter sense West Germany - as can be seen from Table 4.3 occupies the top rank among the listed major Western market economies. For that matter her relative growth rate in terms of real domestic income per head during the 1970s was exceeded only by Japan (also see Table 4.3). Similarly, the relatively favourable performance of the West German economy with respect to capital investment is brought out in Table 4.4. This is not to say that she has no capital stock problems - as will shortly be shown. Nevertheless, in terms of the percentage of nominal domestic income invested she is, again, inferior only to Japan. A more uniform picture emerges, however, if investment in machinery and equipment is assessed.

Since both nominal and real variables in value terms have now been introduced, it is possible to continue this study of growth trends by comparing various income concepts. This may be done by referring to the data presented in Table 4.5. Readers interested in comparing the various nominal and real national income concepts in detail may find the notes on accounting appended to Table 4.5 useful.

Finally, the relative growth of private consumption and savings are presented in both Table 4.6 and Diagram 4.1. In addition to the decreasing rate of growth in private consumption, already discussed in real terms above, two significant features of the propensity to save are demonstrated by both the table and the diagram. First, the growth of savings was greater during the 1950s and 1960s, than during the 1970s as a whole. In fact, the first actual fall on the previous year during the period under review preceded and continued through the 1967 recession. Further statistical evidence of this is found in the OECD, *Economic Outlook* (December 1979, p.134), as is evidence of the second point, namely the sudden dramatic rise in the propensity to save in most industrialised countries during the 1974-75 recession. In West Germany the ratio of savings to disposable income peaked at 17 per cent in the first quarter of 1975, thus frustrating government attempts to stimulate consumption and, therefore, aggregate demand. This exacerbated the 1974-75 recession and it is against such a backcloth that the analysis can now focus on fluctuations in economic activity.

Table 4.3: GDRP per head of the Population: an International Comparison (1975 prices)

| Year | West Germany | Belgium | France | Italy | Nether- lands | Great Britain | USA | Japan |
|------|------|------|------|------|------|------|------|------|
| 1975 = 100 | | | | | | | | |
| 1970 | 91 | 86 | 85 | 92 | 90 | 91 | 92 | 86 |
| 1975 | 100 | 100 | 100 | 100 | 100 | 100 | 100 | 100 |
| 1976 | 106 | 105 | 105 | 105 | 105 | 104 | 104 | 104 |
| 1977 | 109 | 106 | 107 | 107 | 106 | 105 | 109 | 109 |
| 1978 | 113 | 109 | 111 | 109 | 108 | 109 | 112 | 113 |
| 1979 | 118 | 112 | 114 | 114 | 110 | 110 | 114 | 118 |
| 1980 | 120 | 114 | 115 | 118 | 109 | 108 | 113 | 123 |
| (1981 | 118 | 113 | 115 | 118 | 106 | 106 | 114 | 127) |
| GDP per head[a] | 13310 | 11820 | 12140 | 6910 | 11850 | 9340 | 11360 | 8910 |

Note: (a) US$ at current prices and exchange rates (1980).

Sources: BMWi, Table 3.3, p.35 (writer's translation) and OECD, *Economic Surveys* (Germany), June 1982, Statistical Annex.

Table 4.4: An International Comparison of Real Gross Fixed Capital Formation in Construction, Machinery and Equipment[a]

| Annual or average annual percent- age change | West Germany | France | Great Britain | Italy | Japan | USA |
|------|------|------|------|------|------|------|
| 1951–55 | +12.7[d] | +4.6[d] | . | +12.8[d] | . | +3.5 |
| 1956–60 | +6.8[d] | +6.9[d] | −5.5 | +7.8 | +17.6 | +1.6 |
| 1961–65 | +5.8 | +9.1 | +5.3 | +2.7 | +13.6 | +6.9 |
| 1966–70 | +3.8 | +6.5 | +3.7 | +7.5 | +17.6 | +1.2 |
| 1971–75 | −1.0 | +3.6 | +1.0 | −1.0 | +3.3 | −0.1 |
| 1976–80[b] | +5.1 | +1.9 | −1.0 | +2.8 | +5.4 | +3.4[c] |
| (1981[b] | −2.9 | −2.3 | −7.5 | −0.3 | +2.3 | +0.5) |
| Percentage of GDP (1979)[e] | 22.6 | 21.4 | 17.8 | 18.9 | 32.1 | 19.4 |
| Ditto – machinery and equipment only | 9.1 | 9.2 | 9.3 | 8.0 | 10.7 | 7.4 |

Notes:
(a) Measured in national currencies at constant 1975 prices.
(b) Provisional estimates.　　　　(c) Private investment only.
(d) 1970 prices.　　　　(e) At current prices.

Sources: IdDW, Table 78 (writer's translation); OECD, *Economic Outlook*, July 1982, p.144, and OECD, *Economic Surveys* (Germany), June 1982, Statistical Annex.

Table 4.5: Nominal and Real (1970) Values of National Income (DM billion)

|      | 1950[a] | 1960  | 1970  | 1980   |
|------|---------|-------|-------|--------|
| GDP  | 98.0    | 302.8 | 678.8 | 1494.7 |
| GDRP | 143.5   | 428.7 | 678.8 | 896.0  |
| GNP  | 98.1    | 303.0 | 679.0 | 1497.5 |
| GNRP | 143.6   | 429.5 | 679.0 | 897.5  |
| NNP  | 76.9    | 240.1 | 533.1 | 1155.4 |
| Yd   | 65.0    | 187.9 | 425.9 | 946.1  |

(a) excl. Saarland and Berlin; 1962 prices for real income variables.

Notes on national income accounting:

Gross domestic product at current (market) prices + net factor income from abroad = gross national product at current prices.

Gross domestic (real) product at constant prices + net factor income from abroad = gross national (real) product at constant prices.

Gross national product at current prices – depreciation – indirect taxes + subsidies = net national product at factor cost (known in Germany as *Volkseinkommen* or national income).

Net national product at factor cost – undistributed profits – corporate direct taxes and employers' social insurance contributions + transfer payments = personal income.

Personal income – personal direct taxes and employees' social insurance contributions = Personal disposable income (Yd) or private consumption + personal (household) savings.

Sources:  BMA, Tables 1.1 to 1.17;  MRDB, November 1981, Table VIII (1).

Table 4.6:  Private Consumption and Personal Savings as Percentages of Personal Disposable Income

|        | Consumption | Savings |
|--------|-------------|---------|
| 1950   | 96.8        | 3.2     |
| 1955   | 93.6        | 6.4     |
| 1960   | 91.5        | 8.5     |
| 1965   | 87.8        | 12.2    |
| 1970   | 86.3        | 13.7    |
| 1975   | 84.7        | 15.3    |
| 1980   | 86.6        | 13.4    |

Source:  Calculated from BMA, Tables 1.14 and 1.15.

Diagram 4.1: Growth in Personal Disposable Income, Private Consumption and Personal Savings, 1950–1980

(a)

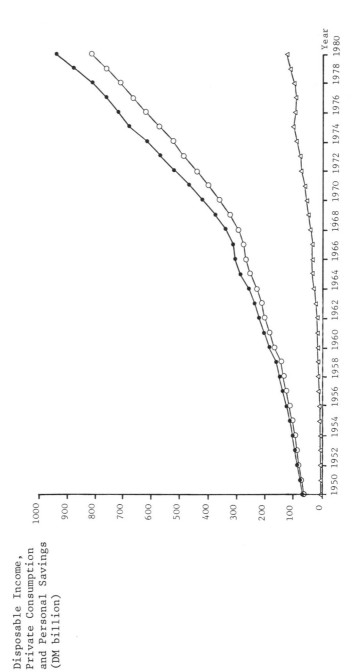

Disposable Income,
Private Consumption
and Personal Savings
(DM billion)

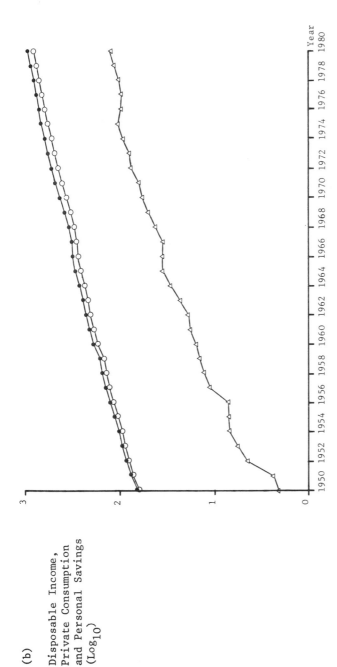

(b)

Disposable Income,
Private Consumption
and Personal Savings
(Log$_{10}$)

Key • Disposable income

○ Consumption

△ Savings

Sources: Plotted from Dresdner Bank, *Statische Reihen*, p.8; BMA, Tables 1.14 and 1.15.

Economic Fluctuations

As well as displaying a marked downward trend in
growth during the period 1950-1980, economic
activity began to display increasingly larger fluctuations (Donges, p.186). These fluctuations are best
shown by plotting the percentage changes in some of
the variables already introduced earlier in this
chapter. This has been done in Diagrams 4.2 and
4.3, where fluctuations in real national income, real
investment in machinery and equipment, real investment in construction, and industrial production are
all related to one another. An additional variable
is introduced for the first time in so far as the
Central Bank's Discount Rate has been added. This
is for comparative purposes - as a proxy for the
general behaviour of interest rates, although this
particular topic will be dealt with in more depth
in the next chapter.

It is apparent from these diagrams that there
have been absolute falls in industrial production in
1967 (-2.8 per cent), 1974 (-2.0 per cent), 1975
(-6.2 per cent) and 1980 (-0.2 per cent). Real
national income fell in both 1967 and 1975, by -0.1
and -1.8 per cent respectively. As would be expected,
real investment in machinery and equipment displayed
the most pronounced fluctuations: its percentage
change on the previous year was negative in 1957,
1966, 1967, 1972 and 1974. During the two recessionary years of 1967 and 1974 the percentage changes in
real investment were -7.4 and -10.2 respectively,
whereas during the boom years of 1955, 1960 and 1969
the increases on the previous year were +25.0, +17.6
and +23.0 per cent.

These peaks and troughs in economic activity are
presented schematically in Table 4.7. As Donges
points out (p.186) these developments may correct
simplistic notions about economic miracles in West
Germany. In fact, along with what has been said
about growth trends, they correspond well with
analyses of long-term cycles in West Germany's growth,
the last one of which peaked in 1960.


EMPLOYMENT AND PRICE LEVELS

The trends and fluctuations in economic activity which
have just been analysed were reflected in the labour
market. Item (i) in Table 4.8 is designed to reveal
an important implication of this derived influence of
aggregate demand levels. It will be seen that the
ratio of the stock of unfilled vacancies to the stock

Table 4.7:    Troughs and Peaks in GNRP, 1951-1979

| Troughs | | | Peaks | | |
|---|---|---|---|---|---|
| 1954 | } | 4 years | 1955 | | |
| 1958 | | | 1960 | } | 5 years |
| 1963 | } | 5 years | 1964 | } | 4 years |
| 1967 | } | 4 years | 1969 | } | 5 years |
| 1971 | } | 4 years | 1973 | } | 4 years |
| 1975 | } | 4 years | 1976 | } | 3 years |
| 1977 | } | 2 years | 1979 | } | 3 years |

Source:    See Diagram 4.2.


Table 4.8:
  (i) Ratio of the Number of Unfilled Vacancies to the
       Number Unemployed
 (ii) Percentage Change of the Retail Price Index on
       the Previous Year

|  | (i) | (ii) |  | (i) | (ii) |  | (i) | (ii) |
|---|---|---|---|---|---|---|---|---|
| (1950 | 1.0:13.6 | -6.2) | | | | | | |
| 1951 | 1.0:12.2 | 7.7 | 1961 | 3.1:1.0 | 2.3 | 1971 | 3.5:1.0 | 5.2 |
| 1952 | 1.0:11.7 | 2.1 | 1962 | 3.7:1.0 | 3.0 | 1972 | 2.2:1.0 | 5.6 |
| 1953 | 1.0:10.0 | -1.8 | 1963 | 3.0:1.0 | 2.9 | 1973 | 2.1:1.0 | 7.0 |
| 1954 | 1.0: 8.8 | 0.2 | 1964 | 3.6:1.0 | 2.3 | 1974 | 1.0:1.8 | 7.0 |
| 1955 | 1.0: 4.6 | 1.6 | 1965 | 4.4:1.0 | 3.3 | 1975 | 1.0:4.6 | 6.0 |
| 1956 | 1.0: 3.5 | 2.5 | 1966 | 3.4:1.0 | 3.5 | 1976 | 1.0:4.5 | 4.3 |
| 1957 | 1.0: 3.3 | 2.0 | 1967 | 1.0:1.5 | 1.7 | 1977 | 1.0:4.5 | 3.7 |
| 1958 | 1.0: 3.4 | 2.2 | 1968 | 1.5:1.0 | 1.7 | 1978 | 1.0:4.1 | 2.7 |
| 1959 | 1.0: 1.9 | 1.0 | 1969 | 4.2:1.0 | 1.9 | 1979 | 1.0:2.9 | 4.1 |
| 1960 | 1.7: 1.0 | 1.4 | 1970 | 5.3:1.0 | 3.3 | 1980 | 1.0:2.9 | 5.5 |
| | | | | | | (1981 | 1.0:6.1 | 5.9) |

Notes:   (i) Calculated from annual averages.
              1950-56 excl. Berlin.   1950-58 excl. Saarland.

          (ii) 1950-61 excl. Berlin.   1950-59 excl. Saarland.
               Until 1962 4-persons household with average
               income; from 1963 all private households.
               1976 = 100 in both cases.

Sources:   Calculated from Dresdner Bank, *Statische
Reihen*, p.3; BMA, Tables 2.10, 6.11 and 6.19; IdDW,
Table 7;   BMWi, Tables 1.26 and 2.31.1.

42

Diagram 4.2: Annual Percentage Changes in GNP, GNRP and Real Gross Capital Formation, 1950-1980

(a)

Annual percentage change in GNP and GNRP

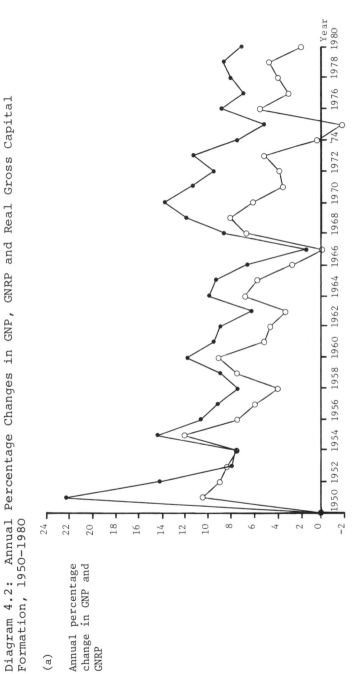

Key • GNP
    ○ GNRP

(b)

Annual percentage
change in
Real Investment

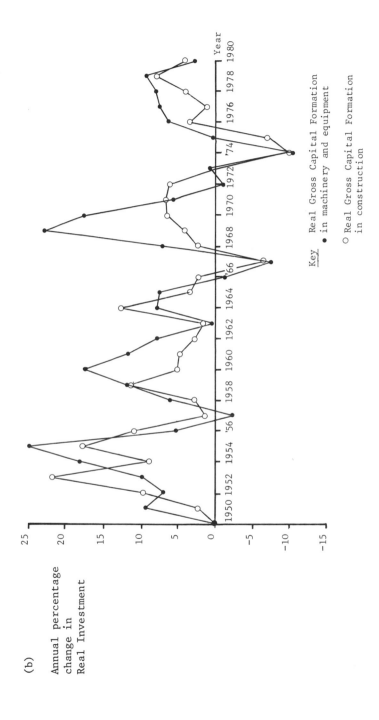

Key   Real Gross Capital Formation
      • in machinery and equipment

      ○ Real Gross Capital Formation
        in construction

Source:  Plotted from Dresdner Bank, *Statische Reihen*, p.1.

Diagram 4.3: Annual Percentage Changes in GNRP, Industrial Production, Real Gross Capital Formation and Interest Rates, 1950-1980

(a)

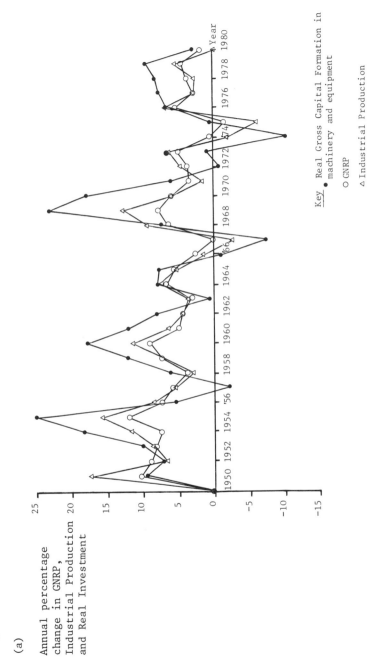

Annual percentage change in GNRP, Industrial Production and Real Investment

Key Real Gross Capital Formation in machinery and equipment

● GNRP

○ GNRP

△ Industrial Production

(b)

Annual percentage
change in Industrial
Production, Real
Investment and
nominal interest rates

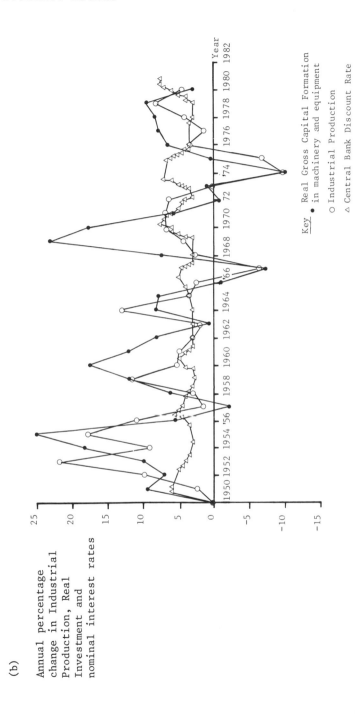

Key: Real Gross Capital Formation
   ● in machinery and equipment
   ○ Industrial Production
   △ Central Bank Discount Rate

Source:   Plotted from Dresdner Bank, *Statische Reihen,* pp.1–2.

of unemployment has been calculated for the three decades under review. Over such a fairly long-run period this produces a rather crude measure of the relationship between the demand for labour and its supply.

Again, there are significant trends by decade. During the 1950s, there was a sizeable pool of unemployment. As already shown in Chapter 3, this emanated from supply side factors, including the refugees and expellees who flooded into the western area of the country. There was also considerable mobility out of agriculture into industry. These structural changes in the labour market had two results.

First, the labour force grew by almost 6 million to reach 26.3 million by the end of the decade - a valuable contributory factor to economic growth. Consequently, until 1960 the supply of labour grew more rapidly than the demand for this factor, although the rapid downward trend in unemployment can be seen from Diagram 4.4. After the Berlin wall had been built in 1961, there was a virtual stability in the size of the labour force during the second decade, while a fall in the size of the labour force was recorded during most of the third decade. Between 1961 and 1973 - apart from 1967 - the demand for labour exceeded its supply, although after 1967 there were greater fluctuations on the demand side.

Secondly, during the 1950s the proportion of the labour force in industry (defined here to include energy, coal mining, manufacturing and construction industries) grew by 5 per cent while the agricultural labour force fell by 10 per cent. In the 1960s there was a continued movement from agriculture into the more highly productive industrial sector: agricultural employment fell from 13.6 per cent to 8.5 per cent of the labour force. Between 1970 and 1978 the proportion of the labour force in industry (defined as above) fell from 49 per cent to 45 per cent. Movement out of agriculture slowed down and the service sector of the economy expanded more rapidly: from 42 per cent of employed persons in 1970 to 49 per cent in 1979.

Average annual growth rates 1950-1962 reflected both the increase in the size of the labour force and the re-allocation of resources from agriculture to high productivity industry. For example, in the UK these growth rates were 2.29 per cent compared to 7.26 per cent in the FRG. The growth in labour input contributed 0.6 per cent to total growth in the UK, while in the FRG the equivalent contribution was 1.37 per cent. Improved allocation of resources contributed 0.12 per cent to the UK's growth rate whereas in

Diagram 4.4: The Decrease in Unemployment in the 1950s

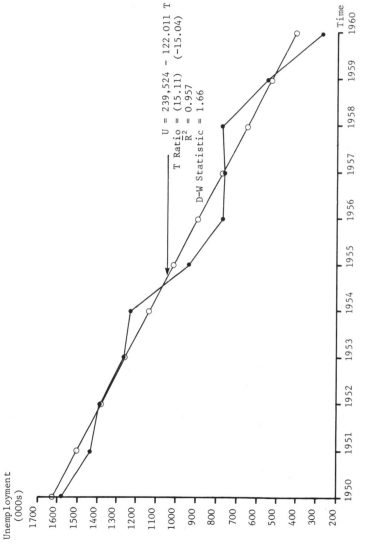

$$U = 239,524 - 122.011 \, T$$
$$\text{T Ratio} = (15.11) \quad (-15.04)$$
$$\overline{R}^2 = 0.957$$
$$\text{D-W Statistic} = 1.66$$

Source: Plotted from Dresdner Bank, *Statische Reihen*, p.3.

the FRG the contribution was 1.01 per cent (Denison
quoted by Ford, pp.238-239).

Finally, it can be seen from both Diagram 4.5
and Table 4.8 that a fall in aggregate demand brought
about a fall in the demand for labour in the two
recessionary years of 1967 and 1975. It will be
necessary to return to the reasons for the secular
fall in the demand for labour from 1974, which can
also be gauged from Table 4.8. On the supply side,
towards the end of the 1970s, the trend in unemployment, seasonally adjusted, seemed to be downwards,
but during 1980 it turned upwards again - with predictions of 2 million unemployed by 1982 confidently
being made. Nevertheless, in nine of the years between 1960 and 1973 unemployment was below 1 per cent.
Only in 1967 did unemployment exceed 2 per cent.
After 1974 the ratio was around 4 per cent in the
seven years up to, and including, 1980.

Each of the three decades under review had its
own peculiarities in terms of price inflation. By
again referring to Table 4.8, it can be seen that
prices fell 1953 on 1952 but increased considerably
1951 on 1950. Another such large increase and fall
had been experienced after the Currency Reform, so
that for the period from the second half of 1948 to
1953 the average change in prices was zero. In the
following five years (1953-58) the average annual
increase in prices was 1.9 per cent (1950=100).
From 1958-1963 the average rise was 2.3 per cent,
while from 1948-1963 it was 1.3 per cent (MRDB,
December 1963, p.13). During the 1950s trade unions
displayed wage restraint and in any case their bargaining strength was possibly undermined by the influx
of refugees. Labour's share in the national income -
adjusted for increases in the size of the employed
labour force - fell from 75 per cent in 1950 to 65
per cent in 1960. On the other hand, the gradual
abolition of price control caused large increases in
public transport fares, postal charges, rents and
food, heating and lighting prices. Nevertheless,
because of the high rate of economic expansion during
the 1950s, real wages rose 63 per cent between 1950
and 1960.

Perhaps the most striking feature of the 1960s -
with the exception of 1967 - was the high level of
excess demand in the labour market. The OECD has
reported (*Economic Outlook*, December 1979, p.131)
that during the relatively stable full employment
years of 1961-66 inclusive, West Germany's inflation
rate was consistently, although marginally, above
that of the average weighted rate for seven OECD

Diagram 4.5: Annual Average Percentages of Unemployment and the Rate of Change in the Retail Price Index, 1950–1980

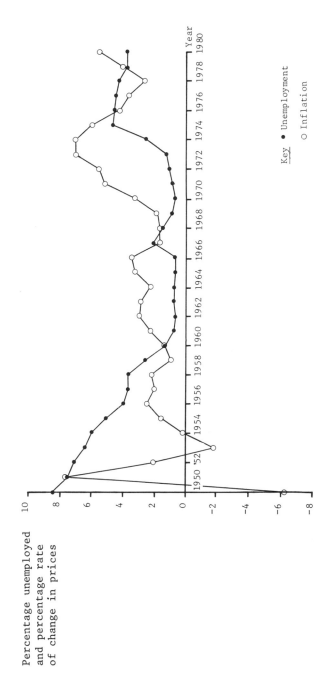

Percentage unemployed
and percentage rate
of change in prices

Key ● Unemployment
○ Inflation

Source: Plotted from Dresdner Bank, *Statische Reihen*, pp.3–4.

countries including the Federal Republic - the other
six being the USA, Canada, UK, Japan, Italy and
France.  This was in contrast to the period 1953-1960
when the FRG, along with the USA, recorded a total
rise in prices of 11 per cent.  Italy's total was 15
per cent; the UK 21 per cent and France 34 per cent
(Stolper, p.282).
     *Economic Outlook* later reported (July 1982,
p.151) that from 1967 to 1981, with the exception of
1971 and 1972, the Federal Republic was able to re-
gain her below average position among the seven OECD
countries mentioned in the previous paragraph.  On an
unweighted compound basis the FRG had an average
annual inflation rate of 5.1 per cent between 1970
and 1980.  During the same decade the rate in the USA
was 7.8 per cent, followed by Canada (8.0 per cent),
Japan (9.0 per cent), France (9.7 per cent), the UK
(13.7 per cent) and Italy (13.8 per cent) (BMWi,
Table 2.31).  Nevertheless, the high degree of excess
demand which had characterised the West German economic scene during the 1960s - and on a fairly stable
basis in the first half of that decade - gradually
gave way to an excess supply situation in the 1970s.
Inflation, on the other hand, remained above the
level of unemployment between 1960-1976, except during the 1967 recession.  This can all be seen in
Table 4.8 and Diagram 4.5.

## Measures of Efficiency

Business enterprises in the FRG expanded rapidly in
the 1950s because of the rapid expansion in labour
supply, savings and ploughed-back profits.  Trade
union pushfulness was moderated.  In the 1960s, the
savings ratio continued to rise, as did investment.
The capital/output ratio, which had fallen during
the 1950s, rose in the 1960s, and capital intensity
therefore increased much more than it had during the
1950s (Hennings, p.47).  After 1967 wage inflation
became more of a problem.  Technical progress, in
spite of increased research and development (R&D)
expenditure, slowed down and there was a marked increase in the average age of the capital stock.
Although investment remained high, there was a need
for a still higher level to replace the capital stock
built up during the two previous decades.  There was
also a need for capital deepening as well as widening
(Hennings, p.66).  In fact there was more deepening
than widening during the 1970s.  Productivity, profits and savings also increased at slower rates.  All
these trends must therefore be examined in a little
more depth.

The quantitative aspects of investment can be summarised as follows. There was a fall in the proportion of GNRP accounted for by both private and public consumption in the 1950s. Real investment, on the other hand rose (at 1962 prices) from 21 per cent to 25 per cent of GNRP. At 1970 prices there was then a relative stability of the investment function during the 1960s, followed by an initial decline but then a revival to 24 per cent of GNRP in the later 1970s. All the signs were that investment would stagnate thereafter. In real terms, both private and public consumption increased during the 1970s and reached 1950 levels (BMA, Table 1.2a). Relative to other OECD countries, using 1970 prices and exchange rates, the decline in investment began in 1970 from 11.1 per cent of investment undertaken in OECD countries in 1970 to 9.5 per cent in 1975 (*Die Zeit*, 19/76, p.19). Moreover, the amount of industry's capital equipment older than eleven years increased from one-third in 1960 to one-half in 1976 (Gruhler, p.15). Fixed capital always shows such a tendency to age when new capital formation slows down. The fall in the ratio of gross fixed real capital formation to GNRP, less depreciation and excluding construction and the public authorities' contributions, was even more dramatic and prolonged: from an average of 17.5 per cent in 1961-64 to 10.5 per cent in 1974-79 (MRDB, January 1980, p.14). This point was raised in another context in Table 4.4 above, where it was shown that (nominal) gross capital formation in machinery and equipment alone is relatively much more uniform among the six OECD countries included in the table. Hence those countries with a relatively high investment rate are nowadays spending more on infra-structure (Lloyds Bank Economic Bulletin No.33).

During the 1970s some concern was expressed within the FRG about the effect of the fall in investment on aggregate demand, national income and employment levels. One calculation placed the total of jobs lost annually at 150,000. Such a calculation was based on the gap between the actual rate of growth in investment and the extrapolated growth rate of this variable during the 1960s. The gap was calculated to be DM 53.3 billion in 1975. In order to close the gap and reduce unemployment to 500,000 - or approximately 2.5 per cent of the labour force - the Federal Ministry of Labour calculated that investment would have to increase by 8 per cent per annum in real terms (*The Times*, 24 November 1975). It can be gauged from what has been said that this was not achieved.

Moreover, when investment revived it was heavily concentrated, as in other recent years, on rationalisation and replacement; very little being allocated to
expanding productive capacity.

Turning to the qualitative aspects of changes in
the capital stock, it is first necessary to recall
that the increase of, and mobility within, the labour
force contributed 1.37 per cent and 1.01 per cent
respectively to the FRG's average annual economic
growth rate of 7.26 per cent during the period 1950-
1962. A further 1.41 per cent was contributed by
investment and 1.61 per cent by economies of scale,
compared to 0.51 per cent and 0.36 per cent in the
case of the UK. Advances in knowledge contributed
0.76 per cent in each country; 'other' factors contributed the remaining 1.1 per cent in the case of
West Germany (Ford on Denison, pp.238-239). More
recently, however, the smaller growth in the capital/
labour ratio indicated in the previous two paragraphs,
was accompanied by a slower growth in productivity -
in line with the long-term trend. This was due not
only to the ageing of the capital stock, but also
another qualitative factor, namely a falling return
on technical progress (Vollmer, p.587). It has been
pointed out that the quality and pace of technical
progress often develop in waves which do not solely
depend on the expenditure on research and development (MRDB, January 1980, p.13). Significantly,
capital productivity, measured as potential GDRP per
unit of fixed capital, decreased at an average rate
of 1 per cent per year after the 1974-75 recession.
Qualitatively, however, the rise in R&D expenditure
which took place in the 1970s should presumably have
resulted in at least a degree of technological change
(Hennings, p.47). R&D expenditure in the ten most
important OECD countries doubled between 1971 and
1978 to reach DM 180 billion. By 1978 absolute
expenditure in the USA had reached DM 89.4 billion;
in Japan it was DM 30.9 billion; in the FRG DM 23.8
billion; France DM 15.4 billion and in the UK
DM 10.6 billion. In per capita terms the FRG came
second (DM 388) to the USA (DM 409), then came France
(DM 289), Japan (DM 271) and the UK (DM 184). Approximately half the R&D expenditure in the FRG was
undertaken by private companies, the other half by
the State (*Die Zeit*, 47/79, p.19). However, where
the government makes R&D grants, it has been argued,
it favours the large companies and thereby undermines
the potential competitive and innovative spirit of
the smaller companies (Horn, pp.59-60).

Having examined the performance of capital, it

is now necessary to turn to labour inputs, although
a full analysis of the quantitative and qualitative
aspects of this factor will be postponed until the
labour market chapter is reached. What matters here
is that if cyclical fluctuations are eliminated the
long-term trend of labour productivity gains in West
Germany, in common with virtually all the industrialised market economies, seem to have declined (MRDB,
January 1980, pp.11-12). Since international competitiveness in terms of labour costs is functionally
related to relative productivity gains, the trends in
such gains are important. Relative labour costs
themselves are functionally related to differing rates
of pay settlements and, above all, to fluctuations in
exchange rates.

For reasons to be developed shortly, the DM exchange rate appreciated rapidly against the US dollar
in the 1970s but then depreciated during 1980. In
order to demonstrate the full effects of such a change
in exchange rates, Table 4.9 shows a selection of the
relative movements in total hourly labour costs between early 1978 and 1981. (Where the table to be
extended, further support to the points about to be
made would be found.)

Table 4.9:   Productivity and Labour Costs in Seven
Industrial Market Economies (manufacturing industry
only)

| | Total hourly labour costs[a] | | | Productivity[a] | | Unit labour costs[b] | |
|---|---|---|---|---|---|---|---|
| | 1981 | 1981 | 1978 | hourly 1981 | per head 1978 | 1981 | 1978 |
| | DM | | | West Germany = 100 | | | |
| West Germany | 25.00 | 100 | 100 | 100 | 100 | 100 | 100 |
| United States | 24.50 | 98 | 89 | 102 | 124 | 96 | 72 |
| Netherlands | 24.10 | 96 | 101 | 97 | 116 | 99 | 87 |
| Italy | 19.90 | 80 | 59 | 68 | 51 | 118 | 114 |
| France | 18.40 | 74 | 65 | 83 | 78 | 89 | 83 |
| Japan | 16.20 | 65 | 69 | 78 | 76 | 83 | 91 |
| United Kingdom | 14.20 | 57 | 43 | 50 | 52 | 114 | 83 |

Notes:
(a) At current (DM) exchange rates.
(b) Labour costs ÷ productivity.
(c) Further points of clarification are contained in the text.

Source:   Selected from Dresdner Bank, *Economic
Quarterly*, August 1978 and November 1981.

It will be seen that at current DM exchange rates,
and including social insurance contributions and
fringe benefits, total labour costs in West Germany
are high by international standards. However, allowing for differences in annual working hours, the
changes in relative positions since 1978 are also
apparent - one reason for the selection of the
countries in Table 4.9. Changes in 1981 on 1980 were
particularly dramatic. For example, whereas in 1980
hourly labour costs in West German manufacturing
industry had averaged DM 23.40 compared to the equivalent (at US$ 1 = DM 1.82) of DM 18.20 in the USA, it
can be seen from Table 4.9 that by autumn 1981 this
relatively (at US$ 1 = DM 2.20) was DM 25.00 to
DM 24.50.

Total labour costs are not all that meaningful
in this context, however. Hourly output per employee
is much more significant. Such a measure is also to
be found in Table 4.9, again at current DM exchange
rates. It is apparent that, with the exception of
Italy, high labour costs and high productivity, or
conversely low labour costs and low productivity,
tend to be fairly closely associated - another reason
for the selection of countries in Table 4.9. West
Germany scores quite highly in terms of productivity.

Random exchange rate fluctuations can be eliminated if hourly labour costs and productivity are
related to each other. Hence in the final column of
Table 4.9, indices of relative unit labour costs are
presented. These are the acid test of a country's
competitiveness in terms of international trade,
regardless of currency movements. At any given rate
of exchange Japan, France, the United States and, if
only by a small margin, the Netherlands, all therefore possessed a competitive edge on West Germany.

In fact, West Germany's competitive position
displayed a deterioration during the 1970s as the DM
exchange rate increased. In order to show the full
effects of this, both in relative and absolute
senses, the OECD in its *Economic Survey* (1979, p.21)
examined the trends in the growth of unit labour
costs in common (DM) and local currencies. In common
exchange rates (1970=100) all the selected countries
in Table 4.9 had higher rates of growth in unit
labour costs in manufacturing during the 1960s. In
the 1970s, measured in these terms, only the Netherlands and Japan (also because of the appreciation in
their exchange rates) experienced higher growth in
unit wage costs. (Japan's DM 16.20 hourly labour
costs in Table 4.9 had rocketed from DM 12.35 the
year before.) But the effects of domestic wage

inflation can best be gauged from measuring in local
currency terms. When this is done (1970=100), only
the United States (and Switzerland) among West
Germany's trading partners witnessed a smaller cumulative growth in unit costs in manufacturing. In
other words, West Germany's cost competitiveness decreased (common currency terms) but her domestic wage
inflation (local currency terms) was at once relatively low and largely absorbed, part of the adjustment being borne by decreasing profit margins - a
subject to which the analysis now turns.

Emphasis has already been placed on the fiscal
policies which were used to increase both personal
and business sector savings during the economic
recovery. Such policies also favoured the retention
of profits and provided direct incentives for their
re-investment. Hence profits were given policy priority over wages, and investment priority over consumption. In all probability profits were consequently higher than they would otherwise have been;
there is also some evidence that profits have been
generally higher than in all other OECD countries,
except Japan and the USA during the 1960s (Hill
quoted by Hennings, pp.30 and 98). In spite of
numerous measurement problems when making international comparisons, however, it is probably true to
say that the profits picture within West Germany has
changed during the three decades under review.
Basically, this change has consisted of decreasing
profits.

One indication is that labour's share in the
national income at factor cost - adjusted for increases in the number of employees - followed a
general upward trend from 1960 onwards (BMA, Table
1.5). Labour's share reached a peak of 71 per cent
in the recession years of 1974 and 1975, subsequently
falling to 69 per cent by 1980. Measured as a residual,
that is after the deduction of income from employment,
rent, interest and self-employment, 'profits' in 1974
and 1975 declined to an average of 5.5 per cent of
national income at factor cost. There was then a
recovery and the proportion reached 9.0 per cent in
1979, but declined to 7.4 per cent in 1980 and 6.0
per cent in 1981. At this level, therefore, 'profits'
were under half of the 14.6 per cent achieved in 1960
(IdDW, Table 18).

Another indication is that profit margins on
turnover seem to have fallen, although such margins
give no direct indication of the return on capital
and labour inputs. 'Profitability' in this latter
sense - that is the return on capital employed or

profit per employee - could be moving in the opposite
direction from profit margins. However, since evidence of a falling growth trend in both capital and
labour productivity has just been presented, it is
improbable that measures of profitability would
reveal a tendency to expand, unless volume and price
increases compensated for the fall in productivity
(also see NEDO, 1981b, para.13). The evidence already
presented in terms of falling economic growth trends
and low inflation implies that this has not occurred.
In any case, differences in the quantity of capital
employed in different sectors and the decline in
labour input in manufacturing tend to make such
measures of profitability misleading. Hence, the
margins presented in Table 4.10, with the appropriate
qualifications at the foot of the table, have been
selected for three reasons. First, a distinction is
made between pre- and post-tax profits. Second,
support for what has been said about the falling trend
in profits, with fluctuations around the trend in boom
and slump, seems to be presented. Third, the rise in
labour costs, also emphasised in this section, is
brought out.

A final point concerns the financing of investment. In the 1950s over a third of average annual
gross investment of enterprises was financed by undistributed profits. By the 1970s this average had
fallen to below 10 per cent. On the other hand,
depreciation allowances accounted for an increasing
proportion of gross investment expenditure - as
would be expected from what has been said about the
growing size of the capital stock, yet the falling
ratio of gross fixed real capital formation to GNRP.
By 1980 over half of gross investment was attributable to deductions for depreciation. More specifically, the gross investment of enterprises in 1980
was financed by depreciation (52.3 per cent), undistributed profits (7.5 per cent), borrowed capital
(27.7 per cent) and the balance of asset transfers
(12.5 per cent) (IdDW, Table 14).

The implications for income distribution of what
has just been said will be reviewed in Chapter 6. At
the moment, the discussion of macro-economic trends
continues with an analysis of the balance of payments.


THE BALANCE OF PAYMENTS

Perhaps the most significant aspect of the FRG's
balance of payments was her undervalued exchange rate
during the 1950s (Opie, p.16). In all probability

this continued during most, if not all, of the 1960s
(Horn, p.21). The rate was arguably pitched on the
low side after the Currency Reform, but the rapid
productivity gains of the 1950s had the effect of
increasing the degree of undervaluation. Moreover,
until the 1970s import prices of raw material inputs
tended, if anything, downwards. This all clearly
gave German exporters a certain degree of competitive
advantage, although export prices were perhaps not
the only factor which influenced foreign demand. As
export surpluses secularly grew, however, speculative
pressure was brought to bear on the exchange rate.
In addition, as capacity utilisation reached relatively high levels, inflationary pressure increased.
Hence in 1961, 1969, 1971 and 1973 economic external
balance had to be restored by revaluing the DM
exchange rate against the dollar. On the one hand,
this policy was designed to increase imports and
decrease exports thus relieving the pressure of
demand on German industry. On the other hand, it
would reduce the inflow of funds which were boosting
the internal money supply. Since the issue of exchange rate adjustment is connected with monetary
policy, therefore, a full investigation is postponed
until Chapter 5.

In 1980 the exchange rate of the DM against the
US$ increased (depreciated) from DM 1.73 to DM 1.96
(see Diagram 5.7). The appreciation of the DM since
1973 had undermined price competitiveness and so the
reversed trend in 1980 came as a relief to West
German companies. Goods manufactured in the FRG
remained in relatively high demand at the end of the
period under review, although the Japanese in particular were making inroads into some markets (Vollmer,
p.578). West Germany's electrical, chemical and
mechanical engineering industries, the latter including vehicles, were the main contributors. Iron
and steel and, somewhat surprisingly perhaps, textiles also made important contributions (BMWi, Table
5.26). Nuclear and coal-fired power stations, civil
engineering projects, oil refineries, chemical and
steel plants were being built by German companies in
the USSR, East Europe, China, Latin America and the
Middle East (*Die Zeit*, 52/79, p.17). It is, however, her Common Market neighbours who provided the
FRG, along with the USA, with her most important
trading partners by nominal value (see Diagram 4.7).
In 1980 and 1981 the top half dozen nations to which
the FRG exported goods were, in rank order: France,
the Netherlands, Italy, Belgium/Luxembourg, the UK
and the USA. Similarly, by 1981 the major origins

Table 4.10: Selected Ratios of all Enterprises submitting Annual Accounts to the Bundesbank

| Item – as percentage of turnover | 1965 | 1966 | 1967 | 1968 | 1969 | 1970 | 1971 | 1972 | 1973 | 1974 | 1975 | 1976 | 1977 | 1978 | 1979 |
|---|---|---|---|---|---|---|---|---|---|---|---|---|---|---|---|
| Stocks | 13.3 | 13.4 | 12.7 | 13.3 | 13.5 | 13.5 | 13.4 | 13.2 | 13.1 | 13.1 | 13.2 | 13.2 | 13.1 | 13.3 | 13.4 |
| Short-term claims | 15.0 | 15.2 | 15.1 | 17.3 | 18.3 | 18.9 | 19.5 | 20.5 | 19.8 | 18.7 | 18.7 | 18.4 | 17.5 | 18.5 | 18.5 |
| Labour costs | 16.9 | 17.8 | 17.4 | 18.2 | 18.2 | 19.2 | 20.2 | 20.8 | 20.9 | 20.6 | 20.5 | 19.9 | 20.0 | 20.2 | 19.7 |
| Interest paid (net)[a] | – | – | – | – | – | – | 1.2 | 1.1 | 1.4 | 1.6 | 1.3 | 1.0 | 1.0 | 0.9 | 0.9 |
| Gross earnings | 38.0 | 38.5 | 38.7 | 38.5 | 38.3 | 38.5 | 39.4 | 40.3 | 40.1 | 38.6 | 38.1 | 37.6 | 37.3 | 38.0 | 37.5 |
| Internal resources[b] | – | 7.4 | 7.3 | 8.1 | 8.0 | 8.0 | 7.6 | 7.5 | 6.8 | 6.2 | 6.3 | 6.8 | – | 6.3 | 6.2 |
| Profit for the year | 3.7 | 3.3 | 3.3 | 3.6 | 3.9 | 3.6 | 3.3 | 3.2 | 2.6 | 2.2 | 2.2 | 2.7 | 2.4 | 2.5 | 2.4 |
| Pre-tax profit for the year | 8.8 | 8.3 | 8.4 | 7.3 | 7.3 | 6.6 | 6.3 | 6.4 | 5.7 | 5.0 | 5.1 | 5.6 | 5.4 | 5.6 | 5.5 |

(a) Interest paid less interest received.
(b) Profit for the year plus depreciation of fixed assets and change in provisions.

Note:

The data on enterprises' annual accounts are based on balance sheets and profit and loss accounts submitted to the branches of Land Central Banks in connection with rediscount transactions. About 90 per cent of the balance sheets evaluated were drawn up to comply with tax regulations; in general, commercial balance sheets are submitted only by public and the larger private limited companies.

The source material contains an above-average proportion of enterprises whose financial position is relatively strong and which satisfy the Bundesbank's solvency requirements. Weaker enterprises whose bills of exchange are obviously not 'eligible for discount at the Bundesbank' frequently do not submit any balance sheets at all. In addition, large enterprises, particularly those organised in the form of public limited companies and thus subject to disclosure requirements, carry greater weight in the source material than in the enterprise sector as a whole.

In order to offset the distortion of the source material – particularly the over-representation of large enterprises – and to obtain data on the development of balance sheets and profit and loss accounts over time, even though the range of enterprises included varies from year to year, the annual accounts are as a rule extrapolated and published in that form.

Sources: 'Jahresabschlüsse der Unternehmen in der Bundesrepublik Deutschland 1965 bis 1976', *Sonderdrucke der Deutschen Bundesbank*, Nr.5, p.9; 'Verhältniszahlen aus den Jahresabschlüssen der Unternehmen in der Bundesrepublik Deutschland für 1977', *Sonderdrucke der Deutschen Bundesbank*, Nr.6, p.10; MRDB, November 1981, p.26.

of imports were (again in rank order): the Netherlands, France, the USA, Italy, the UK and Belgium/
Luxembourg (BMWi, Tables 5.24.3 and 5.24.4).
  Table 4.11 illustrates the changing current
account and foreign trade balances which have been
so important in influencing foreign confidence.

Table 4.11:  Average Annual Foreign Trade and Current
Account Net Balances, 1951-1980

| | DM million (at current prices) | | | |
|---|---|---|---|---|
| | Foreign Trade Balance | | Current Account Balance | |
| | Mean | Median | Mean | Median |
| 1951-1960 | 2953.4 | 2797.5 | 3984.9 | 4012.5 |
| 1961-1970 | 9785.4 | 7286.5 | 2993.6 | 2087.0 |
| 1971-1980 | 30275.0 | 33724.0 | 5350.4 | 9706.5 |
| 1951-1980 | 14338.0 | 7286.5 | 4109.6 | 3771.0 |

Source:  Calculated from Dresdner Bank, *Statische
Reihen*, p.5.

The foreign trade balance was positive in 29 out of
the 31 years between 1950 and 1980, the two exceptions
being 1950 (-DM 3,012 million) and 1951 (-DM 149
million).  Further, both the mean and the median
values markedly increased in magnitude in each of the
three decades, thereby underlining the importance of
export-led growth.  In other words, export surpluses
often compensated for deficiencies in domestic aggregate demand.  As Shonfield remarked (pp.274 and 289),
the boom in world trade kept German order books
filled, irrespective of fluctuations in domestic consumer demand.  This compensatory element was particularly valuable during the 1967 and 1974-75 recessions,
when the balance of trade surpluses were well above
the trend line and mean values for the respective
decades.  However, the increased degree of variability each decade (see the upper sections of
Diagrams 4.6 and 4.7) culminated in the huge surplus
of 1974 and a relatively minor surplus in 1980.  This
presented a number of policy problems, especially
when the increasing oil bill, mounting invisible
deficits and capital outflows are all taken into
account.  There was a corresponding deterioration in
the real terms of trade (IdDW, Table 72).

Dependence on imported oil is now West Germany's major economic weakness: oil imports amounted to one-fifth of the total import bill in 1980. The extent of the rise in imported crude oil prices is shown in Diagram 4.6. Together with the gradual increase in deficit invisible items (also shown in Diagram 4.6), these developments meant that the net current account balances did not, relative to the foreign trade balances, mount in magnitude to any great extent - as the means and medians in Table 4.11 indicate. Indeed, the 1960s were in this sense down on the 1950s. Moreover, the deficits, when they occurred, mounted in magnitude: 1950, -DM 0.4 billion; 1962, -DM 1.6 billion; 1979, -DM 9.6 billion; and 1980, -DM 29.0 billion. (In 1981 the deficit was -DM 17.3 billion but predictions indicated that the eradication of the deficit by 1982-84 was the only bright spot on the macro-economic horizon: growth would stagnate and unemployment would continue to rise.) Yet it is arguably the current account balance which is the crucial indicator of economic welfare, or a nation's well-being.

As shown in Diagram 4.6, there have been important invisible net outflows on current account which were financed out of the favourable foreign trade balance. Of primary significance here were, first, net travel expenditure (services account) and, secondly, remittances made by foreign workers (transfer payment - foreign workers are treated as residents from the economic point of view). Another group of transfer payments which tended to increase the deficit were official expenditures, the total of which exceed official receipts. However, receipts from foreign military agencies and the European Community's agricultural fund remained buoyant positive items (cf. MRDB, January 1982, p.17). Quite clearly, then, export surpluses are of central importance in assessing the FRG's economic performance.

As will be shown in more depth in Chapter 5, in spite of exchange rate adjustments speculative funds continued to flow into the FRG, along with the foreign exchange inflows resulting from large balance of trade surpluses. Foreign currency reserves therefore secularly increased. At the end of the 1970s the FRG had the largest reserves in the industrialised world. Since her gold reserves remained constant at about DM 14 billion, they have become a smaller proportion of her total reserves. In 1979 and 1980 the current account deficits were financed from these reserves and they consequently decreased. But the significant short-term capital inflows gave West

Diagram 4.6: Current Account Performance, 1950–1980

(a)

Current, Trade and
Services + Transfers
(Balances in
DM billion)

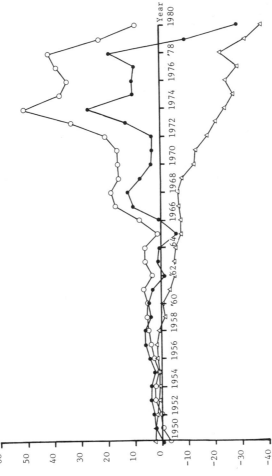

Key • Total current account balance

○ Trade balance

△ Balance of services and
transfer payments

(b)

Annual percentage
changes in imported
crude oil prices

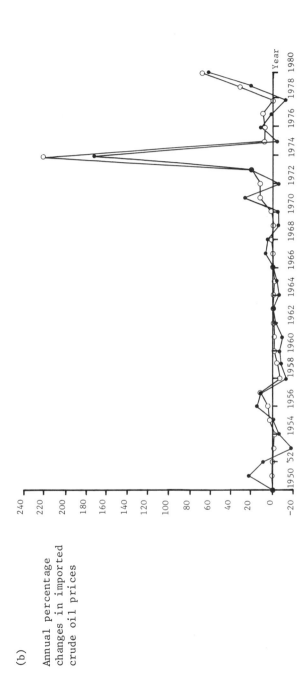

Key  • Annual percentage change in
        crude oil prices (DM basis)

      o Annual percentage change in
        world market price of crude oil
        (US$ basis)

Source:  Plotted from Dresdner Bank, *Statische Reihen*, pp. 4-5.

Diagram 4.7: West Germany's Share in World Trade, 1950–1980

(a)

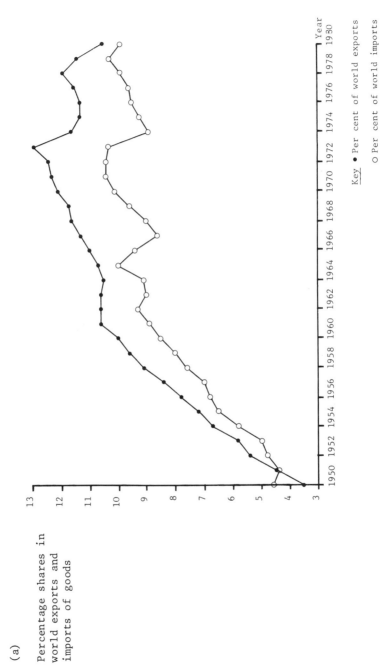

Percentage shares in
world exports and
imports of goods

Key • Per cent of world exports

 ○ Per cent of world imports

(b)

Percentage shares of
West Germany's exports

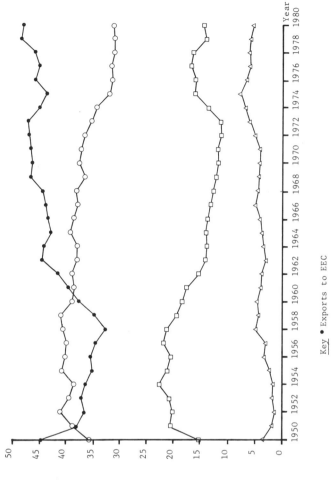

Key • Exports to EEC

○ Other industrial market economies

□ Developing countries

△ Communist countries

Source: Plotted from Dresdner Bank, *Statische Reihen*, p. 4.

German companies the means, and probably the increasing domestic labour costs and appreciating DM exchange
rate were the reasons, for the long-term capital inflows which occurred during the 1970s.  Prior to the
1970s, German companies had in any case concentrated
on the re-construction of the domestic economy, to say
nothing of the apprehension arising from the fact that
they had twice had foreign assets confiscated following the two World Wars.

Interest in the context of long-term capital outflows is, for the present, focused on direct investment.  (Portfolio investment has been erratic, this
being caused not least by the behaviour of bond purchases.)  When analysing direct investment in and by
the FRG, one encounters two statistical problems.

First, the Bundesbank and Economics Ministry
definitions of direct investment differ.  The Bundesbank records those transactions by companies which are
regarded as attempts to gain influence within another
organisation.  The Economics Ministry records capital
assets which create a permanent economic commitment.
It seems that the latter is more preferable for the
present purposes (especially because the data are
recorded net of loan repayments, liquidations, sales
of holdings and book transfers).

Second, German direct investment abroad **has been**
recorded since 1952, whereas foreign direct investment in the FRG was not recorded until 1961.  It is,
however, the increased outflow of direct investment
in the late 1960s and 1970s which are particularly
pertinent here, although the activity around all the
periods of revaluation is also worthy of note.  One
estimate is that total capital outflows by 1962 had
reached DM 5 billion, whereas inflows totalled DM 15
billion (IdDW, Table 69).  A dramatic change in the
situation, especially after 1975, resulted in outflows by 1980 totalling DM 74 billion and inflows
DM 71 billion.  (By 1981 outflows were DM 84 billion
and inflows DM 75 billion.)  Table 4.12 gives a breakdown of the relative importance of both recipient and
source countries.  It can be seen that most of the
capital outflows have been to the industrialised
world.

In terms of the FRG's export trade, direct investment remains relatively small.  Overseas subsidiaries of American owned companies produce four times
as much of the exports as their parent organisations;
similarly UK foreign subsidiaries produce twice as
much as their parent companies export.  When this
comparison is applied to the FRG the ratio drops to
one-third (*Die Zeit*, 13/79, p.26).  Nevertheless, the

Table 4.12: Direct Investment: Rank order of
recipient and source countries

Percentage of total flows, 1980

| The most important recipients (i.e. flows out of the FRG) | | The most important sources (i.e. flows into the FRG) | |
|---|---|---|---|
| USA | 21.1 | USA | 35.3 |
| Belgium/Luxembourg | 9.8 | Switzerland | 15.1 |
| France | 9.2 | Netherlands | 12.6 |
| Switzerland | 7.9 | UK | 11.7 |
| Brazil | 7.2 | France | 5.9 |
| Canada | 6.5 | Belgium/Luxembourg | 5.7 |
| Netherlands | 5.9 | Japan | 2.5 |
| Spain | 4.9 | Iran | 2.4 |
| UK | 3.5 | Sweden | 2.3 |
| Italy | 2.9 | Italy | 1.1 |

Source:   IdDW, Table 69 (writer's translation).

trend has been unmistakably one of increasing direct
investment overseas.  When measured by the stock of
direct investment in industrial market economies, the
FRG moved up from sixth to third position between
1967 (2.8 per cent of the total) and 1976 (6.9 per
cent of the total).   In this period the USA's share
fell from 53.8 per cent to 47.6 per cent, while the
UK's share fell from 16.6 per cent to 11.2 per cent
(Hood and Young, p.18).
     As one would probably expect, the main impetus
of overseas investment comes from the large German
companies in her traditional export industries, namely
chemical, electrical and mechanical engineering –
including motor vehicles.   Of the DM 74 billion of
direct investment between 1952 and 1980, DM 11 billion
was in chemicals, DM 7 billion in electricals, DM 6
billion in machine tools and DM 5 billion in motor
vehicles.   A further DM 6 billion was invested in iron
and steel production – in other words about half the
total was invested by these industries (BMWi, Table
5.52.21).   Whereas in the USA 300 firms are responsible for 70 per cent of foreign direct investment,
and in the UK 165 firms provide 80 per cent, only 82
West German companies own 70 per cent of the stock of
direct investment abroad.   (The link between West
German industry and banking again becomes apparent
from the fact that foreign direct investment by the
banks also reached DM 6 billion in 1980, having been

only DM 0.8 billion in 1970.) The USA in particular
has attracted investment from both German chemical
and motor vehicle manufacturers. For example, VW
Golfs are assembled and marketed under the name of
Rabbit in the USA. Beetle models are now manufactured only in South Africa, Brazil, Mexico and
Nigeria. In short, an increasing proportion of total
turnover and employment are accounted for by foreign
subsidiaries of major German companies. On the other
hand, average exports of the parent company seem so
far to have been barely affected. It may also be the
case that the deficit on current invisibles will be
reduced by an earnings inflow. But the financing of
overseas investment at a time of falling demand and
employment in the domestic economy has its obvious
negative side.


CONCLUSION

Summarising, then, one is struck by the richly contrasting features of the performance of the German
economy during the period 1950-1980. The rapid
economic expansion, and equally rapid diminution in
unemployment, during the 1950s, ushered in a period
of firm consolidation and full employment until 1966.
Thereafter, fluctuations in economic activity became
relatively more severe. These fluctuations were
combined, after 1973, with balance of payments problems emanating from relatively high unit labour costs,
a mounting crude-oil import bill, an appreciating
exchange rate and increased investment abroad. Hence
the next chapter investigates the reactions of policy-
makers to these changing economic circumstances.

Chapter Five

ECONOMIC POLICIES

INTRODUCTION

Four basic features have characterised economic
policies in the FRG. First, the nature of the policy
problems themselves changed during the three decades
under review. Secondly, as a result of this factor
there has been a gradual movement away from the orthodox model of economic control to counter-cyclical
aggregate policy instruments. Thirdly, such a policy
development was accompanied by attempts to moderate
cost inflation, as well as the implementation of a
more active labour market policy. Fourthly, a number
of autonomous authorities have contributed to overall
economic policy. It will therefore be necessary to
briefly outline the role of these institutions.

THE AUTHORITIES

Because interest here is focused on macro-economic
policy-making, the principal authorities to be reviewed are the Federal Ministries of Finance and
Economics, the Federal Bank and the Federal Labour
Office. At the Federal level the Finance Ministry is
in charge of fiscal policy, the Economics Ministry
has powers for economic planning and the Bundesbank
(Central Bank) has wide powers in the field of monetary policy. The Federal Labour Office has labour
market responsibilities. There has been a clearly
discernible trend towards centralisation in economic
decision-making. Having said this, it is important
to note that only a half of the total expenditure and
revenue of the public authorities is included in the
Federal budget. The governments of the eleven Länder
(federal states) and 25,000 local authorities account
for the other half. Clearly some aspects of these

latter levels of government will have to be covered.
Emphasis, however, must be placed on the growing degree of centralisation and counter-cyclical policy
at the Federal level.

The system of decentralised public finance
(re-)created by the Allies placed most public expenditure and revenue-raising powers in the hands of the
Länder and local authorities. Because the power to
levy taxes was so diffused, with the Länder deriving
the bulk of the revenue, the central government tended
to over-insure in order to make certain that its minimum needs were met. It was only after various tax
reforms, and constitutional amendments, between 1955
and 1969 that the central government was able to assert a regular and more substantial claim to a share
of the revenue from income, corporation and turnover
taxes - the latter being, since 1968, the sum of the
tax revenue from value added tax and the turnover tax
on imports. The negotiations leading up to these reforms were somewhat acrimonious; even today the annual
negotiations over the division of the revenue from the
turnover tax are regarded as a round of poker (*Die
Zeit*, 2/79, p.22). But the process of centralisation
has been evident. Above all, the Act to Promote Economic Stability and Growth (*Gesetz zur Förderung der
Stabilität und des Wachstums der Wirtschaft* - StWG)
recreated the relatively more centralised fiscal
system which had eventually been established in 1922,
the Allies having decentralised the system so that the
Länder had again been the more powerful fiscal partner.
However, the tax structure remains complex and somewhat
unwieldy, while in the late 1970s the expenditure side
caused the fiscal balance to lurch very markedly into
deficit - the opposite of the surpluses amassed in the
period 1952-56. It is possibly these complexities of
the West German fiscal system which have resulted in
the relative neglect of the role of fiscal policies in
West Germany. Neo-liberal ideological reasons may
also be partly to blame (Stolper and Roskamp, p.387).

In turning to the role of the central bank in
West Germany, one also detects the decentralising
influence of the Allies (Reuss, p.51). Central banking activities were confined to the Länder level until
shortly before the Currency Reform of 1948 when all
previous banking legislation was repealed and the
autonomous Bank deutscher Länder (BdL) was established.
Under the legislation which founded the BdL in the
western zones of occupation, however, the Länder banks
remained legally independent entities (Denton, p.169).
It was 1957 before the Länder banks were transferred
to the more centralised control of the newly founded

Deutsche Bundesbank. Many of the functions in the field of social
security spending which impinge on the labour market
are carried out by the Federal Labour Office, a self-
governing body incorporated under public law. It is
not directly associated with the Federal Government,
although it is subject to legal supervision by the
Ministry of Labour and Social Affairs. Again some
centralisation is evident, because the Federal Labour
Office assumed several additional functions as a
result of the Employment Promotion Act, 1969. Through
its Länder and local employment offices it promotes
vocational training and employment opportunities. It
is also responsible for the payment of unemployment
benefits and assistance as well as child allowances.
When the social security funds were accruing massive
surpluses in the 1950s and early 1960s their managers
had a considerable degree of investment freedom.
Because large amounts were deposited in the banks,
thus increasing bank credit, the Bundesbank regarded
this absence of effective control as a serious policy
weakness. Under the Promotion of Economic Stability
and Growth Act (1967), however, the Federal Government and the Bundesbank may require the Federal
Labour Office to purchase treasury bills out of its
job creation and pension funds, although the growth
in unemployment benefits and rise in other social
security spending during the 1970s forced the Federal
Labour Office into deficit.

Having mentioned the major authorities involved
in economic policy-making, it is possible to proceed
to an analysis of economic policy itself. Basically,
it is intended to show that conventional monetary
policy proved to be just as inadequate in tackling
the problems of economic affluence - particularly the
balance of payments side of things - as it had been
in the period following the Currency Reform. After
the 1961 revaluation, therefore, the search began for
anti-cyclical fiscal policies. This search resulted
in the appointment of a Council of Economic Advisers
and increased attempts at government planning. It
also led to the growing centralisation of budgetary
control. In addition, there were reforms of the tax
system. All these policy developments are first
placed in their historical context.


SOME NOTABLE DEVELOPMENTS

In an attempt to absorb the large excess supply of
money which was the legacy of the Nazi régime, the

Allies introduced in 1946 the highest income tax in
German history (Denton, p.188; Horn, p.10). At the
time of the Currency Reform, corporation tax rates
were reduced but income tax rates were not lowered
to the extent advocated by the German Economic Council
chaired by Erhard. In order to increase incentives,
therefore, the German side of the Council resorted to
tax privileges and concessions, most of which were
directed at stimulating capital formation by encouraging savings and ploughed-back profits. In other
words, the accelerated depreciation provisions of the
tax laws, plus a willingness to go on investing in
order to have something to write off, and the
ploughing-back of the profits thus generated, were
all responsible for the tremendous upsurge in the
initial self-financing of business recovery (Mendershausen, pp.75-76; Wallich, pp.161-162). Forced saving in this sense therefore played a large part in
this recovery.

Nevertheless, in an unsuccessful attempt to ward
off another budgetary deficit, and to reduce inflationary pressure, several of the concessions had
to be rescinded in 1951; a number of taxes were also
increased. The four notable exceptions were, first,
the special export incentives, which expired in 1955.
(Export sales remain exempt from value added tax
(VAT), of course.) Secondly, a tax incentive to the
shipbuilding industry was withdrawn in 1954 when the
industry was already over-capitalised, although tax
exempt grants and loans continued even when excess
capacity existed in 1962 (Reuss, pp.200-203). Thirdly,
bottleneck industries where price control was still in
operation - mainly coal, steel and electricity -
received the proceeds of a levy placed on other industries, together with specially accelerated depreciation allowances under the Investment Aid Act of 1952
(Shonfield, p.275). Fourthly, housing subsidies and
tax remissions on all investment continued (Reuss,
p.197). But Federal budgets now moved into surplus
and it is necessary to see why - not least because
it was another form of forced saving.

Reference has already been made to the role
played at the Economics Ministry by Professor Ludwig
Erhard during the economic recovery (Chapter 3). The
first of Erhard's contemporaries at the Finance Ministry was Fritz Schäffer (CSU), while the President
of the Bank deutscher Länder was Dr Wilhelm Vocke.
Between 1952 and 1966 Schäffer ran the Federal budget
in surplus (Hardach, p.175). These surpluses were
frozen at the Central Bank and they became known as
the 'Julius Tower' - a historical reference to the

fortress in Spandau where the Prussian kings had
stored their war treasures (Shonfield, p.284n).
The surpluses were partly the result of an underestimate of revenue, but mainly came about as a result
of an overestimate of future defence commitments. In
fact, rearmament and other increases in expenditure
were accomplished without increasing taxation because
they could be financed from the budget surpluses.
While the Julius Tower was at its maximum, the surpluses probably helped damp down the boom of 1955-56
- unlike the inflationary effects of FF 5 billion
reparation payment from France which increased expenditure in the early 1870s because only RM 120
million was secreted away in the war chest at Spandau
(Henderson, p.162). The Schäffer surpluses were
unintentionally expenditure switching because they
skimmed off internal demand, and probably also served
as an added incentive to West German industrialists
to look for overseas markets. On the other hand, the
very success of stabilising West German prices aggra-
vated the balance of payments problem of subsequent
years (Stolper and Roskamp, p.399).
        Schäffer went to the Justice Ministry in 1957
and was replaced as Finance Minister by Franz Etzel.
Although not a Keynesian, Etzel was prepared to view
his budgetary calculations in terms of modern national
income accounting; in the same year, Vocke also
retired (Shonfield, p.285). Vocke had been a staunch
representative of traditional German finance (Hartrich, pp.165 and 169). He was replaced by Karl
Blessing in the year - 1958 - that the more centralised Deutsche Bundesbank started to operate (Keesing's
Contemporary Archives, 1957, 15715). By 1962 Rolf
Dahlgrün of the FDP had become Finance Minister.
Dahlgrün succeeded Heinz Starke who had been in office
for only one year.
        Hence as Germany entered the phase of full employ-
ment and imported inflation in 1959-1960, the emphasis
gradually changed from one of financial orthodoxy to
one of active anti-cyclical intervention, an example
of which were the powers given to the Finance Minister
in the 1961 budget to increase the tax allowances for
new investment, without recourse to parliament. Such
policies would be based on his judgment of cyclical
trends. In the same year an official enquiry was
jointly launched by the Finance and Economics Ministries, with advice from the Bundesbank, into the
adequacy or otherwise of anti-cyclical policy instruments. Adenauer seemed to lose electoral support,
and the absolute parliamentary majority gained by his
party in 1957 was lost in 1961. Both the absolute

majority, and the fact that the 1961 setback had not
been greater, may be attributable to Erhard's repu-
tation as Minister of Economic Affairs. Eventually
Adenauer resigned - in 1963 - and Erhard became
Chancellor. This was only a few weeks after the Act
which established an independent Council of Economic
Advisers reached the statute book. They were to be
charged with the duties of observing and advising on
economic developments, although the extent to which
their views revised orthodox economic thinking is a
topic mentioned in Chapter 6. Four goals were included in the Act and Professor Schiller (see below)
was to join the Advisers in quantifying same (Wallich,
1968, pp.354 and 364). In fact Schiller had much more
in common with the Advisers than Erhard (*ibid.*,
pp.352, 368-369 and 376).

Erhard's stated economic policy goals and instu-
ments were either inadequate or ignored. The changes
in West German budgetary policy which gradually took
place in the first half of the 1960s amounted to a
new determination to use fiscal and expenditure policy
for anti-cyclical purposes alongside monetary policy
(Denton, p.226; Shonfield, p.287). Erhard was unable
to achieve his declared policy aim of public spending
not increasing more rapidly than national product.
Moreover, his apparent inability to prevent public
expenditure and revenue from moving apart was com-
pounded by his insistence on the micro policy front,
in spite of continued objections from industry, that
resale price maintenance should be abolished. On
this latter issue he was not supported by the new
Economics Minister, Kurt Schmücker (CDU), or the new
Deputy Chancellor Erich Mende of the FDP (Marburg,
p.97). On the other hand, much to the consternation
of exporters, he was a party to the revaluation of
the DM in 1961; he was also a party to the enactment
of what became known as 'Lex Abs' which was a move to
restrict the number of supervisory board chairmanships
any one individual could hold (Chapters 7 and 8 above;
Englemann, p.66). Of significance here, however, is
that the concept of the social market economy was
increasingly regarded as 'old fashioned' (Horn, p.19).

Budgetary deficits now arose, culminating in a
record level during the election year of 1965.
Erhard's CDU party was returned but again without an
overall parliamentary majority. His Free Democrat
(FDP) coalition partners resigned the following year
when he attempted to decrease the budget deficit by
increasing taxes. He was himself in turn forced to
resign and was replaced on 1 December 1966 by Dr Kurt
Georg Kiesinger (CDU) of Baden Württemburg. Herr

Franz Josef Strauss, his party colleague from the CSU
wing, became Finance Minister and Professor Karl
Schiller of the Social Democrats (SPD) became Economics Minister - two very different personalities in
the so-called Grand Coalition. Schiller was also
something of a Keynesian who, among other things,
agreed with the stress placed on economic growth as
a variable to set alongside the more traditional ones
of high employment, price stability and balance of
payments equilibrium. A 'magic square' of these four
macro-policy goals was formally substituted for the
former 'magic triangle' of three variables (Bendix,
pp.58-59). However, the Grand Coalition initially
took vigorous steps to prune public spending and
raise public revenue at a time when the German economy was moving into recession. For example, shipbuilding had been through a crisis and period of
rationalisation in 1966, followed by Krupps in 1967
and coal in 1967 and 1968. Hence, to counter this
trend two special public investment programmes were
undertaken later in 1967. As already shown in
Diagrams 4.2 and 4.3 and the surrounding discussion,
the economy rapidly moved into a boom. Whether
Schiller's reflationary measures, or Blessing's des-
perate reduction of interest rates was primarily
responsible, is not absolutely clear (Denton, pp.172-
173; Hallett, p.82; Hartrich, p.169).
    What is clear is that in 1967 the final break
with what might be termed orthodox fiscal policy was
made. It was replaced by Keynesian demand management
in the sense that fiscal policy was formally assigned
a role for the purposes of stabilisation and counter-
cyclical intervention. An Act to Promote Economic
Stability and Growth (StWG) reached the statute book
in that year (Owen Smith, 1979, p.165). The original
Erhard plans were transformed into the more ambitious
Schiller mode - the 'magic square' was given legal
status (Spahn, p.61). Schiller still espoused the
neo-liberal social market: 'as much competiton as
possible, as much planning as necessary' was his
maxim. But his StWG Act was so far-reaching that a
constitutional amendment was required (Denton, p.228).
Basically, the StWG provided the Federal Government
with a wide range of planning mechanisms and stabilisation instruments; it also linked the three levels
of government budgeting more closely together;
finally, it introduced what proved initially to be a
successful means of restraining the growth of money
wage rates - the so-called Concerted Action (Owen
Smith, 1981, p.201).
    A number of other important changes were also

75

introduced. For example, the 1969 Employment Promotion Act (AFG) resulted in the Federal Labour Office
assuming further responsibilities for such services as
placement, vocational training and counselling, job
creation, mobility incentives and wage subsidies.
The Office saw these measures as a method of achieving an 'improved balance between supply and demand in
the labour market' (Stingl, p.203). Both the number
and expertise of its staff were increased. Also by
1969 another series of Acts had reached the statute
book which brought a further accretion of power to
the Federal Government by giving it the right to
participate in policy formulation in a number of areas
which were previously within the exclusive competence
of the Länder. Again, these Acts followed procedural
delays and constitutional amendments (Grosser, p.159).
Ironically, it was regional policy which was at issue.
Financially weaker Länder (especially Schleswig-
Holstein, Lower Saxony, Saarland and Rhineland-
Palatinate) found from the beginning that the Federal
system of fiscal equalisation (see below) did not
resolve their specific economic problems (Spahn, p.26).
In addition to this revenue-sharing system, therefore,
Federal grants-in-aid were directed towards such pol-
icy areas as housing, regional and agricultural devel-
opment.

A Regional Planning Act (ROG) had been passed in
1965 (Schöller, pp.11-13). However, following the
specially enacted constitutional amendments just
referred to, joint planning responsibilities were,
from 1969, undertaken by the Federal and Länder
governments in the fields of university construction
and extensions, research and education, regional policy, agricultural structure and coastal preservation.
In effect, Federal grants-in-aid were extended so as
to cover not only housing and local transport, but
also urban renewal, housing modernisation and hospital
construction (Spahn, p.28n). A further reform in 1974
resulted in the local authorities being included in
the StWG commitment of taking overall economic equilibrium into account when formulating budgetary policy,
although local authorities have less latitude in their
revenue policies.

The important conclusion to the last three paragraphs is that the StWG, AFG and the other Acts of
1969 all committed the Federal Government to 'planning'
for full employment. However, the achievement of both
internal and external balance had now become more
difficult. It is equally important to see why.

Following the election in 1969 of an SPD/FDP
coalition, and therefore the departure from office of

the CSU Finance Minister (Strauss), Alex Möller became the first of a series of SPD Finance Ministers
during the 1970s.  Rather like Adenauer, Chancellor
Brandt took less interest in economic policy than he
did in foreign affairs (Hartrich, pp.159; Prittie, p.77;
Vogl, p.24).  Hence, when Möller resigned in 1971
because he could not support the fiscal policy of the
new coalition government, Schiller became joint Finance and Economics Minister, and as such he headed a
huge department of state.  But Schiller found that
his social market views were becoming unpopular within
the party organisation of the SPD, and he found himself becoming steadily isolated from his Cabinet and
colleagues (Hallett, pp.80-81).  Curiously enough, the
final confrontation over exchange controls involved
the then President of the Bundesbank - Dr Karl Klassen.
(He had replaced Blessing in 1969 and his office enables him to attend Cabinet meetings.  Klassen joined
the Bundesbank direct from the Deutsche Bank and was
a member of the SPD - Hartrich, p.287.)
    These differences over exchange controls, and
exchange rates in general, are of crucial policy
significance.  More will be said shortly on the wider
policy implications, but Schiller's views are relevant
here.
    In 1968 Schiller had sided with the Council of
Economic Advisers in advocating a further revaluation
of the DM in order to reduce imported inflation.
Schiller was supported by Blessing, even though the
latter was associated with the CDU (Keesing's Contemporary Archives, 1969, 23442 and 23697).  Strauss
opposed the revaluation proposal on the grounds that
it would undermine the competitiveness of German goods
abroad.  He also thought that the economic strength
and price stability of the FRG was the reciprocal of
the economic weakness and inflation among her trading
partners.  Strauss was supported by the Federation of
German Industry (*Bundesverband der Deutschen Indus-
trie*) and Chancellor Kiesinger.  Following the election in 1969 of an SPD/FDP coalition, and therefore
the demise of Strauss's influence, the DM was revalued.
    Schiller and the Council were at one over this
issue because they saw the received theory of flexible
exchange rates, the free international movement of
capital and the control of the money supply for stabilisation policy as all being essential to the successful
operation of free market forces (Hallett, p.80; Spahn,
p.71; Wallich, 1968, pp.358 and 369).  Fiscal policy
was, however, valuable as an aid to boost confidence
during recessions.  Further, the private sector was
assumed to be inherently unstable and there was a

need for an incomes policy - both of which are, of
course, at odds with the pure monetarist doctrine
(Spahn, p.80). The evidence is that the public
sector has taken up the inherent instability of the
private sector (OECD, *Economic Survey*, 1973, p.29,
and 1982, p.46).
It was during the renewed speculative pressures
in the period 1970-71 that the controversy over economic policy reached new heights. Schiller felt able
to accept the *Bardepot* measures at the end of 1971,
whereby the Government could impose reserve requirements, sometimes up to 100 per cent, on certain
foreign loans contracted by German companies. This
was in order to reduce the destabilising effects of
capital inflows. As will be seen later in this
chapter, these funds are deposited interest-free at
the Bundesbank. In June 1972, however, Klassen persuaded the Cabinet to impose tight exchange controls
by requiring foreigners to seek Bundesbank approval
for their purchases of domestic bonds. (In the first
half of 1972 foreign purchases of West German securities, mainly fixed-interest bearing bonds, reached
DM 10 billion - Vogl, p.28.) Schiller believed this
to be an unwarrantable constraint on the free market
system. He also expected that this would lead to
more controls and in any case disagreed with his Cabinet colleagues on budgetary questions. He consequently resigned from the Government, being replaced
as Economics and Finance Minister by Helmut Schmidt -
a minister who believed that '5 per cent inflation
was better than 5 per cent unemployment'.
As things transpired both inflationary pressure
and unemployment increased. This was shown in Diagram 4.5 and the surrounding discussion, though some
sense of proportion is necessary: the annual rate of
inflation rose from 5.6 per cent in 1972 to a plat-
eau of 7.0 per cent in 1973 and 1974. Meanwhile, the
OECD weighted average of the inflation rates in the
FRG, UK, USA, Canada, Japan, Italy and France rose
significantly above the West German domestic rate
taken in isolation: a peak of 13.3 per cent in 1974
compared to 7.0 per cent (OECD, *Economic Outlook*,
July 1982, p.151). Unemployment peaked at 4.7 per
cent in 1974 and although this meant over a million
unemployed, the problem was to become even worse in
the early 1980s.
Herr Schmidt left the Finance Ministry to become Chancellor in 1974. Hans Apel, the next Finance Minister, was in 1978 persuaded to take over
the Defence Ministry and his successor was another
SPD member of the Federal Cabinet - Hans Matthöffer,

a man somewhat feared on his appointment for his left
wing views. As pressure over budget deficits increased, Matthöffer was to request a move to the less
demanding Federal Post Office Ministry in 1982. Two
FDP members, Hans Friderichs, in 1972 and, in 1977,
Otto Graf von Lambsdorff, were given the Economic
Affairs Portfolios. Friderichs took over the chai-
manship of the Dresdner Bank on leaving ministerial
office. He was to become involved in the AEG rescue
operation (Chapter 8). Lambsdorff was a more robust
free marketeer than Friderichs, and he did not always agree with Matthöffer on the increasing level
of government expenditure. Lambsdorff also opposed
any further planning instruments. However, before
he became a minister, Lambsdorff was chairman of his
party's economic committee and a member of the econ-
omoic committee of the federal lower house. In 1974
he compared Germany's export surpluses to the winnings
of a consistently successful card gambler during his
days in a prisoner of war camp hospital. Ultimately
the card games could only continue when this persis-
tently successful gambler had been robbed. He pointed
out that deficit countries would not be permanently
content with their lot and even if they were, they
would eventually lose their creditworthiness (*Die
Zeit*, 28/74, p.35). He later referred to 1978 as a
year of recovery with more growth and stability, this
being due to the economic policy pursued by the
Government.

Dr Otmar Emminger replaced Klasen as President
of the Bundesbank in 1977. Emminger had been a member of the Board of Governors of, first, the Bank
deutscher Länder and, secondly, the Deutsche Bundesbank, since 1953. Herr Karl Otto Pöhl was appointed
his deputy at the same time. The latter had worked
in 1970 at the Economics Ministry with Schiller. In
1971 he moved to the Chancellor's office where he
worked with Brandt, while in 1972 (at only 43) he became State Secretary at the Finance Ministry, where
he worked with Chancellor Helmut Schmidt. He held
the Finance Ministry post until his appointment to
the Bundesbank. On 1 January 1980 he succeeded
Emminger as President. (Matthöffer's successor at
the Finance Ministry in 1982 - Manfred Lahnstein -
had also served as a state secretary at the Finance
Ministry and the Chancellery. A state secretaryship,
as opposed to Parliamentary secretary, virtually
represents the political appointment of an outsider
to an influential position within a ministry. Lahnstein was not a member of the Federal Parliament.)
Summarising the evolution of stabilisation

policy, then, it is clear that remnants of the Julius
Tower proved invaluable when economic growth slowed
markedly in 1958, for they provided the means for
deficit financing and tax cuts (Shonfield, p.286).
From 1960 it became increasingly necessary to overtly
use the budget for stabilisation purposes (Denton,
p.173). The 1961 revaluation gave the authorities a
breathing space, although expenditure was blocked in
the interests of stability in 1962 and 1963 (*ibid.*
p.226). In 1964 income tax cuts were used to stimulate economic activity, followed by a stabilisation
programme.

When the economy slowed again in 1967 the Federal
Government took further powers and the efforts to pursue an anti-cyclical fiscal policy were on the whole
successful (OECD, *Economic Survey*, 1973, pp.26 and
73). This success continued until the second half of
1969, but between then and the end of 1971 expenditure policy could be applied contractively only to a
limited extent (MRDB, November 1973, pp.11 and 21).
In 1973, therefore, the main weight of the measures
to curb economic activity was applied to the revenue
side. In 1974, on the other hand, the public authorities made an important contribution to mitigating
the slowdown in business activity (MRDB, April 1975,
p.10). Public expenditure injections were considerably greater than tax leakages. This was as well
since savings were greater than investment, although
exports were far greater than imports. This strong
expansion in public spending, along with several income tax cuts, typified the second half of the 1970s.

The above account of the evolution of policy
problems and prescriptions thus sets the stage for
the remaining sections of this chapter, namely the
analysis of fiscal, social and monetary policies.


FISCAL POLICY

The Revenue Side: the Structure of Taxation
Two points must be made by way of an introduction to
the structure of taxation. First, there has been a
shift in the tax burden away from indirect to direct
taxation, and particularly away from VAT to taxes on
the earnings of employees. Secondly, the structure
of taxation is rather complex. Some of the latter
complexities of the German tax structure will be
demonstrated when the distribution of tax revenue is
analysed in the next section. Basically, it will be
seen that there are two joint taxes accruing to the
Federal, Länder and local authorities; there are

four further joint taxes accruing to the Federal and
Länder governments; the Federal authorities exclusively levy several taxes, as do the Länder and local
authorities.
     The seven categories of personal income defined
by the income tax law are: income from agriculture or
forestry, from business, from professional services,
from employment, from capital investment, from rent-
als, and from specially listed sources such as annuities (Mueller, 1978, p.143). The principal features of the income tax system as a whole are as
follows:

1. Income Tax (*Einkommensteuer*) charged on the
   total income of an individual and which, for
   collection purposes, is divided into:
   (i) Assessed tax on total income,
   (ii) Wages Tax (*Lohnsteuer*) deducted at
        source from salaries, wages, pensions,
        etc.,
   (iii) Capital Yields Tax (*Kapitalertrag-
         steuer*) deducted at source from divi-
         dends, interest, etc.,
   (iv) Directors Tax (*Aufsichtsratsteuer*)
        deducted at source from directors'
        fees receivable by non-resident super-
        visory directors.
2. Corporation Tax (*Körperschaftsteuer*) on the
   profits of companies and other bodies
   (Board of Inland Revenue, p.1).

     In principle, there is only a single tax on the
income of an individual, namely the income tax; the
wages tax, capital yields tax and directors tax
(applicable only to non-resident directors) are merely
methods of collection of the income tax at source,
credit for tax so deducted being given against assessed tax on total income, where appropriate. A taxpayer's net income in each of the above seven categories is computed separately, according to separate
rules. In order to determine total liable income,
the net income from each category is aggregated (a
deficit in any category may normally be set off
against income of other categories) and from the
aggregate a deduction is allowed for special expenses.
Personal reliefs are given in the form of deductions
from total income. In general, the income tax is
collectible by means of an assessment on the taxpayer, credit being given against the tax assessed
for corporation tax, advance payments of tax and tax
deducted at source by way of wages tax, capital

yields tax and directors tax. When the principal
source of income is wages or salaries, subject to
deduction of tax at source, an assessment is made
only in certain circumstances.

An employer must determine the wage tax for
each individual employee, deduct the tax from wages
or salaries, and report it to the tax office. The
same procedure applies to the so-called church tax
(*Kirchensteuer*), which amounts to 9 per cent of the
wage tax. The sole proprietor of a business or the
partner of a partnership must report his business
profit, even if it is not withdrawn from the business.
Shareholders of registered companies must not include
the profits of the company in their income prior to
distribution. Since January 1977, domestic shareholders have been entitled to a credit for the corporation income tax paid by the distributing German
company (see below). The tax amount so credited must
be included in their taxable income. The profits
distributed as dividends are also deducted (capital
yields tax) at the rate of 25 per cent, which is also
deducted at source. It is not an additional tax but
qualifies as a full tax credit against the recipient's
income tax if the recipient is a resident taxpayer.

In Table 5.1 some further features of the
structure of taxation in the FRG are illustrated.
For the purposes of comparison the equivalent UK data
have been included in parts (a) and (b) of the table.
The most striking aspect of this comparison is the
significantly different levels of social insurance
contributions. Part (a) demonstrates that these
regressive taxes are higher in the FRG. This had
the effect of gradually increasing the total tax
ratio, plus social insurance contributions, to above
British levels by the mid-1950s, the first half of
the 1960s, and again in the later 1970s. Indeed,
the reason why the total incidence fell below British
levels between 1966 and 1971 was the increase in
British tax ratio net of social insurance contributions - as can be surmised from part (b) of the
table. Social insurance contributions in the FRG in
1970 were 10.9 per cent of GNP (33.6 - 22.7), whereas
in the UK they were 5.2 per cent of GNP (37.7 - 32.5).
By 1980 the ratio in the FRG had risen to 14.0 per
cent; in the UK it was 6.3 per cent. Contributions
made by West German employers and employees are high.
In 1980 insured employees in the FRG subscribed 22
per cent of the total social budget receipts, whereas
employers and the self-employed contributed a further
23 per cent (plus 16 per cent in direct fringe benefits - *Sozialbericht 1980*, p.151). The effect on

Table 5.1: Personal and Corporate Taxation, 1950-1980

(a) Total taxation†† and social insurance contributions as a percentage of GNP*

|     | 1950 | 1955 | 1960 | 1965 | 1970 | 1975 | 1979 | 1980 | (1981) |
|-----|------|------|------|------|------|------|------|------|--------|
| FRG | 30.3 | 32.2 | 33.9 | 32.4 | 33.6 | 36.8 | 38.3 | 38.4 | (38.4) |
| UK  | 32.5 | 29.0 | 27.6 | 30.0 | 37.7 | 36.2 | 34.4 | 35.3 | (39.4) |

(b) Total taxation†† as a percentage of GNP*

|     | 1965 | 1970 | 1975 | 1976 | 1977 | 1978 | 1979 | 1980 | (1981) |
|-----|------|------|------|------|------|------|------|------|--------|
| FRG | 23.0 | 22.7 | 23.4 | 23.8 | 24.9 | 24.7 | 24.5 | 24.4 | (24.3) |
| UK  | 25.2 | 32.5 | 29.6 | 29.4 | 28.5 | 28.1 | 28.2 | 29.0 | (32.8) |

(c) Total taxation††, taxes on employment income**, and on corporate income† as a percentage of GNP* (FRG only)

|            | 1951 | 1955 | 1960 | 1965 | 1970 | 1975 | 1980 |
|------------|------|------|------|------|------|------|------|
| Total      | 22.7 | 23.3 | 22.6 | 23.0 | 22.7 | 23.4 | 24.4 |
| Employment | 2.3  | 2.4  | 2.7  | 3.7  | 5.2  | 6.9  | 7.4  |
| Corporate  | 3.8  | 4.1  | 5.1  | 5.0  | 3.6  | 3.7  | 3.9  |

* At market prices (therefore includes indirect taxes but not subsidies: see Table 4.5).
** *Lohnsteuer* (= taxes on wages and salaries, on which an additional 9 per cent of the tax is levied as a *Kirchensteuer* or church tax).
† *Veranlagte Einkommen- u. Körperschaftsteuer* (= taxes on assessed income plus corporation tax).
†† Tax revenue received by the Federal, Länder and local authorities plus compensatory deductions (see text).

Sources:
(a) Shonfield, p.265n; BMWi, Table 8.5; *Die Zeit*, 38/82.
(b) BMWi, Table 8.6.
(c) BMA, Table 1.20 (1950 and 1955 excl. Saarland).
(cf. MRDB, Tables VII)

labour costs in the FRG has already been pointed out, and it is still to be examined in more detail. The cost of the industrial injuries and occupational disease scheme is borne entirely by the employer (up to 2 per cent of earnings). Both the employer and employee contribute an equal percentage of earnings for sickness, pension and unemployment benefits. The ceilings on these payments are increased annually to take account of increases in earnings. On the employees' side, social insurance deductions averaged 8 per cent of gross earnings per employed person in

1950. A fairly uniform upward trend meant that by
1980 this proportion had reached 14 per cent. When
the rising incidence of income tax on employees'
earnings is taken into account, total deductions have
shown the same inexorable trend: 13 per cent of average gross earnings in 1950 to 30 per cent in 1980
(calculated from BMA, Tables 1.10 and 1.12).

Indeed, the significant feature of part (c) in
Table 5.1 is the secular increase in the tax on earnings compared to the relative stability of corporate
taxes. This rising trend in the tax burden may be
illustrated as follows. The average incidence of
taxes and other deductions on the income of employees
had reached 31 per cent by 1981 and was predicted to
rise to 36 per cent by 1985; the marginal burden on
each additional DM earned was expected to reach 60
per cent in 1982, compared to 45 and 40 per cent in
1980 and 1981, and only 16 and 27 per cent in 1978
and 1979 (Dresdner Bank, *Economic Quarterly*, July
1982, p.2). These ratios are, of course, averages.
If only because of the progressive system of employees' income tax, therefore, it will be necessary
to say something about the burden on specific groups
when the other implications of the tax ratios have
been analysed. It will also be necessary to say
something about the real, as opposed to the nominal,
burden.

Turning first to the total tax ratio, however,
it may be noted from Table 5.2 that between 1971 and
1980 tax revenue increased by some 9 per cent per
year (compound), whereas (nominal) GNP increased at
an annual average compound rate of about 8 per cent.

Table 5.2:  Relative Increases in GNP and Total Tax
Revenue

|  | Average annual percentage increases | | | |
|---|---|---|---|---|
|  | GNP | | Tax Revenue | |
|  | Geometric Mean | Median | Geometric Mean | Median |
| 1951-1960 | 11.3 | 9.8 | 12.7 | 11.1 |
| 1961-1970 | 8.5 | 9.0 | 8.6 | 6.5 |
| 1971-1980 | 8.3 | 8.2 | 9.1 | 9.1 |
| 1951-1980 | 9.4 | 8.8 | 10.1 | 9.6 |

Source:  Calculated from Dresdner Bank, *Statische
Reihen*, p.6.

Such a development was more or less in line with
experience over the three decades taken as a whole.
Perhaps one should add that the rapid recovery of
tax revenue in the 1969 boom (+19.3 per cent) had
the effect of making the tax revenue distribution
for the 1960s somewhat less symmetrical than the GNP
distribution. (More specifically, the GNP ratio of
the 1960s was the only negatively skewed distribution. Further, the ratio of the percentage increase in tax revenue to the percentage increase in
GNP exceeded unity in sixteen of the thirty years.
This usually occurred during peaks in the business
cycle, the notable two exceptions being in 1967 and
1977.) Incidentally, the impressive growth of tax
receipts during the 1950s should not detract from
the crucial importance of the various tax concessions
which generated economic recovery. One estimate of
the value of these deductions from taxable income for
the period 1949-1957 is DM 28.4 billion or about 6.6
per cent of total budget receipts (Stolper and
Roskamp, pp.388-389).

Nonetheless, the overall tax ratio of 25 per
cent in 1977 (Table 5.1b) was a record level,
although the corporation tax reform introduced on
1 January of that year had the temporary effect of
slightly exaggerating the ratio. Basically, double
taxation of corporate profits was eliminated, tax
credits on distributed profits being granted by
companies to shareholders. This was only the second
reform of corporate taxation. The cumulative turnover tax, which had encouraged vertical concentration, was not reformed until the introduction of
VAT in 1968. Yet a Finance Ministry advisory group
had advocated such a change in 1953 (Denton, p.193).
Under the new law, the tax rate for distributed
earnings is 36 per cent, the rate for retained earnings being 56 per cent (Mueller, 1978, pp.123-124).
Domestic shareholders are entitled to a credit for
the 36 per cent corporation income tax on distributed earnings. On the other hand, they must include
the credit in their taxable income. Thus, the individual shareholder pays only the difference between
36 per cent and his individual income tax rate, or
receives a tax refund if his individual tax rate is
below 36 per cent. Corporate shareholders pay an
additional 20 per cent unless they re-distribute the
dividends received. This was to cause a fall in the
revenue from dividend taxes in 1979-1981 (MRDB,
February 1980, p.17). In spite of this special
factor, however, the tax ratio remained over 24 per
cent for the rest of the decade. In 1977 it was

85

1.25 percentage points higher than the average of
the 1960s and more than 1.5 percentage points above
the average of the 1950s (MRDB, November 1978, p.21).
On the other hand, the average tax ratio for 1970-75
had hardly risen over the average of 1965-69 (MRDB,
August 1976, p.16).

Yet it is the period 1975-1980 in which important nominal tax changes were introduced. A tax reform which became effective on 1 January 1975 followed proposals first made in 1969 when the SPD/FDP
coalition was formed. Initial proposals were tabled
as early as 1971. Income tax allowances for single
persons (double for married couples) were as follows.
The basic tax-free allowance was increased from
DM 1,680 to DM 3,000, and the bottom rate of income
tax was raised from 19 per cent to 22 per cent. This
rate was paid on taxable income to DM 16,000 per year
- twice the previous level. Above this level of income tax was progressive, starting at 30.8 per cent
and reaching a top rate of 56 per cent at an income
of DM 130,000. These new allowances and tax rates
meant tax reductions for individuals earning up to
DM 40,000 per year. Deductible expenses for each
child, as well as social security, pensions, sickness
and life insurance contributions, and payments to
building savings banks were all increased.

From 1 January 1979 the basic tax-free allowances were raised to DM 3,690/7,380 for single/
married employees. The step increase in the marginal
schedule from 22 per cent to 30.8 per cent at
DM 16,000/32,000 taxable income was removed - as is
demonstrated in Diagram 5.1. The scale now rises
slowly in this area. This purported to maintain the
neo-liberal concept, eventually introduced in the
1958 reform, of a curve rising (at that time) from
an entry stage of 20 per cent to a proportional exit
stage of 53 per cent (Denton, pp.191 and 194; Horn,
p.11; Reuss, p.87; Shonfield, p.286). From 1965 the
entry stage was lowered to 19 per cent, but the
imposition of a 3 per cent surtax on incomes over
DM 16,020 raised the exit stage to 56 per cent.

Another adjustment of the tax scale in 1981
further reduced the constant rate (lower proportional)
zone. There was also a further levelling out in the
progressive zone. Other changes in the late 1970s
included the introduction of a child care allowance
and increases in the tax-free allowance on Christmas
bonuses from employers. The general structure of
the personal income tax schedule has, therefore,
remained unchanged since 1958. There are five main
regions:

Diagram 5.1:   Effects of the 1979 Personal Income Tax
Amendments

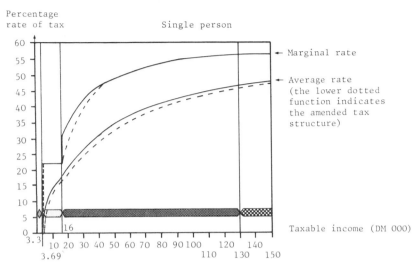

Percentage
rate of tax                     Single person

Marginal rate

Average rate
(the lower dotted
function indicates
the amended tax
structure)

Taxable income (DM 000)

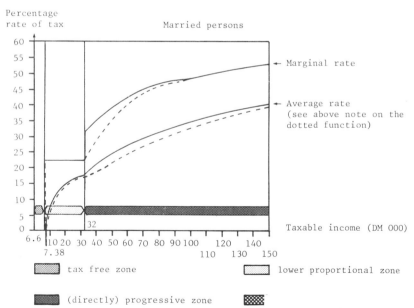

Percentage
rate of tax                     Married persons

Marginal rate

Average rate
(see above note on the
dotted function)

Taxable income (DM 000)

tax free zone                          lower proportional zone

(directly) progressive zone

Source: Based on: Der Bundesminister der Finanzen,
'Die Massnahmen zur Stärkung der Nachfrage und zur
Verbesserung des Wirtschaftswachstums', *Reihen:
Bürger-Informationen*, December 1978, p.17.

1. A number of allowances (family, social
   security contributions) which may be set
   against gross income in arriving at taxable income.
2. An initial income band (up to DM 4,200 in
   1980) which incurs no tax.
3. A lower tax band (from DM 4,200 to DM 18,00)
   within which tax is levied at a proportional
   rate (22 per cent in 1980).
4. A middle region, from DM 18,000 to DM 130,000,
   within which the marginal tax rate climbs
   steeply from 22 to 56 per cent.
5. An upper band, for incomes over DM 130,000,
   subject to a fixed marginal rate of 56 per
   cent.

These rates are in addition to the social security
contribution levied at a rate of 16 per cent on wages
and salaries in 1980. In *real* terms the shape and
position of the marginal rate curve have changed very
little since 1965, although there had been some increase in marginal rates at the upper end of the distribution. Changes to the tax structure in 1975, 1978,
1979 and 1981 have compensated for inflation but have
left unchanged in *real* terms the starting point of the
middle, progressive tax region (OECD, *Economic Survey*,
1982, p.42 - emphasis added).
    Whether such a structure conforms to the neo-
liberal ethic underlying the social market theory (low
marginal rates stimulating effort), the reader alone
may judge. Some statistics on the incidence of personal taxation may be helpful in the formulation of
such a judgement. In 1980 employees earning less than
DM 25,000 a year represented 46 per cent of all taxpayers. They paid 7 per cent of the total revenue
from wages and salaries. Persons earning between
DM 25,000 and DM 50,000 (34 per cent of taxpayers)
paid 28 per cent of tax revenue, whereas the remaining 65 per cent was paid by the 20 per cent of taxpayers earning more than DM 50,000. The reasons are
not difficult to find. The general rise in real
incomes has propelled an increasing percentage of
taxpayers from the lower, flat rate, tax band into
the middle, progressive one. This proportion rose
from about 6 per cent in 1965 to about 40 per cent in
1974, falling back to about 35 per cent following the
adjustments in 1975 and 1979. This shift into the
higher band has also affected the distribution of the
tax yield. Whereas in the mid-1960s the progressive
part of the tax schedule provided only a small proportion of total tax yield, by 1980 taxpayers on the

progressive part of the schedule paid 78 per cent of
the total tax and the 15 per cent of taxpayers with
marginal rates of over 35 per cent provided half of
the total tax (OECD, *Economic Survey*, 1982, pp.42-43).
On the other hand, the standard rate of VAT was
increased by 1 per cent from January 1978, and by a
further 1 per cent in July 1979. These two increases
brought the general rate of VAT to 13 per cent. At
the same time the lower rate on a limited range of
essential goods and services reached 7.5 per cent.
Advance warning of each increase was given - in the
latter case a full seven months. But it will be
shown when the distribution of tax revenue is discussed in the next section that revenue from this
source has fallen. If the reductions in tax rates
just outlined are also taken into account, the heavi-
est burden of this slower growth in total tax revenue falls on the Federal Government. Even so, between 1978 and 1981 the incidence of direct taxes
dropped only half as sharply as it had risen in the
preceding two years. This can be seen from Diagram
5.2 - as can the general rise in the burden of direct
taxation during the 1970s.

Nevertheless, the below-average growth of total
Federal tax receipts is in direct contrast to the
growth of Federal commitments on the expenditure side.
Moreover, the increasing contributions to the EEC are
made entirely from the Federal Budget. Hence the
analysis first turns to the distribution of tax revenue and then to the expenditure side.

The Revenue Side: the Distribution of Tax Revenue
As already indicated, the distribution of tax revenue
in West Germany is subject to a number of complex
formulae. The reader may find Diagram 5.3 of some
introductory value.

From 1980 the yield on income taxes (on both
income from employment and assessed incomes) was distributed 42.5:42.5:15 among the Federal, Länder and
local authorities, whereas corporation and investment
taxes have been shared equally by the Federal and
Länder governments (MRDB, March 1982, Table VII(2)n).
During the 1970s the division of the revenue from the
tax on turnover was subject to marginal adjustments.
For example, in 1970 it was divided on the basis of
70 per cent to the Federal Government and the remaining 30 per cent to the Länder governments; from 1978
the Federal share was 67.5 per cent and the Länder
share 32.5 per cent. The Federal share of income and
corporation taxes amounted to DM 75.8 billion in 1980
(40 per cent of total Federal revenue), while the

Diagram 5.2:    The Incidence of Direct Taxes on Income
in the 1970s

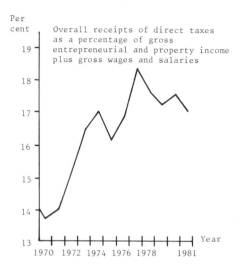

Source:    MRDB, August 1982, p.26.

Diagram 5.3:    Distribution of Shared Tax Revenues,
1980

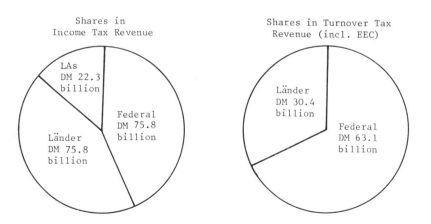

Source:    Based on MRDB, March 1982, Table VIII.

turnover tax share brought in DM 63.1 billion (30 per cent of total Federal revenue). At the Länder level in 1980 the former tax share was, of course, the same in absolute terms, while the latter raised DM 30.4 billion - thus providing 60 per cent and 24 per cent of total tax revenue respectively. Also in 1980 local authorities received DM 22.3 billion as their share in income taxes (43 per cent of their total tax revenue). But the Federal Government then paid DM 6.1 billion of its turnover tax revenue to the EEC and made supplementary grants to the Länder of DM 1.4 billion (BMWi, Tables 8.32 and 8.34). Net tax revenue from all sources accruing to the Federal Government in 1980 amounted to DM 176 billion.

At the Federal level tax revenue is primarily supplemented by petroleum and tobacco taxes. Out of a total revenue of DM 41.5 billion from taxes accruing entirely to the Federal Government in 1980, the petroleum tax raised DM 21.4 billion and the tobacco tax DM 11.3 billion - almost 80 per cent of the exclusive Federal taxes. At Länder level a further 10 per cent (DM 12.6 billion) of total tax revenue accrued from these governments' exclusive taxes on beer, property and motor vehicles. Taxes accruing entirely to the local authorities include a trading tax, a tax on buildings and, until 1 January 1980, a payroll tax. However, local authorities are not as dependent on tax revenue as the Federal and Länder governments. In 1978, taxes provided only 34 per cent of total revenue, with fees for their services (refuse disposal, etc.) providing 20 per cent and 29 per cent of the remainder coming from grants made by the Federal and Länder governments. Some problems connected with the inadequacy of these latter grants developed during the 1970s, however (Newton, pp.15-16 and 29).

A change in the distribution of tax revenue has taken place during the period under review. This is illustrated in Table 5.3, from which the relative decline of the Federal Government's share of tax revenue may be adduced. The Federal share in total tax receipts declined from 54 per cent in 1970 to about 48 per cent in 1980 (IdW, Table 24). All in all the Länder governments were unaffected by the relatively slow growth in turnover tax revenue. By 1980 it accounted for roughly one-fifth of their total tax receipts, whereas its share in Federal Government receipts slumped to 30 per cent. Within this 30 per cent import turnover tax revenue has risen but VAT receipts have fallen dramatically (BMWi, Table 8.32). This was the reason for the secular decline in the

Table 5.3:   The Distribution of Total Tax Revenue
accruing to the Federal and Länder Governments,
1951-1981

| | Average percentage increases in revenue | | | |
| | Federal Government | | Länder governments | |
| | Geometric Mean | Median | Geometric Mean | Median |
|---|---|---|---|---|
| 1951-1960 | 15.0 | 10.7 | 12.1 | 11.2 |
| 1961-1970 | 8.7 | 8.1 | 9.6 | 8.3 |
| 1971-1980 | 7.9 | 8.6 | 9.7 | 10.1 |
| 1951-1980 | 10.5 | 9.2 | 10.5 | 9.2 |

Source:   See Table 5.2.

proportion of turnover tax receipts by the Federal
Government since the Currency Reform, while the proportion of total receipts accounted for by the income
and corporation taxes accruing to the Federal level
has increased (BMWi, Table 8.32; Denton, p.192; US
High Commission Report, p.246).

Finally, two forms of compensatory payments are
relevant to a discussion of the distributive aspects
of fiscal policy.   The first is the system of equal-
ising tax receipts between the Länder - the so-called
system of *Finanzausgleich*, or fiscal equalisation
(Schöller, p.7).   The second group of compensatory
payments are known as *Lastenausgleich*, or equalisation
of burdens.   'Burdens' in this context means the
method of compensating those institutions and persons
who lost property during the war, or who lost savings
by the default of the Hitler government's debt, and
the Currency Reform which effectively wrote-off such
debts (Henning, pp.201 and 238).   The expellees and
refugees were also to later receive aid from the fund
created to administer these payments - the so-called
*Sondervermögen Ausgleichsfonds*.   More will be said
about this fund, and payments, when the social budget,
the Bundesbank's monetary powers and the special purpose banks are all discussed below.   Also included in
the discussion of the special purpose banks in Chapter 8, will be the DM counterpart fund created out of
'Marshall Aid' (*ERP-Sondervermögen*).

What is relevant here is the fiscal equalisation
scheme which operates between the Länder.   The constitution of the Federal Republic lays down two
methods of fiscal equalisation.   First, a vertical
equalisation is attempted by means of the formulae for
the distribution of income, corporation and turnover

taxes between the various levels of government (see above). Second, horizontal equalisation is in turn divided into implicit and explicit categories (Spahn, p.144). The objective here is to implement a flow of tax receipts from the Länder with relatively high tax revenue to those with lower receipts (Grosser, p.159). Implicit equalisation is secured by means of the formula which determines the distribution of joint taxes between the Länder. Under this formula, income tax revenue is distributed on a local revenue basis, while turnover taxes are distributed on a per capita basis - except for a share of up to 25 per cent of turnover taxes which is used for explicit equalisation purposes. This latter 'second round' of redistribution has since 1969 accounted for the full 25 per cent of turnover tax revenue available to the Länder. Part of this amount is used to compensate those Länder whose total per capita tax receipts fall below 92 per cent of the federal average. Those Länder whose receipts reach or exceed the Länder average participate in the remaining sum in proportion to their populations. In 1981 DM 2.5 billion was transferred to those Länder with lower than average tax receipts (*Die Zeit*, 2/82, p.19). Hence the recipient Länder were Lower Saxony, Bavaria, Bremen, Saarland, Rhineland-Palatinate and Schleswig-Holstein. The donor Länder were Baden-Württemberg, North Rhine-Westphalia, Hesse and Hamburg. West Berlin is a special case, as will be seen when the structure of labour markets is discussed in Chapter 6. At the moment the object is to continue the discussion of fiscal policy by turning to the expenditure side.

The Expenditure Side: State Spending
The overall size of state participation in the FRG is quite considerable. The combined expenditure of the Federal, Länder and local authorities' budgets amounted to 38 per cent (DM 565 billion) of GNP in 1980. If the social security funds, whose spending has increased especially sharply, are included, the proportion of GNP rises to 47 per cent (DM 706 billion), which was 10 percentage points higher than in 1968 (IdDW, Table 26).

The share of each budgetary level in total state spending, when allowance is made for various grants and transfers among these levels, is 50 per cent at the Federal level, 30 per cent at the Länder level and 20 per cent at the local level. The Federal Government is responsible for the social welfare system (34 per cent of the expenditure out of the 1980 Federal budget), defence (19 per cent), road

building (4 per cent), and subsidies to the Federal
railways, Berlin and agriculture (BMWi, Table 8.33).
Shonfield (p.438) calculated, for 1961, that the
magnitude of subsidies and tax concessions to industry and trade were far greater than in the UK. The
relative totals for all sectors were 23 per cent of
the Federal Budget compared to 9 per cent in the UK.
In a more recent and extensive comparison, Peacock
*et al.* (para.4.10) refer to the 'uninterrupted expansion of total subsidies between 1966 and 1978 (in
West Germany) ... the major recipients of government
aid have been agriculture, mining and industries
located in less favoured regions. These subsidies
have been devoted primarily to the maintenance of
employment for social and strategic reasons.' Moreover, the Finance Ministry's detailed and informative
biennial Subsidy Reports (*Subventionsberichte*) indicated in 1981 (pp.22, 24 and 303) that by 1980 the
total value of Federal and Länder tax concessions and
subsidies had risen to over DM 55 billion (Owen Smith,
1979, p.171). Länder housing subsidies reached an
estimated DM 7 billion by 1980. They have been
criticised for favouring high income families and
preventing market prices from reflecting the steep
rise in building costs (*Die Zeit*, 14/81, pp.33-37,
and 37/81, pp.24-25; the 1974 Tenancy Protection Act
was also criticised for holding rents below market
values). In its 1981 *Annual Report* (p.42) the Bundesbank referred to the 'distorting' effects of government regulations which, together with the high level
of interest rates, had caused a pronounced setback in
new housing completions.
    But as Peakcock *et al.* also indicate (para.4.37)
the figures for the UK are misleading as an indication
of subsidies to industry. This is because loans and
grants are aggregated and no account is taken of tax
concessions. Nevertheless, they are able to conclude
(para.4.54) that although comparisons of tax allowances involve numerous problems, UK industrial aid
in 1977 and 1978 (excluding support for the national-
ised industries) totalled approximately DM 11 billion,
whereas the total in West Germany was DM 4.9 billion.
This difference almost entirely reflected the more
widespread use of subsidies in the UK. A comparison
of individual programmes in the two countries revealed that grants and loans to aerospace, coal mining and innovation were greater in West Germany.
Expenditure on regional support was broadly similar,
though there was a greater emphasis on tax concessions in the FRG. But, while in the UK almost all
manufacturing industries received some degree of

selective subsidisation, financial aid to West German
manufacturing industry was restricted to very few
industries, notably shipbuilding. In other words,
the maintenance of declining industries and unprofit-
able firms has been accorded a far greater priority
in the UK (Peakcock, para.4.58).
Yet in both countries governments have also
stressed the need for structural intervention to be
directed towards the promotion of industrial growth
and technological advance. In 1980 an SPD Federal
minister for research claimed that subsidies had
saved the German watch industry, encouraged technical
change in the computer industry and supported the
machine tool industry – the nation's top exporter.
He saw this as necessary intervention to correct the
market mechanism, although his FDP cabinet colleague
at the Economics Ministry (Lambsdorff) disagreed (*Die
Zeit*, 23/80, p.19). Such selective intervention
seems to be borne out by the Peacock study – at least
as far as the computer industry is concerned (paras.
5.61 and 5.68).

The Expenditure Side: Public Sector Debt
As a proportion of GNP, Federal Government spending
during the period 1950-1980 remained more or less
constant at about 14 per cent (BMWi, Table 8.31).
Moreover, it can be seen from Table 5.4 that serious
deficits only started to emerge after 1975. However,
if the growing total debt of the Länder is also taken
into account, the cumulative problem of the growth in
total expenditure outstripping the growth in total
revenue becomes more apparent. Various data illus-
trating this trend, and the consequential debt positions in 1980, are presented in Table 5.5 and
Diagram 5.4. (Only the Federal and Länder Governments
have been included because they are responsible,
particularly the former, for economic management. The
rate of increase in local authority debt actually decreased during the 1970s.)
The problem, then, is the rapid rise in the total
public sector debt during the 1970s, especially during
the second half of the decade when the national debt/
GNP ratio jumped from the 20 per cent mark around
which it had hovered since 1950, to over 30 per cent
in 1980. In static terms the FRG still faired quite
well by comparison to, say, the 50, 60 and 70 per
cent ratios of the USA, UK and Italy respectively.
But because she started from a lower base, the rate
of growth in her public sector debt was greater than
the USA and UK. Predictably, two economic issues became topical in the FRG, namely the price of debt

Table 5.4:   The Federal Budget, 1950-1980

|  | Total Revenue | | Expenditure | |
|  | DM billion | 1950=100 | DM billion | 1950=100 |
|---|---|---|---|---|
| 1950 | 11.4 | 100 | 12.4 | 100 |
| 1955 | 26.0 | 228 | 22.4 | 181 |
| 1960[a] | 30.2 | 265 | 30.3 | 244 |
| 1965 | 63.1 | 554 | 64.2 | 518 |
| 1970 | 88.4 | 775 | 88.0 | 710 |
| 1975[b] | 123.8 | 1,086 | 156.9 | 1,265 |
| 1980[b] | 188.1 | 1,650 | 215.7 | 1,740 |
| (1981 | 195.0 | 1,711 | 233.0 | 1,879) |

Notes:
(a) In 1960 the fiscal year was adjusted to coincide with the calander year. Hence this period ran from 1 April to 31 December 1960.
(b) Excl. special anti-cyclical spending (DM 1.9 billion and DM 9 million in 1975 and 1980 respectively). As from 1975 the EEC share of turnover tax has been deducted from the Federal share of the revenue from this source (MRDB, March 1982, Table VII).

Source:   BMWi, Table 8.31 (writer's translation).

Table 5.5:   The Growth in Public Sector Debt, 1950-1980

|  | DM billion | | | | | |
|  | Total[a] | | Federal Government | | Länder Governments | |
|  | Mean | Median | Mean | Median | Mean | Median |
|---|---|---|---|---|---|---|
| 1950-1980 | 132.64 | 83.70 | 57.90 | 33.70 | 35.7 | 17.4 |
| Totals 1980 | 469.10 | | 232.3[b] | | 137.3 | |
| (1981 | 507.73 | | 257.9 | | 156.8) | |

Notes:
(a) Federal, Länder, local authorities, ERP and Equalisation of Burdens funds.
(b) Includes DM 2.6 billion Equalisation of Burdens Fund.

Source:   Calculated from Dresdner Bank, *Statische Reihen*, p.6; *Die Zeit*, 42/82, p.34.

Diagram 5.4:  The Growth in Federal and Länder Debt,
1950-1980

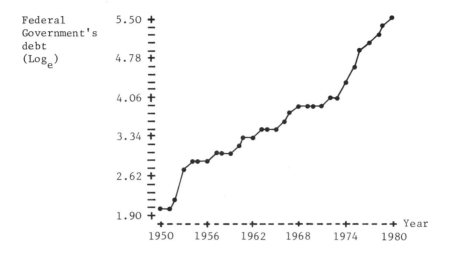

Federal
Government's
debt
$(\text{Log}_e)$

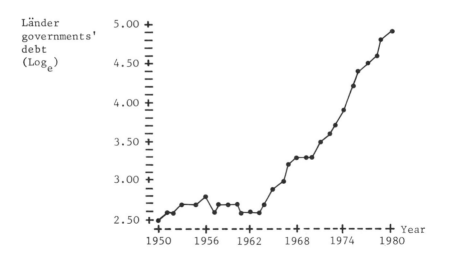

Länder
governments'
debt
$(\text{Log}_e)$

Source:  Plotted from Dresdner Bank, *Statische Reihen*,
p.6.

and the size of the borrowing requirement.
In the case of the former - the price of debt -
there was an increase in the interest payments required to service the debt for two reasons. First,
clearly the absolute size of the debt increased during the 1970s. Second, interest rates were generally
higher during the 1970s than they had been in the two
previous decades - as will be shortly shown in more
detail. Because of the high level of international
interest rates, however, the Bundesbank was able to
make increased contributions to Federal revenue out
of its profits. Nevertheless, the ratio of the
interest paid on debt to total expenditure doubled to
reach 8 per cent by the end of the decade.
In the case of the borrowing requirement there
was also a sizeable increase. Total borrowing by the
three levels of budgetary authorities rose not only
in absolute terms, but also relative to the budget
volume. Between 1969 and 1973 the proportion of
expenditure financed with borrowed funds (5 per cent)
was more or less what it had been during the 1960s.
Between 1974 and 1978 it jumped to an average of 11
per cent, the highest figure being reached in 1975
(18 per cent) (MRDB, July 1979, p.17). The increase
in the Federal Government's net borrowing requirement
was particularly marked. During the period 1975-1980
it averaged DM 26 billion. In 1981 it grew to DM 35
billion and the main economic preoccupation of the
Federal Government by 1982 was reconciling the SPD
demands for high levels of expenditure with the FDP
demands to reduce the net borrowing requirement to
DM 26 billion. (It was at this stage that Herr
Matthöffer requested a transfer from the Finance Ministry to the Post Office Ministry.)
It is worth emphasising that the Federal Government has found it increasingly difficult to reduce
the gap between tax revenue and expenditure due to
income tax reforms (see above), increases in family
allowances and other social policy expenditure (see
below) and meeting EEC commitments (beyond the scope
of this book). Although the Länder do not quite share
the revenue problems of the Federal Government, they
too have had to contend with rapidly increasing personnel costs in recent years. Further, the mounting
budgetary deficits of the second half of the 1970s
stand in stark contrast to mounting surpluses in the
first half of the 1950s. But the reasons for this
policy contrast become more obvious when viewed
against the backcloth of the changes in economic trends
which have occurred over the three decades under review.

As already indicated, social policy expenditure has also increased. Hence, more detail is given in the next section.

## SOCIAL POLICY

It has been seen that there is a high social welfare contribution from the Federal Budget (34 per cent). Historically, both the public budgets ratio to GNP, and the proportion of those budgets allocated to social expenditure have risen: in 1913-14 the public budget was 14 per cent of national income, and 15 per cent of this budget was allocated to social expenditure; by 1925-26 the annual average had risen to 25 per cent and 28 per cent respectively; in 1950 they were 36 per cent and 34 per cent (Mendershausen, p.78). Only the extraordinarily comprehensive German social security system kept the Currency Reform from being a completely intolerable burden by putting a floor under those who otherwise would have fallen into an economic void (Wallich, p.72). Much the same can be said of the relatively high tax burden in the early 1950s, especially when social insurance contributions are included. This too was mitigated by the high proportion of transfer payments (*ibid.*, p.142). In short, both social insurance contributions and benefits are high in West Germany.

Total social spending is actually even higher than implied by the above ratios. For planning purposes this has been spelt out during the 1970s in the annual social budget. The various components of the social budget are shown schematically in Figure 5.1 and Diagram 5.5. It will be seen that this budget constitues a comprehensive account of social expenditure in its entirety. Estimates of projected expenditure are also included when the budget is drawn up. Of particular note is the fact that the social budget covers not only social security as such, but also other direct payments such as statutory public sector employees' benefits, additional payments to other employees ('fringe benefits'), compensation such as reparations and payments to war victims, social assistance, public health services and sponsorship of private asset formation. Direct payments under these heads totalled DM 405.7 billion in 1980. The remaining 10 per cent of the budget (DM 43.8 billion) was accounted for by tax relief (DM 37.8 billion) plus housing concessions (DM 6.0 billion) (*Sozialbericht 1980*, p.150). A clear upward trend in the social budget during the period

Figure 5.1:  The Scope of the Social Budget

| Social Security | |
|---|---|
| General Insurance Schemes | Old age pensions, health and accident insurance, employment promotion (including unemployment benefits, etc.), child benefits |
| Special schemes | Old age assistance for farmers and various rural professions (doctors, veterinary surgeons, etc.) |
| Public servants' scheme[a] | Pensions, family supplements, allowances |
| Supplementary schemes | Supplementary insurance in the public service and individual professions |

| Direct payments made by employers |
|---|
| Earnings protection, contractural and voluntary benefits[b] |

| Compensatory payments |
|---|
| War victims and refugees, victims of Nazi oppression, other compensation |

| Social assistance and services |
|---|
| Social assistance, youth schemes, promotion of vocational training, housing allowances, public health services, asset formation |

| Indirect Contributions |
|---|
| Tax reductions, tax concessions for housing |

Notes:
(a) 'Public Servants' = *Beamte* - see Owen Smith, 1981, pp.192-194.
(b) For an indication of 'fringe benefits' see 'Remuneration and other Terms and Conditions of Employment', Chapter 6.

Source: *Sozialbericht 1980*, p.67 and Part B(IV) (writer's translation).

Diagram 5.5:  The Components of the Social Budget, 1980

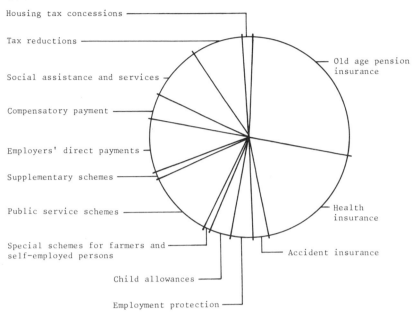

Housing tax concessions

Tax reductions

Social assistance and services

Compensatory payment

Employers' direct payments

Supplementary schemes

Public service schemes

Special schemes for farmers and self-employed persons

Child allowances

Employment protection

Old age pension insurance

Health insurance

Accident insurance

Source:  *Sozialbericht 1980*, p.94 (writer's translation).

Table 5.6:  Trend of the Social Budget in West Germany, 1950-1980

| Year | Social budget | |
|---|---|---|
| | DM billion | Percentage of GNP (at market prices) |
| 1950 | 16.7 | 17.1 |
| 1955 | 29.5 | 16.4 |
| 1960 | 62.8 | 20.7 |
| 1965 | 112.7 | 24.5 |
| 1970 | 174.7 | 25.5 |
| 1975 | 330.3 | 31.9 |
| 1980[a] | 449.5 | 30.1 |
| 1984[b] | 576.7 | 29.3 |

Notes:  (a) provisional; (b) estimate.

Sources:  BMWi, Table 7.12;  IdDW, Table 29; *Sozialbericht 1980*, p.93.

1950-1980 is evident from the data given in Table
5.6.
      Between 1965 and 1969 total social security
expenditure from the social insurance funds increased
at an average annual rate of 11 per cent (see the top
section of Figure 5.1). A deficit of DM 2 billion
was recorded in 1967, followed by one of DM 1.8 billion in 1968 (MRDB, November 1975, pp.22 and 26). By
1970-75 the average rate of increase had reached 16.5
per cent which was about twice as fast as the increase
in GNP. The financial situation of the social security funds deteriorated so badly that crisis proportions were reached in the mid-1970s. Even so the
deterioration was not as dramatic as the deficits
incurred by the public budgetary authorities. Nevertheless, after a surplus averaging about DM 6 billion
a year between 1970 and 1974, a deficit of almost
DM 11 billion was recorded in 1975 (MRDB, March 1980,
p.20). In 1976 and 1977 the rate of increase in both
social security expenditure (6 per cent) fell below
that of GNP (*ibid.*, p.21). Expenditure and receipts
were largely back in balance again by 1979. In this
respect the social security funds differ markedly
from the budgets of the public authorities. Apart
from the incidental nature of the anti-cyclical
mechanism inherent in social security funds, however,
the role of the budgetary authorities and social security funds are not comparable.
      What are the allocational and distributional
implications of such a rising trend? Among other
things, as life expectancy increases, but the length
of the working life decreases, some social security
expenditure rises with time. This is because of the
longer periods of education and a reduction in the
retirement age. Other items which would cause a rise
in expenditure would be a fall in the death rate,
with perhaps no comparative proportionate fall in the
birth rate. (Some illustrative demographic trends
will be found at the beginning of Chapter 6.) Legal
changes have extended the scope of social security
expenditure in West Germany, while the number of employed persons subject to compulsory insurance has
increased. In Table 5.7 the rising trend in social
security expenditure in West Germany, which has
crucial policy implications, is demonstrated. The
numerator chosen is total social security expenditure,
the bulk of which is funded from the social insurance
funds. Since the emphasis here is on the financing
of the scheme by the working population, the national
income demoninator chosen in Table 5.7 is current NNP
at factor cost.

Table 5.7:   The Trend in Social Security Expenditure

| Year | Absolute expenditure (DM billion) | Percentage of NNP (at factor cost) |
|------|-----------------------------------|------------------------------------|
| 1949 | 7.2 | 10.3 |
| 1952 | 12.9 | 12.1 |
| 1960 | 40.8 | 17.3 |
| 1971 | 117.4 | 20.2 |
| 1978 | 279.5 | 27.8 |
| 1980 | 312.4 | 27.0 |
| 1984[a] | 403.9 | – |

Note:   (a) estimate

Sources:   1949-1971 Henning, p.240; 1978-1984 calculated from BMA, Table 1.5, and *Sozialbericht 1980*,
p.150.

The *coverage* of the social security system has
also increased with time. During its early stages
in the 1880s the social security system was designed
by Bismarck as a means of enticing the working class
away from socialism. By the early 1950s, however,
there were statistically more transfer recipients
than people, because not only many households, but
also many individuals, are multiple benefit recipients
(Reuss, p.181). Since the German system of social
security is a composite of many types of protection,
financed by an extremely complex contribution system
and government subsidies, valid generalisations about
the direction of transfer flows cannot be made (*ibid.*,
p.185). This is all, of course, the result of a
conscious policy choice. As is obvious from Table
5.6, the Germans embarked on a major extension of
their social security system in the second half of
the 1950s, while in the UK the objective of tax reduction took priority over social security extension
(Shonfield, p.266; Table 5.1). All this expansion in
social welfare has been achieved, not surprisingly,
at great cost – both in opportunity and absolute
terms. It is therefore apposite to examine some features of the increases in outlay which have characterised the social policy field.
   The general social insurance schemes funded from
the social insurance funds, that is to say, pension,
health and industrial injuries insurance, along with
unemployment benefits, employment promotion and child
allowances, all became increasingly important during
the 1970s. In 1969 the proportion of these payments

in total social security expenditure was 76 per cent.
By 1980 it was 82 per cent (*Sozialberichte 1976* and
*1980*). In 1975 the percentage increased steeply as
a result of the provisions governing child allowances
(see Table 5.8). Once again the reader must judge
the extent to which all these increases conformed to
the social market ethic - and it should be borne in
mind that unemployment benefits have still to be
discussed in detail.

Table 5.8:  The Introduction and Growth of Child
Allowances in West Germany

| Period | Monthly level of benefit (DM) for the | | | | |
|---|---|---|---|---|---|
| | first | second[a] | third | fourth | fifth and each additional child |
| 1. 1.1955 to 30. 9.1957 | – | – | 25 | 25 | 25 |
| 1.10.1957 to 28. 2.1959 | – | – | 30 | 30 | 30 |
| 1. 3.1959 to 30. 3.1961 | – | – | 40 | 40 | 40 |
| 1. 4.1961 to 31.12.1963 | – | 25 | 40 | 40 | 40 |
| 1. 1.1964 to 31. 8.1970 | – | 25 | 50 | 60 | 70 |
| 1. 9.1970 to 31.12.1974 | – | 25 | 60 | 60 | 70 |
| 1. 1.1975 to 31.12.1977 | 50 | 70 | 120 | 120 | 120 |
| 1. 1.1978 to 31.12.1978 | 50 | 80 | 150 | 150 | 150 |
| 1. 1.1979 to 30. 6.1979 | 50 | 80 | 200 | 200 | 200 |
| 1. 7.1979 to 31. 1.1981 | 50 | 100 | 200 | 200 | 200 |
| 1. 2.1981 to 31.12.1981 | 50 | 120 | 240 | 240 | 240 |
| from 1.1.1982 | 50 | 100 | 220 | 240 | 240 |

Note:
(a) Paid only to persons whose monthly income did not exceed
(DM):   until 31.12.1964:   600     until 31.12.1972: 1,250
        until 31. 8.1970:   650     until 31.12.1973: 1,400
        until 31.12.1971: 1,100     until 31.12.1975: 1,530
From 1.1.1975 there was no upper income limit, although this
became policy issue in the early 1980s.
Source:  BMA, Table 8.18.

Moreover, there was a sharp rise in the cost of
non-cash benefits in the 1970s, particularly hospital
costs.  Spending on hospital treatment therefore became a policy problem.  For example, in the three
decades under review the average daily cost of treatment per patient in a Hamburg hospital rose from

DM 10 in 1951 to DM 23 in 1961 and DM 70 in 1971. By 1977 this cost had risen to DM 178.40. Perhaps significantly, these costs include, from 1962, ancillary costs and, from 1974, heart/lung machinery (*Die Zeit*, 12/78). Hospital spending is also strongly affected by personnel costs and all these factors led to the 1977 Act to curb the expansion in costs of health insurance (MRDB, March 1980, pp.23 and 27). Some reduction in cost expansion has been accomplished as a result of this measure, although by the end of the review period daily average costs of treatment per patient stood at over DM 200 (*Die Zeit*, 46/81, p.25). Indeed, total health service expenditure nearly trebled during the 1970s: from DM 70.3 billion in 1970 to DM 205.5 billion in 1980.

The rate of increase in the spending of the pension insurance funds did not slow down significantly until 1978. Pensions have been index-linked since 1957. Owing to the influence of the time-lag in the adjustment procedure, however, pensions did not reflect the relative high wage increases of 1974 until 1975, 1976 and 1977 when pensions were increased by 35 per cent in all. In 1977 the pension of an insured person with forty-five eligible years of insurance, whose earnings had always been equivalent to the average, came to about 74 per cent of average net earnings, against 64.5 per cent in 1974 (MRDB, March 1980, p.22). This ratio fell to 72 per cent in 1979 and was expected to continue to fall marginally, due to a series of measures in the Pension Adjustment Acts (*ibid.*, pp.22 and 27). In the case of a person with forty eligible years this certainly happened - from a peak of 65.5 per cent of average net earnings in 1977 to 63 per cent in 1981 (MRDB, April 1982, p.16). The financial deficit of DM 10 billion in the pension insurance funds (1977) was therefore reduced to a surplus of DM 3 billion in 1980 and 1981, although deficits were expected to re-appear in 1982 and 1983 (*ibid.*, pp.14 and 18).

Until the end of the 1960s, three items of expenditure largely determined the spending of the Federal Labour Office: unemployment benefit, promotion of year-round working in construction and administrative costs. In 1969, however, the Employment Promotion Act placed a new emphasis on an active labour market and employment policy, mainly with the objective of improving the occupational and social mobility of the labour force. The allowances for participation in such vocational training, further training and re-training measures were generous, partly no doubt because of the financially prosperous

position of the Federal Labour Office at that time.
Such allowances exceeded unemployment benefit until
1974 (MRDB, April 1970, pp.16 and 19). Moreover,
legislation passed in 1978 required the Federal
Labour Office to meet the pension insurance contributions of unemployed persons. Finally, from 1979
this pension insurance contribution scheme was extended to cover benefits paid to workers laid off
because of inclement weather. (As in the case of
short-time working payments, inclement weather benefits are paid by employers and 75 per cent of the
cost is refunded by the Federal Labour Office.) But
during the 1974-75 recession unemployment benefits
were increased to 68 per cent of the net wage or
salary previously received. By 1975, therefore, the
expenditure of the Federal Labour Office had risen
to DM 18 billion, or to two-and-a-half times its
1973 volume (MRDB, April 1979, p.18). Structural
unemployment, or a hard core of unemployed persons
difficult to place in existing vacancies, also became a policy problem during the 1970s (MRDB, *loc.
cit.*; *Report*, FRG Embassy, London, 8 October 1979,
p.2).

As a result of these policy decisions, the total
expenditure of the Federal Labour Office rose from
DM 4 billion in 1970 to DM 22 billion in 1980 (MRDB,
August 1981, p.33). The 1980 figure contained the
following components: DM 10.5 billion unemployment
benefits; DM 6.5 billion vocational training; DM 2.0
billion promotion of winter construction and DM 3.0
billion for administration.

In the face of the rapidly deteriorating
financial situation during the 1970s the Federal
Labour Office raised its total unemployment insurance contribution, which had stood at 1.3 per
cent of wages and salaries since 1964, to 1.7 per
cent at the beginning of 1972. (Employers and employees pay half of this figure each, in addition to
the other social insurance contributions.) This
still did not prevent a deficit of DM 2.4 billion in
1974, followed by a record DM 8.6 billion in 1975.
Contributions were therefore raised to 2 per cent
and then 3 per cent from the beginning of 1975 and
1976 respectively. In addition, the Federal Government provided financial assistance of DM 7.28 billion
in 1975. Small surpluses in 1977 and 1978 again gave
way to deficits from 1979, culminating in a figure of
DM 8.4 billion in 1981. Since the Office had exhausted its own liquid reserves, financial assistance
from the Federal Government was again sought. In
other words, it had become impossible for the Office

to form even modest reserves as a cushion against
the cyclical fluctuations in the demands on its
finances. This is, of course, another common social
insurance problem. However, the numbers unemployed
in 1979 and 1980 were lower than the mid-1970s. It
was the additional vocational training expenditure
and pension contributions made on behalf of the unemployed which added materially to the sharp increase in the Office's expenditure (MRDB, August
1981, p.29). Further, unemployment in 1980 again
started to increase.

There is a poignant conclusion to be drawn from
the fact that the unemployment insurance contribution
was again increased in 1982 - this time to 4 per
cent. That had been the contribution rate in 1950
when (if West Berlin is included) there had also been
nearly 2 million unemployed. During the 1950s, the
sharp decline in unemployment (Diagram 4.4) resulted
in this rate falling to 3 per cent in 1955 and 2 per
cent in 1957 (BMA, Table 7.5). During the 1960s the
rate fell to 1.4 per cent in 1962. Indeed at one of
the peaks in this full employment era (Table 4.8),
no employment insurance contributions were payable
between August 1961 and March 1962 inclusive.

In Chapter 6 there will be a further analysis
of the costs of unemployment. But in order to conclude this review of economic policy, the discusssion
now turns from social to monetary policy.


MONETARY POLICY

Central Banking and Supervision
Introduction. In the Federal Republic of Germany,
the main statutory bases of monetary policy are the
Deutsche Bundesbank Act (*Gesetz über die Deutsche
Bundesbank* - BBankG) of 1957, the Act to Promote
Economic Stability and Growth (*Gesetz zur Förderung
der Stabilität und des Wachstums der Wirtschaft* -
StWG) of 1967 and the External Trade and Payments
Act (*Außenwirtschaftsgesetz* - AWG) of 1961. The
functions of monetary policy dealt with in these
Acts are the responsibility of either the Deutsche
Bundesbank or the Federal Government. The basic
provisions on the supervision of the banking system
are to be found in the Banking Act (*Gesetz über das
Kreditwesen* - KWG) which entered into force at the
beginning of 1962. These four Acts will be used as
a means of analysing the legal and constitutional
framework of monetary policy.

BBankG. It will be shown below that the Bundesbank's main powers are those of fixing interest and discount rates, fixing minimum reserve ratios up to the limits set out in the Act, and laying down the principles of its credit and open market operations. But the absolutely crucial phrases of the BBankG have been emphasised by the writer in the following excerpts:

Section 3. Duties
The Deutsche Bundesbank shall regulate the volume of money in circulation and of credit supplied to the economy, using the monetary powers conferred on it by this Act, *with the aim of safeguarding the currency*, and shall make banking arrangements for domestic and international payments.

Section 12. Relationship of the Bank to the Federal Government
Subject to the discharge of its duties, the Deutsche Bundesbank shall be required to support the general economic policy of the Federal Government. In exercising the powers conferred on it by this Act it *shall be independent* of instructions from the Federal Government.

Section 13. Co-operation
(1) The Deutsche Bundesbank *shall advise* the Federal Government in monetary policy matters of major importance and shall furnish it with information at its request.
(2) The members of the Federal Government *shall have the right* to participate in the discussions of the Central Bank Council. They shall have no right to vote, but may propose motions. If they so request, a decision shall be deferred for up to *two weeks*.
(3) The Federal Government *shall invite* the President of the Deutsche Bundesbank to take part in its discussions on important matters affecting monetary policy.
(BBk, pp.64-65 and 69)

It has already been implied by the discussion of Inflation and the Currency Reform in Chapter 2 that the contraction of the money supply and re-organisation of public debt once again required in 1948 led the Allies to establish the predecessor of the Bundesbank (the Bank deutscher Länder - BdL). The BdL was given considerable legal autonomy and a substantial degree of operational independence from

the later-established Federal Government (Hardach,
p.153). It should not, however, be assumed that the
independence of the Bundesbank has been consistently
regarded as an inviolable constitutional principle.
Indeed, considerable political controversy has been
aroused by the Bundesbank's interpretation of its
'safeguarding the currency' mandate. This is because
balance-of-payments and exchange-rate objectives have
been accorded priority over internal stability.
Successive Federal Governments on the other hand
strove for internal stability (Hennings, p.44). Other
changes at the Bundesbank - for example, in the personalities at the head of its organisation - have not
brought about any significant change in its exchange-
rate policy. At the end of the 1970s, for that
matter, the policy survived a disagreement between,
on the one hand, the President and his five fellow
directors (collectively known as the Directorate or
*Bundesbankdirektorium*) and, on the other hand, the
eleven presidents of the Bundesbank at Länder level
(*Landeszentralbankenpräsidenten*), who together with
the six members of the Directorate constitute the
governing council of the Bundesbank (*der Zentral-
bankrat*) which also contains non-voting representatives of the Federal Government - see Section 13(2)
of the Bundesbank Act above). Basically, the disagreement emanated from the Directorate's view that
there should be a change to influencing interest
rates from the previous view that direct control of
the money stock should be attempted via the money
market, a point which will be taken up later (*Die
Zeit*, 9/80, p.21).
Opposition to Bundesbank policies outside of the
bank itself emanates from several sources. The Federal Government was opposed to the high interest rate
policy of the Bundesbank on two occasions during the
1970s. First, in 1973 there was extensive discussion
of a change to the Bundesbank Act which, while
strengthening the bank's powers in some respects,
would have deprived it of some of its autonomy. The
proposed amendment was dropped in the face of the oil
crsis. Secondly, the Federal Government sharply
criticised the higher interest rates imposed during
1981 in the belief that they would still further
restrict the hopes of economic recovery. One qualification which should be made here, however, is that
during the review period the state-owned specialist
banking institutions, as will be seen in Chapter 8,
were more compliant as instruments of government
policy (Hardach, p.154).

Criticism has also come from other institutions. The trade unions have been fairly consistent critics of the effects of monetary policy on employment levels. They were joined on occasions by the employers and other parts of the banking sector. Even the five normally conservative economic research institutes were critical of Bundesbank policies during 1981.

StWG and AWG. The former Act provided the Federal Government with a wide range of planning mechanisms and instruments to counter cyclical movements. It was seen earlier in this chapter as a notable postwar development in economic policy.

A crucial point here is that the StWG not only supplemented the Federal Government's short-term economic policy instruments, but the Act also increased the Bundesbank's freedom of action (BBk, p.6). Some of the instruments have an indirect and others a direct significance for monetary policy. Among the indirect instruments, the Bundesbank has the right to participate in the proceedings of the Public Authorities' Council on Economic Trends - an advisory body set up to harmonise the ways in which the various central, Länder and local authorities manage their budgets (*ibid.*, p.58). This council also examines ways and means of meeting the borrowing requirement of public authorities.

Among the instruments directly significant for monetary policy, the technicalities of which are dealt with below, are three methods of mobilising or immobilising government debt and revenue in order to control the money supply in an anti-cyclical manner. First, the Bundesbank's room for manouevre in open market operations was widened considerably by investing the central bank with the unrestricted right to mobilise treasury bills' sales of claims (*Lastenausgleich*) on the public authorities arising either directly or indirectly out of the Currency Reform (*ibid.*, pp.48 and 60). Proceeds from the sales are immobilised by the Bundesbank and used only to redeem bills falling due or re-purchased before maturity by the central bank. Secondly, the Federal Government and the Bundesbank may require the Federal Labour Office to purchase treasury bills out of its job creation and pension funds, although the growth in unemployment benefits and rise in other social security spending during the 1970s forced the Federal Labour Office into deficit. Thirdly, net tax revenues released through cuts in public spending will be either mobilised or immobilised by transferring them into or out of a special Bundesbank reserve account in order to exert some control over the potential influence on demand of the central, regional and local authorities.

The AWG is relatively less important. It basically empowers the Federal Government, in certain circumstances, to control and restrict by regulation the various sectors of foreign trade and payments. Doubt must be cast on the efficacy of this Act in view of what will be said about the international aspects of West German banking.

KWG. Banking institutions (*Kreditinstitute*) are subject to the official supervision of the Banking Supervisory Authority (*Bundesaufsichtsamt für das Kreditwesen*). Section 1 of the KWG defines the term 'banking institution' as meaning enterprises engaged in banking business which, in turn, are defined as follows:

1. The acceptance of monies from others as deposits, irrespective of whether interest is paid (deposit business or *Einlagengeschäft*);
2. the granting of loans and acceptance credits (credit business or *Kreditgeschäft*);
3. the purchase of bills of exchange, promissory notes and cheques (discount business or *Diskontgeschäft*);
4. the purchase and sale of securities for the account of others (securities business or *Effektengeschäft*);
5. the custody and administration of securities for the account of others (custody business or *Depotgeschäft*);
6. the transactions designated in the investment Companies Act (investment business or *Investmentgeschäft*);
7. the incurring of the obligation to acquire claims in respect of loans prior to their maturity;
8. the assumption for others of guarantees and other sureties (guarantee business or *Garantiegeschäft*); and
9. the effecting of transfers and clearings (giro business or *Girogeschäft*).
   (Schneider, pp.32-33)

It will be immediately apparent that Section 1 of the KWG has a wide-ranging application. Any of the types of business listed above, even if only a small part of total business, constitutes a 'banking institution', providing the business requires a commercially organised operation. There are, however, a number of institutions specifically exempted from supervision under the KWG (Section 2). These include the Bundesbank and the state-owned Reconstruction and Development Loan Corporation, which is subject to the direct supervision of the Federal Government. Insurance companies which do not typically carry out banking, the social security departments of the Federal Labour Office and the Post Office savings bank/giro operations are also among the exempt institutions (Schneider, pp.33 and 63).

Any banking institution operating in the Federal Republic, including branches of foreign-owned banks, must obtain a banking licence from the Supervisory Authority. Further, the Supervisory Authority operates in close co-operation with the Bundesbank, the latter passing on the various financial reports made by the banks. Under Section 44 of the KWG the Supervisory Authority is also entitled to launch its own investigations into the affairs of a particular banking institution (*ibid.*, pp.134-137). The Supervisory Authority has exercised its powers under the KWG to issue the so-called Principles 1 and 1a which respectively control the domestic loan/equity capital and the foreign currency/equity capital ratios of the banking sectors. Finally, the keystone of the Second Amendment to the KWG was the new powers accorded to the Supervisory Authority enabling it to virtually step in and conduct the affairs of a bank in financial difficulties. It will be necessary to return to many of the points made in this paragraph when the banking sector is examined (Chapter 8 below).

### Instruments of Monetary Policy

It has been seen thus far that the Bundesbank's targets are the control of the banking system and the supply of money in co-operation with the Supervisory Authority. Capital and liquidity requirements are used in this process. Hence, with the instruments available to it, the Bundesbank endeavours to influence monetary demand by influencing two basic sets of indicators, that is, bank liquidity and interest rates, which are, of course, also instruments. The interest rates so affected are those charged or paid in the banks' credit and deposit business, together with those on the money and capital markets. Instruments of liquidity policy (minimum reserves, rediscount *quotas* and open market operations with non-banks) always affect interest rates as well, since

they change the supply-demand relationship on the
money market (BBk, p.28). Some instruments of
interest rate policy also exert an influence on bank
liquidity, in that the cost of converting liquid reserves into central bank money is raised or lowered.
Interest rate instruments are the discount *rates*,
Lombard rates (to be defined below), along with open
market operations in money market paper. The latter
comprises the treasury bills and 'funds' of the public
authorities. Treasury 'bonds' (*U-Schätze*) are dis-
counted like bills. Hence to avoid confusion with
long-term fixed-interest bonds, treasury bills and
'bonds' are best collectively known as 'treasury
bills'. The various instruments are summarised in
Figure 5.2. It will be seen that there are several
ways in which the goals of internal and external balance of the StWG can be affected.

An important distinction has to be made between
the various interest rates of the Bundesbank, on which
more detail will be found in Diagram 5.6 and Table
5.9. The discount rate approximates to the former
bank rate and minimum lending rate in the UK, or the
rediscount rate elsewhere. In other words, discount
operations are used as a method of changing bank
liquidity and hence the money supply. This rate
determines the price at which commercial and treasury
bills offered by the banks will be rediscounted. For
example, a DM 100 bill may be rediscounted (sold) a
month prior to the date it is due for redemption for
DM 99.50, in which case the rediscount rate is 0.5 per
cent per month or just over 6 per cent compound per
year. From Diagram 5.6 it can be seen that the discount rate has varied between 3 and 7.5 per cent during the period under review, with the record highs and
most variability being registered during the 1970s, a
point to be taken up again shortly. Discount policy
(*Diskontpolitik*) also consists of fixing rediscount
limits for each bank which determines the potential
level of liquidity.

A second interest rate instrument is known as
the Lombard rate. This is the rate at which secured
advances will be made by the Bundesbank to the banks
(*Lombardpolitik*) (Stein, 1977, p.11). Securities
which may be pledged in this way include treasury
bills and fixed interest securities (BBk, pp.32-33).
It will be seen from Diagram 5.6 that the Lombard
rate has been varied at levels of between 0.5 and 2.0
percentage points above the discount rate, that is to
say between 3.5 and 9.5 per cent. It will also be
seen from Diagram 5.6 that there is a special Lombard
rate which has generally been 3 percentage points

113

## Figure 5.2: Instruments of Monetary Policy

In the Federal Republic the wholesale money market is a market in bank deposits at the Bundesbank. Minimum requirements are set by the Bundesbank and the system is geared to maintain them. The boxes at the top show normal retail operations of the banking system that may affect banks' deposits at the Bundesbank. The lower half shows the methods available to the Bundesbank to iron out any distortions created by the retail operations, as well as to ease or tighten monetary policy. If there is a shortage of deposits at the Bundesbank as a whole, i.e. after inter-bank lending, interest rates will rise.

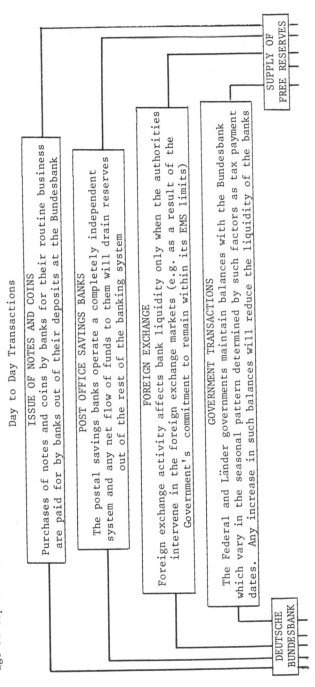

Day to Day Transactions

**ISSUE OF NOTES AND COINS**

Purchases of notes and coins by banks for their routine business are paid for by banks out of their deposits at the Bundesbank

**POST OFFICE SAVINGS BANKS**

The postal savings banks operate a completely independent system and any net flow of funds to them will drain reserves out of the rest of the banking system

**FOREIGN EXCHANGE**

Foreign exchange activity affects bank liquidity only when the authorities intervene in the foreign exchange markets (e.g. as a result of the Government's commitment to remain within its EMS limits)

**GOVERNMENT TRANSACTIONS**

The Federal and Länder governments maintain balances with the Bundesbank which vary in the seasonal pattern determined by such factors as tax payment dates. Any increase in such balances will reduce the liquidity of the banks

SUPPLY OF FREE RESERVES

DEUTSCHE BUNDESBANK

Monetary Policies

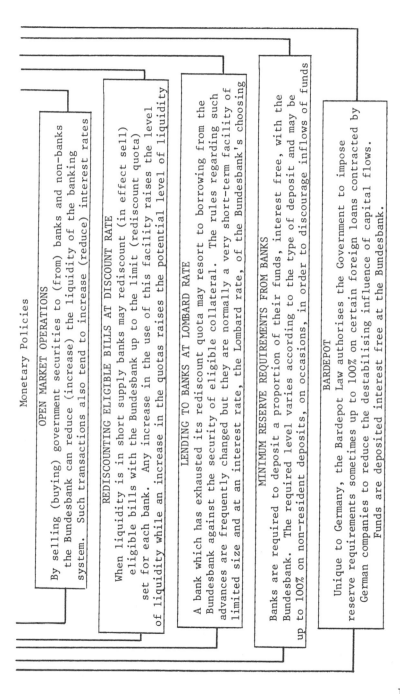

OPEN MARKET OPERATIONS

By selling (buying) government securities to (from) banks and non-banks the Bundesbank can reduce (increase) the liquidity of the banking system. Such transactions also tend to increase (reduce) interest rates

REDISCOUNTING ELIGIBLE BILLS AT DISCOUNT RATE

When liquidity is in short supply banks may rediscount (in effect sell) eligible bills with the Bundesbank up to the limit (rediscount quota) set for each bank. Any increase in the use of this facility raises the level of liquidity while an increase in the quotas raises the potential level of liquidity

LENDING TO BANKS AT LOMBARD RATE

A bank which has exhausted its rediscount quota may resort to borrowing from the Bundesbank against the security of eligible collateral. The rules regarding such advances are frequently changed but they are normally a very short-term facility of limited size and at an interest rate, the Lombard rate, of the Bundesbank's choosing

MINIMUM RESERVE REQUIREMENTS FROM BANKS

Banks are required to deposit a proportion of their funds, interest free, with the Bundesbank. The required level varies according to the type of deposit and may be up to 100% on non-resident deposits, on occasions, in order to discourage inflows of funds

BARDEPOT

Unique to Germany, the Bardepot Law authorises the Government to impose reserve requirements sometimes up to 100% on certain foreign loans contracted by German companies to reduce the destabilising influence of capital flows. Funds are deposited interest free at the Bundesbank.

Source: *Barclays Bank Review*, August 1979.

116

Diagram 5.6: Movements in the Discount, Lombard and Special Lombard Percentage Rates, 1950–1980 inclusive

Discount, Lombard
and Special
Lombard rates
(per cent)

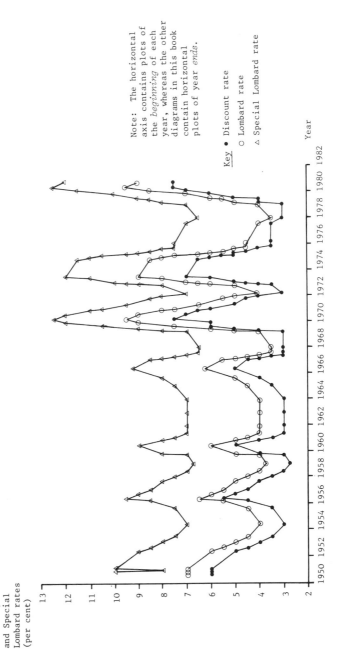

Note: The horizontal axis contains plots of the *beginning* of each year, whereas the other diagrams in this book contain horizontal plots of year *ends*.

Key ● Discount rate
○ Lombard rate
△ Special Lombard rate

Year

Source: Derived from data in MRDB, August 1981, Table V(1).

Table 5.9:   Frequency Distribution of the Discount,
Lombard and Special Lombard Percentage Rates

Discount rates   (N = 73; class size = 0.5)

| Group No. | Frequency | Mid-Point | Group No. | Frequency | Mid-Point |
|-----------|-----------|-----------|-----------|-----------|-----------|
| 1 | 0 | 2.5 | 7 | 2 | 5.5 |
| 2 | 15 | 3.0 | 8 | 9 | 6.0 |
| 3 | 10 | 3.5 | 9 | 2 | 6.5 |
| 4 | 12 | 4.0 | 10 | 3 | 7.0 |
| 5 | 7 | 4.5 | 11 | 3 | 7.5 |
| 6 | 10 | 5.0 | | | |

Mode   = 3.1         Standard deviation      = 1.3
Median = 4.2         Pearson's second measure
Mean   = 4.5           of skewness*          = +0.7

Lombard rates   (N = 73; class size = 0.5)

| Group No. | Frequency | Mid-Point | Group No. | Frequency | Mid-Point |
|-----------|-----------|-----------|-----------|-----------|-----------|
| 1 | 3 | 3.5 | 8 | 5 | 7.0 |
| 2 | 13 | 4.0 | 9 | 3 | 7.5 |
| 3 | 8 | 4.5 | 10 | 3 | 8.0 |
| 4 | 11 | 5.0 | 11 | 2 | 8.5 |
| 5 | 7 | 5.5 | 12 | 4 | 9.0 |
| 6 | 7 | 6.0 | 13 | 2 | 9.5 |
| 7 | 5 | 6.5 | | | |

Mode   = 4.1         Standard deviation      = 1.6
Median = 5.4         Pearson's second measure
Mean   = 5.8           of skewness*          = +0.75

Special Lombard rates   (N = 73; class size = 0.5)

| Group No. | Frequency | Mid-Point | Group No. | Frequency | Mid-Point |
|-----------|-----------|-----------|-----------|-----------|-----------|
| 1 | 3 | 6.5 | 8 | 4 | 10.0 |
| 2 | 13 | 7.0 | 9 | 3 | 10.5 |
| 3 | 8 | 7.5 | 10 | 3 | 11.0 |
| 4 | 12 | 8.0 | 11 | 2 | 11.5 |
| 5 | 7 | 8.5 | 12 | 4 | 12.0 |
| 6 | 7 | 9.0 | 13 | 2 | 12.5 |
| 7 | 5 | 9.5 | | | |

Mode   = 7.1         Standard deviation      = 1.6
Median = 8.3         Pearson's second measure
Mean   = 8.7           of skewness*          = +0.75

\*   $\dfrac{3(\text{mean}-\text{median})}{\text{standard deviation}}$

Note: Other medians and means quoted in this book are for
ungrouped data.

Source:  Derived from data in MRDB, August 1981,
Table V(1)

above the Lombard rate. This special rate is used
to penalise banks for failing to meet the minimum
reserve requirement, although for the month of June
in 1973 and from 20 February 1981 to 6 May 1982, all
'normal' Lombard loans were suspended. In effect,
the closure of the Lombard 'window' in this manner
represented a particularly severe form of credit
rationing, some of the implications of which must be
examined in a little more depth.

Taken together, all three rates represent a central element in the Bundesbank's interest rate policy.
Changes in these rates usually entail a shift in the
pattern of interest rates in the Federal Republic.
The tendency is for interest rates to change much more
in short-term business than in long-term business,
that is more sharply on the money market than on the
capital market, and more sharply for short-term lending than for long-term lending. But the relative
economic instability of the 1970s, culminating in the
generally poor banking profits of 1980 can be further
illustrated by examining the pattern of Bundesbank
interest rates during this period - if only because
short-term rates were presumably an indicator and
long-term rates a target of monetary policy (Dennis,
p.22). This poor profitability was in spite of the
endowment effect of high short-term interest rates
(see Chapter 8).

Not only were the three Bundesbank rates unstable during the 1970s (Diagram 5.6) but their general level was also relatively high, a point which
can also be demonstrated by reference to Table 5.9.
The instability was not new: between the formation of
the Bank deutscher Länder in 1948 and 1961, the discount rate was altered twenty-three times - more often
than in any other European country (Opie, p.14). The
relative high average levels were new, however. Virtually all the positive skewness in the three distri-
butions is, of course, attributable to the right-hand
tail. This tail almost exclusively contains data from
the 1970s. In the case of the two Lombard rates, the
top 14 observations range respectively from 7.5 to
9.5 per cent and from 10.5 to 12.5 per cent, the mid-
points coinciding with the actual rates in each group.
In the case of the discount rate, the top 17 observations lie in the range 6.0 to 7.5 per cent, with
the mid-points again coinciding with the actual rates.
All the high Lombard rates were in operation at various times during the period September 1969 to September 1980. Similarly, 14 of the top discount rates
were applied at intervals during the 1970s, the other
three (all 6 per cent) lying in the very early 1950s.

Some further implications and consequences of high interest rates will be examined in the final part of this chapter. It is first necessary to review the instruments designed to act directly on interest rates, bank liquidity and the monetary base. These instruments are open market operations (*Offenmarktpolitik*) and minimum reserve requirements (*Mindestreservepolitik*). In order to compare theory and practice in these two policies, a short digression on theory follows in the next paragraph.

The theory behind open market operations is that the banks' own deposits at the central bank can be controlled by the latter's purchases and sales of government securities. Should the central bank purchase DM 1,000 of these securities, it increases the reserves of the banks held at the central bank by DM 1,000. If the banks observe a reserve/deposits ratio of 1:12 then the money supply is increased by up to DM 12,000. (Where 'reserves' equal central bank deposits and loans create bank deposits. Also where a number of factors - particularly the profitability of credit expansion - determine the extent to which the money supply is increased.) If the central bank purchases government securities from the non-bank public, both the reserves of the banks held at the central bank, and the deposits of the non-bank public held at their banks, increase. Hence some observers would regard the monetary base, plus the banks' assets and liabilities, as critical indicators (see Dennis, pp.178-180 for a succinct analysis of the differences in long-term/short-term and bank/non-bank public open market operations. The monetary base, or high-powered money, consists of reserves held at the central bank plus currency in circulation with the non-bank public.)

In turning to the practice, it must first be noted that the Bundesbank's open market transations with the banks in instruments of short-term indebtedness must be considered as relating to interest-rate policy rather than liquidity policy (BBk, p.53). If, as already indicated, the discount rate influences the whole level of interest rates, the effect of the selling and repurchase rates also have far-reaching effects. This is because borrowers bid up short-term interest rates in other markets.

Further, the Bundesbank's open market policy is closely related to the special features of the German money and capital markets. Money market transactions, as regards dealings in both central bank funds and treasury bills, are conducted mainly, in the case of the former, between banks or, in the case of the latter, between the central bank and banks (BBk, p.46).

On the capital market the Bundesbank takes a direct
decision on the amounts of long-term securities
(bonds) it wishes to purchase and sell. As would be
expected the *total* sales of long-term bonds by value
far exceeds the sale of (short-term) treasury bills.
In consequence, the total amount of bonds outstanding
in December 1980 totalled DM 548.6 billion compared
to DM 6.2 billion in shorter term instruments (MRDB,
August 1981, Tables VI(4) and VII(8)). The bond
market is in any case dominated by the banks:
DM 413.3 billion (or just over three-quarters) of the
DM 548.6 billion outstanding in December 1980 had
been issued by the banks, and the banks themselves
held DM 227.9 billion (or over 40 per cent) of these
bonds as assets (MRDB, August 1981, Tables VI(4) and
III(17)). Nor do the peculiarities of the German
system end here. It has already been seen that the
StWG gives the Bundesbank wide discretionary powers
over the sale of treasury bills. In effect, this
gives the Bundesbank power to create these short-term
instruments irrespective of the financing requirements
and policies of the public authorities. The treasury
bills issued under these arrangements are known as
'mobilisation paper' (Currency Reform) and 'liquidity
paper' (additional powers) (BBk, pp.48-50).
      Since 1955, when open market operations began,
a substantial amount of surplus funds, mainly arising
from the heavy foreign exchange inflows into the Federal Republic, have also at times been placed into
mobilisation paper. This represented an attempt to
sterilise the effects of such inflows. The importance
of such intervention by the Bundesbank can be easily
demonstrated: coupled with the later mobilisation and
liquidity powers under the StWG, such interventions
have resulted during the 1960s and 1970s in the banks'
treasury bill holdings (including mobilisation and
liquidity paper) always exceeding, often quite substantially exceeding, the value excluding such paper
(MRDB, June 1974, Table III(12) and August 1981,
Table III(15)). Finally, in the middle of 1967 open
market operations entered a new phase. Although the
Bundesbank increased bank liquidity, the banks invested it abroad. Hence in order to engineer the
desired fall in interest rates, the Bundesbank itself
purchased a substantial holding of bonds, which it
disposed of two years later.
      Minimum reserve requirements are at once the
most important yet most complex instrument with which
the Bundesbank influences bank liquidity (Stein, 1977,
p.11). These requirements derive from section 16(1)
of Part IV (monetary powers) of the Bundesbank Act.

(The Bank deutscher Länder had possessed similar powers.) Under this section, the banks have to deposit a given minimum percentage of liabilities on an interest-free basis with Bundesbank (Schneider, p.183). Such reserves vary in amount according to the type of bank deposit and type of banking institution. The respective maximum percentages for sight, time and savings deposits are 30, 20 and 10, although for liabilities to non-residents the maximum percentage is 100 per cent. Even within these ratios there is a further variation in sight and savings deposits according to whether a bank is situated near to an office or branch of the Bundesbank. The reason for this is that a bank not in such a location will be obliged to retain more till money.

If the use to which the minimum reserves has been put is considered, the fairly clear trend has been one away from their use as a means of controlling the money supply. In 1971, the Bundesbank could assert that the minimum reserve regulations were used to 'prevent either a major rise or drain in liquid reserves' (BBk, p.44). From 1974 money supply growth targets were introduced on an experimental basis (Stein, 1979, p.10). The target was defined in terms of central bank money - a concept using cash in circulation and the minimum reserves held at the Bundesbank which differs from the monetary base defined above since total bank reserves were not included. But the targets for 1975, 1976 and 1977 were all overshot. Moreover, the actual developments in both real GNP and inflation diverged appreciably from the assumptions made by the Bundesbank planners - that is, their growth was lower than expected. Finally, with the shift towards a greater holding of cash relative to income and turnover, the velocity of circulation fell. Hence, the Bundesbank council decided in December 1977 to set a target (again 8 per cent) for central bank money growth in 1978, but then a gradual exchange-rate induced change started to take place. Its result has been the transformation to another type of monetary control, namely the increases in costs to the banks of borrowed reserves. The later increases in the discount and Lombard rates reviewed above came about partly as a result of this policy change (Diagram 5.6, Table 5.9 and the surrounding discussion).

The Balance of Payments and Monetary Policy
In Chapter 4 the change from a net inflow of direct capital investment in the 1950s and 1960s, to a net outflow in the 1970s was analysed. The behaviour of

portfolio investment has been much more erratic, this
being caused not least by the behaviour of bond purchases. In the first half of the 1970s there were
large speculative inflows before the introduction of
floating exchange rates in 1973. This was followed
by a post-1973 outflow once capital gains had been
made. The relatively high real interest rates in
1979 attracted an inflow of DM 4 billion into the
bond market. This compared to DM 687 million and
DM 124 million in 1977 and 1978 respectively (MRDB,
various, Table IX(5)). Moreover, in order to cover
both the current account deficits and the large
government borrowing requirement at the end of the
1970s, exchange controls were relaxed. Foreigners
were, for the first time, allowed to invest in German
government securities of less than four years' life.
(Securities of over four years' life are not taken
into account when determining the minimum reserve
requirements or calculating the M3 money stock -
MRDB, August 1981, Table I(1).) Technically non-
resident purchases of short-term fixed interest
securities had never been banned. Instead they had
been made subject to Bundesbank approval, which was
invariably withheld. During 1980 public authorities
imported a total of DM 23 billion of long-term funds,
mainly from Saudi Arabia. Also in 1980, German exporters scored particular successes in their trade
with OPEC countries (MRDB, December 1981, p.7). In
short, every effort was made to capitalise on the oil
dollar surpluses of the OPEC countries.

As well as changing the physical controls over
capital inflows, which had precipitated Schiller's
resignation earlier in the decade, the second type of
reaction to counter large speculative inflows or outflows of currency was to adjust interest rates. As
already pointed out, there was a shift from fixed to
free exchange rates in 1973. These two régimes
brought different types of problems and Diagram 5.7
aims to illustrate some of the underlying features.
The revaluations of 1961 and 1969, together with the
1971 period of floating and the introduction in 1973
of the free exchange rate régime, are all discernible.
Various fluctuations after 1973 consist of further
gains by the DM against the dollar, with the exceptions of 1975 and 1980. It is therefore necessary to
briefly review the interaction of the exchange rate
and interest rates. Such a review will show that
after the Korean War massive currency inflows led to
policy debates about the methods of achieving both
internal and external balance. Revaluations were
virtually forced on to the authorities in 1961 and

Diagram 5.7:   DM Exchange Rate against the US$, 1950-
1980

US$ 1 = DM

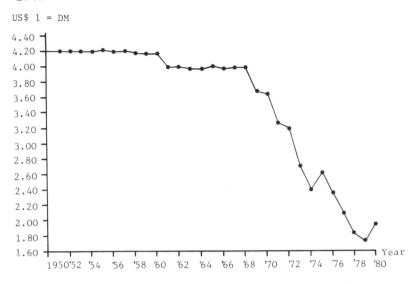

Technical Note: In order to arrive at a geometric index for the
purpose of calculating the weighted exchange rate of the DM,
the various indices for the external values of the DM against
the currencies of trading partners are multiplied by each other
after having been raised to the power of the respective foreign
trade shares for the purpose of weighting (MRDB, April 1979,
p.23). When weighted in this manner against the currencies of
13 other industrial countries, the *nominal* DM exchange rate was
much the same in 1981 as in 1978. Since the FRG's inflation
rate was lower, however, the *real* DM exchange rate was about
11.5 per cent lower (MRDB, March 1982, pp.19 and 27). But the
rise in the DM nominal exchange rate against the dollar in 1980
and 1981 led to the FRG recovering some of her competitive
advantage in unit labour costs and all her export unit competitiveness (1970=100 - OECD, *Economic Survey*, 1981, p.28; Table
4.9 and the surrounding discusssion). This enabled West German
exporters to recapture some lost markets, although both costs
and currency values are not always strictly reflected in the
prices charged (Dresdner Bank, *Economic Quarterly*, November
1981, p.2; MRDB, March 1982, p.19). Further, exports in real
terms continued to expand more rapidly than imports, but the
net contribution from this sector in nominal terms was expected
to be smaller because of the relatively more rapid rise in import prices (Dresdner Bank, *Economic Quarterly*, April 1982, p.2).

Source:   Plotted from Dresdner Bank, *Statische Reihen*,
p.5.

1969.  In the 1970s economic instability was even
more exacerbated by monetary policy.

Following the Currency Reform, bank credit, the
money supply, budget deficits and prices all seemed
to be getting out of hand.  As can be seen from Diagram 5.8, in 1949 and 1950 there was a drain on
foreign currency reserves.  Unemployment was high but
the Bank deutscher Länder gave priority to currency
stability and achieving a balance of payments equilibrium (Wallich, p.85).  Its job after mid-1950 was
made considerably easier by external events: aggregate demand was increased by the international increase in output during and after the Korean war
which drew German industry back into world markets.
Equally important, the imports bill was kept within
tolerable limits by the ERP aid, special EPU credits
and a fall in raw material prices from the Korean
peak.  The Bank deutscher Länder also persuaded a
reluctant Erhard to re-impose physical import controls
(*ibid.*, pp.90-91).  During the Korean crisis the Bank
maintained a highly unpopular restrictive policy from
October 1950 to May 1952 - in fact until prices were
falling (Hartrich, p.167).  In order to constrain
rising prices during the first post-Korean boom
(1955-56), the Bank again intervened vigorously, by
raising interest rates, increasing minimum reserves
and using open market sales (Denton, p.170).  This
move met with the disapproval of both the Federal
Government and industrialists (Hardach, p.154).

Quite apart from the role of the specially
created public banks in offering alternative sources
of credit (see Chapter 8), yet another factor in this
early period enabled the Bank to pursue a restrictive
course.  For that matter it also indirectly allowed
the Federal Government to abstain from stabilisation
policies and amass huge budget surpluses.  This factor
was the undervalued exchange rate of the DM, which
increased in degree as rapid productivity gains were
made.  Both the consequent export surpluses and the
liberalisation of capital movements attracted large
inflows of speculative money - in the expectation
that the DM was to be revalued.  As a result Germany's
monetary reserves grew by gigantic proportions.  It
was at this stage, however, that the Bank was to find
the money supply increasingly difficult to control.
The steep growth in foreign exchange reserves during
the 1950s is plotted in percentage terms in Diagram
5.8.  'Imported inflation' therefore became a principal policy problem from 1957 - ironically the year
that the Deutsche Bundesbank succeeded the Bank
deutscher Länder.

Given a fixed exchange rate, 'imported inflation' in its broadest sense is construed here to mean inflationary pressure stemming from, first, the inflow of foreign exchange which increases domestic liquidity; secondly, from the excess export demand placed on German industry (cf. Wallich, 1968, p.376) and, thirdly, from importing goods from economies where inflation rates are higher than in the FRG. It is extremely difficult for orthodox (classical) monetary policy to deal with this problem: increased liquidity from abroad gives private institutions greater independence from the central bank. If interest rates are raised to combat this problem, more capital will be attracted from abroad. Further, attempts to counteract the effects of inflows by physical intervention are not consistent with the free market philosophy. As Denton *et al.* astutely observe (p.171) the orthodox response to an increase of reserves is to let internal prices rise until the net inflow of foreign exchange is checked. But assuming that price stability is considered to be an equally important goal there is clearly a conflict at work. Hence, the unorthodox monetary remedy is to revalue the currency. This issue sparked off considerable political controversy, both between 1957 and the 1961 revaluation, and before the 1969 revaluation (Hardach, p.203; Hennings, p.62).

Between 1957 and 1959 the Bundesbank lowered discount rate to discourage the inflow of hot money, but used minimum reserves and open market operations to restrict liquidity at home (Denton, p.171). In addition to this somewhat ambivalent stand against imported inflation, the export of capital was encouraged (Hardach, p.193). This policy at first seemed to meet with some success: in 1959 West Germany recorded her first overall balance of payments deficit since 1950 (Diagram 5.8).

In the face of another boom and a massive inflow of capital in 1960, the Bundesbank still initially opted for the orthodox (classical model) response: by reducing its interest rates and relaxing minimum reserve requirements the Bundesbank formally acknowledged that balance of payments objectives had taken - priority over internal considerations. Finally, in March 1961 the Federal Government and the Bundesbank agreed to revalue the exchange rate so that US\$ 1 = DM 4.00. Such a decision meant that import prices would decrease by (4.00 - 4.20)/4.20 x 100 = -4.76 per cent, whereas export prices would increase by (4.20 - 4.00)/4.00 x 100 = 5 per cent.

The 1961 revaluation succeeded in producing the

Diagram 5.8:  (a)  Annual Net Foreign Exchange Balances, 1949-1980;
              (b)  Total Gold and Foreign Currency Reserves, 1951-1980

(a)

Annual net foreign
exchange balances
(DM billion)

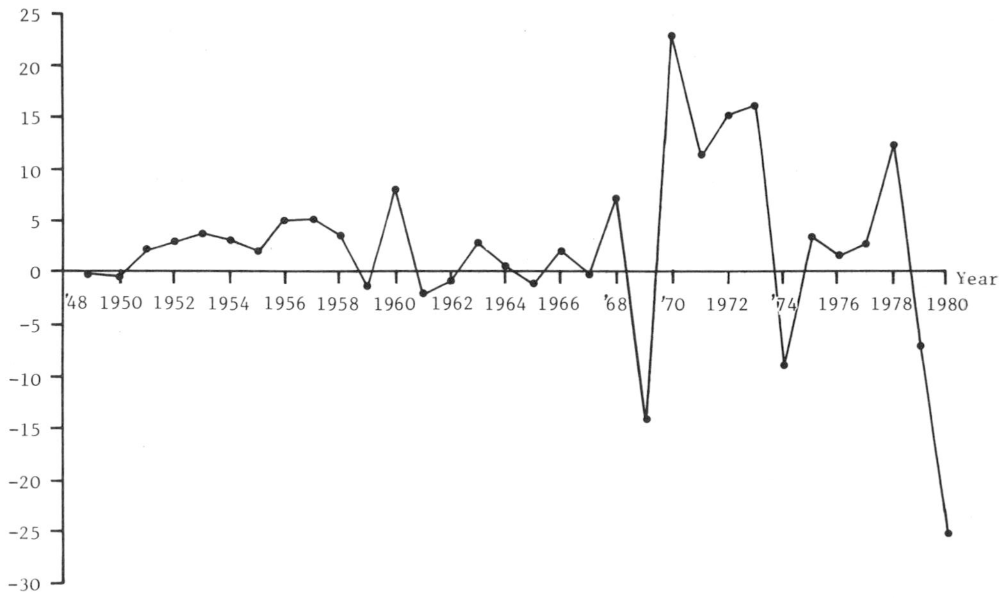

Note:  The secular worsening of the five current account deficits between 1950-1980 (Diagram 4.6) contrasts to the variability in magnitude of ten balance of payments deficits (DM billion):  1950, -0.6;  1959, -1.7;  1961, -2.3;  1962, -0.9;  1965, -1.3;  1967, -0.1;  1969, -14.4;  1974, -9.1;  1979, -7.3;  1980, -25.7. The mean value 1949-1980 is +2.1, the median is +2.3, while 22 of the 32 observations lie between -2.5 and +7.5 (standard deviation = 8.8).

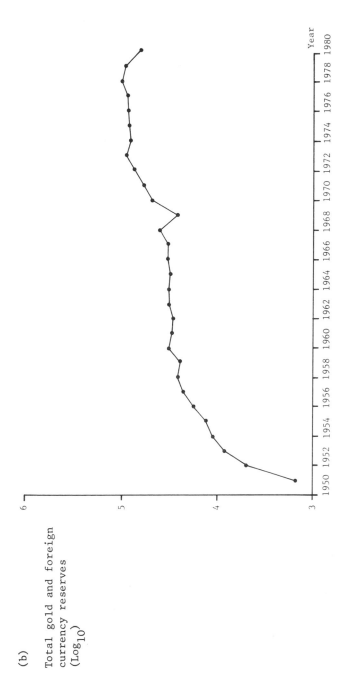

(b)

Total gold and foreign
currency reserves
($\text{Log}_{10}$)

Year

Note: The DM −664 million foreign exchange debt in 1950 could not, of course, be plotted. Reserves in 1949 stood at +DM 379 million.

Source: Based on Dresdner Bank, *Statische Reihen*, p.5.

desired objective: over DM 8 billion had poured into
Germany during 1960, whereas in 1961 and 1962 there
were net outflows of DM 2.3 billion and DM 0.9 billion
respectively (Diagram 5.8). Moreover, the deflationary measures taken by Germany's neighbours, together
with a 25 per cent tax on the capital earnings of non-
resident holders of fixed interest securities, enabled
the Bundesbank to hold its interest rates stable between May 1961 and January 1965. In consequence, the
foreign currency reserve position stabilised at an
extremely healthy level (Diagram 5.8). Export surpluses, particularly at the end of the 1960s, were
quite high. But this was again in spite of, rather
than because of, Bundesbank policies. Rising prices
had caused it to intervene vigorously and interest
rates reached a peak in 1966, but were adjusted des-
perately in 1967 when a fall in internal demand produced recessionary trends.

Because of the destabilising effects of monetary
policy, the search began for alternative fiscal
measures. In any case, there was another massive
inflow of currency during 1968 which eventually forced
another revaluation to US$ 3.66 in October 1969. This
time import prices decreased by -8.5 per cent and export prices were increased by 9.3 per cent. Both
before and after the revaluation the Bundesbank attempted to curb boom conditions and imported inflation
by raising the discount rate from 3 per cent in April
1969 to the post-war record of 7.5 per cent in March
1970. Nevertheless during 1969 there was a considerable outflow of currency and a consequential fall in
foreign exchange reserves. Another problem of the
1960s was highlighted at this stage. The Bundesbank
had not effectively controlled the money supply,
because a fixed exchange rate and muted sterilisation
resulted in its attempts to do so increasing interest
rates. This in turn meant an inflow of foreign funds
which undermined the restrictive stance of monetary
policy.

In practice, the Bundesbank could control the
money supply only as long as foreign interest rates
were higher (Hennings, p.58). But in 1970 foreign
rates were lower than those in the FRG (Vogl, p.18).
Hence the relative volatility of the 1970s was
ushered in by a net inflow of DM 22.6 billion, a
signal for a period of further growth in foreign
exchange reserves. Schiller unsuccessfully pleaded
for tax increases and the Federal Government was un-
willing to reduce public expenditure (*ibid.*, p.18).
In spite of the 1971 floating and post-1973 free exchange rates - which in effect meant a process of

continual revaluation throughout the decade, except
in 1975 and 1980 - the reserves reached DM 90.5 billion in 1973 and DM 100.3 billion in 1978 (Diagrams
5.7 and 5.8).
Although the introduction of free exchange rates
in 1973 led to an outflow in 1974, the Bundesbank
made full use of the freeing of exchange rates to continue its restrictive stance at home (Hennings, pp.76
and 80). This stance had been initiated during the
boom of 1973 and was continued in 1974, possibly
supported by a change in fiscal policy. The Bank was
determined to mop up the cost-push effects of the
unusually bitter wage round of 1974. At the end of
the decade there was another kind of problem, namely
large current account deficits. These deficits led
to outflows in 1979 and 1980. Consequently the reserves stood at DM 67.4 billion at the end of 1980.
Table 5.10 shows, however, that the FRG still possessed the world's highest foreign currency reserves.
Hence the level of these reserves has to be sharply
contrasted to the problems created by the pattern of
their flows. The interest rate backcloth to the volatility of foreign exchange flows was discussed above
(Diagram 5.6 and Table 5.9 and the surrounding discussion). The change in monetary policy from one of
money supply targets to interest rate management was
also discussed.

Table 5.10:   Rank Order of Total Official Reserves

|  | US$ billion | |
|---|---|---|
|  | 1980 | 1979 |
| West Germany | 52.3 | 56.9 |
| France | 31.0 | 21.4 |
| USA | 27.4 | 20.0 |
| Italy | 26.1 | 21.2 |
| Japan | 25.7 | 20.6 |
| UK | 21.5 | 20.7 |
| Switzerland | 19.4 | 20.3 |
| OPEC countries | 93.2 | 74.1 |

Source:   Deutsche Bundesbank, *Annual Reports*, 1979,
p.57, and 1980, p.54.

For most of the 1970s the main preoccupation of
the West German authorities almost paradoxically

became the defence of the US dollar. Under the
régime of fixed exchange rates, surplus countries
like West Germany had been forced by inflows of
foreign exchange to increase the money supply, although there was no corresponding cut in the money
stock of the USA, the main deficit country. The
transition to floating exchange rates did not completely resolve the problem: the value of the US dollar was not stabilised because of the current account
deficit in the USA. The Bundesbank not only had to
intervene to smooth the erratic, downward trend of
the dollar, thus undermining the domestic money supply
target and feeding inflation, but each year the dollar
component of foreign reserves had to be written down.
In 1977, for example, the write down was DM 7.8 billion. It seems that the transition from fixed to
flexible exchange rates had an even larger impact on
the West German economy than the rise in crude oil
prices (Hennings, p.77; cf. Wallich, 1968, p.376).

Efforts to defend the value of the US dollar can
also be seen in interest rate policy. The aim here
was to encourage the flow of currency to the USA by
decreasing nominal interest rates relative to those
obtainable in the USA. Bundesbank interest rates
were therefore gradually decreased between 1974 and
1979. Indeed for the whole of 1978 they were at their
lowest levels since the mid-1960s (Diagram 5.6). This
was thus caused not just by the favour shown to monetary targets at the Bundesbank during this period,
it was also due to a conscious effort by the bank to
accentuate the trans-Atlantic interest differential.

But in 1979-1980 West Germany developed, so to
speak, problems of her own. The exchange rate of the
DM against the US$ started to decline; her foreign
reserves started to fall as her current account
deficit rose and her foreign trade balance fell. The
decline of the DM, by increasing the costs of oil and
other imports, was leading to the opposite form of
'imported' inflation hitherto experienced. A weak
currency, it was felt, could feed domestic inflationary fires. Hence, the decision of the Bundesbank to
increase interest rates to the levels of the early
1970s. This was to emulate, rather than accentuate,
US interest rates (OECD, *Economic Survey*, 1981,
pp.21-24).

In other words, the Bundesbank was giving notice
that the DM must remain a 'hard' currency. To achieve
this the DM would have to maintain its attractiveness
in the eyes of foreign investors. When the 7.5 per
cent discount rate did not of itself arrest the decline of the DM - it reached US$ 1 = DM 2.25 at one

stage - the bank suspended its Lombard rate (in
February 1981) and replaced it with special Lombard
rate.  Although the slide of the DM exchange rate
was at first not completely stopped, it was arrested
somewhat.  However, the unprecedented interest rates
again became a live political issue.  Ironically the
relatively low rate of inflation in West Germany
meant that real interest rates were among the highest
in the industrialised world, although as the inflation
rate in the USA was reduced, but nominal interest
rates remained unchanged, the real interest rate differential between rates in the USA and the FRG did
tend to fall.  High mortgage rates hit the construction industry, and high hire purchase rates hit the
motor industry.  This placed the Bundesbank under a
great deal of pressure but an easing of interest
rates in the money and capital markets was not 'tol-
erated' until the DM 'strengthened in the foreign
exchange markets' (MRDB, December 1981, p.7).  Only
when this condition existed did the bank ease its
special Lombard rate from 12 to 11 per cent in October 1981, then to 10.5 per cent in December, although the bank also warned against any increase in
anti-cyclical spending by the government.  In January 1982 the top Lombard rate was further decreased
to 10 per cent, in order to keep the rate in line
with lower money market rates.  These lower rates
had in turn been engineered by the Bundesbank purchasing large amounts of government stock on the open
market.  The 'normal' 9 per cent Lombard rate was
finally restored on 6 May 1982, the 'special' rate
having been reduced to 9.5 per cent in March.  The
necessary condition of a trend to a current account
surplus had been met.


CONCLUSION

The three decades reviewed in this chapter contrast
as much in policy terms as they did in economic
trends.  Budget surpluses gave way to deficits.
Social security expenditure and contributions, as
well as the taxation of earnings, increased secularly.
Real and nominal interest rates were at record heights
at the end of the period, although their volatility
throughout was remarkable.  Normally strong perform-
ances in the foreign trade field were undermined in
the 1970s by an appreciating exchange rate.  Speculative inflows of currency exerted pressure on both
the exchange rate and money supply in the 1960s and
1970s.  Fiscal policy and central planning became

increasingly more important, in order to supplement
monetary policy.  But the Federal Government's tax
revenue did not keep up with its expenditure commitments.
     It is now time, however, to apply what has been
said thus far to some in depth micro studies of the
labour market, banking and the industrial sector.

Chapter Six

THE LABOUR MARKET

INTRODUCTION

Although there are a number of labour market features
common to most industrialised market economies, it is
the *degree* to which some of these factors have influenced the German economy which impresses the observer.
Demographic variations have been caused by the two
world wars, economic conditions and migration.  There
have been largely consequential changes in the deployment and participation rates of the labour force.
Moreover, structural imbalances between supply and
demand, along with recessionary trends, have resulted
in the introduction of a more active labour market
policy.  In order to explore all these factors, the
analysis commences with a brief demographic survey,
followed by accounts of regional and structural variations in employment.  Some aspects of migration are
then explored.  This is followed by sections on labour
market policies, human capital formation and, finally,
remuneration and hours of work.  Having gained all
these insights, it will be possible to see the major
policy questions of the 1980s.

A BRIEF DEMOGRAPHIC SURVEY

As Wallich (p.264) indicates, the population pyramid
of a normal population resembles a Christmas tree:
it is narrow at the top and slopes uniformly down
to a broad base, both sides (male and female) being
symmetrical.  Wallich goes on to point out that the
American population pyramid roughly resembles this
shape.  Nikolinakos (p.82) shows how the population
pyramid of Germany in 1910 was of similar dimensions.
However, Figure 6.1 supports what both of these
authors emphasise about the effects of the two world

Figure 6.1:   Total and Working Population by Age,
Sex and Nationality, 1976

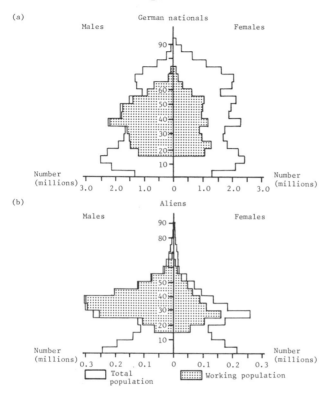

(a)

German nationals

Males                                    Females

90

60
50
40
30
20
10

Number                                   Number
(millions) 3.0    2.0    1.0    0    1.0    2.0    3.0    (millions)

(b)

Aliens

Males                                    Females

90
80

50
40
30
20
10

Number                                   Number
(millions) 0.3    0.2    0.1    0    0.1    0.2    0.3    (millions)

☐ Total          ▦ Working population
  population

Notes:   A population pyramid is published annually in the *Statisches Jahrbuch für die BRD* (p.61 in both 1980 and 1981).   As a
result of the growth in the number of foreign children, the
participation rate among foreigners fell dramatically between
1973 and 1980, but it still stands above that of the native
population (cf. Martin and Miller, p.322).   Since the vast
majority of foreign workers are employees, a comparison of the
two participation rates may be expressed as the ratio of employees to the relevant population.   Hence foreign workers =

1973: $\dfrac{2.5}{3.97}$ x 100 = 63%          1980: $\dfrac{2.0}{4.45}$ x 100 = 45%

But for the native population =

1973: $\dfrac{(22.6 - 2.5)}{(63.05 - 3.97)}$ x100 = 34.6%   1980: $\dfrac{(22.3 - 2.0)}{(61.66 - 4.45)}$ x100 = 35.5%

Source:   Huber and Wiegert, p.185 (writer's translation).

wars and economic crises. For example, in that part
of the pyramid above the age of 50 it is still possible to distinguish the larger number of females.
The main reason for this difference is the number of
males killed in the two world wars. Moreover, there
were distinct periods where the low birth rates during the two world wars and the economic depressions
of 1930-32 and 1945-48 affected the shape of the pyramid. The first Chancellor of West Germany, Konrad
Adenauer (p.148), regarded the demographic structure
of his country's population in 1949 as no less than
'terrifying'. Referring to Germany as a whole, he
said that 'there are 28.9 million men and 36.2 million women ... for every 100 men of thirty there are
more than 300 unmarried women of twenty-six or under.'
West Germany's population at this stage was in the
process of being swollen by what was to be the first
of two migratory flows, namely the influx of expellees
and refugees from the East, a flow which by the time
the Berlin wall was built in 1961 added nearly 14 million to the basic population. It was seen in Chapter
2 that much of this flow arrived in rural north Germany during the early post-Second World War years.

Between 1961 and 1967 more than a million people
were born in the Federal Republic every year; since
then the trend has been one of continuous decline.
There were only 576,500 live births in 1978, the lowest figure in the history of the FRG (IdDW, Table 2).
Since 1972 the indigenous death rate has exceeded the
indigenous birth rate, so that by 1978 the difference
was -146,800, although this difference fell back to
-93,500 in 1980. The net result is that the total
population decreased after 1974 to reach 61.3 million
by 1978 but 61.7 million in 1980 (*ibid.*, Table 1).
Reference to the foot of Figure 6.1 clearly reveals
this decrease in the birth rate. On the basis of
present evidence, a total population of 56.2 million
is forecast by the year 2000.

There are two separate effects of these phases of
relatively high, followed by relatively low birth
rates. The first effect is the increased flow on to
the labour market during the late 1970s and early
1980s as the cohort who were around thirteen years of
age in 1976 (Figure 6.1) swell the size of the labour
force. This was in contrast to the fairly constant
size of the labour force in the 1960s, and the decline
between 1970 and 1977. It was calculated in 1980 that
approximately two million more jobs will be required
by 1985-1990 to accommodate this increased flow, some
of whom were already in higher education (*Die Zeit*,
7/81, p.20). This in turn implied the need for a

4.5 per cent annual growth rate in order to avoid
increasing the already comparatively high levels of
unemployment. The peak in demand for places in
higher education would be reached by 1983, whereas
the expansion in the size of the potential labour
force would come to an end by 1990. Beyond this date
the labour force would fall, but only the growth rate
of 4.5 per cent would be sufficient to restore full
employment by 1995. A growth rate of 2.5 per cent,
and assuming net annual migration of +55,000, would
produce 5 million unemployed by the year 2000 (*Die
Zeit*, 35/82, p.10). Since the provisional growth
rates for 1981 and 1982 were zero and 0.5 per cent
respectively, the future for employment levels seems
bleak.

The second effect stems from the more recent
fall in the birth rate. In primary schools the entry
figure is already noticeably lower; it is estimated
that by 1995 the total school population will be 8.2
million - a third below the 1976 total. By 1985,
there will be as many pensioners as children under 15
years of age. In 1950 there were 4.8 million pensioners (9.3 per cent of the total population) compared to 11.9 million children under 15 (23.3 per
cent) (IdDW, Table 4). All this shows the reasons
for the two clear social policy trends in the 1970s:
increasing child allowances by stages for the second,
and third and subsequent children, and reducing the
rate of increase in pensions (Chapter 5).

A final demographic factor concerns the second
post-war wave of migration into the FRG, a wave
which gathered momentum after the building of the
Berlin wall in 1961. This time the flow was mainly
from the southern extremities of Europe, as opposed
to the eastern fringe of the continent in the first
post-war wave. Figure 6.1 shows the complete contrast in the population pyramid of these aliens in
1976. They were chiefly young and middle-aged persons whose presence in Germany was due to what was
defined in Table 4.8 as an excess demand for labour.
At an early stage of the recession in the 1970s (on
23 November 1973), the Federal Government suspended
the recruitment of foreign workers in countries where
large pools of untapped labour had been discovered.
The countries most affected were Greece, Spain, Port-
ugal, Yugoslavia, Morocco, Tunisia and Turkey. This
ban could not, of course, be extended to EEC nationals.
Even with increased migration from other EEC countries,
however, the total number of foreigners initially fell
from a peak of 4.13 million in 1974 to 3.98 million in
1978. The number rose again to 4.14 million in 1979

(6.8 per cent of the total population); by 1980 there
were 4.45 million foreigners (7.2 per cent). However,
the number of foreigners in the labour force fell
from a peak of 2.5 million in 1973 to 2.0 million in
1980.

There was thus a sharp fall in immigration following the prohibition of non-EEC recruitment, as can
be seen by comparing columns (4) and (5) in Table 6.1.
In other words, the average number of foreigners increased by 128 per cent between 1967 and 1974. The
marginal increase in this so-called third-country
group of foreigners since then is attributable to a
large extent to the number of dependants joining
workers now well settled in German factories and with
little desire to leave. The pay is comparatively much
better, social allowances liberal and many now feel at
home - particularly the second generation to whom the
country of their parents' origin is much stranger than
Germany.

In 1979, the largest number of foreigners were
Turks, 1,268,000 (31 per cent), followed by Yugoslavs,
621,000 (15 per cent), Italians, 594,000 (14 per cent),
and Greeks, 297,000 (7 per cent). Since 1974 the
number of Turks had increased by 240,000 (23 per cent),
whereas the number of Yugoslavs had declined by 87,000
(12 per cent), Italians by 35,000 (6 per cent) and
Greeks by 110,000 (27 per cent). (The absolute size
of all these groups increased in 1980, but the relative magnitudes remained the same; foreigners then
totalled 4.4 million - *Statisches Jahrbuch*, 1981,
Table 3.18.) As shown in Table 6.1, Berlin (West)
had in 1979 the highest proportion, 101 foreigners
for every 1,000 head of population, followed by Baden-
Württemberg with 93, Hesse 84, Hamburg 78 and the
country's most populous Land, North-Rhine Westphalia,
with 75. (Figure 6.2 and Table 6.2 have been included for readers unfamiliar with the geography of
the Federal Republic; various aspects of regional
policy will be analysed shortly.)

The birth rate among foreigners is relatively
high. Indeed, in 1971 the 48,000 difference between
births and deaths was, so to speak, exclusively attributable to babies born to foreigners, whose registered births exceeded registered deaths by 72,000.
German nationals registered 24,000 more deaths than
births. Since 1972, however, the birth rate among
foreigners has not been sufficient to compensate for
the fall in the birth rate of the native population
- hence the fall in total population described above.
But all foreign workers are required by law to sub-
scribe to the German social security system. In

Table 6.1: Foreigners in Relation to Total Population

| Land | (1) Population as at 30.12.79 (000s) | Rank | (2) Foreigners as at 30.9.79 (000s) | Rank | (3) (2) as percentage of (1) | Rank | (4) Growth since 1967 1974 1967=100 | (5) 1979 1967=100 |
|---|---|---|---|---|---|---|---|---|
| Baden-Württemberg | 9,190.1 | 3 | 852.1 | 2 | 9.3 | 2 | 221.9 | 206.9 |
| Bavaria | 10,871.0 | 2 | 652.3 | 3 | 6.0 | 7 | 212.5 | 197.2 |
| Berlin (West) | 1,902.3 | 8 | 192.9 | 6 | 10.1 | 1 | 342.1 | 407.8 |
| Bremen | 695.1 | 11 | 43.4 | 10 | 6.2 | 6 | 289.1 | 314.5 |
| Hamburg | 1,653.0 | 9 | 129.8 | 8 | 7.9 | 4 | 190.2 | 216.3 |
| Hesse | 5,576.1 | 5 | 467.8 | 4 | 8.4 | 3 | 220.4 | 232.4 |
| Lower Saxony | 7,234.0 | 4 | 261.3 | 5 | 3.6 | 10 | 261.8 | 248.1 |
| North Rhine-Westphalia | 17,017.1 | 1 | 1,277.0 | 1 | 7.5 | 5 | 233.7 | 248.6 |
| Rhineland Palatinate | 3,633.2 | 6 | 148.3 | 7 | 4.1 | 8 | 241.2 | 230.6 |
| Saarland | 1,068.6 | 10 | 40.7 | 11 | 3.8 | 9 | 148.3 | 138.4 |
| Schleswig-Holstein | 2,599.0 | 7 | 78.3 | 9 | 3.0 | 11 | 261.2 | 269.1 |
| National totals/averages | 61,439.3 | - | 4,143.8 | - | 6.8 | - | 228.4 | 229.4 |

Source: (based on) *Statisches Jahrbuch für die BRD*, 1980, Table 3.18, and 1981,
Table 3.9; *Wirtschaft und Statistik*, 11/74, p.767.

Figure 6.2:   The Federal Republic of Germany

Länder as at 1.1.1980

Table 6.2:   Areas of Länder (in rank order - 1,000 km²)

| | | | |
|---|---|---|---|
| Bavaria | 70.5 | Schleswig-Holstein | 15.7 |
| Lower Saxony | 47.4 | Saarland | 2.6 |
| Baden-Württemberg | 35.8 | Hamburg | 0.8 |
| North Rhine-Westphalia | 34.0 | Berlin | 0.5 |
| Hesse | 21.1 | Bremen | 0.4 |
| Rhineland Palatinate | 19.8 | Total | 248.6 |

Sources: *Statisches Jahrbuch für die BRD*, 1980, p.19
and Table 2.2.

return they receive the same benefits as their German
analogues. During the 1960s their contributions exceeded the benefits received (Martin, p.37). However,
child allowances are in most cases payable whether or
not the subscriber is accompanied by his children.
(Schooling is compulsory in a case where his eligible
children are living with him in Germany, although
those born in Germany do not automatically become
citizens - Martin and Miller, p.321.) Altogether,
the number of foreign workers entitled to child allowances was 420,290 in 1973 - 71,926 accompanied,
348,364 unaccompanied (Federal Labour Office, p.35ff).
Of the 5.4 million children who were beneficiaries,
868,000 (16 per cent) lived overseas. The total expenditure on child allowances was DM 3.2 million
(BMA, Table 8.16). After the 1975 reform of child
allowances, together with subsequent increases
(Table 5.8), total expenditure had climbed to DM 13.5
million by 1980. When compared to 1973, the proportion of beneficiaries living overseas (14.7 per
cent) had not fallen as much as the proportion of unaccompanied parents (from 14 to 11 per cent - BMA,
Table 8.16).

The argument thus far is summarised in Figure
6.1. The first thing to note is the relative size
of the shaded areas in parts (a) and (b). This illustrates the low participation rate of German nationals
compared to foreigners, although a qualification
appears at the foot of the figure. Secondly, the
cohort of young German nationals who will be entering
the labour market during the early 1980s is readily
apparent from the upper portion of the diagram.
Thirdly, the marked contrast in the birth rates of
Germans and foreigners is shown by the lower portions
of each population tree. Finally, the considerably
larger proportion of persons over retirement age
among German nationals is clearly indicated by the
plain area at the top of the German's population
tree.

EMPLOYMENT TRENDS

## The Structure of the Labour Force

Because of the first post-war wave of migration, together with mobility out of agriculture and into industry, the employed labour force increased during
the 1950s by 43 per cent or from 14 million to 20 million. In the 1960s, only a further 2.3 million employees were added. Thus by 1970 the figure reached
22.3 million. This number remained unchanged in 1980,

although the absolute size of the labour force actually fell in the mid-1970s (BMA, Table 2.6). Various factors played a role in slowing down the labour supply in the 1960s and 1970s: the building of the Berlin wall; the slow build-up of the birth rate during the 1950s; a rise in retirements and increased higher education opportunities.

Whereas unemployment is partly responsible for the variation in employment levels during the 1970s - as will shortly be shown - there are other implications of the above employment trends. Activity rates - i.e. that proportion of the total population (self-employed + employed + unemployed) available for work - fell from 47.8 per cent in 1960 to 44.2 per cent in 1970 and to 43.4 per cent in 1980, having reached 42.5 per cent in 1976 (*ibid.*, Table 2.3). Also between 1960 and 1980, the activity rates of males decreased from 64 to 56 per cent, whereas female rates remained at about one-third.

There were also a number of other structural changes in the labour force. The number of employees increased as a proportion of the economically active population (employees + self-employed - unemployed). In 1950 this proportion was 69 per cent; in 1960, 77 per cent; in 1970 82 per cent and by 1980 86 per cent (*ibid.*, Table 2.5). The number of white-collar workers (public servants and staff employees) over the total number of employees increased from 29 per cent in 1950 to 51 per cent in 1980 (*ibid.*, Table 2.6). There was also a significant change in the sectoral location of the labour force: the number of employees in mining, energy supply, manufacturing industry and construction rose from 8.7 million in 1950 to 12.5 million in 1960. By 1970 the number was 13.0 million, but it decreased to 11.6 million in 1980 (*ibid.*, Table 2.4). In percentage terms, industrial employment (as defined) decreased from 48.8 per cent of the employed labour force in 1970, to 44.8 per cent in 1980 (BMWi, Table 1.25). The service sector of the economy, on the other hand, accounted for 42.7 per cent of the employed labour force in 1970, but 49.3 per cent in 1980. But the dramatic fall in agricultural employment (from 25 per cent of the employed force in 1950 to 13.7 per cent in 1960 and 8.5 per cent in 1970) slowed down during the 1970s. By 1980, 5.9 per cent of the labour force were in agriculture.

The proportions of employees in the various sectors of the economy in 1980 are summarised in Table 6.3, as are the proportions by Länder.

Table 6.3: Employment Indicators by Länder, 1980

| | Total employment[a] (millions) | Percentages in | | | |
|---|---|---|---|---|---|
| | | Industry | Agriculture | Commerce and Transport | Other Services |
| Baden-Württemberg | 4.3 | 52 | 5 | 14 | 29 |
| Bavaria | 5.2 | 45 | 10 | 17 | 28 |
| Berlin (West) | 0.8 | 35 | 1 | 17 | 47 |
| Bremen | 0.3 | 34 | 1 | 29 | 36 |
| Hamburg | 0.7 | 32 | 1 | 28 | 39 |
| Hesse | 2.4 | 46 | 4 | 17 | 33 |
| Lower Saxony | 3.1 | 41 | 8 | 19 | 32 |
| North Rhine-Westphalia | 6.9 | 49 | 2 | 18 | 31 |
| Rhineland Palatinate | 1.6 | 44 | 6 | 17 | 33 |
| Saarland | 0.4 | 51 | 2 | 16 | 31 |
| Schleswig-Holstein | 1.1 | 34 | 6 | 20 | 40 |
| Federal level | 26.9 | 45 | 5 | 18 | 32 |

Note: (a) Not directly comparable with Table 6.6 – agriculture and other services include some unpaid family helpers.

Source: Dresdner Bank, *Wirtschaftsberichte, 33*(2), p.11.

Regional Variations
It will also be seen from Table 6.3 that there are a
number of regional factors which impinge upon employment trends.   In the case of West Germany the significance of these factors could easily be underestimated because her overall prosperity has tended
to conceal her regional problems (Donovan, p.1).  But
merely a perfunctory glance at Tables 6.1, 6.3 and
6.4 illustrates the wide diversity of the eleven
Länder in terms of population, employment and economic
prosperity.  (Figure 6.2 and Table 6.2 will also be
helpful for readers not familiar with the geography
of the Federal Republic.)  Financially weaker Länder
(especially Schleswig-Holstein, Lower Saxony, Saarland and Rhineland-Palatinate, where large, negative
deviations from the Federal average GDP per head are
recorded in Table 6.4) found from the beginning that
the Federal system of fiscal equalisation did not
resolve their specific economic problems (Spahn,
p.26).  In addition to this revenue sharing system,
therefore, federal grants-in-aid were directed towards such policy areas as housing, regional and agricultural development.  As seen in Chapter 5, joint
planning responsibilities were, from 1969, undertaken
by the Federal and Länder governments in the fields
of university construction and extensions, research
and education, regional policy, agricultural structure
and coastal preservation.  Federal grants-in-aid were
also extended.  In short, 'a market mechanism to
correct regional disparities may exist in theory but
not in practice'; hence the introduction of a wide-
ranging regional planning scheme known as *Raumordnung*
(Kluczka in Schöller, p.11).
    Twenty-one development areas have been pinpointed.
They cover 60 per cent of the land area of the FRG and
37 per cent of her population (Donovan, pp.1 and 4;
Owen Smith, 1979, pp.168-169).  The 40 per cent of
land area relatively free from employment and infra-
structure problems stretches roughly down the centre
of the country - from Hamburg in the north to most of
Baden-Württemberg in the south.  There is a similar,
but smaller, belt north of Munich (the capital city
of Bavaria).  It was these relatively prosperous
regions which attracted the second wave of migrants -
see Table 6.1.
    There are five areas where employment problems
are particuarly pronounced.  The first two are the
traditional coal, iron and steel areas around the Ruhr
and Saar rivers.  The second two are the parts of
Lower Saxony and Eastern Bavaria which lie adjacent
to the border with East Germany and Czechoslovakia -

Table 6.4: Various Measures of Gross Domestic Product by Länder

| | GDP[a] 1979 | | GDP[a] per head | | | | | GDRP[a] average increase (per cent) |
| | Absolute (DM million) | Percent of total | Deviations from Federal average (in percentages) | | | | 1979:DM | |
| | | | 1950 | 1960 | 1972 | 1979 | | |
|---|---|---|---|---|---|---|---|---|
| Baden-Württemberg | 220,143 | 15.8 | +1.5 | +2.5 | +2.7 | +6.0 | 24,038 | 36.7 |
| Bavaria | 236,710 | 17.0 | −14.8 | −12.1 | −4.6 | −3.8 | 21,826 | 37.5 |
| Berlin (West) | 49,548 | 3.6 | − | +2.9 | +7.0 | +14.7 | 26,019 | 22.7 |
| Bremen | 21,419 | 1.5 | +55.6 | +36.3 | +31.4 | +35.6 | 30,743 | 22.4 |
| Hamburg | 66,114 | 4.8 | +81.9 | +74.0 | +67.6 | +75.8 | 39,874 | 25.2 |
| Hesse | 130,750 | 9.4 | −2.4 | +0.1 | +5.7 | +3.7 | 23,514 | 33.8 |
| Lower Saxony | 140,671 | 10.1 | −19.8 | −13.5 | −15.9 | −14.1 | 19,469 | 35.1 |
| North Rhine-Westphalia | 382,859 | 27.5 | +17.9 | +9.4 | +1.4 | −0.7 | 22,530 | 25.8 |
| Rhineland Palatinate | 73,825 | 5.3 | −16.5 | −23.2 | −5.7 | −10.3 | 20,332 | 37.9 |
| Saarland | 21,354 | 1.5 | −14.8 | −7.2 | −12.1 | −12.0 | 19,959 | 36.5 |
| Schleswig-Holstein | 47,677 | 3.4 | −28.4 | −19.3 | −15.8 | −19.0 | 18,379 | 36.6 |
| Federal level | 1,391,070 | 100.0 | 0.0 | 0.0 | 0.0 | 0.0 | 22,679 | 32.0 |

Note: (a) National income concepts are clarified in the footnote to Table 4.5.

Sources: *Statisches Jahrbuch für die BRD*, 1980, p.513, and Dresdner Bank, *Wirtschaftsberichte*, 25(2), p.7, and 33(2), p.11 (writer's translation).

the so-called 'frontier corridor'. The fifth area
is East Friesland. When employment levels in these
regions, particularly the coal and steel areas, did
not participate in the slight economic recovery of
1978, the Federal Government launched a DM 500 million employment programme (Schmid and Peters, pp.99
and 106). Through a budgetary technicality the final
sum allocated in early 1981 was increased to DM 860
million.
    Firms investing in development areas receive
government subsidies. They also receive accelerated
depreciation allowances and tax concessions. Between
1975 and 1980 the regional development plan cost the
Federal Government DM 294 million annually. Investment grants cost an additional DM 325 million annually - shared on a ratio of 4.7:4.7:0.6 by the Federal, Länder and local authorities (BMWi, Table
10.3.1). In other words, the authorities in development regions have attempted to attract industry or
diversify the industrial base. As early as 1962,
Opel took advantage of the redundancies in the Ruhr
coal mining industry by establishing a large assembly
plant at Bochum (Mellor, p.252). Financial inducements from the Land and Federal governments, along
with the extreme labour shortage and high wage rates
around its plant in the Rhine/Main area, were responsible for this decision (Burtenshaw, p.112). Similarly, manpower was readily available to Ford when
it decided in 1966 to build an assembly plant in
Saarlouis. Moreover, subsidies and redundancies in
shipbuilding attracted Mercedes Benz in the 1970s to
Bremen - away from its Baden-Württemberg base, where
serious labour shortages still existed in 1981. In
addition, official promotional bodies in all the
development areas attempt to attract investment from
overseas. Publicity is given to the various
financial and other inducements.
    West Berlin, by virtue of its geographical lo-
cation, is a special case. Towards the end of the
1970s, Ford joined the fairly large number of manufacturing companies (including Siemens and AEG) with
significant operations there, although 200,000 jobs
in manufacturing industry had disappeared since 1960.
Cash subsidies, European Recovery Programme loans at
low rates of interest, several tax concessions and
accelerated depreciation allowances, are all used to
attract new industrial investment. In order to encourage inward labour migration, income tax concessions, bonuses and increased family allowances
have been introduced. Yet the total population continues to fall and skilled workers are among those

who leave the city. Foreign workers account for an
increasing proportion of the labour force. Indeed,
a problem was caused by alien immigrants arriving
without work permits and then taking up employment
illegally. Most of the illegal immigration of foreign
workers into the FRG consists of clandestine flows into West Berlin by way of the eastern sector of the
city (cf. *Sozialbericht 1973*, p.21).
    Table 6.5 indicates unemployment levels in the
various Länder during the 1970s. For comparison, the
Federal average is also included. The differing levels
of unemployment derive from the regional diversity of
the industrial structure. This is particularly true
of Baden-Württemberg, the northern part of which has a
strong manufacturing industry base. There is no primary industry and agriculture tends to be concentrated
in the southern part of this region. In Bavaria, on
the other hand, unemployment tends to be lower than
the national average in the industrial south, whereas
the large tracts of agricultural land in the north
would tend to pull the overall Land level above the
national average. Berlin, as might be expected from
what has been already said about its severe locational
problems, had a higher than average unemployment level
in the late 1970s. Bremen's shipbuilding and steel
base also result in high unemployment levels, while
nearby Hamburg has a relatively prosperous industrial
and commercial base - hence its relatively low unemployment level.
    Hesse, with its below average figure, contains
the highly industrialised Rhine/Main region. But
Lower Saxony, in spite of being the location of most
of the Volkswagen plants and domestically-produced
hydrocarbons, has a large agricultural area. This
latter factor, together with the land-locked Saltz-
gitter steel plant and a portion of the 'frontier
corridor', make Lower Saxony a relatively high unemployment area. North Rhine-Westphalia was once the
powerhouse of Germany, since it contains the Ruhr coal,
iron and steel industries. These are now in decline.
Although the Rhineland-Palatinate is largely agricultural, the presence of, for example, one of the FRG's
three large chemical combines tends to keep its unemployment level around the national average. Saarland,
like North Rhine-Westphalia, has an over-representation
of coal, iron and steel - hence its relatively high
unemployment levels. Finally, Schleswig-Holstein has
to depend on agriculture and shipbuilding which has
tended to pull its unemployment to above-average levels.

Table 6.5: Yearly Averages of Unemployment by Länder, 1970-1980

| Year | Federal level | Baden-Württemberg | Bavaria | Berlin (West) | Bremen | Hamburg | Hesse | Lower Saxony | North Rhine-Westphalia | Rhineland-Palatinate | Saarland | Schleswig-Holstein |
|------|------|------|------|------|------|------|------|------|------|------|------|------|
| 1971 | 0.8 | 0.4 | 1.2 | 0.8 | 1.1 | 0.5 | 0.7 | 1.2 | 0.8 | 0.9 | 1.2 | 1.1 |
| 1972 | 1.1 | 0.5 | 1.2 | 1.2 | 1.7 | 0.6 | 1.0 | 1.7 | 1.2 | 1.1 | 1.5 | 1.5 |
| 1973 | 1.2 | 0.5 | 1.3 | 1.1 | 1.6 | 0.8 | 1.0 | 1.8 | 1.3 | 1.1 | 2.0 | 1.6 |
| 1974 | 2.6 | 1.4 | 2.7 | 2.0 | 2.6 | 1.7 | 2.4 | 3.2 | 2.9 | 2.8 | 3.9 | 3.2 |
| 1975 | 4.7 | 3.5 | 5.2 | 3.7 | 5.4 | 3.7 | 4.5 | 5.4 | 4.8 | 5.1 | 6.1 | 6.2 |
| 1976 | 4.6 | 3.4 | 4.9 | 3.9 | 5.6 | 4.0 | 4.4 | 5.4 | 4.9 | 4.8 | 6.7 | 6.2 |
| 1977 | 4.5 | 2.9 | 4.6 | 4.5 | 5.4 | 4.2 | 4.0 | 5.5 | 5.0 | 4.6 | 7.2 | 5.2 |
| 1978 | 4.3 | 2.6 | 4.2 | 4.6 | 5.4 | 4.3 | 3.6 | 5.2 | 5.0 | 4.3 | 7.6 | 4.8 |
| 1979 | 3.8 | 2.1 | 3.6 | 4.0 | 4.9 | 3.6 | 2.9 | 4.6 | 4.6 | 3.7 | 6.5 | 4.2 |
| 1980 | 3.8 | 2.3 | 3.5 | 4.3 | 5.3 | 3.4 | 2.8 | 4.7 | 4.6 | 3.8 | 6.5 | 4.2 |

Source: *Statisches Jahrbuch für die BRD, 1981*, Table 6.11.

Other Characteristics of Unemployment
        During the 1950s - when the first inflow of mi-
grants was being absorbed into the labour force and
labour-using industrial capacity was being rapidly
expanded - the level of unemployment was higher than
the number of unfilled vacancies (Table 4.8). There
was an excess supply of labour in this sense. For
the period 1960-1973, with the exception of the recessionary year of 1967, unemployment in West Germany
was extremely low - both relative to other industrialised market economies and to the national levels of
unfilled vacancies (Hanby and Jackson, pp.84-85).
In contrast to the 1950s, therefore, this was a
period of excess demand for labour. There were many
reasons why Germany was able to retain such a favourable position. These included the advantageous economic climate, the numerical decline in the domestic
labour force and the highly developed employment services (Stingl, pp.200-201).
        However, during the 1967 recession activity was
decreased, not least because the proportion of
foreigners in the labour force fell. Short-time
working also increased. Further, recessionary trends
after 1973 contributed to a comparative and absolute
deterioration in West German unemployment levels.
During the period since 1973, short-time working remained relatively high and activity rates decreased.
Predictions for the 1980s can only be pessimistic.
As mentioned above, flows into the labour market, not
least on the part of those entering higher education
in the late 1970s and early 1980s, would necessitate
an annual growth rate of 4.5 per cent if the average
unemployment levels of over 4.0 per cent in the late
1970s are not to be exceeded. Since the annual average growth rate of the 1970s was 2.9 per cent, the
required expansion in job opportunities (2 million
between 1985 and 1990) is unlikely to be achieved.
Hence, the 1.3 million unemployment figure for January 1981 was almost certain to increase. Strictly
speaking, such a prediction assumes that there will
be no changes in retirement and school-leaving ages,
as well as the length of the working week and annual
holiday entitlements. For example, at the supply of
hours level Gennard (p.77) estimated that unemployment in Germany would have been 280,000 higher in
1975 had short-time working not been substituted for
normal working time. Diagram 6.1 shows how unemployment, unfilled vacancies and short-time working have
interacted during the period 1950-1980.
        This supply-side problem in the West German
labour market is poignantly illustrated by the fact

Diagram 6.1: The Interaction of Unemployment, Short-time Working and Unfilled Vacancies, 1950–1980

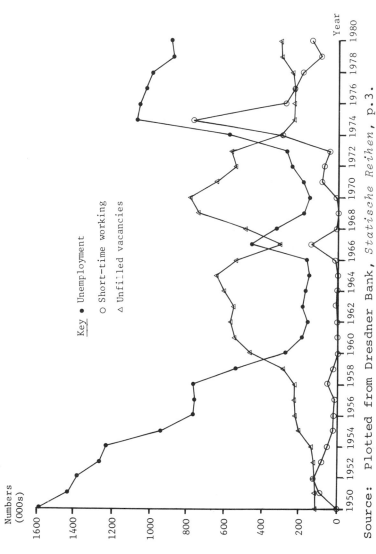

Key  •  Unemployment

      o   Short-time working

      △   Unfilled vacancies

Source: Plotted from Dresdner Bank, *Statische Reihen*, p.3.

that the baby-boom of the 1960s had by the later
1970s reversed the numerical decline in the domestic
labour force. Whereas in the early 1970s about
700,000 young people entered the labour market, the
subsequent increase was expected to peak in 1982 -
when the annual flow was expected to be in the region
of 950,000. Moreover, the published data do not reveal the full extent of the problem. Some young
people have failed to register as unemployed. Emergency training programmes and uncounted young
foreigners have also concealed the significance of
the problem (Pettman and Fyfe, pp.11-12). But the
young job seeker has not just been badly hit by
supply side factors. There have been some extremely
important demand-side changes.

The reasons for the demand for young workers
changing so dramatically have important policy implications. New vocational training laws have increased
costs. At the same time rationalisation has lowered
skill requirements in the large industrial companies.
In the more traditional handicraft sectors, where
special training facilities do not exist, apprentices
tended to be a source of cheap labour and many of
them are dismissed when their apprenticeships are
completed (*ibid.*, p.15). Yet for many years a stable
demand function for apprentices existed in the economy as a whole: as demand in the industrial sector
fluctuated with the business cycle, the handicraft
sector compensated during down-swings by employing
more apprentices.

But in the 1970s the absolute number of apprenticeships decreased. Moreover, the cost factors
responsible are also reflected in the decreased demand for young semi-skilled and unskilled labour:
employers are legally constrained from allowing juv-
enile workers on assembly lines and shiftwork. In
addition, young workers under 18 years of age are
obliged to spend one remunerated day per week at a
vocational school. Finally, far fewer young aliens
are trained than their native counterparts (Gaugler,
1978, p.200). In any case, legal restrictions were
initially placed on the employment of foreign young
persons joining their parents. These restrictions
were modified during the second half of the 1970s.
First, the latest date of arrival for work-permit
eligibility was extended to the end of 1976 (*Sozialbericht 1978*, p.18). Secondly, the work-permit restrictions were reduced in 1979, while in 1980 the
efforts to integrate young foreigners were increased.
However, further restrictions on their entry were
imposed in 1981, at least partly because unemployment

among foreign workers was above the national average,
even though they are generally concentrated in areas
of relatively high labour demand.

Hence, comparatively more young people seeking
apprenticeships, more of those who have completed
their apprenticeships, a higher proportion of those
looking for unskilled and semi-skilled work, and
young foreigners, are all faced with the spectre of
unemployment. The trade unions hold the employers
responsible for the shortage of apprenticeships.
They have also condemned the general rise in youth
unemployment. They have advocated special policy
measures to combat this increase, particularly among
females, the handicapped and foreign youth. However,
it may be these groups who, in turn, form part of
those marginal groups of any labour force who seem to
face increasing difficulties in obtaining stable jobs.
Foreign workers as a whole, as well as part-time
workers, are other such groups. In West Germany, the
substantial improvements in job security achieved by
means of collective bargaining and legislation have
benefited only core workers (Hanby and Jackson, p.88;
Pettman and Fyfe, p.114). While aggregate demand was
usually high, and recessions therefore short-lived,
unemployment among these disadvantaged groups fluctuated with the trade cycle. 'Temporary workers' in
Japan have also provided such a buffer (Allen in Owen
Smith, 1981). But the increasing proportion of disadvantaged, hard-to-employ workers in the labour
force make it difficult, if not impossible, to reach
full employment. Resorting to aggregate demand expansion would further increase the rate of inflation
(Pettman and Fyfe, p.114). This element of dualism
in the labour market has become more intractable as
employment opportunities have fallen, but the proportion of the labour force willing and able to effectively withdraw from the market has also fallen.

Summarising, then, it is possible to say that
the proportion of the total population in the labour
force fell gradually during the 1960s and 1970s.
Within the labour force itself there were a number of
changes. These changes, when related to the total
population, can be classified as proportionate increases on the part of employees generally, and on
the part of white-collar workers, immigrants and females in particular. Conversely, the percentage of
self-employed, males and industrial employment registered decreases. These changes are represented
graphically in Diagram 6.2 and summarised in Table
6.6. Finally, there were equally significant changes
in the location and structure of unemployment. In a

Diagram 6.2: Various Participation Rates in the Labour Force, 1950-1980

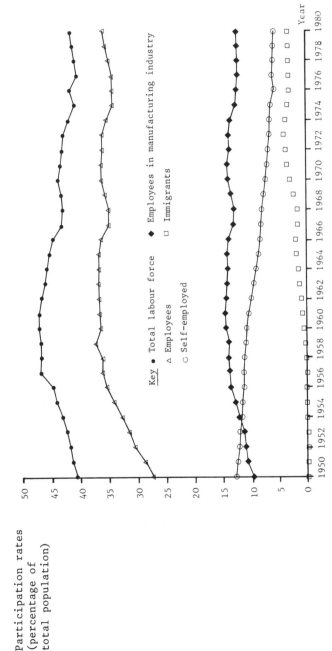

Participation rates
(percentage of
total population)

Source: Plotted from Dresdner Bank, *Statische Reihen*, p.3.

Table 6.6: Various Participation Rates, 1950-1980 ((i) millions, (ii) percentage of the total population)

| (Total Population) | Total labour force (i) | (ii) | Self-employed (i) | (ii) | Employees Total (i) | (ii) | Manufacturing industry[a] (i) | (ii) | Immigrants (i) | (ii) | Activity Rates[b] Male (i) | (ii) | Female (i) | (ii) |
|---|---|---|---|---|---|---|---|---|---|---|---|---|---|---|
| 1950 (50.2) | 20.4 | 40.6 | 6.4 | 12.8 | 13.8 | 27.5 | 4.9 | 9.8 | – | – | 14.2 | 63.8 | 7.7 | 30.2 |
| 1955 (52.4) | 23.2 | 44.3 | 6.1 | 11.6 | 17.1 | 32.6 | 6.8 | 13.0 | 0.1 | 0.2 | 15.4 | 65.7 | 8.7 | 32.7 |
| 1960 (55.4) | 26.2 | 47.3 | 6.0 | 10.8 | 20.3 | 36.6 | 8.1 | 14.6 | 0.3 | 0.5 | 16.7 | 64.2 | 9.8 | 33.4 |
| 1965 (59.0) | 26.9 | 45.6 | 5.1 | 8.6 | 21.8 | 36.9 | 8.5 | 14.4 | 1.1 | 1.9 | 17.2 | 61.9 | 9.8 | 31.9 |
| 1970 (60.7) | 26.7 | 44.1 | 4.4 | 7.2 | 22.2 | 36.6 | 8.6 | 14.2 | 1.8 | 3.0 | 17.2 | 59.5 | 9.6 | 30.3 |
| 1975 (61.8) | 25.4 | 41.1 | 3.9 | 6.3 | 21.4 | 34.6 | 7.9 | 12.8 | 2.1 | 3.4 | 16.6 | 56.2 | 9.8 | 30.4 |
| 1980 (61.6) | 25.8 | 41.9 | 3.5 | 5.7 | 22.3 | 36.2 | 7.7 | 12.5 | 2.0 | 3.2 | 16.5 | 56.3 | 10.2 | 11.6 |

Notes: All data for 1950 and 1955 excl. Berlin and Saarland, except total population for these years which includes Berlin. For an analysis of white-collar activity rates, and trade union density for all groups, see Owen Smith, 1981, pp.190-193.
(a) incl. mining – approx. 230,000 in 1979 and 1980 – *Statisches Jahrbuch*, 1981, Table 9.3.
(b) absolute numbers include unemployed; percentages of total male and female populations respectively.

Sources: Calculated from Dresdner Bank, *Statische Reihen*, p.3; BMA, Table 2.3.

sense it is to these latter problems that most of the
remaining parts of this chapter are devoted.


SOME ASPECTS OF MIGRATION

The First Wave of Migrants
At the end of the Second World War there were large-
scale population movements. While the collapse of
the Third Reich released for resettlement in their
own countries the 8 million forced labourers brought
to Germany by 1945, an almost identical number of
German nationals expelled from former eastern territories of the Third Reich flooded into western Germany. A further 4 million expellees fled to the
Russian zone of Germany, although about 3.5 million
inhabitants of the Russian zone later migrated to
Western Germany as political refugees. The inflow of
expellees into the western areas of Germany came
to an end by the late 1940s. (Their arrival coincided
with the return of 4 million German ex-POWs - Henning,
p.196). The political refugees from East Germany continued to flow into West Germany between 1950 and the
building of the Berlin wall in 1961, with a peak occur-
ring in the mid-1950s but the annual number falling
below 200,000 in only 1959 (Stolper, p.337). After
1961 the flow fell to a little over 20,000 per year,
before dwindling to a complete halt. By 1965 there
were almost certainly 14 million expellees and refugees in the Federal Republic (over 22 per cent of the
total population), although the real figure was probably 10-12 per cent higher because of non-registration
(Mellor, p.189). Approximately 6.5 million (4.7 million expellees and 1.8 million refugees) were of working age on arrival (Henning, p.196).
    Well over 50 per cent of the expellees arriving
in the western sectors settled in the three rural
states closest to their points of origin: Schleswig-
Holstein, Lower Saxony and Bavaria. Gravitation to
the rural areas was prompted by the housing and food
shortages in the cities - shortages which had also
caused the former populations of those cities to drift
to the countryside (Stolper, p.233). In 1951 35.8 per
cent of the total population in Schleswig-Holstein
were expellees (742,000) and refugees (131,500).
Equivalent percentages for Lower Saxony and Bavaria
were 32.0 per cent and 23.3 per cent respectively
(Wallich, Table 34, p.273).
    By 1950, with the re-building of the bombed towns
and industry reviving under the stimulus of the Korean
crisis, there was a strong current back to the urban

areas as accommodation gradually became available.
Many of the newcomers in the over-crowded northern
rural areas sought employment in the Rhine and Ruhr
industrial districts, which also became a focus for
the refugees arriving from East Germany (Mellor,
p.193). In 1954 it was estimated privately that some
4 million expellees had moved to the industrial areas,
but as a result of re-settlement programmes and of
private migrations an equal number remained in less
than optimal areas (Wallich, pp.275-276).
   Hence, there were two longer-term advantages of
this first post-war wave of migrations. The first
advantage was the elastic labour supply with respect
to the growth in aggregate demand. In his now classic
study, Kindleberger (pp.27-37) sees this as being the
single most important factor in Germany's post-war
recovery. Without this substantial flow of population,
then, the rapid rate of expansion in output achieved
in the Ruhr and other industrial areas would not have
been possible. This leads to the second point, which
applies to the migrants in both post-war waves: there
was an exceptionally high degree of labour mobility,
as the immigrants were under great pressure to suc-
ceed (Mann, p.860). In the case of the first wave,
the expellees intensified competition wherever they
went and local firms found themselves faced with
immigrants who brought new techniques and new ideas
(Wallich, p.283). Competition for jobs in the industrial centres tended to depress wage levels somewhat,
especially since the uprooted natives of western Germany were also seeking work. Nevertheless, the de-
pressant effect on wages was not all that strong.
This was because of the maldistribution of manpower
due to the housing-shortage, which meant that the
demand for labour was high in the industrial conurbations and unemployment was at its worst in the rural
areas (*ibid.*, p.284).
   Bitter rivalry for housing sometimes developed
between the newcomers and the bombed-out members of
the local population, although the newcomers generally
tended to be more badly housed than the local population at large. This rivalry, and the bitterness
felt by the immigrants, only gradually subsided during
the 1950s - a trend partially due to the integration
of second-generation immigrants and the enormous output of housing (Stolper, p.311). In any case income
per head was rising rapidly during the 1950s and the
excess supply of labour fell quite rapidly. Hence,
there is another important inference to be drawn at
this point, namely that the smooth integration of a
sizeable inflow of migrants, albeit that in this case

they were of the same nationality, is more likely to occur during periods of economic expansion.
    There was a further important characteristic of the refugees from East Germany who flowed into West Germany during the 1950s. Qualitatively the migrants of working age either tended to possess above average skill levels, or they had at least completed their schooling. For that matter, the expellees were also a highly select group (Mellor, p.149). Among them were nearly 2 million Sudeten Germans, an alert people with an excellent educational background. Other groups, too, were especially well qualified in various respects. They had all been through a brief but ruthless process of natural selection: many of their weaker bretheren had not survived the rigors of expulsion and the long trek to safety (Wallich, pp.282-283).
    Any country of immigration greatly benefits from the fact that the expenses of child rearing and education embodied in the immigrants has been borne in the country of origin (Blitz, p.479). Furthermore, the typical age and sex composition of immigrants is such that they will seek employment to a greater extent than the native population. Although this latter view has to be qualified somewhat in respect of the expellees, it has been seen that their mobility and educational backgrounds were a positive asset during the 1950s. Moreover, they were German speaking nationals. In other words, as a country of immigration, the FRG derived an added value from this inflow (Ergun, p.187). For example, among the refugees from the GDR there were skilled workers, doctors, technicians and scientists (Stolper, p.338). After the building of the Berlin wall, the first secretary of the GDR (Walter Ulbricht) claimed in 1962 that the loss sustained by his country because of migration to the FRG amounted to DM 30 billion or approximately DM 10,000 per person - presumably at 1962 prices (Blitz, p.481; Stolper, p.310). Blitz also reports that of the 2.5 million refugees who reached the FRG by 1957, 1.5 million (60 per cent) were of working age. This represented an outlay on education and bringing-up in the GDR of DM 15,000 per head to the state and family - a total of DM 22.5 billion. Extended to 1961 this figure increases to DM 28.5 billion. Output added in the FRG - a measure of income or human capital as opposed to cost - has been estimated at DM 36 billion.
    Immigration, however, also imposes costs on the receiving country. A fuller cost-benefit analysis of immigration will appear below when the details of

the second wave of immigrants have been reported. The four types of costs imposed by the first wave are nevertheless quite similar to those imposed by the second wave. First, additional capital equipment had to be supplied, although the high and expanding level of aggregate demand - to which the migrants contributed - was in itself an investment incentive. The growing share of profits in the national income, along with various other investment incentives introduced by government, were also conducive to a high level of capital accumulation. Moreover, without migration there may well have been a serious labour-shortage constraint due to the numbers killed and badly wounded in the Second World War. (About 4 million combatants and about 3 million non-combatants, including expellees, died during and immediately after the war - Henning, p.184; Mellor, p.153; Milward, p.113.) Having said all this, however, the capital absorbed by the migrants would have been quite high: when they numbered between 3.4 and 4 million, Wallich (p.285) estimated a non-agricultural per capita requirement of DM 12,000. Somewhat more controversially, in view of the contents of this paragraph, Wallich goes on to infer that productivity per man hour would have risen substantially more if there had been an intensive improvement of the capital equipment used by the 'existing' labour force.

A second cost imposed by an influx of migrants is the additional strain placed on the social infra-structure - that is on schools, roads, railways, hospitals, housing and so on. Since much of the social infra-structure lay in ruins when the bulk of the expellees arrived, they further exacerbated the shortages which already existed. Such were the degrees of devastation and recovery, however, that it would be difficult, if not impossible, to disentangle the later costs and benefits of the first migratory stream in this respect.

Thirdly, there is the increase in the tax burden attributable to the expellees. In 1950, it was estimated that they received about 40 per cent of the various social security benefits, more than twice their share of the population (Wallich, pp.285-286). But the social security system was generally extended from the second half of the 1950s onwards, while the tax burden initially fell. At the very least it can be said the degree of economic recovery and expansion therefore concealed the tax burden problem.

The fourth and final point is concerned with the costs to the balance of payments. On the one hand, further food had to be imported because of the food

shortage which already existed when the expellees began to arrive. In 1949, on the basis of a relatively
low volume of imports, the foreign exchange costs attributable to the expellees were put at US$ 450 mil-
lion annually (*ibid.*, p.286). On the other hand,
some of the expellee industries were export intensive,
while others were important in economising imports.
Moreover, in terms of the net effect on the balance
of payments, they evidently raised no serious ob-
stacles to the achievement of equilibrium and even a
large surplus (Chapter 4).

The Second Wave of Migrants
An alternative source of labour was required once the
Berlin wall effectively stemmed migration from the
east (Giersch, p.18). At that time (1961), the FRG's
economy had entered a phase of excess demand for
labour (Table 4.8). Such a situation obtained from
1960 until 1973, with the exception of 1967 when there
was an economic recession. Further, the number of
hours supplied annually by the native labour force
was falling. This reduction was due to lower birth
rates, delayed entry into the labour force because of
more extensive education, longer holidays and a
shorter working week (Blitz, p.483). The gap created
by the prolongation of compulsory military service
from 12 to 18 months in the early 1960s was another
factor to bring about a need for immigrant workers
(Völker, p.64). Foreign workers from southern Europe
were therefore recruited. Table 6.7 charts the growth
of this second post-war inflow of labour. There are
a number of similarities to the earlier flow of refugees from the GDR. First, during the 1970s the second
inflow reached on average a level equivalent to the
earlier inflow of persons of working age. Secondly,
the ban on the further recruitment of employees in
1973 came after roughly the same time period as the
earlier inflow. Thirdly, the growth in the number of
foreign workers, and later their families, was little
short of dramatic. In 1961 barely 12 inhabitants out
of 1,000 was a foreigner; by 1967 the number was 30;
by 1973 it was on average 64; and by 1980 it had
reached 72. Another similarity to the earlier inflow
from the GDR, therefore, was that by 1973 the total
inflow of immigrants reached roughly the same proportions.
    Throughout the 1960s the most important sending
country was Italy, although by the end of the decade
Yugoslavia, Turkey and Greece had also become major
sending countries. The absolute number of Italians
decreased after 1972 while the number of Turks,

Table 6.7: Migrant Employees in the FRG

| Year | Total (Annual Averages) (000s) | Of which females (per cent) | Percentage of total employed labour force |
|------|------|------|------|
| 1960 | 279 | 15.5 | 1.3 |
| 1961[a] | 507 | n.a. | 2.5 |
| 1962 | 629 | 18.1 | 3.1 |
| 1963 | 773 | 20.9 | 3.7 |
| 1964 | 902 | 22.4 | 4.3 |
| 1965 | 1,119 | 23.2 | 5.3 |
| 1966 | 1,244 | 25.5 | 5.8 |
| 1967 | 1,014 | 29.3 | 4.7 |
| 1968 | 1,019 | 29.9 | 4.9 |
| 1969 | 1,366 | 29.8 | 6.5 |
| 1970 | 1,807 | 29.3 | 8.5 |
| 1971 | 2,218 | 28.7 | 9.8 |
| 1972 | 2,285 | 29.4 | 10.5 |
| 1973 (est.) | 2,450 | n.a. | 11.0 |
| 1974[a] | 2,331 | 31.1 | 11.2 |
| 1975 | 2,061 | 31.6 | 10.2 |
| 1976 | 1,925 | 31.4 | 9.6 |
| 1977 | 1,872 | 31.2 | 9.4 |
| 1978 | 1,857 | 31.0 | 9.2 |
| 1979 | 1,924 | 30.8 | 9.3 |
| 1980 | 2,018 | 31.0 | 9.6 |

Note:
(a) End of June.

Sources: Federal Labour Office, 1974 (pp.5 and 70) and *Presse Informationen*, 14/81; BMA, Table 2.7

Yugoslavs and Greeks continued to rise. It is evident from Table 6.8 that by 1973 both Turkey and Yugoslavia had overtaken Italy, a situation which was still the case in 1980. It will also be seen from Table 6.8 that foreign workers from the Iberian peninsular constituted a fairly significant group. By 1980 West Germany's liberal political asylum laws were attracting further immigrants. In the first four months of 1980 nearly 50,000 foreigners seeking political asylum arrived - or approximately as many as the whole of 1979 (MRDB, June 1980, p.28). By October 1980, just before the regulations were tightened, the number had reached 100,000. The countries of origin were Turkey, the India sub-continent and

Table 6.8:  Migrant Employees by Nationality

| Country of Origin | End of January 1973 | | End of June 1980 | |
|---|---|---|---|---|
| | Number | Percentage | Number | Percentage |
| Turkey | 528,414 | 22.5 | 590,600 | 28.5 |
| Yugoslavia | 465,611 | 19.8 | 357,400 | 17.3 |
| Italy | 409,448 | 17.5 | 309,200 | 14.9 |
| Greece | 268,408 | 11.4 | 133,000 | 6.4 |
| Spain | 179,157 | 7.6 | 86,500 | 4.2 |
| Portugal | 68,994 | 2.9 | 58,800 | 2.8 |
| Morocco | 15,261 | 0.7 | a | a |
| Tusisia | 11,124 | 0.5 | a | a |
| (sub-total) | 1,946,417 | 82.9 | (1,535,000) | (74.1) |
| Other nationalities | 400,383 | 17.1 | (536,200) | (25.9) |
| Total | 2,346,800 | 100.0 | 2,071,000 | 100.0 |

Note:
(a) Separate statistical records of Moroccans and Tunisians are
no longer kept.  The category 'other nationalities' is therefore not strictly comparable in 1973 and 1980.  However, since
these North African states sent only 1.2 per cent of the total
in 1973, the relativities reported remain instructive.

Sources:  Federal Labour Office, 1974, p.11, and
*Presse Informationen*, 14/81.

other parts of Asia and Africa.
    A very important policy change took place be-
tween the end of the 1967 recession and the recruitment ban of 1973 (Federal Labour Office, pp.6-7).
This change consisted of a gradual move from a continuous, administratively enforced *rotation* of una-
companied foreign workers on fixed term contracts to
immigration for an indefinite period with the possi-
bility of workers being joined by their families -
the so-called *integration* principle (Feix; Schiller,
p.338).  A comparison of the two troughs in economic
activity which were reached in 1967 and 1975 brings
out the effects of the policy change.  In both recessions the index of industrial production (1970=
100) decreased: from 78.7 in 1966 to 76.5 in 1967,
and from 112.8 in 1973 to 110.5 (1974) and 103.6 in
1975.  There was a consequent rise in unemployment -

from 0.7 per cent in 1966 to 2.1 per cent in 1967,
with a similar increase between 1973 (1.3 per cent)
and 1975 (4.7 per cent). But whereas the percentage
of foreign workers in the labour force fell by 1.1
percentage points between 1966 and 1967, the fall between 1973 and 1975 was 0.8 percentage points. Translated into absolute numbers this meant a decrease from
1.313 million to 0.991 million in the period October
1966 to September 1967, and 2.6 million to 2.3 million
in an eighteen months period following the 1973 recruitment ban (Federal Labour Office, p.5; Schiller,
p.350n). Moreover, the number of foreign workers increased by 130 per cent between 1967 and 1974 (Table
6.7) and the total number of foreigners increased by
128 per cent (Table 6.1). Hence a smaller proportion
of foreigners returned home during the second recession (MRDB, December 1974, p.5). Further, there
was every indication that they were being increasingly
joined by their families and 'temporary migration' was
becoming 'permanent settlement'(Martin, p.34).

Economic activity recovered somewhat between 1976
and 1979, even though unemployment remained at relatively high levels. The total number of foreigners
in the FRG initially fell slightly but then returned
to the 1974 level by 1979 (Table 6.1). Foreign
workers were reluctant to leave - not least because
unemployment benefits had been substantially improved
since 1967. At first foreign workers were, however,
reluctant to register as unemployed during the 1974-
75 recession. Fear that unemployment might accelerate
loss of residence rights seems to have been part of
the explanation of low reported unemployment rates
for foreign workers at the beginning of the recession
(Paine, p.219). In addition, some car manufacturers
also granted fairly generous severance payments to
any workers prepared to leave and the offer was
accepted by several thousand foreign workers. Instead
of leaving the country, however, they took up employment in other sectors (Schiller, pp.343-344).

But as the recession became firmly entrenched,
and after existing savings and other assets had been
used up, economic pressure forced immigrants to register as unemployed (Paine, p.219). Hence, the number
of foreigners registered as unemployed increased from
16,000 in 1973 to 67,000 in 1974 and 133,000 in 1975
(OECD, *Economic Survey*, 1980, p.15). Between 1976
and 1979 an annual average of 81,500 foreigners were
unemployed. Expressed as a percentage of foreign
workers, registered unemployment among foreigners
rose from being marginally below total unemployment
in 1976 (3.8 per cent compared to 3.9 per cent) to

0.7 above the total rate in 1979 (3.9 per cent compared to 3.2 per cent - *ibid.*). By February 1981
these two percentages were 7.3 and 5.6 respectively.
The incidence of unemployment among foreign
workers is perhaps better demonstrated by expressing
their unemployment as a percentage of total unemployment. At the end of the 1970s this statistic stood
at over 10 per cent (77,000 out of 737,000 in 1979,
for example - Deutsche Bundesbank, *Annual Report*,
1981, p.47). By 1980 and 1981 it was 12 and 14 per
cent respectively. The basic reason for this relatively high level of unemployment among foreigners
is that they generally tend to possess a low level of
education and training. Not only does this mean that
foreigners tend to work in the more insecure, un-
pleasant and unsocial jobs, but also that some German
nationals have been able to move up the social hierarchy to the more secure and pleasant jobs. For
example, the number of German nationals employed in
mining and industry decreased by over 870,000 between
1961 and 1971, whereas the number of foreigners increased by 1.1 million. In the tertiary sector both
types of employees have increased, but the foreigners
increased their numbers by 344 per cent (90,000 to
400,000) compared with a German expansion of nearly
13 per cent (8.10 million to 9.2 million). By 1973
22 per cent of all employees in building and construction were foreigners (Federal Labour Office,
1974, pp.15-16). Similarly, between 1961 and 1973
about 3 million German workers switched to white-
collar jobs. About half the jobs set free were taken
by foreigners. Further, turnover rates among indigenous workers seem to exceed even the large turnover
rate among foreigners once the ratio of alien to
natives exceeds 50 per cent (Gaugler, 1978, p.201).
In all these senses there was an inexorable substitution of alien for indigenous workers; competition
would come later when the foreigners attempted upward
mobility or recession limited the number of jobs
available to both aliens and natives (Martin and
Miller, pp.319 and 325).

Only a minority of the migrants from southern
Europe were skilled workers. Those migrants who
arrived in possession of skills, however, were much
more likely to settle permanently in the FRG (Böhning,
p.270 and pp.272-273). The cost to Turkey and Yugoslavia of such permanent emigration has been particularly significant (*ibid.*; Ergun, pp.195-196; Martin,
p.40). Moreover, two-thirds of the migrants from
Turkey have been educated to primary school level, a
rather high percentage for a country where almost half

the population is illiterate (Ergun, p.196). The
cost of this is also enormous. For example, Blitz
demonstrates (p.501) that for the period 1957-1973
the FRG has benefited greatly from the immigration of
foreign workers because the child rearing and educational costs of this imported human capital were
borne abroad. Although it would take only a fraction
of the time and cost for the FRG, because of her superior factor and training endowments, to convert
these inexperienced workers into semi-skilled workers,
however, many of those who returned home were still
untrained (Böhning, p.272). This is because they had
been used in unskilled or non-industrial work (Berger
and Mohr, p.78).
     An alternative to the human capital theory ex-
planation of migration is the classical/neo-classical
model. In the case of the former, a cost-benefit
model is used and migration is viewed as being determined by the present value of future net earnings
which the individual can receive from migrating.
Maldonado, on the other hand, has tested a fairly
sophisticated version of the classical/neo-classical
model which predicts that labour will move from regions with surplus labour and low wages to regions
with excess demand for labour and high wages (see
particularly p.8 of her article). In addition, she
attempts (p.9) to estimate the chain effects of cumulative migration as earlier migrants provide potential
migrants with information and assitance. Non-material
aspirations such as a better education for the children of migrants also enter the equation (Feix,
pp.40-64). Although Zell criticises both Maldonado's
data and her model, her findings on the determinants
of Puerto Rican migration to the USA are similar to
those of Ergun (pp.144-149 and p.213) on migration
from Turkey to the FRG. In both cases, the presence
in the home country of higher unemployment, lower
wages and lower welfare payments are seen as an in-
ducement to migrate. Such migration was possible
because there were not enough German workers willing,
at the wages offered, to do the low-paid manual jobs
(Berger and Mohr, p.118). Franz (pp.599-601) has
modelled and tested the employment and real wage inducements described here. But the huge savings which
the foreign workers remit home are not generally
utilised to finance industrialisation in the sending
countries: those workers who return home find they
have financed, at best, a re-equipped peasant holding or small holiday hotel (Berger and Mohr, p.78;
Blitz, pp.498-499; Ergun, pp.181-186).
     Another shortcoming of the human capital

approach is that the private costs to employers of
hiring foreign workers may be lower than the social
ones (Martin, p.34). However, one cannot conclude
from the estimates made by Schiller (p.352) that it
was foreigners who caused the deficiencies in the
social infrastructure. In the larger conurbations
in the FRG, where foreign workers tend to congregate,
social demands for education, housing and child-care
are already high (*Sozialbericht 1973*, pp.19-20). In
any case, immigrant demands for these services will
initially be low since active members typically migrate alone in the early stages (Blitz, pp.500-501;
Ergun, p.66). However, the availability of additional and mobile manpower in the form of foreign
workers may be said to have accelerated regional
agglomeration and industrial concentration (Schiller,
p.337). In reality, however, immigrant workers have,
at least in the first place, been recruited to alleviate labour shortages in existing workplaces
(Ergun, p.67). Finally, the inflow of young and able
foreign workers may have reduced employment opportunities for women and older workers, as well as
obstructing technical progress (Schiller, pp.337 and
342). Evidence on the former possible effect is
mixed, whilst probably one immediate result of the
Berlin wall, however, was to induce further capital
intensity (Giersch, p.18).

The *Deutscher Gewerkschaftsbund* (DGB) has for
many years attempted to integrate foreign workers
into the German trade union movement, making it plain
that they have the same rights and obligations as a
German worker. To this end, the DGB has always opposed the use of the term *'Gastarbeiter'* (or 'guest-
worker'). The expression 'foreign worker' is preferred in order to stress that the immigrant worker
does not seek anything different from his German
analogue. Foreign workers had apparently themselves
criticised the term 'guest-worker' (DGB, *Geschäftsbericht*, 1962-65, p.79). Three years later (1968)
the DGB regretted that the term 'guest-worker' was
still in common use among trade unionists. It was
maintained that the use of this term not only dis-
criminated against members, but was also psychologi-
cally undesirable. The use of the term could only
lead to the German population imagining that the
employment of foreign workers was a transitional
phenomenon. However, the DGB continued, since a
community of European people was in the process of
being established, foreign workers would become a
permanent feature of the German economy. The term
'guest-worker' was therefore inappropriate because

these workers were the European workers of tomorrow
(DGB, *Geschäftsbericht*, 1965-68, pp.83-84). As
Martin and Miller (p.318) indicate, this was partly
a reaction to the political extremists of the right
who sought to maintain the 'temporary' nature of
immigration.

On the other hand, claims have also been made
that political extremists of the left have attempted
to organise foreign workers. For example, as early
as 1961 the DGB claimed that a group of Turkish in-
tellectuals in Cologne were attempting to usurp the
official trade union movement. This move was opposed
by both German and Turkish trade union officials
(DGB, *Geschäftsbericht*, 1959-61, p.75). In August
1973 there was a wave of unofficial strikes, including one involving Turkish workers at the Ford works
in Cologne. *The Times* (20 August 1973) referred to
the 'small groups of well organised political extremists involved in prolonging the strike at Fords
after workers at other companies had settled their
unofficial strikes' (cf. Geiselberger, p.84ff and
Jacobi, p.161ff and p.176ff).

After the recruitment ban, as unemployment
among foreign workers became an increasingly vital
question, the DGB created a special central department to deal with the problems of foreign workers
(DGB, *Geschäftsbericht*, 1972-74, pp.462-463). An
assurance that unemployment alone was not sufficient
grounds for the authorities to rescind entry visas
and work permits was also secured by the DGB. News-
letters in the various langugages of the six principal groups of foreign workers (see Table 6.8) were
also published and seminars for several thousand
workplace representatives and works council members
- including females - were organised for these six
national groupings (DGB, *Geschäftsbericht*, 1975-77,
pp.439-440).

One conclusion to this section is that the
problem of unemployment has again arisen. The next
question to ask, therefore, is whether the various
imbalances in the labour market can be corrected by
active labour market policies.


LABOUR MARKET POLICIES

Intervention in the labour market began to develop
in Germany after the First World War. On the unemployment benefit side, the first measures were of a
limited nature: they applied only where unemployment
resulted from the war or indigence (Stingl, p.198).

165

On the labour exchange side, the first offices were
established - with equal representation of both employers' associations and trade unions.  The various
developments during the 1920s culminated in the Placement and Unemployment Insurance Act of 1927.  The
National Placement and Insurance Office was established as an independent, self-governing body responsible for the administration of both the placement
service and the new compulsory, contributory unemployment insurance system (Braun, p.214; Henning, p.130).
This Office also assumed responsibilities for vocational guidance and the placement of apprentices.
The Nazis placed the Office under direct control, but
in 1952 a Federal office with the same title was
placed under the tripartite control of employers,
trade unions and government (at local, Land and Federal levels).  On 1 July 1969, the 1927 Act was replaced by the Employment Promotion Act.  Labour market policy remained a Federal matter and the relevant
central co-ordinating institution now became known as
the Federal Labour Office.  Just as the Placement and
Insurance Act was put to test during the world economic crisis of the 1930s, the Employment Promotion
Act has been confronted since 1974 with the longest
and deepest recession of the post-war years.

Policy-makers in the FRG are required by statute
to maintain high employment levels.  In confirming
this in 1980, the Federal Minister of Labour rejected
any idea that the government should allow the level
of employment to be determined by the free play of
market forces.  Further, the re-creation of full employment was a principal policy goal in the late
1970s (*Sozialbericht 1980*, p.11).  The trade unions
have also consistently advocated the need for such
intervention.  However, when the OECD came out in
favour of 'active manpower policies' in 1964, unemployment was relatively low and there was a relatively small core of structural unemployment.  As
these problems grew, policies designed to increase
mobility have been supplemented in most member
countries by job creation measures.

In the case of West Germany, the 1969 Employment
Promotion Act resulted in the Federal Labour Office
assuming further responsibilities for such services
as placement, vocational training and counselling,
job creation, mobility incentives and wage subsidies.
Both the number and expertise of its staff were increased.  The Office is emphatic about its responsibility for placing an unemployed person in a suitable
job (Mukherjee, p.27).  This view arises not merely
from its legal obligation but from a full commitment

to the notion that an effective placement system is
an indispensable pre-condition for a properly functioning labour market.  In theory, the provision of
reliable and sophisticated information to decision-
takers in the labour market is regarded as imperative
(Stingl, p.202).  In practice, the system inevitably
runs into difficulties when it comes to placing the
unqualified, older workers and females.  Moreover,
the system has been criticised for its bureaucracy
and the short period of time allocated to interview-
ing job-seekers, although officials became hard-
pressed.  Since competition for jobs increased in the
mid-1970s, only one-quarter of appointments are secured through employment exchanges.  Hence the
vacancies notified to the exchanges clearly do not
accurately reflect the actual demand-side situation
(Krautkrämer, p.241).  Successful placement is also
constrained by the disposition on the part of the
indigenous labour force not to move house in order to
find a new job, together with other inhibitions such
as an understandable reluctance to accept lower remuneration, demotion and longer travelling time.

The cost of the new functions assigned to the
Federal Labour Office by the 1969 Employment Promotion Act and various amendments made in the 1970s,
along with the steep rise in unemployment benefits
from 1975, pulled the previously healthy balances of
the Office into a precarious financial state (*Employment Gazette*, June 1976, p.586; Stingl, p.205).  From
1970 to 1973 the increase in both unemployment and
benefits was only moderate, whereas they became extremely pronounced thereafter.  Total benefits rose
faster than total unemployment over the whole period.
Thus, average benefits per head increased continu-
ously.  A number of factors accounted for this dyna-
mism of unemployment benefits, among which the fol-
owing were considered of major importance:

(i)    the total amount of unemployment;
(ii)   the proportion of unemployment insured;
(iii)  the structure of unemployment (age,
       professional level, duration, etc.);
(iv)   the level of benefits;
(v)    the duration of benefits.
                          (OECD, 1979, p.188)

Taking (i) first, it has already been demonstrated that the total amount of unemployment increased after 1973 (Table 4.8).  Turning to (ii),
note must be taken of the fact that the already very
high average of unemployment insurance contributors

rose to approximately 95 per cent of the dependent
labour force during the 1970s (OECD, 1979, pp.189-
190). With respect to the structure of unemployment
(iii), it has already been stressed that there has
been an increase in youth unemployment. However,
school-leavers are not eligible to receive benefits.
Moreover, where employment of young people proves to
be temporary, they subsequently receive a low level
of unemployment benefit because of the short period
of time previously spent in employment, and their
relatively low incomes whilst they were employed.
Hence, it was the dramatic increase after 1973 in unemployment among those entitled to full benefit which
was mainly responsible for the escalation of benefits.

An increase in the level of benefits (iv) was
introduced from 1 January 1975. First, the supplement of DM 12 paid to the unemployed for each depend-
ant was replaced by the payment of the full child
allowance (*ibid.*, p.195). Secondly, unemployment
benefit for an insured, unemployed person was raised
to the equivalent of 68 per cent of the net earnings
received while in employment. In effect, family
status thus again influenced the total benefit payable. This amount was payable for a maximum period
of twelve months. Thereafter anyone who is still
unemployed may apply for unemployment assistance but
in this case 58 per cent of previous net earnings are
payable. Those receiving assistance, as opposed to
insurance, are means-tested in so far as the income
of other domicile close relatives is taken into account. Under the subtle headline 'Grandma must pay
if necessary', *Die Zeit* (34/76, p.21), after giving
examples of family income being deducted from '*Alhi*'
(as assistance is colloquially known), went on to
point out that the family home and jewellery - even
the family car - need not be sold. Savings deposits,
bonds and shares would, however, be taken into account. (Sight deposits would not be, since unemployment benefit or assistance is normally paid into the
recipient's bank account.)

The final factor (v) which accounts for the dyna-
mism of unemployment benefits is the duration of unemployment. The clear trend in the 1970s was for the
proportion of the unemployed who were out of work for
less than one month to fall. (From 33.2 per cent in
1971 to 17.7 per cent in 1980 - OECD, 1979, pp.193
and 195; *Statisches Jahrbuch*, 1981, Table 6.10.) At
the other end of the scale the proportion unemployed
for more than twelve months rose from 5.3 per cent
in 1971 to 17.0 per cent in 1980.

The consequence of the steep rise in unemploy-

ment itself, as well as unemployment benefits, is
that the annual percentage change in total benefits
with respect to the annual percentage change of total
unemployment (the so-called 'elasticity' of %ΔB/%ΔU)
has generally been greater than unity in both real
and nominal terms (OECD, 1979, pp.191 and 194, modified and up-dated by the writer). The costs of unemployment were also estimated for the FRG in 1975,
when the contribution loss to pension and insurance
funds of every 250,000 persons unemployed was put at
nearly £200 million. An extra £500 million had to
be found for payments of benefits (*Employment Gazette*,
October 1975, p.981). Estimates in the UK, based on
1980-81 tax and benefit rates, earnings and so on,
indicated a cost to the Exchequer of £340 million for
an increase of £100,000 in the number employed. This
estimate included the cost of losses in tax receipts
and national insurance contributions, increases in
benefits, rent and rate rebates and administration
costs. Redundancy payments and wider, but less
direct, consequences were excluded (HM Treasury,
*Economic Progress Report*, No.130). Converted into
DM at current exchange rates the annual average cost
in 1975 for the FRG was DM 14,000 per head and the UK
(1980) estimate was DM 13,600. By 1980 the figure
for the FRG - this time including lost tax revenues
- was DM 20,000. Hence, the precarious state of the
Federal Labour Office's finances stems mainly from
the high level of unemployment. In other words, this
financial deterioration, with a consequent need for
Federal subsidies, dates from the mid-1970s.
     At this juncture, it is perhaps necessary to
very briefly mention that the alternative social insurance policy of reducing unemployment benefit at a
time of rising unemployment was part of the continu-
ously deflationary policies which were used during
the rise of the Nazis. In any case, unemployment
still entails significant financial losses to the
individual, along with serious social and psychologi-
cal problems. Nevertheless, the policy debate on
social security spending in general, and unemployment
benefits in particular, became more intense at the
beginning of the 1980s. (The extent to which such
assistance undermines initiative, it will be recalled,
is an important aspect of the social market economy
debate.) As a result unemployment insurance contributions, and the minimum qualifying period for entitlement to benefit, were increased. Further, the
penalties for not accepting a job offer considered
to be suitable by the employment exchange official
were tightened. But expenditure on job creation was

increased and it is to this aspect of labour market policy that the analysis now turns.

With the increasing severity of the recession since 1974, then, the Federal Government was obliged to introduce, through the Federal Labour Office, a series of measures designed to alleviate unemployment among certain disadvantages groups. The increase in placement activity has already been noted earlier in this section. The increased importance attached to vocational training - particularly among young people - will be dealt with in the next sextion (Human Capital Formation). A final aspect of policy relevant here is the job creation programme (*Arbeitsbeschaffungsmaßnahmen*).

Between 1977 and 1980 job creation activity commanded an average annual outlay of about DM 858.5 million or 5 per cent of the total budget of the Federal Labour Office (*Statisches Jahrbuch*, 1981, Table 18.7.2). Unemployment benefits, on the other hand, account for about half of the Office's expenditure, but this should not be allowed to conceal the importance attached to its job creation programme: under the terms of the enabling Act, both Federal and Länder governments may contribute grants which match those of the Federal Labour Office (Hanby and Jackson, p.93).

The scheme is operated at the local employment exchange level of the Federal Labour Office. Technically, the local tripartite committee appraises a suggested scheme. In practice, a forceful local director might actively solicit job creation schemes (*ibid.*, pp.93 and 106). The depth of penetration of the scheme could, however, be fostered or frustrated according to the attitude of employers' organisations, trade unions and the relevant Land government (*ibid.*, pp.98-102). Nevertheless, there has been a considerable national increase in the number of jobs created annually under the scheme: from 3,000 in 1974 to 40,000 in 1980. It was estimated in 1977 and 1978 that almost as many jobs again were being indirectly created by the general effects of the scheme (*Sozialbericht 1978*, para.16). In addition, the female and long-term unemployed groups were successfully placed by the public works creation element of the regional employment measures discussed above (Schmid and Peters, pp.107, 117 and 119). Further measures proposed in the early 1980s were, however, the subject of controversy between, on the one hand, the SPD and, on the other hand, the CDU and FDP.

## HUMAN CAPITAL FORMATION

Although training and skills are not in themselves an infallible protection against unemployment, the acquisition of suitable vocational skills is one of the most decisive factors determining an individual's prospects on the labour market; in an industrialised society it is also of crucial significance in terms of the development of the economy as a whole. A European comparison by Saunders and Marsden (p.296) has shown that formal vocational training among manual men is most fully developed in West Germany. This system must, therefore, be described.

The core of the German vocational training scheme is the so-called 'dual system' which may be described by reference to five main characteristics:

1. After leaving compulsory schooling (*Haupt-* or *Realschulen*, followed where necessary by one year at *Berufsschulen*) at the age of 16, training for the qualified school-leaver is organised on a contractual basis. The practical in-firm training is combined with compulsory part-time education between the ages of 16 and 18 in vocational schools (*Berufsschulen*).

2. Private firms are responsible for the in-firm training which, however, is regulated, guided and controlled since 1969 by Federal legislation (Vocational Training Act - *Berufsbildungsgesetz* - BBiG). The chambers of industry and commerce conduct examinations.

3. Apprenticeship training is mainly financed by the firms themselves, with some help from the State in special cases.

4. An apprenticeship lasts approximately 2 or 3 years, depending upon the candidate's educational qualifications and his progress. At the end of the apprenticeship, there is an official written examination and the candidate prepares a piece of practical work (*Gesellenstuck*). An apprentice who passes these examinations receives a certificate and becomes a qualified *Facharbeiter* (skilled worker).

5. At a minimum age of 25 the *Facharbeiter* may decide to enrol for a *Meister* course, which again will conclude with a written and practical examination, usually set by the Land government. Possession of the *Meisterbrief* (foreman's certificate) awarded to success-

ful candidates gives the *Meister* a great
deal of kudos and supervisory powers, al-
though in small firms a foreman may not
possess a certificate.
(EEC, European Documentation, Periodical 6/80, p.12;
Hutton and Lawrence, pp.13-16; Lawrence, pp.157-161;
NEDO, 1981a, pp.5 and 22; Prais, p.52; Sadowski;
Winterhager, pp.3 and 6.)

An indication of the importance of the dual
system is that in December 1978 there were over 1
million apprentices in Germany, representing over 50
per cent of young people in the 16-19 age-group.
Over 70 per cent of young people who leave full-time
school at 16 enter an apprenticeship. However,
Sadowski (p.240) concludes that firms do not train
the number of apprentices justified by their self-
interest as a group. Hence, if the overall supply
of apprentices did not exceed demand by 12.5 per cent
on a given day each year, the *Ausbildungsplatzförder-
ungsgesetz* (APFG) of 1976 enabled the government to
impose a maximum levy of 0.25 per cent of the payroll on all firms whose payrolls exceeded DM 400,000.
This levy was meant to create additional apprenticeships, and only to a limited degree to subsidise the
replacement of existing apprenticeships. But this
was another Act which provoked controversy (Sadowski,
p.241; compare both Chapter 5 above and Owen Smith,
1981, pp.184 and 201). In December 1980, the Act was
ruled unconstitutional.
At the end of the 1970s there were nearly 1
million school-leavers, the vast majority of whom
were seeking to swell the total of 1.7 million in
training (BMWi, p.24). Moreover, the groups which
were hardest to place in new jobs were those among
whom training and re-training is relatively neglected.
Such groups have been shown to include women,
foreigners, unqualified school-leavers generally, and
other workers at both extreme ends of the working-age
spectrum; the physically handicapped should also be
added to these structurally disadvantaged groups.
For the first time during the period 1950-1980,
more women than men were unemployed between 1978 and
1980. (Of the yearly average of 889,000 unemployed
in 1980, 463,000 were women - BMA, Table 2.11). A
white-collar union demanded more openings for women
in technical and in the armed services, while the
Federal Government made legislative proposals designed to ensure more equality of opportunity.
Efforts were also made by the Federal Government to
improve training opportunities for female school-

leavers who, in spite of good school-leaving qualifications, were experiencing difficulties in obtaining employment (*Sozialbericht 1980*, para.28). The general position of foreigners in the context of unemployment has already been analysed, as has the position of young foreigners. It must be noted, however, that the number of older workers is declining sharply. Before the 1973 recession, 67 per cent of males aged 60 to 65 were still employed. By 1978 this proportion had fallen to 43 per cent. The trend was the same for females, although not so pronounced - from 19 to 12 per cent.

At the other end of the working-age spectrum, the problem of unemployment among younger members of the labour force was combatted in several ways. First, the Federal Government took further powers under the ill-fated APFG to financially support, where necessary, a voluntary year at a technical or vocational school (*ibid.*, para.43; Winterhager, p.6). Between 1976 and 1979 the number taking such a prevocational training course almost trebled - from 22,000 to 65,000. The Federal Government sought to make this practice mandatory which would have resulted in a minimum school-leaving age of 16. By 1980 this compulsory (or tenth) year of schooling had been introduced either on an optional or compulsory basis in all Länder except Bavaria and Baden-Württemberg. At the same time, the Federal Government introduced measures designed to assist particularly disadvantaged groups of young people in achieving some training. The groups involved here were, above all, unqualified school-leavers, young people with learning difficulties, socially disadvantaged youths and young foreigners. Between 1974 and 1980 the Federal Government made available DM 1.2 billion for the expansion and establishment of training schools and technical colleges (*Sozialbericht 1980*, para.30).

From 1980 measures were taken to offer preparation courses (MBSE) for vocational training to young foreigners who did not possess a German school-leaving qualification, including German language training where necessary. Regular attendance at the one-year MBSE course entitled a young foreigner to a work permit. While attending the course he was entitled to a grant. In 1980-81, 15,000 young foreigners attended such a course. By 1982, 20,000 places were to be made available. According to the Federal Labour Ministry: 'From the mid-1980s when the number of young German people will display a marked decrease, every foreign trainee should be welcomed so as to prevent a threat to the future supply of skilled labour' (*Sozialpolitische Informationen*, 5/81 and 10/81).

At first blush, the various measures introduced during the second half of the 1970s seemed to be paying dividends in September 1979 when for the first time in five years the supply of training places (680,000) was greater than the demand for such places (660,000) (*Sozialbericht 1980*, para.26). Federally-owned training facilities alone had been expanded by 40 per cent on 1977 to reach a total number of 29,500 trainees. By March in the vocational guidance year 1 October 1980 to 30 September 1981 the excess demand widened to 438,000 against 334,000. These figures represented something like 70 per cent of both the total demand and applicants for training places. In March 1982 the total number of training places notified during the previous six months to employment exchanges was down by 11 per cent (389,700), while the number of applicants had increased 14 per cent (381,800). By the end of March (1982) there was again an excess supply: 113,000 vacancies existed for 223,700 searchers. Compared to March 1981 this represented a decrease of 33 per cent in vacancies, but an increase of 20 per cent in searchers. The structural problem was also growing worse, in that searchers were located in areas of relatively high unemployment and/or preferred places in trades where vacancies did not exist. (This latter structural problem is not new since the current pattern of shortages among skilled workers today indicates that training in the past has not been in the appropriate trades; moreover, 42 per cent of trained workers leave their trades for improved prospects elsewhere - BA, *Presse Informationen*, 27/82.)

Although the employers' associations were generally satisfied with the training situation, the trade unions were rather more critical of the micro imbalances between supply and demand, particularly where choice was limited in careers offering an expanding future (FRG Embassy, London, *Report*, 3/81, p.6). In addition, the trade unions estimated that in 1981 some 13,000 young people aged between 15 and 16 will go into jobs without further training; 41,000 will break off their training and 60,000 will complete courses offering no real vocation or skill (*ibid.*, 5/81, p.4). Hence, 114,000 (or nearly 11 per cent of the age group) will enter careers 'with nothing behind them' (*ibid.*). The main reasons for imbalance have already been mentioned: training places are not always provided where they are needed; places are often offered in older industries but not in

newer ones; big firms are more reluctant than small
firms to provide training, yet the former may be more
efficient; far more girls than boys fail to receive
training - twice as many girls as boys are jobless;
the number of young foreign workers drifting into
unskilled work is increasing steadily. As a result,
there is still a critical shortage of the right types
of skilled labour.
    Higher education is clearly another important
aspect of human capital formation. The normal path
to university-level education is via a *Gymnasium* or
grammar school, at which 25 per cent of the country's
school-children are educated. Constitutionally, however, the Länder have autonomy in the field of education. Hence, as the Geimers observe (p.11), the
structural pattern and the functions of the institutions and bodies dealing with policy and promotion
in this area are complex. One reason for this is
that a landmark in the development of scientific life
in Germany was the establishment of separate institutions for technological research and training,
owing to the rapid growth of the natural sciences and
engineering. This latter development took place during the 19th century, particularly after the phase of
rapid economic growth began in the 1870s (UNESCO,
p.14). Hence, the technical universities (*Technische-
hochschulen*) nowadays co-exist alongside the traditional universities (*Universitäten*) and under-
graduate engineering may generally only be studied at
the former (Lawrence, p.63).
    An alternative engineering course is offered by
the *Fachhochschulen*, although this training perhaps
has a somewhat lower status when compared to the
qualification obtained at a technical university
(Hutton, Lawrence and Smith, p.30). Until 1968 the
*Fachhochschulen* had been termed *Ingenieurschulen*.
More recently, particularly in North Rhine-Westphalia,
many *Fachhochschulen* have been incorporated into the
new *Gesamthochschulen*. These are associations of
engineering schools, colleges of art and colleges of
commerce often scattered geographically but grouped
under the generic term of *Gesamthochschulen*. In
practice this has meant bringing together staff from
a variety of higher and further educational establishments (*ibid.*, p.34). Such establishments offer a
considerable range of courses at both university and
sub-university level - the latter being mainly vocational in character (Hutton and Lawrence, p.19;
OECD, 1972, p.51). Entrance to the *Fachhochschulen*
and to the *Gesamthochschulen* is normally via either
a technical school or college (*Fachschulen* and

175

*Fachoberschulen* - ages 15-18). In the case of the *Gesamthochschulen*, entrance may also be via a grammar school. All those who qualify from both of these relatively new higher education institutions would be eligible to go on to a technical university, although the *Gesamthochschulen* have their own university-type engineering course.

In 1967 there were 36 institutions of university rank in the Federal Republic (UNESCO, p.12). But there was a rapid expansion of both the existing universities, together with the founding of 27 new institutions, in the 1960s and 1970s. There are now over 60 institutions of university rank, some of which have developed in a spectacular manner. Bochum, for example, first opened its doors to students in 1964. It now has over 25,000 students. In the winter semester of 1979-80 there were 970,000 students in institutions of university rank and *Gesamthochschulen*, already more than was envisaged by educational planners for 1985 and over three times as many as in 1960. Since further expansion is planned, there will be well over one million students in the early 1980s. A peak of new entrants in 1983-84 will enter the labour market in 1991-92.

Three points about this expansion in tertiary education must be made. First, undergraduates are not uniformly spread by discipline and, above all, university. Some faculties attract many more students than their capacity can reasonably accommodate, while others have seminar and lecture theatres which are grossly under-utilised. Secondly, there is, by British standards, a very high student wastage rate (Hutton and Lawrence, p.39; Prais, p.53). Hence, in spite of the high enrolment rate at the beginning of the approximate six-year period at university, there is a much smaller subsequent flow of highly qualified manpower on to the labour market than the figures in the last paragraph may at first indicate. (For that matter, absenteeism from the vocational training schools is also high - Prais (p.51n) reports 30 per cent.) Nevertheless one must (thirdly) emphasise that the vocational emphasis in higher education results in a high proportion of graduates in engineering, law, economics and management studies. Law, it should be added, is treated as a general entrance qualification for both the civil service and industrial management (Hutton and Lawrence, p.102). Further, a high proportion of gifted students choose engineering, rather than mathematics or pure science (*ibid.*, p.39).

Employers in the late 1970s criticised the

relatively low output of engineers by institutions of
higher education, although one of the trade unions
organising engineers refused to accept that the pattern of sixth-form and first-year university recruitment indicated that there was a potential manpower
shortage in this field. Two pieces of evidence seem
germane. The first is that there are significantly
more engineers with degree level qualifications in
Germany than in France, the USA, Sweden and the UK,
but all these countries are in turn below Japan
(*ibid.*, p.103; Prais, p.50). Secondly, a fairly consistent 18 per cent of German nationals in higher
education between 1975 and 1980 were reading engineering, and over 25 per cent of those receiving first
degrees in the same period were engineers (BMWi, p.27;
Prais, p.54; *Statisches Jahrbuch*, 1980, p.345, and
1981, p.357). On the other hand, at the beginning of
the 1980s there was a growing problem of unemployment
among graduates. As well as the structural problem
involving the excess supply of teachers, social
workers and politics graduates, an increasing number
of pure scientists and engineers were among the unemployed (*Die Zeit*, 21/82, p.21). This latter trend
confirmed the predictions reported by Hutton, Lawrence
and Smith (pp.63-65).

In this section the various assumptions of human
capital theory - such as education being exclusively
a capital good and rates of return being the principal
motivator in job choice - have been uncritically and
necessarily accepted. Some of the other factors entering into the equations of wage determination and
job choice are analysed in the next (and final)
section of this chapter.


REMUNERATION AND OTHER TERMS AND CONDITIONS OF
EMPLOYMENT

Wage Determination and Wage Levels
Between 1970 and 1980 average gross monthly earnings
per employee rose by 120 per cent in nominal terms
(DM 1,148 to DM 2,525) and 36 per cent in real terms
(BMWi, Table 2.13). The compound rate of increase in
average gross monthly earnings per employee was 8.72
per cent in the period 1970-74 but 4.86 per cent in
the period 1975-79. By 1979 negotiated settlements
in wage rates were at their lowest average rate of
increase since 1968, when an incomes policy reduced
rises in money wage rates to a greater extent than
profits (Owen Smith, 1981, p.201). In fact, there
was a profits explosion in 1968. The slackening of

the policy, and a consequential fall in profits, was
brought about by a period beginning with unofficial
strikes in 1969 and culminating in an official strike
in 1974 (*ibid.*, p.199). This latter strike was
brought about by the Federal Government's opposition
to a two digit percentage claim in the public service.
Ultimately, the Chancellor's own political position
was undermined when such a concession was made in
order to secure a resumption of work. Thereafter,
economic recession undermined trade union bargaining
power - hence the difference in average pay increases
in the two halves of the 1970s.

This raises the need to emphasise some features
of the annual wage round in West Germany. Its numerous rituals and highly legalistic aspects should not
be allowed to conceal the extent to which a conflict
of interests may arise. It is only after a wage contract has been signed that a legally-binding agreement comes into being. Normally, this agreement is
observed thereafter and only a conflict of rights can
be pursued by means of litigation (*ibid.*, 182-183 and
196-197). But before contracts are signed there is a
public debate, to which politicians, government departments, the Council of Economic Advisers and the
five Economics Research Institutes all contribute
(Adam, pp.31-32; Owen Smith, 1979, p.166). Whether
the Council should make such specific evaluations,
as opposed to presenting a series of policy options,
is an issue which has been debated since its establishment in 1963 (Wallich, 1968, pp.351-353 and 369).
For example, the resignation of one of its members in
1981 was precipitated by this controversy (*Die Zeit*,
37/81, p.21).

It is usually the country's, indeed the world's,
largest union (*IG Metall*) which commences, and negotiates the key settlement in, the annual wage round
(Owen Smith, 1981, pp.189 and 198-199). This union
organises workers in engineering and motor vehicle
manufacture, as well as the metal manufacture and
foundry sectors. It has been involved in a number of
industrial disputes. Both the union, and the employers' association with which it negotiates
(*AV Gesamtmetall*), are at least at one in regretting
this key bargaining role. A further complication is
that there are separate district negotiating councils
within the 'metal industry', though the North Rhine-
Westphalia or North Württemberg/North Baden districts
usually determine the key settlements. Finally, an
important feature of the pay round is the phenomenon
of 'warning strikes' during negotiations for a new
wage contract. They are used before the previous

wage contract has expired and as such are on uncertain legal grounds. However, the typical warning strike lasts for only a few hours and usually consists of downing tools for a demonstration. No official statistics of their frequency are published.

Having established that the 1979 settlement was relatively low, and having also established the key characteristics of the pay round, the analysis may proceed to a consideration of the 1980 and 1981 pay rounds. Both were relatively hard fought, although the final settlement in the 'metal industry' of 6.8 per cent and 4.9 per cent may seem low. As will be shown below, however, real pay and fringe benefits are relatively high in the Federal Republic and, of course, it has become almost a cliché to point out that the Germans fear inflation.

The 1980 and 1981 pay rounds are compared to the two previous rounds in Table 6.9.

Table 6.9:  Four Recent Pay Rounds

| Increases in basic pay (percentage range) | Percentage of employees | | | |
|---|---|---|---|---|
| | 1978 | 1979 | 1980 | 1981 |
| 4.0 - 4.4 | 8 | 55 | – | 27 |
| 4.5 - 4.9 | 22 | 29 | – | 55 |
| 5.0 - 5.4 | 50 | 11 | 1 | 13 |
| 5.5 - 5.9 | 15 | 3 | 1 | 4 |
| 6.0 - 6.4 | 4 | 2 | 18 | 1 |
| 6.5 - 6.9 | 1 | – | 65 | – |
| 7.0 - 7.4 | – | – | 13 | – |
| 7.5 - 7.9 | – | – | 1 | – |
| 8 or more | – | – | 1 | – |
| Average increase (per cent) | 5.0 | 4.5 | 6.7 | 4.8 |
| RPI increase       ( "       " ) | 2.7 | 4.1 | 5.5 | 5.9 |

Sources:  RPI increases, MRDB, Table VIII(7).  All other data, Incomes Data Services Limited, *International Reports*, Nos 142 and 165.

Two things become immediately apparent. First, the distribution in each year indicates the range and the pace-setting role of the 'metal industry' settlements: 5.0 per cent in 1978, 4.3 per cent in 1979 and, as already pointed out, 6.8 and 4.9 per cent respectively in 1980 and 1981. The second point to note about

Table 6.9 is that in 1981 the general level of pay
settlements was below the general rate of inflation.
For that matter, the average 1982 settlement of 4.2
per cent was also below both the actual and predicted
rates of inflation. However, perhaps such a general
indication of the trend in real pay is open to criticism, not least because taxes on earnings are not
taken into account. Hence Table 6.10 contains a
rather more sophisticated appraisal of the course of
gross, net and real pay during the period 1950-1980.
The absolute fall in average real pay per head of the
labour force recorded in 1980 was unique in the review period. A continuation of such a trend was
expected by the DGB research institute, which predicted that by the end of 1982 employees' real income
would have fallen below the level of 1978 (WSI,
*Pressedienst*, 13/82).

Table 6.10: Average Annual Growth in Gross, Net and
Real Earnings Per Member of the Labour Force, 1950-
1980

| Year | Gross[a] | | Net[b] | | Real[c] | |
|------|------|-----------|------|-----------|--------|-----------|
|      | DM | Per cent[d] | DM | Per cent[d] | DM | Per cent[d] |
| 1950[e] | 2,918 | – | 2,554 | – | 5,528 | – |
| 1955[e] | 4,401 | +7.9 | 3,782 | +7.7 | 7,445 | +6.0 |
| 1960[e] | 6,156 | +9.4 | 5,183 | +8.0 | 9,322 | +6.4 |
| 1965 | 9,336 | +9.1 | 7,731 | +10.0 | 12,118 | +6.5 |
| 1970 | 13,773 | +14.7 | 10,648 | +12.4 | 14,892 | +8.9 |
| 1975 | 22,426 | +7.2 | 16,265 | +7.3 | 16,978 | +1.1 |
| 1980 | 30,273 | +6.5 | 21,170 | +5.0 | 18,250 | -0.3 |
| (1981 | 31,783 | +5.0 | 22,129 | +4.5 | 18,020 | -1.3) |

Notes:
(a) Not including employers' national insurance contributions.
(b) Gross earnings minus income tax and employees' national
insurance contributions.
(c) Net earnings in 1976 prices, deflated by subtracting the
percentage change in the consumer price index for a middle-
income four-family household. (1975 includes a 4 per cent
increase in family allowances.)
(d) On previous year.
(e) 1950, 1955 and 1960 excl. Berlin and Saarland.

Source: BMA, 1982, Tables 1.13, 1.14 and 1.15.

In the 1981 'metal industry' pay round the employers made the anticipated offer of 2.5 per cent -
somewhere around the growth in productivity. The
union had already made clear its intention to include
in its claim what it understood to be an unwritten
convention, namely an element to compensate for inflation. Hence, even though the union intended lodg-
ing a moderate claim in view of the economic situation, an increase in line with productivity growth
alone was unacceptable. The claims lodged varied
between 7.7 and 8 per cent, according to district.
By April 1981 the number of warning strikes had risen
to an unprecedented level and a national engineering
strike was on the cards. From the middle of January
nearly sixty meetings took place between the employers and trade union representatives in the various areas, although both parties agreed that only at
six of these meetings did actual negotiations take
place. As shown elsewhere by this writer (1981,
pp.181-182), the employers are noted for their soli-
darity. It was therefore much to the chagrin of
other branches of the employers' association in 1981
when the North Württemberg/North Baden district made
an eleventh hour settlement of 4.9 per cent on 28
April.

Wage Structures
Despite profound social and industrial changes, the
upheavals of two world wars and a dramatic increase
in median earnings, the dispersion of earnings among
manual workers in Germany and several other countries
has changed very little during this century (Lydall,
pp.187 and 318; Phelps Brown, pp.285-286). This does
not mean that all earnings have increased by the same
percentage, but rather that gains in one occupation
have been offset by losses in another, or by changes
within occupations, such that the overall shape remains the same (Atkinson, pp.23-24). Among other
things, Saunders and Marsden (pp.108 and 176) report
that in West Germany both manual skill and industrial
differentials have displayed remarkable stability.
Table 6.11 summarises part of their research relating
to West Germany. As they emphasise (p.248) each
contributory factor to the dispersion of earnings is
estimated on its own and no allowance was made for
the strong relationship between them. For example,
employees move up the occupational hierarchy with age.
Industry and establishment size are also related, as
are age and length of service.
    From the relatively low coefficient of variation
of 35.7 per cent shown in Table 6.11, the impression

Table 6.11: Percentage of the Overall Dispersion in
Gross Monthly Earnings and the Estimated Factors to
which they were Attributable (All industrial workers,
1972)

|  | FRG | Six country mean[a] |
|---|---|---|
| Occupation | 40.9 | 41.1 |
| Manual/non-manual | 10.8 | 14.1 |
| Sex | 20.6 | 12.7 |
| Age | 7.3 | 11.3 |
| Length of service | 5.1 | 7.7 |
| Industry | 7.9 | 10.3 |
| Establishment size | 1.3 | 4.6 |
| Region | 2.1 | 2.3 |
| Sum[b] | 85.2 | 89.9 |
| Overall coefficient of variation | 35.7 | – |

Notes:
(a) France, Italy, Great Britain, West Germany,
Netherlands and Belgium.
(b) Excl. manual/non-manual which is included in
occupation.

Source:  Saunders and Marsden, p.247.


is given of a relatively small dispersion of industrial earnings about their mean value. In the case
of Britain it was 47.7 per cent. In fact, of the
six countries included in the Saunders and Marsden
study (see Table 6.11), Britain, France and Italy
displayed the greatest degrees of inequality in pay.
West Germany on the other hand, appeared to have the
most egalitarian wage structure (Saunders and Marsden,
p.17). If the industrial labour market is disaggre-
gated into four sub-labour markets (males and females
in both manual and non-manual occupations) then the
FRG remains, on balance, the most egalitarian country.
This applies to the sub-group mentioned, whether
adults-only or all-ages are measured (*ibid.*, pp.24
and 26). Similarly, four non-industrial sectors
(p.36) produced results which showed relatively more
equality in West Germany. Hence. occupational differentials in the FRG are generally smaller than the UK,
but since the overall dispersion of earnings in the
FRG is also smaller, occupations account for a larger
percentage of the total variance.
    But the really significant feature is that in

both West Germany and the UK it is possible to identify two separate occupational hierarchies, one for
manual and one for non-manual occupations with a
good deal of overlap in pay levels between them
(Marsden, pp.310-311). In the case of West Germany,
however, the non-manual/manual differential, measured
as the average earnings for industrial men and women
in the two groups, seems to have widened between 1972
and 1979 from 129.2 per cent to 137.6 per cent.
Within the non-manual workers group, a compression of
the pay structure has taken place (*ibid.*, p.312).
One of the chief causes would appear to be related to
the faster growth in the numbers in the top grades,
and the shift from low-paid commercial functions to
the higher-paid technical ones (Saunders and Marsden,
p.174). Manual workers' occupational pay structures,
on the other hand, appear to be somewhat more influenced by trade union wage policy. Since this factor
is not included in Table 6.11, the manual workers
skill differential will be considered shortly.

In West Germany, as in Great Britain, but not
in France and Italy, sex differentials emerge as the
next most important factor in accounting for differences in earnings. Since Lydall (pp.60-61) had concentrated on the variation in male earnings in order
to arrive at his Standard Distribution, the estimate
in Table 6.11 is of particular importance. Moreover,
Markmann's somewhat more dated time series (1950-1963
- pp.326 and 338) also indicates a significant male/
female differential, in spite of some progress in the
implementation of an anti-discrimination policy and
trade union efforts to bring about greater equality.
As elsewhere, custom plays a large part in this discrimination, which is more pronounced among manual
female workers than among their white-collar colleagues. In 1981 a Federal Labour Court decision
gave an impetus to trade unions to pursue their female members' constitutional right of equal pay for
equal work (*Die Zeit*, 39/81, pp.17-18).

Despite marked changes in the range of industry
differentials, the position of individual industries
in the pay hierarchy has been fairly stable. In both
West Germany and the UK, inter-industrial differentials display a phenomenon well-described by Marsden
(p.317) as a 'concertina' movement: that is to say
that there is a successive compression and expansion
of the spread which affects most industries, with
little change in the rank order. Hence, Marsden
calculates the rank correlation coefficient of the
inter-industry wage structure between 1972 and 1977
to be +0.84.

Coal mining has tended to be in the highest paid
group of industries between 1950 and 1979 (Markmann,
pp.338-339; Marsden, p.316). It was not in the top
five in 1972 but has regained its position in this
group since the oil crisis. (In the case of the UK
two major disputes were sparked off by its fall in
the pay hierarchy - Owen Smith, 1981, pp.141-142.)
The energy sector generally is well-represented among
the top five. By 1980 mineral oil was top of the
table, with electricity and natural gas second and
coal mining fifth (*Die Zeit*, 13/81, p.24). Printing
was at the very top of the West German industry pay
hierarchy for many years, but it had fallen to fifth
in 1978 and third in 1980. In all countries, the new
technology may undermine the unions' traditional bargaining power in this industry. Economic recession
seems to have caused the disappearance of the iron
and steel industry from the top five of the West German earnings hierarchy, although it just remained in
this group in the UK. But the recession appears to
have hit the motor vehicle assembly in the UK much
more than the West German industry: in the UK it has
disappeared from the top five payers, whereas the
German industry still occupies a rank at this level.
There is much more similarity between low paid industries (clothing and textiles) in West Germany, Britain,
France and Italy. Markmann's data also give historical
support to this latter view of the German industrial
pay hierarchy. Increasing international competition
from the developing countries is probably a major
factor at work here and it is particularly important
to note that a higher than average proportion of women
and young people are employed in these industries.

Employers tend to oppose a narrowing of percentage differentials because, they contend, it undermines
the incentive to a worker to invest in training, as
well as reducing employment levels among the unskilled
because it becomes relatively less costly to automate
the processes previously carried out by the unskilled
(*Die Zeit*, 8/80, p21). As already seen above, however,
the tendency at the end of the 1970s was for an increase in the number of potential trainees, albeit not
in the occupations most in demand. But it is true to
say that the level of unemployment among unskilled
workers is relatively high - they represent one half
of the total number of the unemployed, whereas they
constitute only one third of the labour force. Moreover, investment has tended to be of a labour-saving
kind.

The unions, on the other hand, would perhaps prefer to see some narrowing of percentage differentials.

In other words they would wish to see at least some
absolute element in money wage settlements. This is
for reasons of social equity, especially during times
of inflation when price increases in basic commodities
have a larger proportionate impact on the low-paid.
In real terms, therefore, differentials remain fairly
constant.

In the 'metal industry' there has been, for
example, some narrowing of percentage differentials,
most notably between 1968 and 1976. In North Rhine-
Westphalia this was achieved by means of effectively
awarding higher percentage increases to the lower
grade in what at the beginning of the period was a
seven-grade wage structure. Hence, in 1968 grade one
workers earned 73 per cent of the skilled hourly
rate. The grade was abolished in 1972, so that by
1976 grade two workers were receiving 82 per cent of
the skilled hourly rate. While acknowledging this
narrowing, and also one in textiles, Saunders and
Marsden (p.179) conclude that the skill differential
in West Germany has hardly been affected in the 1970s.
This is attributed to the formal system of training
outlined above, which has prevented employers from
using artificial upgradings either as a way of granting covert pay increases, or as a method of reducing
turnover.

Wealth and Factor Shares
In effect, the problem just raised is one of attempting to distinguish between criteria involving economic efficiency and those concerned with social
equity. This issue becomes a controversial social
and political question when the distribution of income and wealth between social classes is considered
(Adam, p.5). Indeed, even within the field of economics income distribution lies 'in the province of
high theory' (Pen, p.158). Yet it is relevant to the
social market economy debate. In this short section,
therefore, it is proposed only to give an overview.

Although there is a greater degree of equality
of earned incomes in West Germany, labour's share in
the national income (at factor cost) tends to be
lower in Germany than in the UK and USA (*ibid.*,
p.163). However, labour's share cannot always be
taken as a reliable economic welfare indicator. In
conditions of economic expansion a falling share
could be associated with an absolute growth in the
income levels of the employed population, whereas in
a contracting economy an increase in labour's share
could be accompanied by an absolute fall in employees'
income. Adjusted for changes in the proportion of

employees in the total labour force (1950=100), labour's share in the period 1925-1970 reached its highest level (71.8 per cent) in 1932 - at the height of the world depression and record levels of unemployment. The lowest level (53.8 per cent) was reached in 1960 when net real incomes from employment were 85 per cent higher than in 1932 and for the first time unemployment was well under 2 per cent (Adam, p.13).

Upward changes in labour's share relative to capital may also, in the longer run, induce capital substitution. Nevertheless, there may be some evidence of trade union pushfulness operating to increase labour's share during the period under review. (In the absence of detailed and reliable profits data, various proxies must be used - *ibid.*, p.17.) The possible effect of collective bargaining may best be seen by taking five sub-periods during the review era - the 1950s; 1960-66; 1967-1970; 1971-74 and 1975-1980. Again assuming a constant employment structure (1970=100), labour's share in the 1950s fell from 71.1 to 65.2 per cent. Union bargaining power had been circumscribed by a number of factors. Until the 1967 recession labour's share then showed an increase to 68.3 per cent. At this stage incomes policy caused a relative decline. After the 1968 'profits explosion' and 1969 unofficial strikes, labour's share displayed an increase from 67.8 to 71.4 per cent between 1970 and 1975. Finally, from 1975 the adjusted labour's share again began to decline.

In order to demonstrate these developments, Table 6.12 draws together the data on post-war cycles and demand in the labour market (Tables 4.7 and 4.8), together with some distributional and wage rate data. Hence, Table 6.12 represents an attempt to capture the trends in labour's share, as well as the cyclical factors which operate. To begin with, there was evidence for the period 1950-1963 that the growth of negotiated wage rates is generally slower than gross wage rates (Markmann, p.326). This seems to be confirmed in Table 6.12. But it also seems evident that negotiated wage rates rose more rapidly during the period of relatively low unemployment. Further, the recovery of wage rates during an upswing is lagged compared to profits, but during periods of low unemployment earnings advanced more rapidly than profits. It was this latter factor which seems to have brought about the upward trends in labour's share.

Much the same kind of distributional picture emerges if the post-war growth cycles are viewed in

Table 6.12: The Trends and Cyclical Fluctuations in Labour's Share, 1950–1980

| Average annual unemployment during cycle (per cent) | | Approximate cycle (calendar years[a]) | Labour's share in the Net National Product at factor cost (per cent) | | Percentage change in average annual earnings on previous year | | Male manual employees annual negotiated settlements | |
|---|---|---|---|---|---|---|---|---|
| | | | unadjusted | adjusted[b] | Gross | Net of tax | 1976=100 | Trend period average (per cent) |
| 8.4 | | 1950 | 58.4 | 71.1 | – | – | 17.4 | |
| 4.7 | TROUGH | 1954 | 59.9 | 68.7 | +11.4 | +9.8 | 19.4 | 9.9 |
| | PEAK | 1955 | 59.3 | 67.0 | +13.8 | +13.6 | 20.5 | |
| 1.6 | TROUGH | 1958 | 60.9 | 67.3 | +7.9 | +6.6 | 25.2 | |
| | PEAK | 1960 | 60.4 | 65.2 | +12.4 | +10.9 | 27.9 | |
| 1.0 | TROUGH | 1963 | 65.1 | 68.3 | +7.3 | +6.8 | 35.2 | 15.2 |
| | PEAK | 1964 | 64.8 | 67.3 | +10.1 | +9.5 | 37.6 | |
| 1.2 | TROUGH | 1967 | 66.4 | 68.3 | 0.0 | -0.5 | 45.4 | |
| | PEAK | 1969 | 66.1 | 66.8 | +12.2 | +10.3 | 50.4 | |
| 2.1 | TROUGH | 1971 | 69.1 | 68.7 | +12.6 | +10.6 | 64.9 | |
| | PEAK | 1973 | 70.7 | 69.8 | +12.6 | +9.0 | 77.8 | |
| | TROUGH | 1975 | 72.3 | 71.4 | +3.5 | +3.6 | 94.8 | |
| 4.6 | PEAK | 1976 | 71.3 | 70.1 | +6.5 | +3.9 | 100.0 | 6.1 |
| | TROUGH | 1977 | 71.5 | 70.0 | +7.1 | +5.9 | 107.0 | |
| 4.1 | PEAK | 1979 | 70.8 | 68.6 | +7.5 | +7.9 | 119.1 | |
| | | 1980 | 71.8 | 69.3 | +7.9 | +6.4 | 126.9 | |

Notes: (a) 1950–1960 excl. West Berlin and Saarland.    (b) Constant 1970 employment structure.

Sources: Derived from Adam, p.27;   BMA, Tables 1.5, 1.10, 1.11, 2.10 and 5.1.

terms of the growth in national income per head (at
factor cost) of the total economically active population compared to the growth in average gross income
per employee (Adam, pp.26-27). In the first two
cycles (1950-54 and 1954-58) national income per head
of the economically active rose more rapidly. In the
next four cycles - 1959-1963, 1963-67, 1967-1971 and
1971-75 - income per employee rose faster. Finally
in 1975-77 national income per economically active
person grew more rapidly. By 1980, the unadjusted
share of labour in the national income was 71.8 per
cent, leaving 15.2 per cent for the self-employed,
5.3 per cent as income from capital and land, and 7.7
per cent corporate 'profits' (IdDW, Table 16).

The distributional picture now emerging still
has to take account of the State and consumer credit.
In order to remedy this shortcoming, it is advisable
to subtract labour's unadjusted share from net
national product at factor cost. The gross income
stream which remains increased by 12.8 per cent in
1976, but 1.4 per cent in 1980. In 1981 it probably
fell by 1.1 per cent (WSI, *Pressedienst*, 8/82). Because of this decrease, average tax liability also
fell, so that the net income stream was higher than
in 1980. Then the large borrowing requirement and
high nominal and real interest rates must be taken
into account. If this growing cost of servicing the
national debt is added to the net income stream, along
with the interest-payment stream from consumer credit,
the provisional estimates indicate an increase of 4.7
and 2.3 per cent in 1980 and 1981 respectively.

Various distributional features mentioned in this
book so far may now be summarised. West German trade
unions became increasingly concerned to achieve a more
equal distribution of factor incomes (Donges, p.188).
Real wages in industry moved to the top rank compared
to other OECD countries. But the real wage push
petered out at the end of the review period. Nevertheless, profits were squeezed by both the real wage
push and, after 1973, the oil-price explosion and
appreciation in the DM exchange rate. In many cases,
however, this reduction of profits started from quite
a comfortable position. Finally, relatively high
factor incomes led to increasing competition from
labour-intensive industries in developing countries
and the need for structural adjustment.

Capital ownership remains highly concentrated:
86 per cent of productive assets (business assets and
shares) are owned by only 20 per cent of the households. Private ownership of business enterprises,
real estate, bonds and equities, cash, savings

accounts and life insurance amounted to a total value
of DM 2,207 billion in 1973. Again, the 20 per cent
of the richest households owned the largest proportion - this time 78 per cent (Mierheim und Wicke,
quoted in *Die Zeit*, 45/78 and 46/78). Much of the
rest of this book will be devoted to this topic, but
for the moment the position of employees is examined.

Capital sharing has been seen as one method of
redressing this inequity. In 1976 there were perhaps
800 companies with some form of capital-sharing
scheme in operation (Gaugler, 1979, p.279). The
schemes in the majority of these firms had been introduced in the previous decade, although other schemes
had been in existence for 25 years or more. Almost
800,000 employees are involved in the various schemes;
they hold capital to a total value of DM 2.3 billion.
The growth in capital sharing has been particularly
marked in the joint-stock companies: 134 companies
out of a total of 2,000 have introduced schemes in
the last few years. Employee-shareholders in these
firms numbered 700,000 in 1976, with further subsequent expansion. But in order to redress the imbalance in capital ownership much more re-distribution
by means of capital-sharing would be necessary (*ibid.*,
p.285). On the other hand, the partial de-national-
isation of companies like Volkswagen was accompanied
by an effort to encourage the small shareholder (Owen
Smith, 1979, p.179).

Productivity and Labour Costs
It would not be accurate to conclude that there has
been no 'wage problem' in West Germany (Denton,
p.278). For one thing, the change in money wage rates
has generally outstripped the growth in productivity
since 1950. For another thing, the growth in fringe
benefits in the 1970s has created a labour cost
problem.

Once recovery was under way, the disparities
between money wage and productivity growth were at
first minimal. Even after 1955, when the gaps became
bigger, the trend did not give immediate cause for
policy concern. This was because the rise in wages
was more vigorous as output expanded but slackened as
the rate of expansion fell. But then the problem
grew gradually worse: wages started to outstrip productivity at the beginning and end of the cycle. In
its first three reports (1964, 1965 and 1966) the
Council of Economic Advisers recommended that guide-
lines based on productivity should be established for
wage negotiations (Denton, p.283). This practice was
initiated in 1967 when the government and both sides

of industry initiated regular talks on how to preserve stability during economic upsurges - the so-
called 'Concerted Action' phase (Owen Smith, 1981,
p.201). These talks were boycotted by the trade
unions in 1977 and abandoned thereafter, but there is
nowadays no shortage of lugubrious, even gratuitous,
advice before each wage round begins. During the
1970s the rise in gross employment income was considerably greater than the rise in productivity. The
rise in unit labour costs reflected this trend.
Table 6.13 summarises the contents of this paragraph.

Table 6.13: Determinants of Wage Inflation (Percentage Changes over Previous Year)

| Year | Gross income from employment per employee[a] | Productivity (GDRP per economically active persons)[b] | Aggregate unit labour costs (Wage costs per unit of output) |
|------|------|------|------|
| 1951[c] | +16.1 | +7.7 | +7.8 |
| 1955[c] | +8.1 | +8.0 | +0.1 |
| 1960[c] | +9.3 | +7.1 | +2.1 |
| 1965 | +9.5 | +5.0 | +4.2 |
| 1970 | +15.5 | +4.7 | +10.3 |
| 1975 | +7.8 | +1.6 | +6.1 |
| 1980 | +6.5 | +1.0 | +5.4 |
| (1981 | +5.4 | +0.6 | +4.7) |

Notes:
(a) Includes employers' social insurance contributions - see
BMWi, Table 2.13.
(b) Includes self-employed - see BMA, Tables 2.3 to 2.6.
(c) Excl. Saarland and West Berlin.

Source:   IdDW, Table 18.


This leads on to a consideration of the other
problem area, namely the increase in fringe benefits
during the 1970s. An illustration of the problem can
be given by making a more specific reference to what
has been said about the relative small rise in real
wage rates in 1979. Gross hourly earnings in the
chemical industry in that year increased by 4.6 per

cent. But due to an extra day's paid holiday and
increased sick fund contributions, the increase in
hourly wage costs was 6.7 per cent. Since 1970 gross
hourly earnings have risen by 107 per cent, whereas
hourly labour costs have increased by 130 per cent.
Hence, by 1980 for every DM 100 paid directly to employees, an additional DM 80 was necessary to meet
further costs. Saunders and Marsden (p.78) found
that in 1975 costs other than direct pay were 60 per
cent of hourly direct pay in the FRG, 30 per cent in
the UK but 100 per cent in Italy. However, the relatively high level of West German total labour costs
in value terms was shown in Table 4.9.

Also in 1979 employers in many sectors entered
into agreements to move away from the traditional
German practice of using age as the determinant of
holiday entitlement. Phased agreements were reached
so that by 1984 *all* employees in iron and steel,
mining, engineering, chemicals, textiles, clothing
and printing will be entitled to a standard six-week
holiday. Trade unions in the public and other sectors
have usually attempted to obtain similar improvements
to the sectors just mentioned. At the end of the review period five weeks paid annual holiday was already
quite commonplace in West Germany. Indeed, by 1981 a
quarter of all employees were entitled to six weeks
paid holiday.

In addition to the significant increases negotiated in paid holiday entitlement, a high percentage
of West German employees receive *extra* holiday pay
and/or an annual bonus known as the '13th month
salary'. The increase in the number of employees included in such agreements is indicated in Table 6.14.
Moreover, as will be shown in the next sub-section,
another source of increasing costs has been the reduction in the working week with no fall in the
weekly wage rate.

It is possible to conclude that both productivity and labour costs have increased rapidly in the
Federal Republic. This becomes even clearer when her
position relative to other industrialised nations is
viewed. Both her labour costs and productivity
levels tend to above those of her trading rivals. A
concomitant of this is that the growth of real wages
in West Germany has been internationally among the
highest: between 1975 and mid-1980 real wages (that
is after taking price increases but not taxation and
social security payments into account) increased by
13 per cent in France, 11 per cent in Germany, 8 per
cent in Japan and 2 per cent in the UK. They fell
by 3 and 4 per cent respectively in the USA and

Table 6.14:   Percentage of Employees Receiving Extra
Holiday Pay and/or an Annual Bonus

| Percentage of Monthly Salary | Percentage of Employees | | |
|---|---|---|---|
| | 1976 | 1978 | 1980 |
| Less than 30 | 15 | 14 | 14 |
| 30  -   60 | 18 | 19 | 3 |
| 60  -   90 | 10 | 8 | 20 |
| 90  -  120 | 49 | 50 | 52 |
| 120  and more | 9 | 9 | 11 |

Source:   Incomes Data Services Limited, *International
Report*, No.142.

and Sweden.   Living standards in the UK in 1977 were
something like 60 per cent of the level in the Federal Republic.

The Supply of Hours and Persons
In 1980, 94 per cent of all employees covered by
collective agreements worked a *standard* (that is,
excluding overtime) 40-hour week;   the other 6 per
cent - mostly in hotel and catering, food, transport
and agriculture - worked between 41 and 43 hours a
week.   A phased reduction of hours to 40 per week was
scheduled over the following few years for some
200,000 workers.   Perhaps it should be emphasised for
British readers that it is not the normal pattern outside the UK for blue- and white-collar workers to have
different standard hours of work.   Hence the 40-hour
standard working week in West Germany applies to both
white-collar and manual employees.
        Progress towards the shorter working without loss
of pay was at first slow.   In 1950 the length of the
average standard working week for both manual and
white-collar employees was 48 hours.   It was again in
the 'metal industry' where the first break-through
was made:   in October 1956 agreement was reached to
reduce the standard working week to 45 hours.   This
agreement was then generally followed throughout the
economy.   The 40-hour week was introduced from 1975
onwards (BMA, *Gesellschaftliche Daten*, 1979, pp.138-
139).
        On average, *actual* paid hours for manual workers,
that is including overtime, were 41.2 in January 1981.
An average figure for one country or industry should,

however, be used with care since some employees may
be working a considerable amount of overtime and
others none at all.  Moreover, accurate inter-country
comparisons are extremely difficult to make.  If
annual hours of work are used to compare countries
then not only weekly hours of work but also differences in annual and public holidays are taken into
account.  Towards the end of the review period, IDS
(*International Report*, No.152) quoted an EEC survey
which indicated that annual hours worked per employee
in the Federal Republic numbered 1,716, compared to
1,969 in the UK, 1,785 in France and 1,643 in Italy.
In terms of *potential* and *actual* working days per
employee in 1980, the standard working week of 40
hours produced 250 and 200 working days respectively
(IdDW, Table 19).  The difference arose from subtracting holidays (28 working days), sickness (13 working
days) and short-time (9 working days).

At the end of the 1970s, the 35-hour week was a
live social and political issue in the Federal Republic.  There were two strands in the trade unions'
argument: first, that it was socially desirable on
health grounds to reduce the working week for older
workers, as well as to relieve the monotony for shift,
piecework and production-line workers.  The second
strand of the argument asserted that it was equally
desirable on employment policy grounds to reduce the
length of the working week of those in employment as
a method of creating work for the unemployed.  In
other words reducing the supply of *hours* per head of
the labour force, increases the supply of *persons*.
Both strands of the argument influenced IG Metall's
bargaining stance in the somewhat bitter wrangle
which took place in the iron and steel industry during the 1979 wage round.  The eventual outcome was
the phased introduction of a six-week paid holiday
and rest periods or extra time off for night-shift
workers and older employees.  This agreement was subsequently used in the 1980 wage round as a model for
numerous others, both in industry and the public
sector.  In the case of the public sector agreements
it was explicitly recognised as a step towards the
35-hour week.

A number of objections to these trends were
raised.  At the macro-economic level, the Council of
Economic Advisers found it a paradox that fewer hours
were being worked when the (oil price-induced) current
account deficits demanded higher output levels.  At
the micro-level, an employer's spokesman expressed
the view that reducing the older employees' working
week would have little effect on unemployment levels,

since there was already a shortage of skilled workers. Bottlenecks and other interruptions to the work flow would therefore be compensated for by utilising more (stressful) overtime working for younger workers and these increased costs would lead to a fall in investment and even less job creation. Nevertheless, given the importance of the work-sharing issue, the next few paragraphs attempt to isolate the main implications.

Ott attempted to model the implications of a reduction in working time as a means of job creation:

$$Nh = Ah_v$$

where N = the employed labour force
h = the current working week
A = the employed (N) + unemployed (U) labour force
$h_v$ = the reduced working week required to eliminate unemployment.

By transformation:

$$\frac{h_v}{h} = \frac{N}{A} = \frac{N}{N+U} \text{ and } h_v = \frac{Nh}{A}.$$

The approximate data for West Germany were:

N = 21 million
h = 40 hours
U = 1 million.

Hence to arrive at $h_v$:

$$\frac{21 \text{ million} \times 40 \text{ hours}}{22 \text{ million}} = 38.18 \text{ or, rounded,}$$
$$38 \text{ hours.}$$

Ott postulates that employers would stipulate constant hourly labour costs, although the increase in indirect labour costs would effectively raise costs. But since unemployment benefit payments would decrease, effective demand could fall. An alternative to money wage cuts for those already employed would be to allow the price level to rise. Whether this reduction in real wages would lead to an expansion of output, or whether the latter causes the former, is a Keynes v Classic issue. Finally, decreasing the number of hours worked tends to raise productivity as was demonstrated by the maintenance of output levels during the three day week in Britain

in the early 1970s (Blyton and Hill, p.42). In other
words, effort per hour is not a constant. However,
if hourly wage costs are to remain constant, hourly
wage rates must be reduced by:

$$\frac{38 - 40}{40} \times 100 = -5 \text{ per cent.}$$

Moreover, if productivity is increasing per time
period, given constant hourly costs, the absorption
of the unemployed by reducing the working week would
result in a constant hourly wage rate for those already in employment *plus* an increase in output requiring a corresponding expansion of demand. Consider
an increase of 10 per cent in productivity, an increase in employment by 10 per cent, and a reduction
of the working week by 9.1 per cent:

$$h_v = \frac{N \times h}{A} = \frac{100 \times 40 \text{ hours}}{110} = 36.36 \text{ hours}$$

$$\therefore \frac{36.36 - 40}{40} \times 100 = -9.1 \text{ per cent.}$$

At a constant hourly wage rate of, say, 0.6875 units:

        110 x 36.36 = 4,000 total weekly hours worked
                        (constant)
but     4,000 x 1.1 = 4,400 units of output per week
                        (increased)
and     4,000 x 0.6875 = 2,750 total weekly wage bill
                        (constant).

(Blyton and Hill (p.43) assume that output remains
unchanged, but that the reduction in the working
week by 10 per cent allows employment to increase by
1 per cent.)
       A fairly obvious criticism of the model, Ott
goes on to argue, is the feasibility of trade unions
accepting either money wage cuts or constant money
wages rates when productivity is rising. Perhaps
the benefits of rising productivity should be 'shared'
by increasing wage rates slightly but also reducing
the working week. Secondly, the structural nature of
unemployment - by region, occupation, sex and age -
would not necessarily be attenuated by reducing the
working week. Thirdly, technical indivisibilities
may constrain any increase in the numbers employed -
for example, each employee in a particular firm may
require one lathe. Fourthly, there will be a minimum
size of firm in which it will be possible to increase

the number employed by reducing the working week,
although paradoxically this constraint diminishes as
unemployment rises. In the case of a reduction to
38 hours, 19 is the minimum employment level:

$$19 \times 40 = 760 \text{ hours per week}$$
$$19 \times 38 = 722 \text{ hours per week}$$
$$760 - 722 = 38 \text{ hours per week.}$$

Finally, if the policy of reducing the working week
to increase employment is a short-run anti-cyclical
measure, then flexibility of working hours upwards
would be required during periods of economic expansion and low unemployment.

Some of these objections are removed if the more
specific notion of job-sharing is introduced. Such a
working method again combines increasing numbers and
reducing working hours. But two or more employees
share the responsibilities of one full-time post,
dividing the hours between them on a daily, weekly or
monthly basis. Job-sharing as a method of reducing
unemployment has received the full support of the
Federal Labour Office, just as the less sophisticated
method of generally reducing working-time did. It is
thought that job-sharing would be a particularly viable measure for combatting rising female unemployment at a time when females account for more than
half of the unemployed labour force.

Job-sharing has to be distinguished from short-
time working where *existing* employees *temporarily*
agree to reduce working hours in order to maintain
employment levels during a downward fluctuation in
demand. Moreover, the Social Democrats and trade
unions have expressed serious reservations about job-
sharing on grounds of its lack of flexibility for the
employee - an aspirant part-time worker may often not
be in a position to extend his or her hours to cover
for an absent partner, and only about one in five unemployed persons is seeking part-time employment.
The unions have added that if job-sharing is to make
any contribution towards relieving unemployment, then
new jobs must be created rather than existing full-
time ones split. On the other hand, the Christian
and Free Democrats support the notion of job-sharing.
Indeed, the former have drawn up their own model, as
have the chemical industry employers (IDS, *International Report*, No.151).

Although the long-term aim of IG Metall remains
the 35-hour week, increasing interest was also shown
in early retirement schemes. The union is in favour
of its members being able to retire at 60. They

should receive 90 per cent of their former net earnings until they reach the age of 63 - the earliest
age at which males are eligible for West Germany's
flexible retirement age scheme. A quarter of all
first-time male pensioners in 1979 had retired under
this state scheme. Moreover, although the jobs of
workers over 55 are legally protected, many employers
were encouraging their employees in this age group to
effectively take early retirement by making up the
difference between their unemployment insurance and
their earnings on leaving.

CONCLUSION

Like other industrial economies, then, the Federal
Republic faced a growing unemployment problem at the
beginning of the 1980s. The duration of time spent
on the dole is also growing. The social and private
costs of unemployment are high. Unregistered unemployment makes the problem worse. At the other extreme, the black economy continues to prosper. However, it is inconceivable that there will be sufficient economic growth to ameliorate the policy
problem of unemployment. The expansion of labour-
using productive capacity has plummeted from being
the largest to the lowest component of total capital
investment. The new major components - rationalisation and labour-saving capital investment - are
exacerbating the unemployment problem. Increasing
training costs and fringe benefits are also likely to
reduce employment prospects. Hence, radical demand-
side improvements in the labour market are unlikely
to occur. Policy prescriptions are accordingly somewhat limited, apart from the fairly obvious need to
identify future employment growth areas and assess
their needs. For example, have the relatively small
and medium-sized business undertakings of Baden-
Württemberg resulted in higher employment growth than
the large units in North Rhine-Westphalia, and do
such small units require more financial assistance in
marketing rather than in technological areas?
    Returning to the supply-side, therefore, viable
policy alternatives seem to be a continued reduction
in both the optional retirement age and the working
week. In addition, increases in job-sharing, the
ages at which full-time education is completed, holiday entitlements and, where necessary, short-time
working may ameliorate unemployment. Moreover,
structural reforms will be necessary to remove hard
core unemployment, as well as correcting the mis-

197

match in vocational training and the skills required
in the labour market. Even if in this latter context
education is treated as a purely capital good with no
leisure implications, there is a need to fundamentally tackle the constraints placed on occupational
mobility by social class (Lydall, Ch.8(3); Phelps
Brown. Ch.7). The two scholarly studies of Lydall
and Phelps Brown put beyond doubt that, to quote the
former (pp.263-264), individuals are somewhat un-
equally endowed at birth, but their environment and
education steadily widen the differences so that the
spread of their earnings also grows. The economic
need for such reform stems from the belief that
human capital formation requires more attention and
support than investment in physical capital assets.

In other words, the central question is one of
resolving the problems created by a growing hard core
of unemployment. Before the beginning of the 1981
pay round, an IG Metall spokesman saw a 'powder keg'
of wider socio-political issues for the 1980s in
terms of declining employment opportunties, long-term
unemployment and increasing relative poverty for many.
This had to be weighed against more leisure and a
more equitable distribution of income for all. He
thought that the solution would be found by either
confrontation or negotiation. As such the problem
of unemployment concerns the whole industrial world.
The stark policy choice lies between totally demoral-
ising both the young and the old by allowing present
unemployment patterns and trends to continue, or
shortening the working day, the working week, the
working year and the working life without proportionate income compensation (also see Blyton).

Allied to the unemployment problem is the amount
of repetitiveness, boredom, stress and humiliation
which constitutes most daily work experience. While
more and better education may improve the individual's
chance of rising above such working conditions it does
not remove them. In any case, many problems lie beyond the educational system: according to one investigation only 30 per cent of unemployed young people
aged 20 and below had successfully completed their
vocational education (Pettman and Fyfe, p.58).

Since 1975 the Federal Government has made
efforts in various directions to improve working
conditions within the framework of its official
'humanisation of working life' programme. The official who was in charge of the programme from 1975
to 1980 has suggested that it has made a contribution to the increasing interest in, and research
into, the organisation of work, developing qualifi-

cations and increasing employee participation in decision-making (WSI, *Pressedienst*, 5/81). One important piece of research under the Federal 'humanisation of work' programme was conducted by the Chemical Workers' Union (*IG Chemie*). The project was concerned with shift-work and was begun in March 1979. A basic dilemma was brought out by the results. On the one hand, although shift-work in the industry is in any case widespread, 65 per cent of the shift workers in the sample responded that they had commenced shift work for financial reasons (IG Chemie, (i) pp.134-135, (ii) p.7). On the other hand, the unattractive domestic, social and health consequences of shift-work were convincingly illustrated by the survey (*ibid.*, (i) pp.199-216, (ii) pp.17-20 and 28).

The official IG Chemie view is that the financial advantages of shift and night work are outweighed by the disadvantages of extra pressure and risk of accidents. Moreover, complex long-term staff planning should be undertaken so that more day work could be made available to older workers, who might be less able to stand up to the stress of night work. The German trade unions' federation is also disturbed about many aspects of industrial disease. For example, it has recently pressed for the addition of noise-induced conditions such as high blood pressure and psychosomatic illnesses to the list of recognised industrial diseases.

Not surprisingly, therefore, the main conclusions of this chapter lie in the fields of employment policy and improving job satisfaction. But it is now time to turn to the organisation and structure of banking and industry in the Federal Republic.

Chapter Seven

THE FORMS AND IMPLICATIONS OF OWNERSHIP AND CONTROL

INTRODUCTION

Now that a picture of income and wealth distribution
has been established it is possible in this relatively short chapter to move on to the forms of business ownership. This is necessary because in both
the banking and the industrial sectors the legal
forms of ownership are quite manifold. Moreover, the
holders of shares in the largest companies fall into
four equally varied categories (Rutherford, p.29;
Vogl, p.43). First, the financial institutions,
mainly the large banks, own strategically placed
blocks of shares. Secondly, there are powerful and
rich families with holdings in important companies.
Among the most important families are the Flicks,
owners of one of the largest companies in West Germany. Others include the Quandts, the Fincks and the
Haniels. Such a list is far from exhaustive. For
that matter, it does not include the families or
individuals such as Siemens (founded in the mid-
nineteenth century) and Grundig (founded after the
Second World War) whose companies played a vital role
in technical innovation and exports. Neither does it
take account of the foundations (*Stiftungen*) to which
families like Bosch and Thyssen hived off respectively 85 and 11 per cent of their shares (Rutherford,
pp.44-45). (The demise of the influence of the
Krupps family will be traced in the next chapter.)
Thirdly, there are assorted types of Federal, Länder
and local authority organisations (Owen Smith, 1979).
Fourthly, there is the traditional owner of a small
shareholding, although it will be shown, again in the
next chapter, that the large banks often exercise
influence on behalf of this latter group.
     When the legal forms of ownership have been
examined, therefore, the structure of large companies

will be analysed.

## LEGAL FORMS OF OWNERSHIP

Figure 7.1 demonstrates that the first important distinction which must be made is between the usually
small one-man (or family) businesses and the various
corporate bodies. The corporate bodies themselves
may, in turn, be divided into partnerships and companies. Some of the larger family-owned companies
are registered in the form of partnerships. However,
most of the very large companies in West Germany are
AGs, that is full public companies with limited liability and quoted shares. The private and unquoted
limited liability companies (GmbH) are usually much
smaller than AGs, although some holding companies,
and firms in trust-ownership such as Robert Bosch,
have taken the GmbH form. There are also some large
share-quoted partnerships (KGaA). The Flick family
holding company is now a KGaA, although for most of
the period under review it was a KG.

## THE CAPITAL STRUCTURE OF LARGE COMPANIES

The share capital structure of the AG and GmbH differ
somewhat (Mueller, 1978, pp.56 and 60). The minimum
share capital of the AG is DM 100,000, whereas that
of the GmbH was DM 20,000. (The GmbHs share capital
is not denominated in equal units and under the 1981
GmbH Act the minimum share capital was increased to
DM 50,000.) But the *Grundkapital* (share capital) of
the AG also differs from the *Stammkapital* (permanent
capital) of the GmbH, since the latter measures the
extent of the capital contributed (*Stammeinlage*).
However, the sheer relative size of the average AG
is apparent from Tables 7.1 and 7.2. For example,
2,000 AGs (rounded) have almost the same total capital as 256,000 GmbHs. When industry alone is taken,
the 876 AGs have a larger capital than the 80,686
GmbHs - and industry in both cases is the largest
user of capital. Further, 60 per cent (155,000) of
the GmbHs out of the total of 256,000 have a permanent capital of under DM 20,000. These smaller GmbH
predominate in the non-industrial sector. It was
really the relatively few large GmbHs which proved
problematical on disclosure grounds until the Acts
of 1971 and 1981. In order to encourage smaller
companies to approach the stock exchange, the Bundesbank (*Annual Report*, 1981, p.22) would like to see

Figure 7.1: Various Forms of Ownership in West Germany

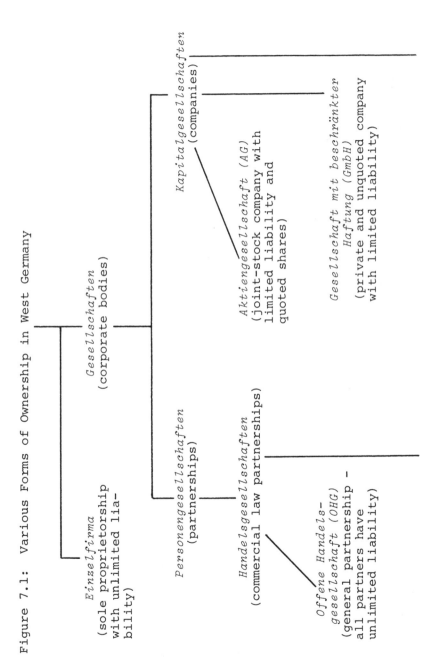

*Einzelfirma*
(sole proprietorship with unlimited liability)

*Gesellschaften*
(corporate bodies)

*Kapitalgesellschaften*
(companies)

*Aktiengesellschaft (AG)*
(joint-stock company with limited liability and quoted shares)

*Gesellschaft mit beschränkter Haftung (GmbH)*
(private and unquoted company with limited liability)

*Personengesellschaften*
(partnerships)

*Handelsgesellschaften*
(commercial law partnerships)

*Offene Handelsgesellschaft (OHG)*
(general partnership – all partners have unlimited liability)

*Kommanditgesellschaft (KG)*
(managing partners - *Komplementäre* - have unlimited liability, while other partners - *Kommadisten* - are liable only to the extent of their commitment. The latter also have a more limited role in running the firm.)

*Kommanditgesellschaft auf Aktien (KGaA)*
(general partnership with unlimited liability of managing partners but with quoted shares)

*GmbH (or AG) & Co KG*
(one or more companies are the sole managing partners with 'unlimited' liability)

In addition, there are publicly-owned undertakings, co-operatives and both mutual insurance and building loan associations. Many public-sector undertakings register their subsidiaries in the AG, GmbH or GmbH & Co form. Subsidiaries of the co-operative banks are registered as *eigentragene Genossenschaften (eG)* - i.e. registered co-operatives with or without limited liability.

Sources: based on Lawrence, pp.30-31; MK, I, II, III and IV; Mueller, 1978, p.49.

Table 7.1: Size Distribution of Companies (GmbH), 1980

| Sector | Total | | Companies with a permanent capital from ... to ... inclusive (DM) | | | | | | | | | | |
| | Number | Permanent capital (DM million) | Below 20000 | | 20000-100000 | | 100000 - 1 mil. | | 1 - 5 mil. | | 5 - 10 mil. | | Over 10 mil. | |
| | | | Number | Permanent capital | Number | Permanent capital | Number | Permanent capital | Number | Permanent capital | Number | Permanent capital | Number | Permanent capital |
| Agriculture, Forestry and Fishing | 1213 | 135.9 | 736 | 14.7 | 363 | 18.8 | 88 | 29.6 | 24 | 56.8 | 2 | 16.0 | – | – |
| Industry | 80686 | 51497.5 | 44415 | 884.5 | 23816 | 1330.7 | 8592 | 3433.5 | 2429 | 6449.1 | 649 | 4944.2 | 785 | 34455.5 |
| Other sectors | 174041 | 47426.5 | 109813 | 2189.8 | 48164 | 2586.3 | 12694 | 4666.1 | 2301 | 5702.8 | 506 | 3836.0 | 563 | 28445.5 |
| Totals | 255940 | 99059.9 | 154964 | 3089.0 | 72343 | 3935.9 | 21374 | 8129.2 | 4754 | 12208.8 | 1157 | 8716.2 | 1348 | 62901.0 |

Source: Extracted from *Statistische Jahrbuch für die BRD*, 1981, Table 7.4, pp.116-117 (writer's translation).

Table 7.2: Size Distribution of Companies (AG; KGaA), 1980 (includes 28 KGaA with share capital of DM 1842.7 million)

| Sector | Total | | Companies with a share capital from ... to ... inclusive (DM million) | | | | | | | | | | | |
|---|---|---|---|---|---|---|---|---|---|---|---|---|---|---|
| | | | Below 1 | | 1 – 10 | | 10 – 50 | | 50 – 100 | | 100 – 250 | | Over 250 | |
| | Number | Share capital (DM million) | Number | Share capital | Number | Share capital | Number | Share capital | Number | Share capital | Number | Share capital | Number | Share capital |
| Agriculture, Forestry and Fishing | 5 | 46.3 | – | – | 4 | 13.3 | 1 | 33.0 | – | – | – | – | – | – |
| Industry | 876 | 59803.9 | 99 | 51.4 | 357 | 1631.1 | 228 | 5554.2 | 80 | 6149.2 | 57 | 8969.6 | 55 | 37448.5 |
| Other sectors | 1260 | 32170.5 | 365 | 148.4 | 504 | 2202.9 | 263 | 6432.3 | 65 | 4700.5 | 42 | 6197.3 | 21 | 12489.0 |
| Totals | 2141 | 92021.7 | 464 | 199.8 | 865 | 3847.3 | 492 | 12019.4 | 145 | 10849.7 | 99 | 15166.9 | 76 | 49937.5 |

Source: Extracted from *Statistisches Jahrbuch für die BRD*, 1981, Table 7.3, pp.114-115 (writer's translation).

further reforms of both company and tax laws.
The various generalisations made so far are supported by the data in Table 7.3. It is, for example,
apparent that about 65 per cent of the top 100 enterprises in the Federal Republic are of the AG form.
When the other two types of companies (GmbH and KGaA)
are added to the AG the proportion in both 1978 and
1980 reached 87 per cent. Further, of the ten partnerships and sole proprietorships, only the Oetker
family business was an industrial concern (MK, III,
para.325). Nevertheless an investigation of the
ownership of West Germany's 100 largest companies
will give valuable insights.

Table 7.3:  Legal Forms of the Top 100 Enterprises

| Legal form | Number of companies | | | | |
|---|---|---|---|---|---|
| | 1972 | 1974 | 1976 | 1978 | 1980 |
| Sole proprietors | 2 | 3 | 2 | 2 | – |
| AG | 68 | 65 | 68 | 66 | 66 |
| KGaA | 1 | 2 | 2 | 3 | 3 |
| GmbH | 17 | 19 | 17 | 18 | 18 |
| OHG | 1 | 2 | 2 | 1 | 1 |
| KG | 6 | 5 | 3 | 4 | 7 |
| GmbH & Co KG | 2 | 2 | 3 | 3 | 2 |
| Others | 3 | 2 | 3 | 3 | 3 |
| Total | 100 | 100 | 100 | 100 | 100 |

Note:
The Monopolies Commission has observed on the relative stability over time in the legal position of
ownership (II, para.265 and III, para.325). Even
under the slightly different criteria employed in
1980 (IV, para.422), this generalisation remains
valid.

Source:  MK, III, para.324 and IV, para.421.

The Monopolies Commission regularly undertakes
an analysis of the Top 100 companies. Its 1978
anaylsis relied on capital ownership, whereas in 1980
shares in value added were used. In 1978 individuals
and families (excluding Stiftungen) had interests in
28 of the top 100 enterprises. In 15 cases these
interests amounted to ownership of over 50 per cent

of the enterprises involved (MK, III, para.332). In
no case did the banks have direct shareholdings of
over 50 per cent, although 22 of their 26 holdings
lay in the 25 to 50 per cent category. State-owned
holdings in the top 100 totalled 16, of which 6 were
over 50 per cent. Another interesting category,
about which a little more will be said in the next
chapter, is the 13 foreign-owned holdings of 50 per
cent and less. These include two holdings by the
Iran government of just over 25 per cent in Friedrich
Krupp GmbH and Deutsche Babcock AG. Kuwait holds
about 14 per cent of the shares in Daimler-Benz AG,
having purchased the Quandt holdings in 1975. The
same country may have expanded its holdings in the
Hoechst chemical combine to just over the crucial 25
per cent level. Yet another interesting category,
this time in 1980 (using value added), was two
companies owned by the trade unions (MK, IV, para.
439).

Finally, a wide range of ownership was reported
by the Monopolies Commission (MK) for 31 enterprises.
This diverse range of ownership applied to over 50
per cent of the holdings in 19 cases. But these 19
included Deutsche Babcock (MK, III, para.342). Also
included in the 19 was Volkswagen AG which is still
40 per cent state-owned and this company will be
used as a 'case study' later in this chapter. The
two other companies to be partially denationalised in
the 1960s - Preussag AG and VEBA AG - were in the
group of 19 (Owen Smith, 1979, p.179). There were
two family firms among the 19, too. They were Thyssen
AG and Siemens AG, although the holdings of the latter
family have decreased over the years (Rutherford,
p.42). Among the most diversified companies in terms
of ownership - with over 80 per cent of their shares
held in small amounts - were the three chemical companies (BASF AG, Hoechst AG and Bayer AG - MK, III,
para.342; Rutherford, p.30). But it should be recalled that the banks often act on behalf of the
small shareholder. In the case of BASF, which for
most of the 1970s was the largest of the three chemical combines, the Deutsche Bank was entrusted with
more than 25 per cent of these proxy votes (MK, II,
para.552). There may be a similar situation at Bayer
(*Die Zeit*, 23/82, p.17). Hence the need to examine
this system of control in the next chapter. At the
moment, however, it is necessary to review some other
general aspects of ownership and control.

Banks and holding companies which are GmbHs are
nowadays subject to statutory supervision (Mueller,
1978, p.59; Vogl, p.65). Moreover, the GmbH with

over 500 employees, and all AG, have a 'two-tier'
board system. Without pre-judging the intricate relationships between the two boards, therefore, it is
necessary first to consider their functions in isolation. The management board of the GmbH is a
*Geschäftsführung*, while the AG has a *Vorstand*. In
both cases the supervisory board is an *Aufsichtsrat*.
As its name implies, the management board is responsible for day-to-day executive decision-making, while
the supervisory board meets about four times a year
to represent shareholders, inspect accounts, approve
long-term investment projects, and, where necessary,
elect or re-elect members of the management board
(Lawrence, p.39 and pp.40-41; Shonfield, p.248 and
pp.251-252). (In addition to the two statutory
boards, many banks have an advisory board which in
the case of the Big Three consists of invited representatives from major industrial and commercial
undertakings.)
    When the British glass company Pilkington ac-
quired a majority interest in the profitable Flachglas AG (see Chapter 9), it was somewhat frustrated
by its inability to exert direct control over the
management board, even though it was represented on
the supervisory board (*Financial Times*, 15 March
1982). Perhaps only routine functions are delegated:
'In the traditional German organisation (there is) a
"hierarchy of labour" underneath board level; in the
USA the distinction between labour and management
would be drawn at much lower hierarchical levels'
(Dyas and Thanheiser, p.104). Decentralisation was
therefore rare in West German companies during the
1950s. There were some permanent changes in this
situation during the 1960s, but the initial enthusiasm faded somewhat and gave way to a renewed consciousness of German tradition (*ibid.*, p.128). Following
the Pilkington takeover of Flachglas top executives
on both sides were, perhaps necessarily, deeply involved in integrating the two companies. It was the
Pilkington chairman, however, who referred to transferring responsibility to 'second level people' -
executives one level down from the board.
    However, the supervisory board also elects its
own chairman who at times of financial crises, takeover bids and similar episodes in a company's evolution becomes an extremely influential individual.
During such periods the AGM and the whole of the
supervisory board may also become involved. The
supervisory board is in turn elected by both the
shareholders (at the AGM) and employees. As the
writer has shown in more detail elsewhere (1981,

pp.183-185 and 202-204), the Co-determination Acts of
1951 and 1976, as well as the Works Constitution Act
of 1952, are the statutes governing employee participation on supervisory boards. Basically, the 1951
Act requires that 50 per cent of the supervisory
boards in the coal, iron and steel industries must be
elected by employees. From 1976, the same proportion
applied to all companies (including GmbHs) with over
2,000 employees. Similarly, all companies with between 500 and 2,000 employees were required to have
one-third representation elected by their employees.
Employees also have an intricate system of representation through their works councils (Owen Smith, 1981,
pp.194-195). But works councils are not immediately
relevant to the present discussion. This is because
they usually react to the long-term policy decisions
made elsewhere.

Company law also requires that the approval of
75 per cent of the shareholders is necessary for
certain actions. Hence, any institution holding 25.1
per cent of a company's shares is in a position to
veto major company decisions (Vogl, p.43). This power
of veto is what institutions may seek and they often
content themselves with a holding of this magnitude.
Clearly, this level of influence may only normally be
gained in the share-quoted AG. Indeed, as Vogl
suggests (pp.65-66) the reason for many companies remaining GmbH is to avoid such influence.


SOME IMPLICATIONS FOR DECISION-TAKING

There are thus three locations of long-term policy
decision-making at company level: the management and
supervisory boards, and the AGM. In a sense it would
be wrong to think of these institutions as being a
hierarchy, as the experience of the motor vehicle
industry exemplifies.

In spite of their undoubted economic success,
all three of the major German-owned motor vehicle
companies - Volkswagen AG, Daimler-Benz AG and BMW
AG - have been to varying degrees the scenes of power
struggles, and their policies have been influenced by
minority shareholders (Dyas and Thanheiser, p.81).
For example, by the late 1950s BMW had liquidity difficulties and the Deutsche Bank executives who were
respectively chairmen of the BMW and Daimler-Benz
supervisory boards proposed that the two companies
should merge (Rutherford, p.39). But the small shareholders of BMW resisted the proposal at an unusually
bitter and protracted AGM. (AGMs are normally fairly

lengthy affairs, which are well attended social
occasions - Vogl, p.57.) After the 1959 BMW AGM,
however, the merger plans were allowed to lapse and
the Quandts became key shareholders. Under the guidance of the new member of the management board (Paul
Hahnemann) sales rocketed - they nearly doubled between 1960 and 1963 (when the company paid its first
post-war dividend), and then grew at an average
annual rate of 23 per cent between 1963 and 1972.
But a new chief executive of the management board was
appointed by Quandt in 1969, and sales executive
Hahnemann was obliged to tender his resignation to
Quandt in 1971. This event remains shrouded in
mystery.

Other chief executives were appointed at an in-
opportune time from the point of view of their future careers. Kurt Lotz of Volkswagen was a good
example. In 1968, he succeeded the legendary Professor Heinrich Nordhoff who had been appointed by
the British in 1948 (Hartrich, p.219). But in spite
of the phenomenal success of the Beetle, Nordhoff
left a narrow product range, heavily dependent on
exports. True, Audi was acquired in 1965, in order
to move up-market. Nevertheless, the VW supervisory
and management boards were at odds about future strategy. Further, the attempt in 1969 to purchase NSU
and merge it with Audi ran into opposition from minority shareholders at NSU (Vogl, pp.58-59). Again,
there were protracted AGMs, this time with legal
representation and threats of law suits. All this
unfavourable publicity, especially bearing in mind
that VW was still 40 per cent public-owned, was an
important reason for Lotz's dismissal in 1971. His
successor, Rudolf Leiding, had been in charge of Audi
and the remaining NSU shareholders almost immediately
accepted a substantially revised VW offer for their
shares.

Between 1971 and 1974 Leiding introduced new
models and on two occasions forced the supervisory
board to dismiss colleagues on the management board
who disagreed with him. Leiding himself left in the
middle of a slump when VW ran up nearly DM 1 billion
in losses over the two year period 1974 and 1975.
He had made himself unpopular with the majority of
the supervisory board, particularly when he appealed
over the heads of the unions for wage restraint
(*Fortune Magazine*, 13 August 1979, p.121). Perhaps
like Lotz before him, he had also underestimated the
influence of the Federal and Lower Saxony SPD governments who are part-owners of VW (Vogl, p.52).

Leiding was replaced by Toni Schmücker, who in

turn was forced by heart trouble to resign in 1981.
His replacement was Carl Horst Hahn. There were two
remarkable aspects about Hahn's appointment by the
VW supervisory board. First, he was one of the members of the VW management board dismissed by the then
supervisory board in 1972 on the insistence of
Leiding. He had been at VW under Nordhoff since 1959.
Secondly, he had subsequently been chief executive of
Conti-Gummi - a tyre group which he pulled back from
near-bankruptcy. Shareholders there received their
first dividend for eight years just prior to Hahn's
re-appointment to VW, although after his departure
profits fell again. This experience should surely
stand him in good stead for the 1980s, for after five
profitable years, VW was again almost in the red by
1981. In this sense Hahn's appointment resembled
that of Schmücker, since the latter re-organised the
roubled Rheinstahl company before joining VW at the
time of the 1975 financial crisis. He was persuaded
to take the VW job by the newly-elected chairman of
the VW supervisory board (Hans Birnbaum). Birnbaum
was also chief executive of the state-owned Saltz-
gitter steel plant which was not only situated near
to the main VW plant at Wolfsburg, but also gave
Birnbaum links within the rationalising steel industry.

   Daimler-Benz was closely associated with the
Flick group, which owned 38 per cent of the company
(Dyas and Thanheiser, p.81). Quandt held another 14
per cent and the Deutsche Bank 31 per cent. These
three owners disagreed among themselves, but their
company was significant among motor vehicle manufacturers in that it remained highly profitable at
the end of the 1970s (*Business Week*, 20 July 1981,
p.100). Foreign-owned holdings in Daimler-Benz have
already been mentioned and a little more will be said
about the changes in ownership of this company in the
next chapter.

   Having assembled the paramount features of ownership and control, the analysis can now draw some conclusions.


CONCLUSION

The rich variety in types of ownership and influence
in West Germany render simple generalisations invalid.
   In any case, reliable information about the extent of family ownership and family management is not
normally available (Dyas and Thanheiser, p.78).
Engelmann's books may be something of an exception.

Normally, however, even books explicitly concerned with the world's richest men tend to overlook the West Germans (Vogl, p.48). Friedrich Flick remained a relatively unknown figure until the end of his life (Rutherford, p.36). In its obituary, *The Times* (22 July 1972) referred to him as 'something of a recluse ... famed for his exceptional modesty ... but also a strong-willed, autocratic individual.' His youngest son succeeded him as head of the Flick industrial empire. This book was nearing completion when the company was alleged to have been involved in a major tax fraud. It was said to involve a number of senior figures (*Der Spiegel*, 9/82, 47/82 and 48/82).

As senior partner in the private bank, August von Finck need not disclose profits, yet his family own a sizeable amount of land in Munich (*Financial Times*, Banking 1982). In West Germany itself the 'power of the banks' and 'trade union state' are the more usual political slogans (Eglau, p.11). More will be said about the former in the next chapter, including the trade union-owned bank. Trade unions and collective bargaining were analysed in Owen Smith (1981). A further indication of the policy issues raised by German trade unions will be found in Koch and Schuster. Yet sufficient has been said, even in this short chapter, to indicate that during the period under review the rich families were also important in the process of decision-making.

When it comes to the structure of companies, there is an equal amount of confusion about where decision-making powers reside. Chief executives perhaps tend to be somewhat harassed, but they are certainly very busy persons. For example, Leiding is reputed to have worked ten hours a day, seven days a week in his first eighteen months at VW, while Abs of the Deutsche Bank claimed in the early 1970s that he had not taken a holiday since 1956 (Vogl, p.97). Rutherford (p.28) claims that these types of working practice are average for West German chief executives. Perhaps understandably, they may tend to be somewhat insular, in that they are not all that well informed about world affairs in general (*ibid.*, p.28). Even more controversially, doubts have been even cast on their efficiency (Vogl, p.96). According to some studies, however, their educational qualifications, or even their achievements as 'self-made men', are highly respectable (Copeman, pp.18-22; Engelmann, p.209). Nevertheless, sufficient has been said in this chapter to indicate that lack of success tends to threaten their positions. In short, while successful they remain highly-paid and receive extremely

generous fringe benefits; in return - although
shielded as far as possible - they have no claim to
uninterrupted leisure time (Englemann, pp.102-103 and
113).

It has also been shown that there is a great
deal of overlap in company control. Chief executives
from another company may chair the main supervisory
board. The chief executive of the same company may
chair the supervisory board of a subsidiary (Vogl,
p.36).

What necessarily follows from this short chapter
is confirmation of a theme gradually developed
earlier - namely that the attitude of German society
to industry, and the locations of decision-taking
power, have not fundamentally changed in the social
market economy. Industry continues to enjoy a high
social standing (Lawrence, p.163). In industry, there
is a strong sense of purpose with an equally strong
dash of egalitarianism (*ibid.*, p.107). Industry has
provided the means for the relatively high living
standards and social security system quantified in
Chapters 4 and 5. Because industry is so important,
and because West German banking is so closely connected to industry, the final two chapters of this
book concentrate on the banking and industrial sectors
of the West German economy.

Chapter Eight

THE BANKING SECTOR

INTRODUCTION

There are three distinctive features of West German
banking. First, the casual observer may conclude that
the West German banking scene is dominated by the Big
Three commercial banks - the Deutsche Bank AG, the
Dresdner Bank AG and the Commerzbank AG. Although
these private-sector banks wield a great deal of market power, however, the bulk of West Germany's banks
lie in the hands of the public authorities and the
co-operative banking movement. This point is demonstrated by the data in Tables 8.1(a) and 8.1(b) where
all three forms of ownership, plus a bank owned by
the trade unions, are shown to be represented among
the economy's top ten banks.

Secondly, the institutions belonging to these
various banking groups - whether publicly or privately
owned - provide a full range of *both* commercial and
investment banking services. Besides accepting sight,
time and savings deposits, these universal banks take
up longer-term funds; conversely, they grant not only
short-term but also medium and long-term credits and
loans. They also provide brokers' services, generally
deal in securities and accept seats on supervisory
boards of non-banking companies. The exceptions to
this general universal banking rule are the specialised banks which confine themselves to narrow fields
such as the financing of mortgages, instalment sales,
the performance of other specialised functions and
the postal giro and savings banks. But in many cases
these specialised banks are either subsidiaries of
the universal banks or are state-owned. Nevertheless,
it would be impossible to fully understand the methods
of funding the national debt, or the post-war recovery, without examining the roles of these financial
institutions.

Thirdly, until recently the public and co-operative sectors felt inhibited by their charters from entering the more risky investment fields. Further, only the central institutions of the public and co-operative banking sectors are allowed to own equity capital in non-banking institutions, whereas the commercial banks, particularly the Big Three, have not been constrained in either of these ways. In short, their industrial influence is extensive. As a result policy prescriptions have ranged from nationalisation to minor corrections.

An examination of the basic structure and legal forms of banking, therefore, is followed by more detailed analyses of the private-sector, co-operative, trade union and public-sector banks. Some general aspects of banking (developments in profitability, competition and the international field), and the reform of banking law are then considered. (Central banking and supervision were examined in Chapter 5.)

## BASIC STRUCTURAL ASPECTS

The banks differ considerably in business structure, size, legal form, administrative organisation and in their main fields of business activities. The structure of the banking system in the FRG is illustrated in Figure 8.1 which confirms the basic divisions between universal and specialist banking. It also illustrates the varying forms of ownership - private, co-operative and public. These three groups of banking institutions are each affiliated to separate central associations which serve as interest and public relations organisations (not shown on Figure 8.1). The private sector banks are affiliated, through their Länder associations, or their specialist private mortgage or shipping bank associations if appropriate, to the Association of German Banks (*Bundesverband deutscher Banken eV*; *eV* = *eingetragener Verein* or registered charity); branches of foreign banks are also represented by this organisation (BdB, 1 July 1981). Some of the public sector banks - the savings banks and their central giro institutions (*Landes-banken*) - are affiliated to the German Savings' and Giro Association (*Deutscher Sparkassen- und Girover-bank eV*), while the Landesbanken again, plus the public-owned mortgage and special purpose banks, are all affiliated to the Association of Public Sector Banks (*Verband Öffentlicher Banken eV*). Finally, the Association of German Urban and Agricultural Co-operative Banks (*Bundesverband der Deutschen Volks-*

Table 8.1(a): The Ten Largest Banks in West Germany, 1975-1980

| Rank | | Bank | Group Balance Sheet Total (DM billion) | | Group net income[b] (DM million) (% change in GNRP: -1.8% +1.8%) | | Change in net income over *previous* year (per cent): 1980/1979 | Ownership/ Sector of Bank |
|---|---|---|---|---|---|---|---|---|
| 1975 | 1980 | | 1975 | 1980 | 1975 | 1980 | | |
| 1 | 1 | Deutsche Bank | 91.5 | 174.6 | 391 | 457 | +7.0 | private |
| 2 | 2 | Dresdner Bank | 74.1 | 123.5 | 251 | 204 | -26.4 | private |
| 3 | 3 | West LB | 67.9 | 114.3 | 183 | 61 | -67.5 | public |
| 4 | 4 | Commerzbank | 56.6 | 100.0 | 189 | 34 | -76.3 | private |
| 5 | 5 | BV Bank | 48.7 | 91.6 | 125 | 151 | +3.3 | private |
| 7 | 6 | Hypo Bank | 40.2 | 83.8 | 80 | 93 | -21.2 | private |
| 6 | 7 | Bayerische LB | 45.7 | 83.3 | 136 | 116 | +3.6 | public |
| 11 | 8 | DG Bank[a] | (35.8)[c] | 65.3 | (59)[c] | 69 | +35.6 | co-operatives |
| 10 | 9 | BfG | 35.1 | 60.5 | 129 | 102 | -40.2 | DGB trade unions |
| 8 | 10 | Helaba[a] | 39.3 | 54.4 | -[d] | 65 | -56.6 | public |

Notes:
(a) The DG Bank in 1976 and the Hessische Landesbank in 1979 were overtaken for tenth position by the public-sector Kreditanstalt für Wiederaufbau (balance sheet total 1980: DM 53.7 billion). The Norddeutsche LB occupied ninth position in 1975 (balance sheet total: DM 35.9 billion). In 1976 and 1977 ranks 11-20 were all occupied by public sector banks (Stein, 1979, p.40).
(b) Peltzer, p.231.
(c) 1976.
(d) Losses - see later in text.

Sources: *Die Zeit*, Annual 'top 100' (various); Annual Reports (*Geschäftsberichte*) (various); Stein, 1979, p.40; *Financial Times*, Banking Surveys (various).

Table 8.1(b): Top Ten Banks, 1981

| Rank 1981 | Bank | Group Balance Sheet totals (DM billion) | | Net income (parent bank) (DM million) | |
|---|---|---|---|---|---|
| | | Total | Per cent change on previous year | Total | Absolute change 1981/1980 |
| 1 | Deutsche Bank | 192.4 | +10.2 | 242 | -101 |
| 2 | Dresdner Bank | 131.5 | +6.4 | 139 | -15.9 |
| 3 | Westdeutsche LB | 124.2 | +8.7 | 45 | - |
| 4 | Commerzbank | 101.3 | +1.3 | - | - |
| 5 | Bayerische Vereinsbank | 98.3 | +7.3 | 101.9 | +9.1 |
| 6 | Bayerische Landesbank | 90.8 | +9.0 | 114 | -1.8 |
| 7 | Bayerische Hypotheken- und Wechsel-Bank | 89.2 | +6.4 | 82 | +28.1 |
| 8 | DG Bank | 65.0 | -0.2 | 40 | -7.5 |
| 9 | Hessische Landesbank | 61.7 | +8.4 | 45 | -20 |
| 10 | Kreditanstalt f. Wiederaufbau | 61.3 | +14.2 | 21.8 | +10 |

Note:
After 1980, the BfG no longer included the Allgemeine Hypothekenbank AG in its balance sheet total. On this basis it was therefore no longer in the top ten.

Source: *Die Zeit*, 34/82, p.17.

Figure 8.1: Number of Banks and Percentage of the Total Volume of Business, May 1981*

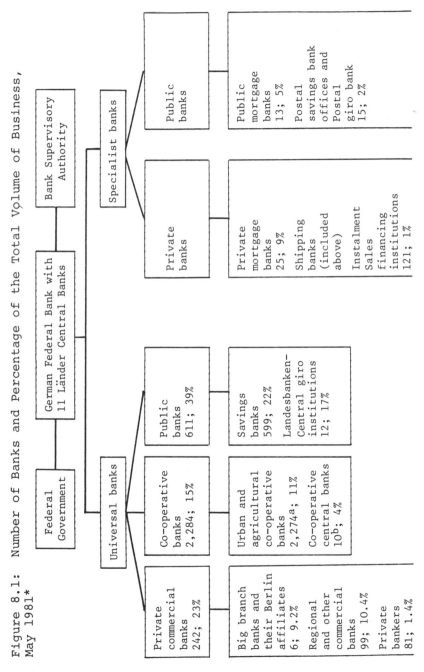

Branches of
foreign
banks
56; 2.0%

Banks with
special
functions[e]
⟍ Totals: 16; 6%

Banks with
special
functions[e]

Other
institutions

Investment
companies
(34)[c]

Security
deposit banks
(8)[c]

Guarantee
banks (incl.
co-operative
credit
guarantee
companies)
(37)[c]

Private
building
savings banks
[18; DM 89.7m.][d]

Public
building
savings banks
[13; DM 45.5m.][d]

Notes:

(a) Co-operatives required to submit returns to the
Federal Bank. Over 4,000 affiliated to their Central
Association.

(b) Including Deutsche Genossenschaftsbank (DG Bank
in Tables 8.1(a) and 8.1(b)).

(c) Not covered in monthly balance sheet statistics –
number given in parentheses.

(d) Separate monthly series. Number and balance
sheet total for May 1981.

(e) Export and investment credit institutions, some
of which are joint public-private enterprises.

*Total volume of business in May 1981 = DM 2.38 trillion ($2.38 \times 10^{12}$).

Sources: Based on BBR, February 1974 (centre-spread); MRDB, August 1981,
Tables III (11), (21a), (22) and (25b); Stein, 1977, p.6.

*banken und Raiffeisenbanken eV*) represents the collective interests of the co-operative banks.
    Although the number of affiliates to the Bund-
esverband deutscher Banken does not exactly coincide
with the Bundesbank data in Figure 8.1, it will be
useful to apply the types of ownership in Figure 7.1
to private-sector banking. In July 1981, the total
number of banks affiliated to the BdB was 220, plus
49 branches of foreign banks represented in the Federal Republic. The Big Three plus other larger banks
in the 'regional and other commercial banks' group
(106 in total) were all AGs. There were also 25
GmbHs. Four banks were of the remaining type of company defined in Figure 7.1, that is KGaA. With the
exception of the Big Three, virtually all private-
sector banks registered as companies are in either the
'regional and other commercial banks' or 'private
mortgage and shipping banks' categories of Figure 8.1.
Finally, the BdB had affiliates from the 'private
bankers' category in Figure 8.1. In fact, there were
85 limited partnerships (KG), general partnerships
(OHG) and relatively small banks which belong to a
sole proprietor (*Einzelfirma*). As their legal form
indicates, management and ownership in the case of
the smaller private banks tends to coincide (Peltzer
and Nebendorf, p.19).


THE PRIVATE-SECTOR COMMERCIAL BANKS

The Big Three and Universal Private-Sector Banking
The relatively sudden transformation of Germany into
a first-rank industrial nation owed much to the
equally dramatic rise of her universal banking system.
Since the undeveloped capital market in those days
could not meet the enormous demands of emerging industry, the banks were encouraged to act as sources of
industrial finance.
    Such was the unique origin of German banking.
It was the beginning of its crucial relationship with
German industry. The Deutsche and the Dresdner Banks,
along with the Commerz- und Discontobank, were therefore the products of the sudden upsurge in banking
activity that followed the founding of the Second
Reich. They were obliged to forge the type of organised credit system which in Britain was apportioned
among numerous financial agencies (Marshall, p.341).
    In 1870 the Deutsche Bank was founded as an AG
under Royal charter in Berlin (Deutsche Bank 1870-
1970, p.6). Later in the same year a new Companies
Act meant that a Government licence was no longer

required and 30 other newly-founded banks were founded in 1870 alone. During the 1973-75 financial crisis, however, nearly 50 banks had to be dissolved. Because the Deutsche Bank initially operated mainly abroad, it had avoided the company promotion fever (*ibid.*, p.10). It began thereafter to take over other banks and rapidly acquired the status of a big bank. From then onwards it became closely involved in electrification with Siemens and AEG. On the eve of the First World War the bank's world-wide activities included interests in electricity, railroads and oil. Its capital, which had already multiplied six times by 1895, stood at 200 million marks. By the time it had merged with the Disconto-Gesellschaft in the late 1920s, the bank was handling roughly 50 per cent of the business done by all the big Berlin banks.

Part of the post-Second World War history of banking was mentioned as early as Chapter 2 (Figure 2.1). It was shown that as part of the western allies' attempts to deconcentrate industrial ownership after the Second World War, the Deutsche Bank was divided into ten separate institutions. As a result of a change in the law in 1952, these ten regional banks were merged into three area banks which covered the northern, central and southern areas of the country. In 1957 another legal change led to these three institutions being in turn merged to form the Deutsche Bank AG. This post-Second World War process, as Shonfield (p.242) suggests, consisted of legal changes which were often adjustments to suit the facts. This was because an inexorable process of reconcentration began almost immediately after the Big Three had been broken up by the Allies. On its formal re-constitution in 1957, the Deutsche Bank had 16,597 employees and a balance sheet total of DM 7.6 billion. By 1980 these figures had reached 44,128 and DM 174.6 respectively. In common with the other two large commercial banks, the head office is nowadays in Frankfurt a.M. with a wholly owned Berlin subsidiary.

The history of the Dresdner Bank follows a similar pattern, except that this bank's administrative headquarters moved to Berlin in 1884 (Dresdner Bank, *Wirtschaftsberichte,* November 1972). The Bank retains the name of the city in which it was founded, along with house colours (white and green) which are the same as the flag of the former Kingdom of Saxony. Again, the small regional groupings into which the bank was divided following the Second World War, were succeeded in 1952 by three larger geographical groups - covering the south, west and north respectively. These three banks were merged to re-form the Dresdner

Bank AG in 1957.
    After its foundation, the Commerzbank took
rather longer to gravitate to Berlin. This is because
its predecessor, the Commerz- und Discontobank, was
founded in Hamburg in 1870, in order to avail itself
of the commercial potential of the norther Länder's
main port (Commerzbank, p.39). Some movement towards
Berlin began in 1891, but it was not until 1920 that
Berlin became its base. Again the deconcentration
process resulted in the bank being divided into nine
separate regional institutions in 1947-48. This was
followed in 1952 by a merger forming three larger
organisations to serve the north, west and south of
the Federal Republic. As in the other cases the original parent body re-emerged in 1957.
    Although a study of the evolution of the Big
Three reveals many similarities, there seem to be traditional differences in management style. The sugges-
tion here is that managerial responsibilities are more
widely shared in the Deutsche Bank than at the Commerzbank, where a more rigidly enforced decision-making
hierarchy exists. The Dresdner Bank perhaps lies between the two extremes. During the Commerzbank's ad-
verse experience in 1980, Herr Lichtenberg was called
back from the chairmanship of the supervisory board
to again become, temporarily, chief executive. This
was because the previous incumbent had resigned on
grounds of ill-health. Lichtenberg took three actions.
First, the supervisory and management boards received
no performance-related payments. Second, he announced
that he expected the staff to work harder and ordered
all bank managers to a meeting at Head Office. Third,
he vigorously embarked on the task of finding a new
chief executive - a post to which Dr Walter Seipp of
the Westdeutsche Landesbank was appointed. Dr Seipp
confirmed that the Commerzbank was overcentralised
and bureaucratic, but unlike other large companies
with such a centralised structure it did not possess
a strong system of financial controls (*Financial
Times*, 30 July 1982).

Regional and Other Commercial Banks
As already noted above, it is really the legal form
of a private-sector bank which determines whether it
is statistically grouped in either the 'regional and
other commercial banks' or the 'private bankers' group.
All banks registered as companies belong to the former.
Moreover, the term 'regional' cannot be taken too literally: while most banks in the group operate only in
a certain part of Germany, some are not confined to
one region and consequently maintain branches in most

parts of the country (Schneider, p.13). The trade-
union owned Bank für Gemeinwirtschaft (BfG) is also
statistically classed in this group, but because of
its origins and ownership it is discussed below.
It will be seen from Tables 8.1(a) and 8.1(b)
that the two largest banks in the 'regional' group
are the Bayerische Vereinsbank (BV) and the Bayerische
Hypotheken- und Wechselbank (Hypo-Bank). These two
Bavarian (*Bayerische*) private-sector banks have a long
history: the Vereinsbank was established in 1780 and
the Hypo-Bank in 1835. In addition to conducting a
full range of universal banking business, these two
banks, together with the relatively much smaller (DM
3 billion balance sheet total) Norddeutsche Hypotheken-
und Wechselbank (Nordhypo Bank), traditionally operate
as mortgage banks on a large scale. In other words,
their long-term loans are secured by long-term bond
issues (Stein, 1977, p.13, and 1979, pp.19 and 42).
Contrary to the practice in other commercial banks,
these institutions are therefore legally permitted to
issue mortgage and communal bonds to finance their
long-term loans. Other commercial banks have to carry
out mortgage business through subsidiaries.
     The BV's mortgage business has always been con-
ducted throughout Germany. It was only in recent
years that its commercial banking business was extended beyond the frontiers of Bavaria. Hence its immediate post-Second World War growth was tied closely to
industrialisation in Bavaria, later followed by a
series of take-overs or part-acquisitions of a number
of small private banks. It also took substantial
shareholdings in cities such as Hamburg, Düsseldorf,
Frankfurt and Saarbrücken. In many ways, however,
the most important merger involving the BV was when
it merged with the formerly Bavarian government-owned
Bayerische Staatsbank in 1971. As a result, the newly
constituted private-sector bank entered *Fortune Magazine's* top fifty international banks outside the USA
(*Fortune Magazine*, August 1972, p.160; Peltzer and
Nebendorf, p.18).
     In the 1970s, the Hypo-Bank has emerged strongly
through its active shareholding policy, particularly
in breweries. These latter holdings sparked off some
controversy, for the Hypo-Bank acquired about 20 per
cent of the Federal Republic's beer market (Rutherford,
p.32). Significantly, two of the large family-owned
firms in West Germany (Oetker and Reemtsma) also diversified into brewing (Bannock, p.111; Dyas and Thanheiser, p.79). Moreover, links between the Hypo and
Dresdner banks resulted in the formation of a company
with a 15 per cent share of the beer market (Peltzer

and Nebendorf, p.18; Vogl, p.47). After a three-year absence, the Hypo returned to the top fifty banks outside the USA in 1975 (*Fortune Magazine*, August 1976, p.244).

Merger activity within the 'regional and other banks' statistical grouping has also resulted in the emergence of the Berliner Handels- und Frankfurter Bank (BHF Bank), as well as the Vereins- und Westbank, Hamburg (Stein, 1977, p.18). These two banks occupy ranks in the top twenties and thirties respectively with balance sheet totals of about DM 17 billion and DM 9 billion (Stein, 1979, p.40) - far behind the Bavarian pair and the BfG. The narrowly interwoven nature of German banking will become even more apparent when the joint holdings of the public-sector Landesbanken and the trade-union BfG are discussed below (Peltzer and Nebendorf, pp.18-19).

Private Bankers
Private banking in Germany has an even longer history than that of the municipal savings banks movement. As recently as 1978, no fewer than 20 of the private banks operating in the Federal Republic were founded before 1800 (Stein, 1979, p.21). But the total number of such banks has decreased rapidly since the 1920s. In 1928 there were more than 2,000 private banks; by 1933 the number had fallen to 750 - one causal factor being a banking crisis. After the Second World War there were 300 private banks in the land area which became the Federal Republic (Peltzer and Nebendorf, p.19). At the end of 1976 there were 113 private banks; in 1978 there were 96 and in 1981 there were 81 (Stein, 1977, p.19, and 1979, p.21; Figure 8.1).

One should not conclude, however, that this group has lost its significance. On the contrary: the group's share in the total business volume has remained nearly static. Hence those institutions which remain have experienced higher than average growth (Peltzer and Nebendorf, p.20). They are distinguishable from the large and regional banks by the fact that they do not carry out mass business, and by the additional fact that they maintain no, or only a few, branches. Given the recent rise in staff and equipment costs (see below), this absence of branches is a cost advantage. On the other hand, a considerable cost disadvantage arises from the relatively low intake of funds from non-bank sources, with the consequent higher-cost need to borrow from within the banking system (*ibid.*, p.20).

On their lending side, there are considerable differences within the group. Some private bankers operate on an international or supra-regional basis, while others are purely local in character (Stein, 1977, p.20). While some private bankers deal mainly with export financing, others favour domestic business. Domestic specialisations for the major private banks are in industrial and investment activities, while the smaller institutions manage instalment sales finance. Hence the larger private bankers tend to resemble the English merchant bankers. Towards the end of the review period, the largest private banks had balance sheet totals which far exceed the average, the top ten all having totals which ranged from DM 1 billion to DM 4 billion (Stein, 1979, p.22). On the other hand, the purely local private banker had a balance sheet total of only a few million (Peltzer and Nebendorf, p.19).

The private bankers have trained some of the economy's most influential figures: for example, Hermann Abs, and Robert Pferdmenges, as well as - his father was also caretaker in the Dreyfus household - the long-serving head of trade union banking and business, Walter Hesselbach (Eglau, p.125; Engelmann, p.191). The latter pioneered the formation, in 1974, of West Germany's largest business group under one roof. The holding company is the Beteiligungsgesellschaft für Gemeinwirtschaft (Hartrich, p.236; IdDW, Table 87). This mammoth organisation includes the BfG which is analysed below. Another influential figure formerly associated with the private bankers is Otto Lambsdorff - the Federal Economics Minister. He was general manager at the Trinkaus Bank.

Abs became banking's most important figure in the post-Second World War era. He had begun his career, before the war, as an apprentice in a small private bank in Bonn (Eglau, p.121; Englemann, p.57). His knowledge of international finance, however, resulted in his being appointed head of the Deutsche Bank's foreign operations while still in his thirties. After the Second World War, it was he who assumed the unofficial managerial responsibilities which were to lead to the Bank's eventual reconstitution (Hartrich, p.233). Although interned by the British after the war, and officially banned from the Deutsche Bank, Abs became the first general manager of the special institution set up to channel Marshall aid into industrial and housing re-development - the state-owned Reconstruction and Development Loan Corporation (*Kreditanstalt für Wiederaufbau* - KfW) (Englemann, p.60; Shonfield, pp.276-278). This institution has become the nation's largest special-purpose bank, specialising in low-interest loans for regional

development.  Moreover, Abs' knowledge of international finance enabled him to reduce West Germany's
reparation payments from DM 20 billion to DM 14 billion (Eglau, p.124).

Even when he had moved back to head the recon-
stituted Deutsche Bank, Abs remained on the KfW's
supervisory board, initially as its deputy chairman,
then as its chairman.  At the Deutsche Bank he remained chief executive for many years, before moving
over to the chairmanship of its supervisory board and,
finally, becoming honorary president.  During the
early 1960s he occupied so many seats on the supervisory boards of other companies that the 1966 Act to
limit the number of such seats any banker could hold
was dubbed 'Lex Abs'.  One of his successors at the
Deutsche Bank - Erhard's nephew, Dr Wilfried Guth,
the bank's joint chief executive - had also served as
a management board member of the KfW.

Abs shared with Pferdmenges the role of advising Adenauer on economic policy and relations with
the Allies, while Erhard, Schäffer and Vocke were
perhaps left to manage the national economy (Hartrich,
p.159).  Vocke also belonged to Adenauer's small group
of advisers, but Pferdmenges, a wealthy partner of
the Sal. Oppenheim private bank, also became a close
personal friend of Adenauer's (Eglau, pp.123-124;
Englemann, p.66).  Among other things, he assisted
with the financial arrangements responsible for the
re-surgence of the August-Thyssenhütte, the Ruhr
steel-making complex.  With Pferdmenges' help the
chief executive who re-built this huge concern for
the Thyssen family (Hans Günther Sohl) was able to
raise finance from the major banks, the Federal
Government and the Marshall Aid funds (Hartrich,
p.216).

Hence one should infer that the private bankers
have a proud tradition and an influential economic
role.  The collapse of the Herstatt bank (see below)
shocked their fraternity.  For the head of Merck,
Finck & Co., for example, it was a catastrophe which,
had it happened to him, would have resulted in his
'never again showing his face in public' (*Die Zeit*,
19/80, p.21).


THE BANKS AND INDUSTRY

Clearly, then, West Germany's highly integrated and
industry-orientated banking system stems from what
became per force a traditionally close relationship
between mutually dependent sectors of the economy.

The banks trade in their corporate customers' shares and advise them on financial matters. Nearly half the sight and time deposits of the corporate sector are held by the private commercial banks (Stein, 1977, p.14). Big commercial banks dominate the business of lending to the giant corporations - in fact, bank loans far outrank stock issues as a source of capital for West German industry (Dyas and Thanheiser, p.56). Further, the commercial banks are collectively important in terms of their loans to small and medium sized firms. However, they face more competition from the savings and co-operative banks in the latter field. But the influence of the big banks from a competition policy point of view, boils down to their direct shareholdings, their proxy voting and representation on their corporate customers' supervisory boards (Eckstein, pp.465-466).

Taken as a whole, the direct shareholdings of all the domestic banks in non-banking companies is ostensibly small. Table 8.2, for example, is based on a fairly recent sample of large companies and the resultant estimate of direct shareholding is about 9 per cent of total share capital. Rutherford (p.32) quotes a Bundesbank survey which put the figure at 8 per cent.

Table 8.2: Bank Holdings in 74 Large West German Quoted Companies, 1974-75

| Banks | Percentage share of equity capital | Percentage share of voting right at AGMs | Percentage share of supervisory board membership | Percentage share of supervisory board chairmanship |
|---|---|---|---|---|
| Deutsche Bank | 3.5 | 18.6 | 5.3 | 24.3 |
| Dresdner Bank | 1.6 | 11.8 | 2.7 | 8.1 |
| Commerzbank | 1.0 | 4.5 | 1.9 | 1.4 |
| All three above | 6.1 | 34.9 | 9.9 | 33.8 |
| Other banks and investment companies | 3.0 | 27.8 | 8.0 | 16.2 |
| Total all banks | 9.1 | 62.7 | 17.9 | 50.0 |

Source: Gessler Commission *Report*, Table 37, p.467 (writer's translation).

However, as Table 8.2 also indicates, the direct
share holdings of the domestic banks in non-banking
companies are heavily concentrated, the Big Three
alone owning about two-thirds of the total. (A Federal Government survey of the early 1960s produced
the same proportion - *Bundestag-Drucksache*, IV/2320.)
Moreover, the Deutsche Bank owns over a quarter of
Daimler-Benz, the Mercedes motor vehicle manufacturer
(Kaufmann; Vogl, pp.44-46). The same bank also has
joint holdings, of over 25 per cent each, with the
West LB and Commerzbank, the latter in Karstadt, the
country's leading chain store. Another of the
country's department stores, Kaufhof, was mainly the
property of the Dresdner and the Commerz, although
the Commerz may have disposed of its stake during the
bank's troubled year of 1980 - partly to cover its
holdings in another troubled company - AEG (*The Times*,
14 January 1981, p.16). Over 50 per cent of Hapag-
Lloyd is jointly owned by the Deutsche and the
Dresdner, while the Deutsche and the Bayerische
Vereinsbank each holds over 25 per cent of the share
capital in Bergmann Elektrizitätswerke (Englemann,
p.63). The Big Three are also strongly involved in
construction and metals. Hence the holdings of the
Big Three are heavily concentrated in certain sectors
(Eckstein, p.467). These holdings often overlap and
it may be the case that all three major banks are
represented in most of the country's top concerns
(Gessler Commission, Table 27, p.457).

These shareholdings are seen as a duty in the
sense that, rather like some trade union leaders,
many executives in the banking world believe that
each social group has a duty to contribute to the
harmonious functioning of the economy - a so-called
*Ordnungsfaktor*. An extension of this view was when
the Deutsche Bank in 1975 bought up the Flick family
holding in Daimler-Benz, thus giving it a total shareholding of 56 per cent. This was to prevent the Shah
of Iran extending his country's industrial ownership
in the Federal Republic, his having already purchased
a holding in the Krupp company. In any case the
Quandt family-holding in Daimler-Benz had been sold
to Kuwait (Eglau, p.176). In 1979 the Bank divested
itself of 25 per cent of the shareholding by creating
a new holding company. When this holding company's
shares were launched on the stock market, two major
vehicle holding companies bought up 50 per cent of
the equity. The Big Three had substantial holdings
in both of them.

There are other ways in which the banks influence industrial decision-making. Above all, the

share of the private-sector banks in the security business far exceeds their share in the balance sheet total for all banks (Stein, 1977, p.13). In *absolute* terms, 3.5 million out of 8.1 million of all security deposits in 1981 were in the custody of the private banks (compared to 3.2 million out of 7.3 million in 1980 - *Beilage zu Statistische Beihefte zu den Monatsberichten der Deutschen Bundesbank, Reihe* 1, Juli 1982, Nr 7, p.2). But by *value* the security deposits held at the private-sector banks represent about two-thirds of all domestic bonds, nearly three-quarters of domestic-issued shares, over 60 per cent of all domestic investment certificates and 90 per cent of foreign banks (*ibid.*, p.2; Stein, 1979, p.14).

Further, of the 3.5 million security deposits held by the private-sector banks in 1981, 2.2 million were held by the Big Three (Deutsche Bundesbank, *ibid.*, p.4). This endows the banks, and particularly the Big Three, with considerable power, for provided a bank has the written permission of its customer it may exercise a proxy voting right at shareholders' meetings - a so-called *Depotstimmrecht.* A Federal Government enquiry in the early 1960s - one of the few relatively early pieces of empirical evidence on concentration in general - found that this proxy voting system gave the banks voting control over 60 per cent of the total capital of stock exchange voted companies (*BT-Drucksache*, IV/2320; Kaufmann, p.264). This proportion was confirmed by the 1970s' Federal Government enquiry - see Table 8.2. According to the 1960s' enquiry, approximately 70 per cent of these proxy votes were cast by representatives of the Big Three (Hartrich, p.223). From the 1970s' sample (Table 8.2), the proportion was estimated at 56 per cent, which is still, of course, quite high. Banks also loan their votes to each other - a system known as *Stimmenleihe* (Shonfield, pp.250 and 252).

There is a positive correlation between the extent of a bank's direct and proxy shareholding and the number of supervisory board seats it controls (Eckstein, p.470). Moreover, the Big Three are virtually the only agencies authorised to buy and sell shares on West Germany's stock exchanges. They therefore effectively control these exchanges. Hence, by virtue of both of their own holdings and their proxy voting rights, according to the larger 1960s' enquiry, the banks held about one in three of the non-employee supervisory board seats in 318 of West Germany's biggest enterprises (Denton, p.70; Kaufmann, p.264). Half of these seats belonged to the Big Three (Shonfield, pp.251-252). When account is taken of the fact that the 1970s' enquiry did not deduct employees' representatives on supervisory boards, the magnitudes of bank representation is almost the same (Table 8.2).

As already seen, in 1966 an Act limited the number of these directorships which could be held by an individual banker to ten. However, in 1972 an analysis of the top nine companies by sales indicated that out of a total of 168 supervisory board seats, 37 were held by bankers, 23 of whom came from the Big Three (Rutherford, p.35). In addition, a bank representative tends to be either chairman or vice-chairman of a supervisory board (Shonfield, p.251). Holders of these two posts are endowed with special responsibilities which distinguish them from ordinary members of the supervisory board. For example, their status entitles them to be consulted, with a right of veto, about capital expenditure plans.

Both the industrial influence of the Big Three, and the growing problems raised by the international expansion of German banking (see below), led to two enquiries during the 1970s. The first enquiry was conducted by the standing Monopolies Commission (MK) - a government advisory body which was established in 1973. A second edition of its 1973-75 report was published in 1977. Chapter III (MK I) was concerned with 'Banking and Concentration'. The Commission returned to the same theme in its 1976-77 report which was published in 1978 (MK II - Chapter IV). A second enquiry was conducted by the specially-constituted Gessler Commission, a body which included authorities from the main banking sectors, the Bundesbank, the supervisory authorities, the universities, Finance Ministry and trade unions. This Commission reported in 1979 and it is the one to which reference has so far been made.

Of these reports, those of the Monopolies Commission adopted a more hawkish assessment of the relationship between banks and industry. Competition was being eroded not just because the bigger banks tended to gain a competitive advantage over the smaller ones, but also because the big banks had access to information on such things as the credit-worthiness of both their existing and newly-formed corporate customers. There was, therefore, a long-term tendency for the banks to acquire bargain-price stakes in enterprises of above-average worth. An examination (MK II, para.553) of the top 100 AGs in terms of turnover revealed that at the end of 1974 the banks held stakes in 56 of them, 41 of which consisted of holdings greater than 25 per cent. Eight of the top 10 AGs were included in the 'greater

than 25 per cent' category. Also in the top 100 AGs,
banking representatives held a total of 179 supervisory board seats, including 31 chairmanships (*ibid.*,
paras 529 and 539). The Big Three held 102 of these
seats and 21 of the chairmanships. Finally, it was
estimated that by far the greatest proportion of the
voting rights in the top 100 AGs was attributable to
proxy voting.

These three methods of influencing industrial
decision-taking, that is to say, direct holdings,
supervisory board seats and proxy voting rights, were
also investigated by the Gessler Commission. This
Commission was also asked to express a view on whether
an upper-limit should be placed on direct-holdings, as
well as looking into the growing problem of banks
using foreign subsidiaries as a means of granting
credit well above the legal limit for their parent
banks. In its report, the Gessler Commission took a
more moderate policy stance compared to the one taken
by the Monopolies Commission. Bank holdings in industry, which were part of the German traditional universal banking system, were not seen as necessarily a bad
thing.

However, the Gessler Commission could not agree
on a maximum holding: the majority recommended the 25
per cent plus one share of a company's capital which
is the legal minimum required to block a change in the
statutes of a West German company (para.99). But a
'substantial minority' proposed that holdings should
not exceed 10 per cent, including any transient holding of up to 5 per cent for share-trading purposes
(para.104). The majority recommendation excluded this
5 per cent holding (para.100). On the other hand,
the MK (I, para.568) had recommended that a bank's
equity holding in a non-banking company should not
normally exceed 5 per cent, and where this limit was
exceeded voting rights should in any case be limited
to an equivalent of 5 per cent.

The Federal Government seemed at one stage to
have settled for a 15 per cent ratio with a large
number of exceptions. But quite apart from the
Finance and Economics ministries being under politicians of differing persuasions, the shaky Bonn coalition was more preoccupied with its budgetary position at the time of writing (Chapter 5). In any case
the banks may have reduced some of their holdings to
25 per cent in anticipation of legislation. Indeed,
at the end of the review period some holdings may have
been drastically reduced to provide reserves normally
provided by profits (see below).

The crucial relationship between banking and

industry is further illustrated by the fact that not
only are the banks represented on the boards of large
companies, but that the large companies are, in turn,
represented on the boards of the Big Three (Annual
Reports). An example of this is the traditional relationship between Siemens and the Deutsche Bank.
Long-standing links of this description are common.
Continuity is also maintained by the practice of
normally appointing a retiring chief executive of a
bank to its supervisory board, usually as chairman
(Denton, p.70). This was seen to be the case when
the careers of Abs and Lichtenberg were discussed
above.

The ownership of the Big Three themselves is not
dominated by any single large shareholder. They also
have, in the main, a record of being remarkably sym-
pathetic shareholders in other companies. The banks
generally have been very restrained in their dividend
demands and have almost always tended to place a
company's long-term interests above the need for
short-term profits. Above all, the economic recovery
of West Germany would have been impossible without
the Big Three and without their long and close relationship to the big industrial and commercial corporations. The German banks were especially well
equipped to know where the worst investment gaps were,
and where the addition of a relatively small amount
of capital - public or private in origin - would remove bottlenecks and produce a disproportionately
large return (Shonfield, p.277).

The banks also took risks with their own capital,
often lending ten and even twenty times their own
capital funds to one borrower (Hartrich, p.230). A
striking example of this risk financing was the re-
organising of the Carl Zeiss Optical Works. (At the
end of the war, the plant in East Germany was taken
over by the Soviet military government.) Another
example of lending money 'on a plan and a promise and
little else' involved the post-war rebirth of the
Pittler Company of Leipzig, for fifty years an important East German machine tool producer (*ibid.*,
p.231). The textiles and glass industries were re-
established in the same way (Mellor, p.149; Wallich,
p.283).

Another industrial role played by the banks -
again led by the Big Three - is that of mounting
rescue operations when companies run into financial
difficulties, a role in Britain readily left to the
state. The Dresdner Bank has its own executive for
retrieving corporate failures - Dr Manfred Meier-
Preschany. In the late 1950s he organised the rescue

of an ailing bicycle and motor cycle concern -
Victoria-Werke in Nuremberg.  In the early 1970s he
led the search for a buyer when the plant engineering
company of Zimmer was failing.  It became one of the
most profitable parts of Britain's Davy Corporation.
His most challenging task, however, was in forming a
consortium of 25 banks in order to inject new capital
of DM 1 billion into the troubled electrical giant
AEG-Telefunken.  This was one of those companies
which had a large number of small shareholders (MK
III, para.342).  When the banks met to consider
further financial aid in 1981, however, they took um-
bridge because Meier-Preschany and not the Dresdner's
chief executive and AEG supervisory board chairman
(Hans Friderichs) chaired the meeting (*Die Zeit*,
46/81, p.24).  More will be said about AEG in Chapter
9.  But by 1982 sharply falling sales and cheap imports in household appliances and electric motors had
also endangered the family-owned Bauknecht company.
In this case 22 banks were involved.

Similarly, in the recession of 1966-67, another
world-famous firm - Krupps of Essen - ran into one of
its recurrent financial crises, the previous ones
having been in the 1870s, 1920s and early 1950s (Manchester, pp.907-908 and 923-924).  No one could imagine that Bonn would permit the troubled company to
go bankrupt, but Abs, Krupp's friend in the banking
world, took a hard line with Schiller's full backing.
At a climactic semi-secret meeting in March 1967 in
Düsseldorf's Dresdner Bank, Schiller, Blessing and
twenty-eight top figures from the world of finance
(quite apart from the confidential nature of the
meeting, there was not room for the 235 savings banks'
and insurance companies' executives entitled to
attend), it was decided that the company would become
public (*ibid.*, pp.928 and 930).  Schiller made it
clear that the government was leaving the rescue operation to 'a few banks'.  Krupp himself had nominated
Abs and Werner Krueger of the Dresdner; they were to
be joined by Otto Brenner of the metalworkers' trade
union, Professor Bernard Timm of the rapidly expanding BASF chemical company, together with an academic
and a research and development expert (*ibid.*, p.934).

When the steel industry as a whole faced the
third post-Second World War recession at the end of
the 1970s, bank lending to this sector increased.  In
effect this reduced both the state subsidies being
paid to the sector and the concomitant need to fund
such subsidies from either public borrowing or tax
revenue.  More specifically, Klöckner, Germany's
third largest steel group, was making heavy losses.

Its capital re-organisation was partly the brain-child of the deputy chairman of its supervisory board, whose full-time employment was membership of the management board of the Deutsche Bank (Dr Alfred Herrhausen). A consortium of twelve banks was formed to raise half of the capital required.

Jürgen Ponto, who until his assassination in 1977 was chief executive of the Dresdner Bank, contributed to the debate on the role of the Big Three by means of the lecture 'The Power of the Banks' delivered in 1971. His principal contention was that the power of the banks was far less than was often thought. For example, the banks have virtually no direct or indirect representation in Parliamentary government, yet because of budgetary deficits and state spending in the modern economy, the banks have become the objects rather than the subjects of politics. For that matter, there was no equivalent of the direct intervention of the Bundesbank in any other economic sector. Further, the massive demand for capital which is a feature of the modern economy is usually supplied from a multiplicity of sources. In any case, 95 per cent of a bank's assets represent, in one form or another, customers' deposits, the contractual repayment of which must be honoured. In terms of ownership, much of the banking industry is in the public and co-operative sectors and trade unions are also represented on supervisory boards. Finally, if 'power' means bringing the knowledge and experience of many banks and many bank employees to bear on economic problems, then this 'power' should be extended, not curtailed.

In short, it is little wonder that the Big Three banks are often known as the 'prefects' of German industry (Hardach, p.152), although their depositors and borrowers are as a rule more interest-minded than those of other banking groups (MRDB, August 1981, p.19). This is of little wonder. In an analysis of 49,400 enterprises in 1976, the Bundesbank showed that 40 per cent of the sources of funds was represented by borrowed capital (*Sonderdrucke der Deutschen Bundesbank*, Nr 5, pp.4 and 80).


THE CO-OPERATIVE AND TRADE UNION BANKS

Co-operative Banks
Co-operative societies, organised along the lines pioneered by Robert Owen, were founded in German during the nineteenth century by Franz Hermann Schulze-Delitzsch (1808-83) and Friedrich Wilhelm Raiffeisen

(1818-88). They followed the principle of self-help
amongst artisans and peasants respectively in an
attempt to defend them against the new claims of industry (Hesselbach, pp.12-13). The Raiffeisen co-
operatives, the first of which opened in Neuwied in
1865, consisted of a network of agricultural credit
institutions which enabled farmers to borrow money
to meet bills which were presented before the revenue
from annual harvests was derived (Henderson, p.129).
Much the same principle - that is providing credit in
anticipation of future revenue - applied to the
Schultze-Delitzsch co-operative banks, which became
known as Volksbanken, and which were established in
*urban* areas in parallel to the Raiffeisen co-operative
banks in *agricultural* areas.

The rural and urban co-operative banks have
flourished. One indication of this success (Table
8.1) is the size of their central clearing bank (the
DG Bank - Deutsche Genossenschaftsbank). The very
nature of the co-operative banks means that their
most important business lies in the savings and short
or medium terms lending business, even though they
increasingly conduct their business as universal banks.
Their business has expanded rapidly because their enabling Act of 1889 allows them to add a further 50 per
cent to their equity capital when determining their
lending ceiling. (Under the KWG a bank's lending must
not exceed eighteen times its equity capital.) This
additional 50 per cent arises from the legal form
which most co-operative banks adopt - i.e. *beschränkte
Nachschußpflicht* or the limited liability of their
members to make additional contributions should their
bank become insolvent. Such a legal concession has
enabled the co-operative banks to expand their business quite rapidly. The savings banks sector, which
contends that the local authority owners have full
liability anyway, would like to see their enabling
Act amended so as to grant them a similar concession.
This would enable them to dramatically expand their
own business.

This leads to a consideration of the role of the
central institutions of the co-operative banks. As
shown in Figure 8.1 they are 10 in number, including
the DG Bank. Their role is similar to the central
institutions of the savings banks (*Landesbanken*),
namely acting as cheque clearing houses and central
banks to the co-operative banks, although the overall
co-ordinating power of the DG Bank is much greater
than its equivalent in the savings banks sector
(*Deutsche Girozentrale*). For example, whereas each
Landesbank went international in its own right (see

below), the international aspirations of the co-operative banks were channelled into the DG Bank. The DG Bank also manages the liquidity of the co-operative banking sector. All this is remarkable since the DG Bank was established in its present form in only 1975 (DG, *Bank History*, pp.7-8).

But the Landesbanken and the central institutions of the co-operatives share the problem of relying on their respective banking systems for their funds, as well as holding their member banks liquidity. In the case of the co-operatives' central institutions such deposits account for three-quarters of their volume of business and the cost of these funds rose sharply in 1980 - costs which could not always be met in the lending business, with a consequent fall in profitability (MRDB, August 1981, pp.18-19).

Trade Union Banks
Around the turn of the century, parallel to the development of consumers' societies, the trade unions began to form insurance companies, hotels, building societies and housing associations (Hesselbach, p.26). Although the desire to manage their own funds dates back to the formation of German trade unions, however, the first trade union banks postdate the co-operative agricultural and urban savings banks.

Trade union banks of the Weimar Republic showed some tendency to universal banking activities, but their primary function was to act as 'house banks' to the trade unions (Hesselbach, p.89). A wider set of objectives were established after the Second World War. As was the case with the Big Three, however, regional banks - six in number in this instance - were established in 1949 and 1950. In 1953, these banks were joined by the Berlin-based Bank für Wirtschaft und Arbeit. Following the Federal Act permitting amalgamation of banking institutions in 1957, one common establishment, the Bank für Gemeinwirtschaft (BfG) was formed. Its headquarters are in Frankfurt and it has become one of the economy's top-ten banks (see Table 8.1).

Another feature which the BfG has in common with the other big banks is its shareholdings in other banks and specialised credit institutions such as hire purchase companies and building societies. In places like Hamburg, Frankfurt and Düsseldorf, it has gone into partnership with well-established private banks which - as seen above - tend to have expertise in investment matters and function rather like the British merchant bank. Finally, the BfG has links with the public-sector savings bank movement (Hesselbach, pp.94-95).

THE PUBLIC SECTOR

The savings Banks (Sparkassen) movement in Germany
has a longer history than both the co-operative and
trade union banks.  At the beginning of the nineteenth century, encouraging the small saver became
the responsibility of the public authorities.  Since
this task was to be undertaken on a local basis, it
was the municipal authorities who either voluntarily
took the initiative of establishing savings banks or,
after 1838, were required by statute to perform this
function.  Nowadays savings banks generate a large
excess of liquidity.  The larger institutions among
them are also some of the world's largest banks.
     In 1909 a giro or cheque clearing system was
introduced into the savings banks' sector.  Today
this system is operated by the Landesbanken which
also act as regional central banks in the various
Länder of the Federal Republic.  In this role they
manage the immense liquidity of the savings banks and
act as house banks to their Land government.  Whereas
the history of some Landesbanken can be traced back
to the mainly specialist 'public' banks established
during the eighteenth century, it was the roles assumed at the beginning of this century which set the
Landesbanken-Girozentralen (to give them their full
title) on the road to their present-day significance
in the West German banking system (VOB, pp.6 and 12).
Moreover, the Landesbanken provide finance for public
sector projects and offer a complete range of commercial and investment banking services - the universal
banking functions emphasised at the beginning of this
chapter (*ibid.*, p.16).  Both the savings banks and
the Landesbanken are subject to statutory control at
the regional level, but the nationwide and international banking activities of the Landesbanken have
excited considerable controversy, as will be shortly
shown.
     Of late the savings banks have widened their
range of services to compete with the commercial
banks (BSA, p.22).  In the past they have largely
concentrated on savings deposit business and the
corresponding long-term lending, whereas nowadays
they are making increasing inroads into the short-
term deposit and credit business.  Although specialising primarily in lending to medium and small-sized
industry and the self-employed, the larger among the
savings banks, and more particularly the Landes-

banken, also engage heavily in large-scale lending
business, providing finance to industry and taking
part in issuing syndicates (BBk, p.9).
Indeed, the customers of the Big Three, Landesbanken and central co-operative banks primarily consist of large-scale borrowers. They have permanent
access to the Euro markets, which operate on small
margins (MRDB, August 1981, p.17). These banking
groups are therefore exposed to keener competition
than the smaller savings banks and credit co-operatives, which supply credit predominantly to medium
and small-sized firms and to individuals who can draw
less readily on the Euro-markets.
The Landesbanken are large by both domestic and
international standards - see Tables 8.1(a), 8.1(b)
and 8.3. A further indication of their size is that
9 of the 12 Landesbanken appear in the top 20 banks
of the Federal Republic (Stein, 1979, p.40). A series
of mergers between 1969 and 1972 created the giant
Westdeutsche, the Bayerische and the Norddeutsche
Landesbanken. In 1969 the West LB was already at
rank number 6 in *Fortune Magazine*'s list of top fifty
banks outside the USA (*Fortune Magazine*, August 1971,
p.156). The Norddeutsche LB first appeared in the
list as number 49 in 1970 (*ibid.*). This was followed
by the first Bayerische LB appearance at number 44 in
1973 (*Fortune Magazine*, September 1973, p.211). By
1973 the Bayerische moved up to rank number 36 because its loans made on a trust basis were included
among its assets (*Fortune Magazine*, August 1974,
p.182 - it is common in Germany for banks to serve
as trustees for loans not provided by the bank themselves but by other corporations). By 1977 the then
head of the West LB (Dr Ludwig Poullain) was thinking
in terms of merging with another Landesbanken in the
top ten, namely the Hessische. This would have created the largest bank in Europe. Later, mergers in
the north between the Norddeutsche and the LBs in
Bremen, Hamburg and Schleswig-Holstein, and in the
south between the LBs in Baden-Württemberg, Saarland
and Rhineland Palatinate were being considered.
Before the Westdeutsche-Hessische merger could
be seriously considered, however, Dr Poullain had
been forced to resign in 1977 after a controversial
and expansionist career at the bank. Soon after his
trial for accepting consultation fees from a
financier had commenced, his successor as chief
executive of the Westdeutsche (Dr Johannes Völling)
was also forced to resign in 1981 as a result of the
losses arising from the need to re-finance long-term
lending through high-cost short-term borrowing; a

Table 8.3:  International Rank[a] of the Large German
Banks

| Bank | Rank in Top Fifty Banks | | | | | | |
|------|--------|--------|--------|------|------|------|------|
| | Excluding US Banks | | | | | | Including US Banks |
| | 1975 | 1976[b] | 1977[c] | 1978 | 1979 | 1980 | 1980 |
| Deutsche Bank | 3 | 1 | 2 | 2 | 3 | 7 | 9 |
| Dresdner Bank | 14 | 9 | 7 | 11 | 7 | 13 | 16 |
| West LB | 15 | 14 | 14 | 13 | 13 | 16 | 19 |
| Commerzbank | 23 | 21 | 16 | 17 | 15 | 24 | 29 |
| BV Bank | 29 | 23 | 20 | 24 | 22 | 32 | 37 |
| Hypo Bank | 42 | 37 | 34 | 34 | 34 | 37 | 42 |
| Bayerische LB | 35 | 28 | 31 | 32 | 29 | 38 | 43 |
| DG Bank | - | - | 45 | 44 | 43 | - | - |
| BfG | 49 | 41 | 39 | 49 | 47 | - | - |
| Helaba | 43 | 47 | 43 | - | - | - | - |

Notes:
(a) By assets, converted to US$ at current rates of exchange.
Hence appreciation of the DM against the US$ inflates the con-
verted asset value.  Depreciation has the opposite effect.
Nevertheless there is a great deal of stability in terms of
membership of the top fifty: in 1979, for example, 47 banks out
of the top fifty in 1978 had re-appeared in the 1979 list.
Further, 33 banks have been in the list since it was complied
in 1969.  Normally exchange rate adjustments have the effect of
changing the ranking within the top fifty.  The only really significant long-term trend has been for British banks to decline
in ranking, while the representation of Japanese banks has
grown: there were 16 Japanese banks in the top fifty in 1980.
(b) The Deutsche Bank climbed from 11 to 1 in four years.  In
1976/1975 its assets rose by nearly 28 per cent.  Six of the
other German banks achieved increases of more than 20 per cent.
Competitive pressure kept profits from growing as rapidly as
assets, however.
(c) Largest combined asset increase (30.8 per cent).  Deutsche
still largest in terms of deposits, DG Bank returned after 8
year absence (36 per cent asset gain).  Commerz 34 per cent
asset gain - up five places.
(d) Norddeutsche LB appeared as 49 in 1970 following merger of
four 'regional' banks.

Sources:  *Fortune Magazine* (various).

similar situation had also led to a re-shuffle at the
Commerz, although health reasons were also a factor
in this case. (Herr Poullain was later cleared by
the courts and the question of his claim for compensation for unfair dismissal further embarrassed the
West LB. He became financial adviser to Max Grundig
in 1982.)

The Westdeutsche had earlier - in 1973 - lost
DM 270 million in foreign exchange deals, while the
Hessische had lost at least DM 2 billion as a result
of ill-judged banking decisions and property speculation. These latter financial disasters led to the
resignation of the then Hessische chief exectutive,
Dr Wilhelm Hankel, who had previously been chief economist at the KfW. Other notable losses were those
incurred by the Norddeutsche (DM 270 million on an
investment in cameras which suffered badly from Japanese competition), the Württembergische (DM 400 million
in high-risk construction company losses) and the
Badische (DM 80 million when the private Herstatt Bank
collapsed). Hence, only the Bayerische among the big
four has avoided financial scandals.

In 1975, Dr Heinz Sippel became the first banker
to be appointed chief executive of the Hessische, and
the first senior commercial banker to defect to the
West LB (Dr Walter Seipp) significantly became head
of its international division in 1974. (Seipp left
a post at the Deutsche Bank which would almost certainly have given him a seat on the board; following
Poullain's resignation he was made a vice-chairman in
charge of international business - *Financial Times*,
Banking 1980, p.18.) But one of Sippel's conditions
in accepting the appointment was that the bank's expansion would not be curbed in order to merely re-
assume its role as manager of the savings banks
liquidity. The new chief executive at the Westdeutsche, Herr Friedel Neuber, possessed 10 years'
experience on the bank's board, along with experience
in both local political circles and in the savings
banks. Since the assets of the Landesbanken have expanded at such a rapid rate during the 1970s, and
since the larger ones are owned on an equal basis by
the appropriate Land government and savings bank
association, banking expertise coupled with an ability to successfully deal with the Land politicans and
savings banks representatives on the board, are pre-
requisites for any Landesbank chief executive. After
all, the Land acts as guarantor, and politicians have
been forced to resign when their Landesbank has had
financial difficulties.

For historical reasons, there are two Landes-

banken in Baden-Württemberg: the Badische Kommunale
LB and the Württembergische Kommunale LB which is
also known as the Landesbank Stuttgart. These banks
were founded in 1917 and 1916 respectively. After
the Second World War they remained separate entities
in spite of the formation of the new Land of Baden-
Württemberg from territory which had formerly been
three independent Länder. Both banks are entirely
owned by the municipal savings banks through their
respective Associations. The local authorities therefore stand as guarantors. There is a separate house
bank for the Land of Baden-Württemberg: the Baden-
Württembergische Bank AG with a land holding of 90
per cent. Another bank - the Landeskreditbank Baden-
Württemberg - carries out the remaining duties normally transacted by the Landesbank: these entail
granting credit for second mortgages and infra-
structure development programmes. One of the biggest
savings banks in the Federal Republic (Landesgiro-
kasse) also operates on an untypically large scale in
the Stuttgart/Württemberg area.

In the Saar, the Landesbank is also exclusively
owned by the regional Association of Savings Banks,
while in Hamburg the Land has a 100 per cent stake in
the Landesbank. The Bremer Landesbank is 50 per cent
owned by the Norddeutsche LB and a further 25 per
cent is owned by the Land of Lower Saxony. This
leaves only 25 per cent of the share capital in the
hands of the Bremen Land government.

It was not until the late 1960s that the Landesbanken became controversial institutions, that is
when they looked abroad for new investment opportunities. Until this time there had been ample investment opportunities in the domestic economy, both
within private industry and with post-war infra-
structure reconstruction. Meanwhile, the larger
savings banks - in Hamburg the local savings bank is
bigger than the Landesbank - had become serious domestic competitors in both investment sectors. They
also began to deposit funds with the private-sector
commercial banks. By entering fields of low profits
and high risks, the Landesbanken inevitably created
problems for themselves. With the exception of the
Hamburg and Bremen, all the Landesbanken now have
the almost mandatory representation in Luxembourg -
something sought by all West German banks going
international. Only the strength of their public
guarantee has saved them from financial disasters
which may have bankrupted a smaller private commercial bank. On the other hand, the Association of
Public Sector Banks emphasises that its affiliates

are not primarily profit-orientated institutions but
rather represent the traditional dual - private and
public - system of banking in the Federal Republic
(VÖB, p.18).


## SPECIAL PURPOSE BANKS

### Reconstruction and Development Loan Corporation
### (Kreditanstalt für Wiederaufbau - KfW)

The role of Hermann Abs in the post-Second World War
formation of this bank has already been discussed
above. What is most significant here is the evolution
of the bank since its establishment in 1948, for, like
all banks in this heterogeneous group, the KfW was
established for a specific purpose. Originally the
KfW was used to administer funds arising from foreign
(mainly US) aid to West Germany under GARIOA (Government and Relief in Occupied Areas) and the European
Recovery Programme (ERP or, more popularly, 'Marshall
Aid'). This special 'ERP special-fund' (*ERP-
Sondervermögen*) is still the official term for the
public funds allocated by the KfW. (Another principal public fund established about this time - the
Equalisation of Burdens or *Sondervermögen Ausgleichsfonds* - also still exists to further social programmes. The banks responsible for the administration
of this fund will be analysed below.)

When the physical goods supplied in the form of
aid were sold to German consumers, a DM counterpart
fund was generated (Wallich, p.365). It was this
fund which was used for vital capital investment in
the process of reconstruction. The credit created
on the basis of the counterpart funds was adminis-
tered by the KfW, initially under the supervision of
the American authorities. Later, the Federal Government assumed responsibility. Credit creation for
capital investment purposes was not inflationary because food imports and consumption were supplied under
foreign aid (Wallich, p.365). Counterpart funds
played a strategic role in German investment; counterpart investment was probably the most carefully
planned of all capital expenditures (*ibid.*, p.175).

As Shonfield indicates (pp.276-277) the KfW became a banker's bank - a valuable source of additional
long-term credit which had two effects. First, the
government could legitimately create credit out of
the counterpart fund in a regimé where its power to
do so was otherwise constrained by the independence
of the central bank. Second, the credit so created
supplemented the exiguous resources of the commercial

banks, since it was their task to recommend and guarantee their customers' applications for investment loans. Hence all the technical competence of Germany's universal banking system, already demonstrated above, was brought to bear on the removal of bottlenecks where small amounts of capital investment would produce a disproportionately large return.

Hence the KfW received interest on its loans and eventual repayment. Its assets expanded until they totalled, in 1980, DM 53.7 billion (*Annual Report*). It was the Federal Republic's eleventh largest bank (Table 8.1(a), note a). By 1981 it was again the tenth largest, with assets of DM 61.3 billion and profits of DM 21.8 million (Table 8.1(b)). As a result of miscalculated interest-rate risks (in common with many other banks) its net income had slumped in 1980 to DM 11.7 million from DM 69.8 million on assets of DM 50.2 billion in 1979. In 1978 the respective figures had been more impressive: DM 81 million on DM 43.4 billion (BMF, 1979, pp.164-165). Its nominal capital of DM 1 billion is held on the following basis: 71 per cent by the Federal Government; 20 per cent by the Länder; 9 per cent by the federal ERP-Sondervermögen (BMF, 1980, p.180 and 1981, p.190).

Today the KfW has three major roles. First, it acts increasingly as a development-aid bank by granting government-approved loans to finance projects in underdeveloped countries (Stein, 1977, p.28). Such projects are assessed by the bank's own expert advisers. Second, the KfW plays an important role in financing direct exports. Third, the bank has become an extremely active agent of official regional policies (Shonfield, p.279). Allied to this domestic regional development function is the amount of aid now given to small businesses: in 1979 20 per cent of the overall capital investment needs of West German companies with under 200 employees were met from KfW supported finance. Hence a longer and wider view of investment prospects are taken by the KfW than would be the case with an ordinary commercial lender (Shonfield, pp.279 and 282). This was exemplified in the preparations for the 1982 federal budget when it was decided that DM 400 million would be paid into the KfW for low-interest loans.

In short, the KfW was launched to balance the ERP books. But over the years it has become an important source of investment credit. The liberal policies of the KfW in this respect probably gave the Bundesbank greater flexibility to pursue its more conservative monetary policies.

Other Public-Sector Special Purpose Banks
The KfW has a 20 per cent holding in the DM 50 million
share capital of the Berliner Industriebank AG, Berlin;
68 per cent belongs to the ERP-Sodervermögen; 4.8 per
cent to the Land Berlin and the remaining 7.2 per cent
to 'other shareholders' (BMF, 1980, p.307). This bank
was founded in 1949 to foster the growth of the economy of West Berlin by granting medium and long-term
loans at favourable interest rates. Again its early
capital was almost entirely supplied out of the ERP
special fund, although later tax concessions under the
Berlin Aid Act attracted some private deposits (Stein,
1977, p.29). In 1979 its balance sheet total amounted
to DM 3.2 billion and its net income to DM 10.3 million
- precisely the same net income which was achieved on
assets of DM 3.1 billion in 1978 (BMF, 1979, pp.285-
286). Similarly, DM 10.3 million was achieved on
assets of DM 3.5 billion in 1980 (BMF, 1980, pp.307-
308). In common with many other banks its profitability improved in 1981: DM 19.9 million on DM 3.8
billion (BMF, 1981, pp.313-314). The existence of
this special-purpose bank is some indication of the
economic problems created by the location of West
Berlin (Owen Smith, 1979, pp.167-168, and Chapter 6
above).
    There are two major banks which owe their origins
to the post-war attempts to integrate the expellees
and refugees. In both cases a second specially created fund (*Sondervermögen Ausgleichsfonds*) was initially used for capitalisation purposes. The two
banks concerned are the Deutsche Siedlungs- und Land-
resrentenbank (DSL - Housing and Agricultural Mortgage
Bank), and the Lastenausgleichsbank (Bank für Vietrie-
bene und Geschädigte), Bonn - where the sub-title
literally translated means 'Bank for Expellees and
(War) Disabled (BfVG)'.
    The former bank (DSL) results from an amalgamation
of two separate banks which carried out each of its
two main functions until 1966. Its basic activity
nowadays is financing rural reform programmes, particularly in areas which attracted a large number of expellees and refugees after the Second World War (BMF,
1979, p.245; Stein, 1977, p.30). As well as raising
capital from the Equalisation of Burdens fund, this
bank attracts capital from the Federal Government,
which is its main 'shareholder'. The remainder of its
capital was owned by various Länder governments, although the Federal share increased to 98.99 per cent
in 1981 (BMF, 1980, p.263). A further source of funds
is the capital market. In 1980 it returned a DM 35
million net income on assets of DM 22.1 billion

(*Annual Report*).
The BfVG was established in 1950 to assist, by means of low-interest loans, in the process of integrating expellees, refugees and war victims into the economic life of the newly emergent Federal Republic (BMF, 1979, p.291; Stein, 1977, p.29). Although the bulk of its nominal capital value is held by the federal Equalisation of Burdens fund (88 per cent), the remaining 12 per cent lies in the hands of the federal ERP special fund. Today the bank promotes many social programmes and supports small business projects. It raises its finance from a wide variety of sources. In 1980 its net income amounted to DM 5.0 million, with assets of DM 10.9 billion. Its profit remained at DM 5.0 million in 1981, whereas its assets had increased to DM 11.4 billion (BMF, 1981, pp.321-322).

Also classified in the special purpose category are the Deutsche Bau- und Bodenbank AG (housing finance); the Landwirtschaftliche Rentenbank (food production finance) and the Deutsche Verkehrs-Kredit-Bank AG (transport finance). All three of these public-sector banks contributed to the elimination of the various post-Second World War shortages. Their assets are in the region DM 4 billion, DM 8 billion and DM 4.5 billion respectively (BMF, 1980, pp.185 and 352; Stein, 1977, p.30). The housing finance institution is nowadays an almost fully-owned subsidiary of the much larger public-sector Deutsche Pfandbriefanstalt. (A *Pfandbrief* is a special kind of mortgage bond issued by German mortgage banks.) In 1980 the Deutsche Pfandbriefanstalt had assets of DM 31.7 billion, and realised a net income of DM 45.7 million (*Annual Report*). It is owned mainly by the Federal Government (51.93 per cent), the Federal Post Office (19.04 per cent) and the Equalisation of Burdens fund has a 7.62 per cent stake (BMF, p.182). However, it is classified as a public mortgage bank in the official statistics. Finally, the sole holder of the nominal capital of the transport industry's bank is the Federal Railways.

As in the case of the KfW, therefore, the major conclusion must be that the reconstruction of the post-Second World War economy owes much to the credit created by the various specially formed, publicly-owned banks.

## Special Purpose Banks Owned by Various Financial Consortia

In 1952 a group of the most significant German export banks founded the AKA Ausfuhrkredit GmbH (export credit company, the legal form of GmbH being adopted

in 1960) (Stein, 1977, p.28). In 1974, the Deutsche
Industriebank, Berlin (established in 1924) and the
Industriekreditbank AG, Düsseldorf (established in
1949) finally merged, having been closely associated
for a number of years (*ibid.*, p.29). The resultant
institution has as its title a compound of the names
of the two banks which formed the new company. It
makes medium and long-term loans to firms which fall
into the median size category. Institutional investors and the issue of bonds supply the bank's funds
and ownership is mainly vested in the large banks and
insurance companies. It assets in 1978 amounted to
DM 9.2 billion (Stein, 1979, p.33).

A final special purpose bank is of particular
interest in an analysis of this nature. It is a
consortium established in 1974 to handle domestic and
foreign payment transactions and to bridge posssible
liquidity shortages in the banking sector (Stein,
1977, p.30). Its title is the Liquiditäts-Konsortial-
bank GmbH and its capital was raised from all groups
in the banking sector: the Bundesbank holds 30 per
cent of the share capital; the private banks also
hold 30 per cent; the savings banks 26.5 per cent;
the co-operative banks 11.0 per cent; the BfG 1.5 per
cent and the instalment sales financing institutions
hold the remaining 1 per cent. Non-banking business
is not handled and the partners can be obliged to
make supplementary payments.

Hence, once again the industry-orientated nature
of German banking may clearly be seen.


## MORTGAGE AND BUILDING SAVINGS BANKS

### The Housing Stock
In relation to incomes, house prices in the UK lie
between 3 to 3½ times average gross earnings, whereas
in West Germany the factor is more in the order of
between 5 and 8 (Bradley, p.941). In other words a
new flat in Germany in the late 1970s cost DM 150,000,
and the figure for a new house was well over DM
200,000 (BSA, p.12). Perhaps not surprisingly, therefore, there is a relatively lower level of owner occupation in West Germany than in the UK - only about 38
per cent compared with 54 per cent (Bradley, pp.938
and 941; BSA, p.11). In the rented sector, by the
mid-1970s, there was hardly anywhere in the country
where the would-be tenant could not find a passable
choice of flats or houses at reasonable rents (BSA,
p.8). How did this come about?

It will be recalled that there was an acute

housing shortage for several years following the
Second World War, a shortage which had been brought
about by both war damage on the housing stock side,
and by the influx of ethnic German expellees and refugees on the demand side. An enormous output of housing induced by subsidies and various tax concessions,
gradually resolved the quantitative aspect of the
problem. By 1980, the housing stock had reached 25.4
million, 16.8 million of which had been completed
since the founding of the Federal Republic (BMWi,
Table 4.42). It will also be recalled, however, that
the expansion of real investment in construction as a
whole fell from an annual average of 9.3 per cent in
the 1950s to 1.8 per cent in the 1970s (Table 4.2).
There were also two absolute falls in the late-1960s
and mid-1970s (Diagram 4.2(b)). Nevertheless,
Diagram 8.1 illustrates this dramatic growth pattern
of housing. Only at the beginning and the end of the
period with which this book is mainly concerned (1950-
1980) did the annual output of housing fall below the
half million mark. Indeed in 21 of the 31 years this
figure was exceeded, with a peak of 714,200 in 1973
when many builders were bankrupted by the speculative
over-building of accommodation intended for renting
(Bradley, p.941).

Hence, Germany has passed from a shortage-situ-
ation in which rent extortioners had a field-day, to
one in which the potential surplus of rented accommodation is a political issue, not least because very
little new rented stock is being built. Further,
about 45 per cent of the completions by 1980 were one-
family dwellings, whereas in 1960 the figure had been
only 20 per cent (BMWi, Table 4.42; Dresdner Bank,
*Wirtschaftsberichte,*June 1982, p.10). In the same
time period the multi-family type housing unit had
fallen from 55 per cent to 30 per cent of all completions. This important qualitative change in the
housing market may be accompanied by a trend towards
a greater degree of owner-occupation (BSA, p.14).
Such a change is taking place in spite of the advantages under income and land tax laws of including a
self-contained flat in newly built accommodation.
Income tax relief is not given on mortgage interest
payments in West Germany. There are, however, numerous other tax advantages of which mortgagors may avail
themselves. Not the least of these attractions is the
Building Savings Premium to which long-term contract
savers with building savings banks are entitled. In
addition, real personal disposable income is relatively high, helped by the maximum 56 per cent income
tax rate and low inflation (Diagrams 4.5 and 5.1).

Diagram 8.1:   Annual Additions to the Housing Stock,
1950-1980

(a)

Completed dwellings
(000s)

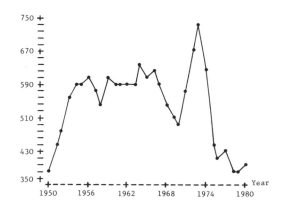

(b)

Growth in volume
of annual expendi-
ture on residential
buildings
(Log$_e$, at current
prices)

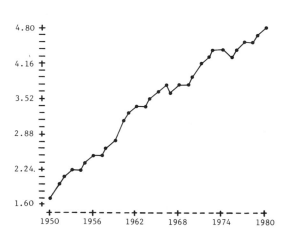

Source:   Based on data from Dresdner Bank, *Statische
Reihen*, June 1981, p.3.

For all the reasons given in this paragraph, therefore, it seems reasonable to predict that the housing
finance institutions will attract a growing clientele.

### The Housing Finance Institutions

The generic term for the institutions providing building finance in the Federal Republic is *Realkredit-
institute*, a term which is clearly linked to the concept of real estate. There are a number of institutions in the field. The reason for this is that it
would be impossible for most people to borrow nearly
all the price of a house because the burden of mortgage repayments, even at low rates of interest, would
represent an intolerably high proportion of net income (Bradley, pp.938 and 941). Hence the mortgagor
usually purchases a property by means of a mortgage
package consisting of a sizeable deposit from his own
funds, a first mortgage supplied by a commercial,
mortgage or savings bank and a second mortgage,
usually provided on the basis of a savings contract
by a building savings bank. Additionally, loans from
the Federal and Länder Governments finance approximately 9 per cent of all mortgage lending (BSA, p.17).

Figure 8.1 indicates that there are 25 private-
sector mortgage banks (Hypothekenbanken). In the
public-sector there are a further 13 mortgage banks
(Öffentliche Hypothekenbanken or Grundkreditanstalten).
Similarly, there are 18 private building savings banks
(Bausparkassen), together with their 13 public-sector
counterparts (Landesbausparkassen).

Four out of the six largest private mortgage
banks, and several smaller ones, are owned by the Big
Three (Bradley, p.940; BSA, p.15). Another of the
six largest in the official statistics is owned by
the DG Bank. The public-sector mortgage banks represent the earliest development in the Landesbanken
system. They stem from the 18th century Landschaften,
Ritterschaften and 19th century Stadtschaften (agricultural and urban societies - VOB, p.6). Today's
largest public mortgage bank (Wohnungsbau-Finanz-
ierungsanstalt des Landes Nordrhein-Westfalen) has a
larger balance-sheet total than the largest private
mortgage banks (Stein, 1977, pp.25-26).

Mortgage banks raise their funds either by issuing mortgage bonds (*Hypothekenpfandbriefe*) or - in
order to finance the increasing amount of lending to
government at all levels - by the issue of communal
bonds (*Kommunalobligationen*). Bonds issued by the
mortgage banks thus constitute a *very* important sector of the fixed-interest securities market (Schneider, p.16).

Predictably, the sales of mortgage bonds have
roughly reflected the fluctuations in house building.
The sales of communal bonds, on the other hand, displayed a rapid growth in the second half of the 1970s.
This growth rate was so dramatic that communal bonds
became much more significant than mortgage bonds in
fixed interest business. It also contributed to the
highly positive skewness of the total bond sales, as
can be seen from the relative sizes of the medians
and means in both communal and total bond sales
(Table 8.4). Similarly, as Table 8.4 also indicates,
other bank bonds and public authority bonds contributed to the rapid expansion of bond sales during the
1970s. In the case of the sales of Public Authority
bonds there was also a significant increase during
the 1967 recession. Finally, it should be added that
some of the privately-owned mortgage banks are engaged in the finance of shipbuilding, an activity
which clearly involves the provision of medium and
long-term loans.

Table 8.4: Medians and Means of Bond Sales (DM million)

| Type | Median | Mean |
| --- | --- | --- |
| Total | 16424.0 | 30666.0 |
| Mortgage | 3782.0 | 4659.1 |
| Communal | 3693.0 | 10339.0 |
| Special Purpose and DG Bank | 1360.0 | 1883.7 |
| Other Bank | 971.0 | 6078.4 |
| Public Authority | 3591.0 | 7130.4 |

Notes:
The Pearson coefficient for mortgage bonds = +0.69,
communal bonds = +1.48, other bank = +1.58, public
authority = +1.26 and total bonds = +1.49.
Some definitions of bonds are given monthly in MRDB,
Table VI(2)n.
'Other Bank' bonds are issued principally by Landes-
banken - see below.

Source: Calculated from Dresdner Bank, *Statische
Reihen*, June 1981, p.7.

Returning to the housing market, it can be noted
that a first mortgage, up to a legal maximum of 60
per cent of the total price of a property, is normally

lent directly by a commercial or savings bank, or
through a mortgage bank (Bradley, p.940). Mortgage
banks specialise in mortgage lending to finance both
owner-occupation and the building of accommodation
for renting. Hence over recent years they have been
induced to change their lending pattern as a result
of the increase in owner-occupation outlined above.
The commercial banks generally sell first mortgages
provided by their mortgage bank subsidiaries, although they are prepared to offer long-term building
finance up to 80 per cent of the total cost or buying
price based on the borrower's creditworthiness and
secured only by a second mortgage. Total mortgage
packages are increasingly offered by the commercial
banks and mortgage finance altogether accounts for 25
per cent of the commercial banks' business (*ibid.*,
p.940). This proportion compares to the 50 per cent
of lending by the savings banks in the form of long-
term loans for housing finance and for capital expenditure by local authorities (BSA, p.23).

But whereas mortgage banks rely on (fixed
interest) bonds for their source of re-finance, the
savings banks attract the largest proportion of savings deposits and bonds (Table 8.5 below). Until
recently the mortgage lending patterns of these two
types of institutions tended to reflect the nature of
their re-financing: the savings banks issued variable
rate loans, repayable over 25 or 30 years, whereas
the mortgage banks issued relatively short-term loans
at over 5 to 7 years at fixed rates of interest, the
maturity of these loans matching the maturity of their
bonds (Boléat, p.11). However, the recent increase
in owner-occupation has tended to have the effect of
lengthening the average mortgage bank loan and increasing the number of fixed rate mortgages offered
by the savings banks (BSA, p.15).

There are large private building savings banks
operating throughout West Germany. Interests in them
have been acquired by the commercial banks (Bradley,
p.940). The two largest are the Schwäbisch Hall and
the Wustenrot, although the DG Bank had a 38.5 per
cent holding in the former (*Annual Report*, 1980, p.25).
Public-sector building savings banks, on the other
hand, operate regionally because they are an integral
part of the Landesbank system (BSA, p.16).

Although they are almost as big as the British
building society movement, German building savings
banks do not dominate the market in the same way: they
provide only 40 per cent of total housing finance,
much of which is concentrated on the financing of new
dwellings. Building savings banks also differ from

British building societies in that both the rate of
interest they pay on savings contracts and the
interest rate which they receive on loans are both
fixed. Hence in respect of variable interest rates,
the savings banks tend more to resemble the British
building societies (Boléat, p.11). Moreover, repayments to building savings banks are kept as short as
possible. Consequently, annuities are high and loans
are usually paid off in eight to twelve years. Finally, unlike the British building societies, the
building savings banks do not operate as major savings
institutions. This is because of the strength of the
savings bank movement which attracts a savings volume
almost four times larger than the private-sector
building savings banks (*ibid.*, p.11; Statistical Sup-
lement, MRDB, November 1981, Tables 7 and 13).

Building savings banks are therefore best seen
as specialist institutions which extend loans to
depositors after completion of a contractual savings
plan, the loans being secured by second mortgages exclusively used for the acquisition, renovation or improvement of private homes (Schneider, p.18). This
system has been succinctly described as indiscriminate, guaranteed and insulated (BSA, p.18). It is
indiscriminate in the sense that anyone may take out
a savings contract. It is guaranteed because anyone
fulfilling contractual obligations has a right to a
loan, and it is insulated because the closed nature
of the business separates it from the interest rates
prevailing in other sectors of the money market.
Hence, the fixed interest rates paid to contract
savers will sometimes be highly competitive, while
at other times they will be substantially below other
nominal rates (Boléat, p.10). But the real value of
the return on savings contracts is greatly enhanced
by the various bonuses paid under the Savings Premium and other Acts (BSA, pp.18 and 23). These
bonuses attract funds from savers who have no intention of purchasing a property with the result that as
much as 25 per cent of total contract savings emanate
from this source, making this the only really developed contractual scheme in the Federal Republic.
Notwithstanding these bonuses, however, the disadvantage of the closed system in which the building savings banks operate is that they are unable to offer
loans sufficient in themselves to finance house purchase. Thus the analysis can now focus on the nature
of the mortgage package as such. This package will
be sold to the borrower at the first point of con-
tact, be it a commercial, savings or building savings
bank. Indeed, arranging such packages, and savings

contracts, are the main functions of a building savings bank office and the British visitor may be
struck by the almost complete absence of cash transactions at these offices. However, it is argued in
West Germany that in this way a mortgage package may
be tailored to suit individual requirements (BSA,
p.19).
    Hence, assuming that a savings contract with a
building savings bank has been observed for an agreed
period (between 18 and 36 months - *ibid.*, p.17), and
also assuming that 20 per cent of the purchase price
is provided from the buyer's own funds, the Dresdner
Bank, for example, would arrange a package of a
further 50 per cent from its mortgage bank and 30 per
cent direct from its own resources (*ibid.*, p.19).
The mortgage bank would issue a matching bond and the
borrower would pay a fixed rate of interest on that
part of the loan. Similarly, the borrower would also
pay a fixed rate of interest, over an agreed period
of the 30 per cent loan. A capital sum equal to half
of the the total loan would have to be repaid by
means of a second mortgage at the end of about an
eight-year period. Since the total loan was equal
to 80 per cent of the purchase price, therefore, a
contract enabling the borrower to repay 40 per cent
of the purchase price at the end of eight years would
be taken out with a building savings bank. Eight
years later, a second contract enabling the borrower
to repay the balance of his loan would be taken out.
A similarly strong vertical integration is to be
found throughout the West German system of housing
finance (Bradley, p.940).


SOME GENERAL ASPECTS OF BANKING

Business Developments in the Period 1950-1980
In the decade 1950-1960, longer-term banking business
became more prominent, with a consequential decrease
in the relative importance of short-term business
(MRDB, March 1961, p.27). As a result, those institutions which engaged more in long-term business -
private and public mortgage banks, savings banks and
Landesbanken - raised their proportion of total banking business. Expressed as a proportion of the total
volume of business the mortgage banks more than
doubled their share (5.9 to 12.8 per cent); the savings banks and their central institutions' share increased from 30.8 to 36.0 per cent. On the other
hand, the commercial banks' share went down from
36.4 to 26.5 per cent (for the Big Three the fall

was from 19.1 to 12 per cent). The co-operatives'
share also fell marginally - from 12.4 to 10.7 per
cent (MRDB, March 1961, pp.28-29).
      In the decade 1960 to 1970 the banks more than
trebled their volume of business, a rate of increase
in excess of that of GNP which, at current prices,
doubled (MRDB, April 1971, p.29). There was also a
fairly large number of mergers in West German banking. The pace of bank growth was, however, no longer
so rapid as in the 1950s when, starting from the very
low base after the Currency Reform, the business volume of the banks increased six-fold. For that matter
the business expansion in the banking sector during
the 1960s was not as rapid as building savings banks
and insurance companies, notably the former which
benefited from government measures to stimulate savings (*ibid.*, pp.29-30).
      Allowing for the break in the continuity of bank-
ing statistics caused by the 1968 revision, developments during the 1960s within the banking sector were
a good deal more uniform than in the 1950s. Of all
three branches of the universal banks, however, the
commercial banks, and therefore the Big Three, recorded the smallest growth rate; the savings banks
and Landesbanken enlarged their lead even further so
that by 1970 they had virtually reached the two-fifths
share of the total business volume they were to still
account for in 1981 (Figure 8.1). Significantly from
the point of view of their 15 per cent share of business volume in 1981 (Figure 8.1), the co-operatives
made the biggest advance during the decade from 1960
to 1970: the reporting ones grew from 8.6 to 11.5 per
cent of the total business volume; including the non-
reporting ones the growth was from 10 to 13 per cent.
This generally more uniform rate was due to the fact
that longer-term lending no longer grew more quickly
than other types of business (*ibid.*, pp.30 and 32).
      Although the volume of business again trebled
during the 1970s business conditions became less
stable (MRDB, August 1981, p.14). Moreover, from
1 April 1967, there was a total abolition of the
interest rate controls imposed during the 1932 banking crisis which, together with a rapid extension of
the branch network, paved the way for more general
competition (MRDB, April 1971, p.31).
      Thus the re-emergence of banking in the Federal
Republic during the 1950s and the 1960s resembles
very much the general expansionary and merger trends
of the economy at large. Similarly, the more cycli-
cally-prone experience of the 1970s is also reflected
in the banking sector, when profitability fluctuated

widely under the influence of the general trends in
interest rates and economic activity (MRDB, August
1980, p.19). The tightening of the Bundesbank's
restrictive course in 1973 confronted the banks with
a new situation (MRDB, May 1974, p.24).

In general terms, the 1970s ushered in a decade
of wide fluctuations in the earnings position of the
banks, as well as a tendency for the proportionate
rise in staff and other operating costs to outstrip
the increase in net interest and commissions - again
two now familiar trends to readers of this book (MRDB,
January 1978, pp.13-14 and 16). Aside from mounting
staff costs, there were also higher rents for office
space and data processing equipment, all of which
were directly connected with the continued strong
expansion in business volume (MRDB, August 1980,
pp.22-23). In this latter sense - the expansion of
business volume - the German banks face the dual
problem of still making profits by keeping the growth
of costs in check and at the same time keeping their
shareholders content after a decade of shareholder
financed capital/asset ratio growth which created the
banks' expansion of their lending limits. This profitability problem probably caught up with the German
banks a full decade after it had hit German industry.

Hence at the end of the 1970s West Germany's
powerful banking industry was experiencing its most
difficult period since its reconstitution after the
Second World War. Two further years of restrictive
credit policy had resulted from the Bundesbank's protracted tight monetary policy. Long-term lending
agreed in 1977 and 1978, when the banking system had
a high level of liquidity, became difficult to re-
finance when the unanticipated balance of payments
deficit led to a restrictive monetary policy. This
helps to explain the descent in international terms
of the seven members of the German top ten banks
which were also among the international top fifty
(see Table 8.3). Moreover, while most of the German
banks registered declines in dollar-denominated assets
- the fall for the group was 5 per cent - the Commerzbank's assets dropped even in domestic currency terms.
This was exceptional: it had only happened to other
banks on three previous occasions while *Fortune Magazine* has been recording data over a seven-year period
(*Fortune Magazine*, 10 August 1981, p.220).

There are thus three features of banking which
require further analysis. First, the fall in domestic
profitability at the end of the 1970s. Second, high
administrative costs, particularly in terms of personnel costs. Third, the profitability crisis in

the domestic economy was exacerbated by international
problems.

Trends in Profitability
In order to examine the profitability record of the
banks in a little more depth it is necessary to de-
fine 'the volume of business', 'operating result (or
net operating income)' and 'pre-tax profits'. This
is because annual data on these variables has been
collected by the Bundesbank since 1968. However,
some caution is necessary when examining these published data because the banks have large reserves on
which they may draw or which they may replenish.

The volume of business represents an enlarged
balance sheet total since it includes endorsement
liabilities and bills drawn by the banks in circulation (MRDB, March 1961, p.26 and October 1979,
p.15n). As from 1976 the volume of business also
included the foreign branches of commercial banks and
in 1979 the statistic was further extended to cover
the foreign branches of the Landesbanken (MRDB,
August 1981, p.14). The operating result is defined
as:

> Interest received - interest paid
> + commissions received - commissions paid
> - administrative expenses
> or
> net interest received + net commission received
> - administrative expenses
> (where net interest received is by far the most
> important source of income for the banks and is
> functionally related to the volume of business
> and levels of interest rates in particular
> periods of time; also where staff costs are by
> far the larger proportion of administrative
> expenses).

Pre-tax profits (taxes on income, earnings and net
assets) are defined as:

> Operating result + excess of other receipts
> over other expenses (where the latter is
> typically a negative item)
> (MRDB, November 1976, pp.16, 18 and 20)

Diagram 8.2 illustrates the low overall profitability of the West German banks in 1973 and 1979,
as well as the high profitability of banking in 1975.
It is also possible to see that the decline of profitability in 1979 was followed in 1980 by an overall

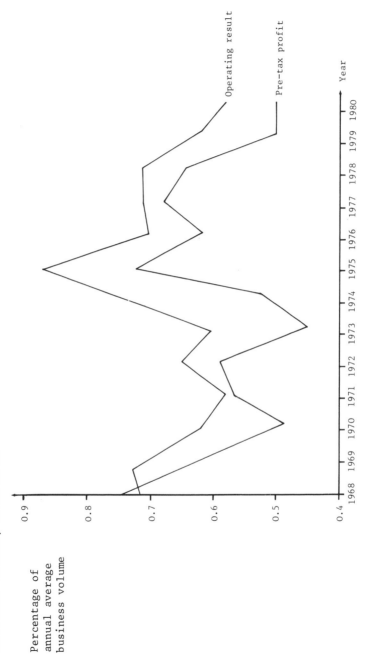

Diagram 8.2: Operating Results and Pre-Tax Profit as Percentages of Annual Average Business Volume, 1968–1980

Source: Based on data from MRDB, August 1981, p.14.

stabilisation. However, there were marked differences in individual cases. Within the top ten group of banks, for example, only four banks produced an increase in profits. As can be seen from Table 8.1(a) three of the four increases were relatively small, especially when viewed in conjunction with the relatively high falls. Only the DG Bank significantly improved on its patchy profit performance of the 1970s, although it too had problems (Table 8.1(b)). Among the top four private-sector banks, only the Deutsche raised its dividend in 1980: from 9 to 10 per cent, a level retained in 1981. The Bayerische Vereinsbank held its dividend at 9 per cent in both 1980 and 1981, while the Dresdner cut its rate from 9 to 6 per cent in 1980, followed by a cut to 4 per cent in 1981. In both 1980 and 1981, the Commerzbank did not pay a dividend at all and offered some of its holding in a mortgage bank for sale. It thus became the first major West German bank in the post-Second World War period to miss its dividend payment and to sell assets to draw on hidden reserves in order to avoid declaring a loss. The BfG also began to dispose of some of its subsidiaries in order to counter its earnings crisis.

What seems to have occurred is that the writedowns for definitive loan losses and for actual and latent risks in national and international banking business all rose sharply. As a result of providing for these risks, the banks' pre-tax profits in 1981 rose less steeply than the operating result. A fillip to profitability was also given by the expiration of fixed interest loans made during the last period of low interest rates. Hence, as measured by the operating result, all banking groups except the Landesbanken and the private mortgage banks were able to improve their profitability in 1981, though to varying degrees. Overall profitability in 1981, as measured by the operating result as a percentage of business volume, was well above the 10-year average for 1971-1980 (0.68 per cent) at 0.75 per cent. Pre-tax profits measured in the same way, however, were still below the average for 1971-1980 (0.58 per cent) at 0.52 per cent (MRDB, October 1982, pp.15-16).

The data for 1975 and 1980 in Table 8.1(a) also indicate the dramatically different profit performance in these two years, both of which were notable for their recessionary trends (Diagrams 4.2 and 4.3; Table 4.7). Yet the 1975 results were the best in banking history. One measure of profitability in 1975 is that net income in some cases was higher in absolute terms than in 1980. Even where 1980 profits were higher in absolute terms, the growth on 1975

was less than the 22 per cent growth in the retail
price index. These high rates of profitability in
1975 were attributable, first, to the interest differential between lending and borrowing rates. Although interest received (DM 93.3 billion) actually
fell by -4.1 per cent on the previous year, interest
paid (DM 64.1 billion) decreased by -11.1 per cent
(MRDB, August 1981, p.14). Hence net interest received increased both absolutely (+DM 29.2 billion)
and as a percentage of business volume, which at 2.24
per cent was the highest in the whole period (1968-
1980) for which comparable statistics exist. A negative change in interest payments in this sense is
wholly untypical, although net interest received as a
percentage of the average volume of business displayed
a downward trend between 1976 and 1980. The extent of
the fall in interest rates and the rapid rise in
liquidity were presumably responsible for both the
unique negative change in interest payments in 1975
and for what was to be the final rise in net interest
received in the decade. Also of significance for
profitability is the fact that the proportionate rises
in interest paid in 1973, 1979 and 1980 were greater
than those of interest received (*ibid.*, p.14).

A second factor which accounts for the profitability peak in 1975 was the booming stock market.
To this must be added, thirdly, the steep rise in the
sales of bonds, particularly communal bonds in 1975.
Public authority and 'other' bank bonds sales had also
generally increased rapidly during the 1970s, reflecting the growth in public indebtedness. The proceeds of 'other' bank bonds, which are principally
issued by the Landesbanken, tend to be extended as
credit to industry and trade (MRDB, October 1981,
p.51*n). Not only did this source of funds become
more costly in 1980, however, but lending to enterprises and private individuals by the Landesbanken
increased by only 6 per cent in 1980, compared to a
16 per cent increase in public-sector lending in the
same year and 17 per cent in 1979. These increases
in public-sector lending stem from the role of the
Landesbanken as principal bankers to the public authorities. While hardly any risks attach to such assets,
they are less lucrative profitability-wise than loans
to private customers (MRDB, August 1981, p.19).
Nevertheless, bond yields generally reached correspond-
ingly high levels during the 1970s. The average
annual yield of 10.6 per cent in 1974 was a post-
Second World War high, with averages over 8 per cent
for eight years during the period 1970-1980, compared
to a post-war (1950-1980) mean of 7 per cent.

Growing Administrative Costs

In Germany a dense network of sophisticated savings
institutions services an economy in which there is a
traditionally high propensity to save (Diagram 4.1;
Table 4.6). Both the emergence of the dense banking
network and savings opportunities owe a lot to the
public and co-operative sectors. Originally the savings banks were opened to everyone, whereas the credit
co-operatives served only their own members, of which
there are now 8 million (BVR, *Zahlen 1980*, p.27).
Over time the agricultural and urban co-operatives
have moved much closer together and the services they
offer are similar to those offered by the savings
banks. Hence all three do not differ radically in
the structure of their business or their customers
(MRDB, August 1981, p.18). However, the co-operatives
remain the property of their members, while the savings banks are still normally owned by the municipal
authorities.

With over 4,000 local co-operative banks and
nearly 600 savings banks, together having 32,343
branches, these parts of the banking sectors provide
the most extensive banking network in Europe (*ibid.*,
Table III(25b)). After the Currency Reform, both
sectors expanded more rapidly than the private sector.
Today, the co-operative and public sector banks
account for over half of the total volume of banking
business (Figure 8.1). Over three-quarters of all
savings deposits and savings banks, as well as over
80 per cent of the country's bank branches, are
accounted for by the co-operative and public sectors
(*ibid.*, Table III(25b); Table 8.5). However, these
sectors do not exert the overwhelming influence that
their massive aggregate business volume suggests.
Both sectors are fragmented, as is borne out by both
their numbers and the size of the branch networks.

Diagram 8.3 also suggests, however, that when
one refers to 'a dense network of savings institutions', one is really nowadays emphasising the
number of branches even more than the number of banks.
The number of credit co-operatives has fallen from
11,795 in 1957 to 4,225 in 1980, whereas in the same
period their branches increased from 2,305 to 15,453
(*ibid.*, Table III(25b) and April 1971, p.31). The
fall in the number of savings banks - from 871 to
599 - was not so dramatic, although their number of
branches more than doubled: from 8,192 to 16,890.
As already shown, the number of private bankers has
also displayed a long-term downward trend, but the
commercial banks generally, and the Big Three in
particular, have made a greater effort in recent years

to build up their personal sector business (BSA,
p.22). In consequence, the Big Three increased their
branches in the above time period from 787 to 3,124.
Hence, despite the decline in the number of banks,
the number of bank branches has risen at a time of
rapidly rising labour costs and rapid changes in
banking technology. West Germany has one bank branch
for every 1,400 members of the population compared to
a ratio of one to 4,000 in Britain and one to 6,000
in the USA (*Die Zeit*, 24/81, p.25).
   In this sense, then, West Germany is 'over-
banked'. The two pressures which will inevitably induce rationalisation are rising staff costs and changing technology. The problem of rising labour costs is
an almost universal one in the German economy: in the
banks such costs represent two-thirds of total administrative costs and they increased by 10.3 per cent in
1980 (MRDB, August 1981, p.17). In 1981, the number
of staff increased still further, although the increase in staff costs (6.5 per cent) was less than the
9.5 per cent increase in the volume of business (MRDB,
October 1982, pp.15 and 18). The staffing problem is
exacerbated by customer conservatism and inertia, although in view of the periodic banking crises and inflation this disposition is probably understandable.
In other words, the German retail banking customer in
particular may have to be cajoled into accepting new
forms of banking service. Another astonishing anach-
ronism in an age of computerisation is the existence
of an independent clearing system in each banking
sector. Moreover, towards the end of the 1970s there
were increasing signs that German savers are shopping
around. This trend was accompanied by a growing interest-rate consciousness among savers (BMWi, 1980,
p.30). Customers tended to move away from low interest savings accounts into short-term instruments
offering higher rates. This trend began at a time
when interest rates were on an upward trend.

International Trends in Banking
The expansion of West German banks abroad was one of
the major developments in world banking during the
1970s. This trend was clearly demonstrated by both
the data and the footnotes presented in Table 8.3.
It is also apparent that the relatively slower growth
in assets and profits brought about some decline at
the end of the decade. The domestic reasons for the
fall in profitability have already been analysed.
Internationally it is clear in retrospect that world
banking as a whole was creating problems for the 1980s.
This was because of the kudos placed on balance sheet

*The Banking Sector*

Diagram 8.3: The Number of Banks and Their Branches, 1958-1980

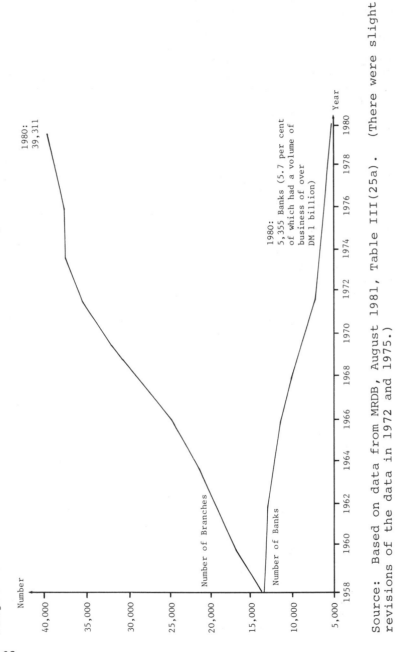

1980: 39,311

1980:
5,355 Banks (5.7 per cent
of which had a volume of
business of over
DM 1 billion)

Number of Branches

Number of Banks

Number

Year

Source: Based on data from MRDB, August 1981, Table III(25a). (There were slight
revisions of the data in 1972 and 1975.)

Table 8.5:  Total General Savings (DM billion)

| Year | Total | Savings Banks inc. Giro | Urban and Rural Co-ops + their central banks | Commercial Banks | PO Savings and Giro Banks | Others |
|------|-------|-------|-------|-------|-------|-------|
| 1972 | 264 | 151 | 51 | 47 | 14 | 1 |
| 1973 | 283 | 158 | 59 | 50 | 15 | 1 |
| 1974 | 313 | 174 | 66 | 55 | 17 | 1 |
| 1975 | 378 | 205 | 84 | 68 | 19 | 1 |
| 1976 | 413 | 222 | 96 | 73 | 21 | 2 |
| 1977 | 441 | 236 | 105 | 74 | 23 | 2 |
| 1978 | 471 | 250 | 116 | 77 | 25 | 2 |
| 1979 | 483 | 256 | 121 | 76 | 27 | 2 |
| 1980 | 490 | 259 | 124 | 77 | 28 | 2 |

Memorandum item:  Bank Savings Bonds (DM billion)

| | |
|------|------|
| 1972 | 10.9 |
| 1973 | 16.4 |
| 1974 | 21.2 |
| 1975 | 30.2 |
| 1976 | 40.6 |
| 1977 | 54.1 |
| 1978 | 64.5 |
| 1979 | 79.6 |
| 1980 | 97.6 |

Note:
77 per cent of all savings bonds in 1975 were issued by the savings banks. Only 1.4 per cent were issued by the co-operative banks. By 1980 68 per cent were issued by the savings banks and 7.7 per cent by the co-operatives (Statistical Supplement, MRDB, Series 1, November 1981, Table 2).

Sources:  BSA (Statistical Appendix), p.2; MRDB, August 1981, Table III(3); *Statisches Jahrbuch für die BRD 1981*, Table 14.5.1.


growth and international expansion. When combined with the liquidity created by Arab surpluses, this led to fierce competition among banks to lend. The profitability and even soundness of such lending played a relatively minor role in credit creation.
    Including foreign branches of the private commercial banks in the Bundesbank's statistics from

1976 resulted in, for that year alone, an average
business volume increase of DM 20.8 billion (MRDB,
January 1978, p.21n). Of this sum, DM 14.1 billion
was attributed to the Big Three, while the remaining
DM 6.7 billion was attributed to the 'regional and
other commercial banks group'. Similarly, including
the foreign branches of the Landesbanken from 1979
resulted in a statistical increase of DM 8.9 billion
(MRDB, August 1980, p.27n). During the two years up
to mid-1979 the total external liabilities of the
banks increased by no less than DM 40 billion to
reach roughly DM 122 billion (MRDB, October 1979,
p.28). By far the greater part of this increase (DM
27 billion) was in the form of longer-term capital
inflows. Mortgage and Landesbanken in particular
placed an increasing amount of DM borrowers' notes
running for more than four years (and therefore not
subject to reserve requirements) in other countries.
In this way they financed a large part of their substantial lending to domestic private and public borrowers, so that the aggregate long-term external liabilities of the banks almost doubled (to reach DM 60
billion) between 1977 and 1979. Since the total external assets of the banks displayed a smaller expansion than liabilities, the overall balance was +DM
16 billion in 1977 but -DM 0.7 billion in 1979.

Every sector of the German banking industry went
international during the 1970s. In effect, this means
that all the major West German banks have either direct or syndicated representation in the principal
financial centres. West German banks therefore lend
and borrow abroad, either as individual institutions
or as part of a syndicate. A further corollary is
that foreign banks sought direct or syndicated representation in West Germany. Three consequences will
therefore be briefly examined: first, the implications
of the Luxembourg subsidiaries of the German banks;
secondly, loans made to East Europe and the Middle
East 'oil dollars'; and, finally, the alleged difficulties experienced by foreign banks in gaining entry
into the German banking system.

Subsidiaries of West German banks were established during the late 1960s and 1970s in Luxembourg
- 'a place known for its liberal banking regulations'
(Commerzbank, 1980, p.5). In other words, the strong
presence of West German banks in Luxembourg resulted
from the fact that they were not required to observe
the minimum reserve requirements imposed by the Bundesbank at home. Domestic regulations also stipulate
that a bank's lending may not exceed its equity capital by more than eighteen times - the so-called

Principle 1 of the Supervisory Authority (issued
under the KWG - Schneider, p.169). In some Luxembourg subsidiaries, much to the consternation of both
the Bundesbank and Bank Supervisory Authority, the
capital to loans ratio reached around 1:28 instead of
the German minimum 1:18. It was in this way that the
German banks used these subsidiaries as vehicles for
their dramatic international growth. What especially
concerned the authorities was the private sector's
inability to build up adequate reserves to cover loan
losses. After a lengthy campaign by the authorities,
and when the banks were facing a profit crisis at the
end of the 1970s, a voluntary agreement was reached
with the private and co-operative banks. Under this
agreement the banks agreed to provide the supervisory
authorities, on a regular basis, with consolidated
accounts including data on wholly-owned foreign subsidiaries.

In turning to the Polish payments crisis as an
example of the difficulties caused by the rapid international expansion of German banking, one must bear
several points in mind. Above all, the German banks
played a vital national role in financing the rapid
recovery of Germany's foreign trade: during the 1950s
and 1960s the Deutsche Bank alone financed about a
third of all the country's foreign trade (Deutsche
Bank, p.43). Further, the strong DM made it relatively easy for the West German banks to raise funds.
Enormous oil-dollar funds flowed on to the Euromarket
- in 1981 alone the total was expected to reach DM
80 billion (*Die Zeit*, 22/81, p.25). Two of these
factors - a strong DM and financing a booming export
trade - increasingly encouraged the pursuit of asset
growth rather than profitability. The risks involved
in extending credit well in excess of equity capital
seemed to be acceptable.

But those risks suddenly became greater at the
end of the 1970s. Interest rates rose to unprecedented heights internationally and the banks found themselves saddled with long-term loans made when rates
had been much lower but re-financed with short-term
funds at higher rates. A mounting balance of payments
deficit added to the problems: such current and capital account problems were new to the West German
authorities during the period under review. Events
in Iran and, more particularly, in Poland were bound
to exacerbate the difficulties in which the West German banks already found themselves. This was because
West German banks are heavily committed in financing
their economy's traditional trade with East Europe as
a whole. Hence in international banking terms

Poland's financial crisis hit Germany's banks hardest.
It was seen in Figure 8.1 that 56 foreign banks
have branches in West Germany. It was also seen that
they account for only 2 per cent of the total volume
of business. There are two reasons for this. First,
although the large US banks have had branches in Germany since shortly after the Second World War, West
Germany only became something of a Mecca for foreign
banks from the late 1960s. Secondly - and this is a
more important, if highly controversial, point - the
small proportion of the business volume accounted for
by the foreign banks is attributed to unfair and
anti-competitive practices of the native German banks.
Discrimination in this sense is frequently alleged;
some Japanese bankers have gone as far as to say that
the West German financial community is a closed
society (BSA, p.26).

Not surprisingly, West Germany's unique universal
banking system is central to the foreign banks' dif-
iculties. As already emphasised, this system has
resulted in extraordinarily close links between the
big domestic banks and industry. The basic allegation
is that this system is used by major German banks to
exclude foreign banks (*Financial Times*, Banking 1979,
V). It has even been alleged that foreign banks may
be asked to temporarily take a loan to a German company back at the end of a financial year so that
problems with the German bankers on the company's
supervisory board can be avoided (*Financial Times*,
Banking 1980, III).

However, business done with some of the larger
German companies may well be booked outside of Germany, even though it is arranged by German staff
(*Financial Times*, Banking 1981, IV). Profits too
may be taken elsewhere. Another method of gaining
access to German corporate companies is, of course,
to take over one of the smaller German banks. For
example, in 1980 the British Midland Bank purchased
a 60 per cent share in one of Germany's largest private banks. Control was actually purchased from the
second largest US bank (Citibank - *ibid.*). For about
£50 million, therefore, the Midland did the German
equivalent of buying one of the City of London's
larger merchant banks. Such moves may also improve
low profitability, for this is another feature which
has tended to characterise foreign banking in Germany
(MRDB, October 1979, p.19 and October 1982, p.28).
One major factor in this respect is that the business
of both foreign banks and private bankers involves a
significant proportion - between a half and two-
thirds - of short-term business. They are therefore

266

better able than other banks to adjust their lending
terms very flexibly to the higher cost of funds
(MRDB, August 1981, p.18).

## THE REFORM OF BANKING LAW

### The Herstatt Failure

Between 1962 and 1974 18 banks were forced into liqui-
dation (*Die Zeit*, 28/74, p.30). By far the largest
of these banks was the Bankhaus I.D. Herstatt KG,
Köln. Its total assets were DM 2.075 billion, but
its losses through currency speculation and fraud
totalled DM 1.2 billion. This disaster roughly coincided with the Westdeutsche and Hessische Landesbanken losses. The major difference, of course, is
that the Landesbanken are in the public sector and
they have the unlimited guarantee of the Länder behind them. In effect this prevented insolvencies in
these latter cases, although the guarantee system
meant that Land politicians were directly involved.
In the case of the Herstatt collapse, the private
banks formed a 'fire-fighting' fund. All small Herstatt depositors were recompensed in full, while half
of the largest institutional investor's assets were
purchased. The idea of a comprehensive joint liability was repugnant to those organisations which
could point to their well-tested deposit guarantee
systems, namely the savings and co-operative banks
(MRDB, July 1976, p.20). However, the major central
associations of the banks agreed to substantially
improve their deposit guarantee facilities. Naturally
enough, the bigger private-sector banks also rail
against the scheme because it has so far been the
smaller banks which have run into liquidity crises.

Banking without any risk at all would, of course,
be hard to imagine - even under a system of massive
control. But the debate over the degree of control
in West Germany became particularly intense following
the Herstatt collapse. There were two issues. The
first issue effectively consisted of agonising about
the degree of control in a social market economy.
The second issue was concerned with preventing a re-
currence of the Herstatt fraud. Basically, it had
been the move from fixed to free exchange rates in
1973 which shifted the costs of foreign currency
speculation from the central bank to the rest of the
banking system. Herstatt made use of its Luxembourg
subsidiary and also made fictitious claims to Swiss
balances, in order to speculate on the forward exchange market. Even after the fraud had been

discovered, it took three years to investigate the
matter and bring charges against the owner and seven
of his bank's officials. Although the main hearing
began in 1979, it took place initially in the absence
through ill health of Herstatt himself and his foreign
currency dealer. By 1981 the case has cost DM 2.8
million and *Die Zeit* (9/81, p.18) was speculating that
proceedings would have to be eventually dropped under
the ten-year rule.

Legal Requirements and Reform
A second amendment to the Banking Act (KWG) which
came into force on 1 May 1976 marked the conclusion
for the time being of the Federal Government's efforts
to remedy the weaknesses in German banking which had
come to light through bank failures - especially the
Herstatt closure - and other difficulties in the banking system. It was made clear that the Amendment had
to be considered in conjunction with:

(i)    The introduction of Principle 1a (*Grundsatz
       1a*) to limit the risks arising from foreign
       exchange deals.
(ii)   The improvement of deposit guarantee facili-
       ties by the banking associations.
(iii)  The appointment of a commission to study
       'basic banking questions' (i.e. the Gessler
       Commission).
                              (MRDB, July 1976, p.17)

     Principal 1a requires that at the close of busi-
ness on each business day a bank's open position in
foreign currencies shall be strictly controlled so as
not to exceed a given proportion of the bank's equity
capital (Schneider, pp.42 and 173-177). Significantly,
Principle 1a had laid down the basic rule that loans
must not exceed 18 times the equity capital, a regulation not always observed by the Luxembourg subsidiaries of the bank.
     The amendment itself sought to restrict large
loans and tighten-up the reporting requirements.
Those provisions concerned with reporting requirements
were related to the Herstatt collapse: they are designed to enable officials at the Bundesbank and the
Supervisory Authority to gain more prompt information
about the actions of bank officials. Under the
clauses dealing with large loans, no individual large
loan - including loans promised - may exceed 75 per
cent of a bank's equity capital; the five largest
loans - including again loans promised - may not exceed three times the equity capital; all large loans

combined - this time only those actually taken up -
must not exceed eight times the bank's equity capital (*ibid.*, pp.77-81). Every other month borrowers
whose indebtedness exceed DM 1 million are reported
to the Bundesbank; the Bundesbank then informs - in
general terms - all affected banking institutions if
any one borrower has several such loans (*ibid.*, pp.
81-82). Lending to the Federal Government and West
German public authorities, however, does not require
equity backing.

Surely the keystone of the amendments lies, however, in the powers given to the Supervisory Authority.
This is because only the Authority may now file a
petition for bankruptcy - and then only after efforts
at re-organisation have failed and when means of compensating depositors have been found (MRDB, July 1976,
pp.21-22; Schneider, pp.141-149). Such measures have
thus far prevented another Herstatt-type failure,
with the consequent serious loss of confidence at
home and abroad. After all, one of the immediate
side-effects of the Herstatt episode was to induce
something akin to near-panic, with a subsequent decline in bank deposits.


CONCLUSION

What is beyond doubt is that there will be further
attempts at legislative reform, although budgetary
and more general economic policy issues preoccupy the
minds of Bonn politicians at the time of writing.
Nevertheless, both the Gessler Commission's recommen-
dations, particularly on the banks' industrial holdings, and the Bundesbank's concern with the lending
loophole created by the presence of the Luxembourg
subsidiaries are both legislative nettles which will
ultimately have to be grasped. As the *Financial
Times* (3 September 1981) suggested, the commercial
banks may hope that further reform can be postponed
until profitability is restored, and perhaps even
until a 'more amenable' Government is ruling in Bonn.
On the other hand, the sudden willingness on the part
of the banks to part with their 'long-treasured'
share-holdings in the non-banking sector has been
seen by *The Times* (10 September 1981) as not just a
result of the squeeze on profits, but also to some
extent the SPD/FDP Government's undertaking to legislate on banking.

Chapter Nine

THE INDUSTRIAL SECTOR

INTRODUCTION

In the previous two chapters, a comprehensive view of
ownership, control and the banking sector has been
assembled. Many of the well-known West German enterprises have been at least mentioned. This makes it
possible to proceed to an analysis of the industrial
sector.
        Hence the first section of this chapter presents
an overview of the legal framework in the fields of
cartels and other industrial restrictive practices.
There then follows an examination of the extent to
which anti-trust law has been successful. In the
third section the various factors which were conducive
to industrial growth and concentration are discussed.
Finally, various major industrial enterprises and
their industries are analysed.

THE LEGAL FRAMEWORK

German law on competitive restraints has evolved separately and independently of the law on unfair competition (Mueller, 1981, p.14). Two major statutes
reflect this distinction. They are the Act against
Unfair Competition (*Gesetz gegen den unlauteren Wettbewerb*) and the Act against Restraints on Competition
(*Gesetz gegen Wettbewerbsbeschränkungen* - GWB). The
former is generally aimed at preventing unethical
business practices, whereas the latter is intended to
preserve competitive market structures (OECD, 1981,
Section 2.1). The latest Act against unfair competition (1977) follows historical precedents and is
similar to statutes in other countries. For instance,
misleading advertising is forbidden.
        It is the history of the GWB which is more com-

plex yet more relevant for policy formulation during
the three decades under review. This is because
cartels of various kinds were historically legitimate
in German law (Gordon, pp.14, 23 and 139). Indeed,
both the Courts and the State displayed a distrust of
competition, and cartels were in some cases compulsory
(Marburg, pp.81-83). Under the 1923 Act the Minister
for Economic Affairs, a supervisory agency and a Cartel Court were all given powers to intervene in the
public interest and prohibit certain abusive practices
of cartels and market-dominating enterprises. Such
powers were never forcefully excercised and effective
control of monopolistic and restrictive business practices was not achieved (Mueller, 1981, p.14; OECD,
1981, Section O.). Indeed, the 1923 Act preceded a
period of strong and comprehensive concentration
(Stolper, p.123).

When Erhard's Economic Council was asked to make
legislative proposals, the decartelisation and deconcentration statutes enacted by the Western Allies
were still in force (Mestmäcker, p.391). The Council,
and later the Federal Government, wanted to legislate
against what Smith and Swann (pp.41-45) isolate as
the two fundamental anti-trust problems: restrictive
business practices and concentration. (The former are
cartel arrangements which either involve horizontal
collusion aimed at enforcing an agreed pricing policy
within an industry and excluding new entrants, or involve vertical attempts to fix the prices at which an
industry's goods are re-sold. The concentration problem, on the other hand, is concerned (rarely) with
pure monopoly, more frequently with market dominance
and, most frequently, with oligopoly.)

First the Allies, and later sections of the CDU
and industry, insisted that the legislators should
concentrate on cartels. In effect, therefore, the
GWB which eventually reached the statute book in July
1957 was a cartel-prohibition law (Marburg, p.92).
When it came into effect on 1 January 1958, however,
there were a number of exemptions to horizontal agreements which considerably weakened the Act (Denton,
p.59; Dyas and Thanheiser, p.54). As Swann indicates
(pp.141-142 and 183-184) horizontal restrictive business practices are prohibited but re-newable exemptions
may be permitted by the Federal Cartel Office in the
event of contingencies such as economic crises, rationalisation and foreign trade regulation. Basically,
Section 1 of the GWB spells out the prohibition,
Sections 2-7 the exemptions, while Section 8 enables
the Economics Minister to override Section 1 in
national emergencies. (Only horizontal agreements

are known as 'cartels' (*Kartelle*) in German termin-
ology - OECD, 1981, Section 2.0, p.l.) Further, an
indication of vertical weakness of the 1957 Act was
that resale price maintenance was legally protected.
Finally, although the newly established Cartel Office
could control the abuse of economic power by dominant
enterprises in certain specified ways, it had no
powers to act against mergers.

After considerable controversy about the operation of the GWB, the Act was amended in 1965. Once
again resistance within the Government's own party
resulted in the continuation of resale price maintenance. However, the amended GWB contained a much more
precise definition of mergers which were to be registered with the Cartel Office, although the exemptions
of certain types of cartels were extended. Taken together the amendments modified but did not fundamentally alter the 1957 Act (Denton, p.61).

But the amendments carried through by the SPD/
FDP coalition in 1973 did radically change the GWB.
Retail price maintenance was abolished, and the control by the authorities of both illegal cartels and
market-dominating companies was made easier. The
Monopolies Commission was also established. About
this time fines were imposed by the Cartel Office on
seven breweries - DM 7 million - and seven leading
enterprises in the special steels industry - DM 2.3
million - for price agreements in their respective
associations (OECD, 1981, Section 3, pp.14 and 19).
A further agreement to the GWB in 1976 brought news-
paper mergers within the scope of the Act - an issue
which was to excercise the minds of the Monopolies
Commission in its third report (III, ch.3). Finally,
the 1980 amendments again intensified the control of
mergers.

Summarising then, it can be said that the GWB
has gradually evolved between 1957 and 1980. Its main
targets are, first cartels which set out to influence
prices, levels of production and other market conditions through restraint of competition. There are
a number of exceptions and a number of areas have not
yet been settled by case law (Mueller, 1981, p.21).
Its second and third targets are the abuse of market
dominant positions and, since 1973, mergers. In 1973
resale price maintenance was also prohibited (with
minor exceptions), although recommended prices are
still allowed (Cable, 1979, p.21). In short, the
large West German enterprises have lived with the doctrine of competition for barely a generation (Dyas and
Thanheiser, p.62). It should be added, however, that
Article 66 of the ECSC (Paris) treaty, as well as

Articles 85 and 86 of the EEC (Rome) treaty, also deal respectively with mergers involving firms in the coal, iron and steel industries and restrictive inter-firm agreements and abuses by market-dominating firms in relation to all other products and services (Markert, pp.294-298).

## THE OPERATION OF THE GWB

In order to gain some insights into the operation of the GWB, it is necessary to have a knowledge of the five institutions which are allocated with powers of enforcement.

First, the Cartel Office (*Bundeskartellamt*) now has wide powers to investigate, search and seize documents, and question witnesses. It is mandatory to notify mergers meeting certain criteria (20 per cent market share; 10,000 employees; turnover of at least DM 500 million) to the Office. In carrying out its duties, the Cartel Office also exercises a quasi-judical function, imposing prohibitions and fines where it deems such action necessary.

Secondly, as already seen in Chapter 8, the Monopolies Commission (*Monopolkommission*) publishes opinions on the development of concentration and competitive structures. It consists of five independent advisers and the titles of its first three biennial reports are indicative of its findings: 'More Competition is Possible'; 'Continuing Concentration among Large Enterprises' and 'Merger Control remains a Top Priority'. A slightly more optimistic view was taken in 1982 ('Progress in the Registration of Concentration').

Thirdly, the first court of appeal against the decisions of the Cartel Office is the Berlin court of appeals (*Kammergericht*). This court reconsiders both the legal and the factual basis of the Office's decisions. Fourthly, the next stage of appeal (the Federal Supreme Court - *Bundesgerichtshof*) is also the highest instance of legal appeal in West Germany.

Finally, in the case of an appeal against a merger prohibition, the Federal Minister of Economics may also become involved. Thus the Minister has investigated several cases and approved appeals on the following grounds (Baur, p.460): the safeguarding of petroleum supplies - Gelsenberg/VEBA (Owen Smith, 1979, pp.182-183); safeguarding energy provision - VEBA/BP; the maintenance of employment - textile machinery manufacturer Artos/Deutsche Babcock; the preservation of technical potential - Hüller/Thyssen;

international competitiveness in, and the domestic
supply of, aluminimum products - VAW/Kaiser. In the
case of VEBA and VAW partly state-owned industries
were involved. In its special reports the Monopolies
Commission supported the Cartel Office's opposition
to the mergers. However, the Minister has made his
approval subject to certain restrictions and conditions (Mueller, 1981, p.99). As Baur (p.461) points
out this gives the Minister the opportunity to mould
the areas of activity of large enterprises according
to his own ideas.

   But the salient point here, as Tillotson (pp.65-
66) lucidly argues, is that the finer points of
national merger law give way to the economic facts of
life. He cites the Karstadt and Neckermann merger.
Karstadt is the largest department store in West Germany, indeed in Europe, while Neckermann before the
merger was the third largest mail order retail company and the second largest operator of package tours
(Markert, p.309). The Federal Cartel Office took the
view that Karstadt, together with three other major
department stores, had to be regarded as a market-
dominating oligopoly that was likely to be strengthened by the acquisition of a major mail order retail
firm. However, it accepted that Neckermann was in
such a critical financial state that only the merger
with Karstadt would avoid bankruptcy and save the jobs
of Neckermann's 19,000 employees. The Office saw that
for it to go through the process of first prohibiting
the merger only for the Minister to later approve it
on the grounds of overriding national interest would
in practice have meant that the rescue of Neckermann
would have come too late. In comparing this case
with the abortive attempt by GKN to take over Sachs
(see below), Tillotson (pp.65-66) concludes that although Karstadt was the largest department store in
Europe, it was German-owned; GKN, on the other hand,
was not German-owned and Sachs did not require res-
cuing. But Karstadt did not bring Neckermann's
losses to a halt. By 1982 losses since the merger
had reached DM 400 million (*Die Zeit*, 47/82, p.23).

   The Federal Government, the Monopolies Commission
and the Federal Cartel Office all shared the view
that it had proved impossible to stop the growth of
concentration, particularly as a result of mergers
involving large and very large enterprises. Two
types of cases were involved (Baur, p.445). First,
mergers as such between large and very large enterprises. The two classic mergers of the early 1970s
were the purchase of considerable holdings in Rheinstahl by August-Thyssen and, similarly, Mannesmann's

purchase of a 51 per cent stake in Demag (Vogl, pp. 232 and 241). In both cases, this represented a merging of steel and engineering interests in the Ruhr (Rutherford, p.44). Schmücker led Rheinstahl into the merger with Thyssen just before joining VW (ch.7 above; *Fortune Magazine*, 13 August 1979, p.122). The other type of merger involved financially powerful and large enterprises purchasing small and medium-sized firms in order to penetrate new markets. The forward integration of chemical firms into the lacquer and dye industry is one example (Baur, p.445).

An example of the trend in merger control is the case involving the British-owned multi-national Guest, Keene & Nettlefolds Ltd (GKN) and the German family-owned Sachs AG. There were many side-issues involved, not least the implications of further foreign intervention and the behaviour of the Sachs family. Of relevance here, however, are the processes by which decisions were made and the implications of the case for merger control. And a complicating factor was the fact that the proposed merger was supranational in character. Hence, Tillotson (pp.47-53) demonstrates that by late 1975 GKN had applied for the necessary consents to the merger from all the appropriate authorities: the UK Office of Fair Trading, the Federal Cartel Office and the European Commission. As the merger involved products falling within the sphere of the ECSC, the European Commission was charged with dual control jurisdiction under both the ECSC and EEC treaties. In view of the absence of Sachs from British markets, the UK authorities did not consider the case relevant; the EEC thought that competition would not be appreciably affected, while the ECSC authorised the proposed merger under Article 66. It was the West German Cartel Office which was opposed to the merger. The GKN/Sachs case therefore merits a little more discussion.

In 1975, GKN declared its intention of eventually obtaining a 75 per cent holding in Sachs. GKN's product range included motor vehicle components and it already held a stake in the West German transmission manufacturer Uni-Cardan. Sachs was part-owner of Fichtel & Sachs which supplied 80 per cent of the West German clutch market. GKN's steel-making division would have been in a position to supply the processing undertakings of the Sachs group with the finished and semi-finished steel products which Sachs previously bought on the open market (*ibid.*, p.43). In addition, GKN's reliance on a vulnerable UK car market (with less than half the output of the West German industry) would have been reduced and Sachs'

turnover would have more than doubled GKN's existing
Uni-Cardan business in West Germany.  Finally, the
management board at Sachs were re-assured by the ex-
cellent relationship between GKN and Uni-Cardan.
But in May 1976 (two months before the ECSC and
EEC announced their decisions) the Cartel Office
issued a prohibition order.  The grounds were that
the proposed merger was contrary to the GWB since it
would lead to a strengthening of a dominant position
through an accretion of financial power.  GKN appealed
to the Berlin high court and, as an indication of its
determination, purchased a 24.98 per cent stake in
Sachs.  Sachs' profits were high at the time and the
chairman of GKN moved on to their supervisory board.
After the Berlin court had upheld GKN's appeal, the
Cartel Office appealed to the Federal Supreme Court.
This time the (1978) ruling went in favour of the
Office, so GKN appealed to the Economics Minister.
However, before the Minister reached a decision, GKN
withdrew its application.  After selling its shares
in Sachs to the Commerzbank, GKN increased its Uni-
Cardan holding to over 80 per cent.  By 1980 the
state-owned Salzgitter steel works was seriously interested in Sachs - although by now the profits picture had deteriorated badly.
Yet the 1980s opened with the successful completion of a merger between two other British and West
German companies - that is between Pilkington Brothers
and Flachglas AG, West Germany's largest glass maker.
Pilkington's motivation had been similar to that of
GKN's: West Germany's economic growth rate was still
expected to be much faster than Britain's and expansion within the European glass market had been a
formally stated tenet of Pilkington's policy since
the early 1970s (*Financial Times*, 12 March 1982, p.
18).  Following a hearing in Berlin and other investigations, the Cartel Office approved the purchase by
Pilkington of a 62 per cent stake in Flachglas.  The
only condition - which proved fortuitous for Pilkington's - was that the British company should abandon
its plans to purchase an ailing pair of Belgian-Dutch
glass companies.  There were two differences from the
abortive GKN/Sachs efforts to merge, however.  First,
the highly profitable Flachglas was already foreign
owned - by the French BSN group.  Second, at the end
of the 1970s GKN turnover (£1.8 billion) was about
six times that of Sachs, while Pilkington's (£629 million) amounted to only around three times that of
Flachglas.  A somewhat more tenuous link between the
two cases is that the controversial chief executive
of Fichtel & Sachs - Dr Walter Trux - became head of

Flachglas in 1981. Why, then, did the GKN/Sachs proposed merger fail?

Undoubtedly, the GKN/Sachs case arose at a time
when mergers and the consequent process of concentration seemed to be getting out of hand. Hence it
is important to emphasise the reasoning behind the
authorities' decisions. The decisive point to the
Office was that the merger would have given Fichtel &
Sachs sufficient financial strength to prevent newcomers from entering the market or to deter competitors (Baur, p.447). Put another way, the Cartel
Office was seeking to distinguish between actual and
potential competition (Tillotson, p.59). Further,
GKN's strong market positions in other fields of motor
component manufacture would bolster Sachs' dominant
market position still further. The Berlin appeal
court, in attempting to emphasise the crucial test of
trade restraint, criticised the Office for its distrust of size alone. For its part, the Monopolies
Commission pointed out that the appeal court was making the assumption that enterprises may be so big
that their market position could not be further
strengthened. In effect, this meant that the largest
enterprises would escape any control of mergers (Baur,
p.448).

When the supreme court published its written
judgement it stressed that potential competitive
forces were already rather weak because of the significant advantage possessed by Sachs. If the merger
were allowed, these forces would disappear completely
as a result of the increase in financial power and
the consolidation of related markets (*ibid.*, p.449).
However, as Baur correctly argues (p.450), this means
that restraint of trade is no longer the major test
but rather the structure and size of the acquiring
enterprise - characteristics independent of the particular market situation. In fact in affirming the
Cartel Office and reversing the Appeal Court, the
Supreme Court went as far as to assert that '... the
highly *conglomerate* and financially very powerful
first party, ... is active in the *vicinity* of the
market to the overall extent of 40 per cent' (Markert,
p.307; Tillotson, p.57 - emphasis added). As Tillotson (pp.57-58) shows, however, it is doubtful whether
GKN could be defined as 'highly conglomerate'. Indeed, conglomerates as such are hardly known in West
Germany (Dyas and Thanheiser, p.90).

In spite of the fact that the West German economy has been dominated by large firms and cartels for
a century, the significance of the GKN/Sachs case is
that it was found to influence legislators when

debating the 1980 amendments. Three factors will consequently now lead to a presumption that a merger has created or strengthened a dominant market position. First, a proposed merger of the GKN/Sachs type where an enterprise with a DM 2 billion turnover in its previous financial year, attempts to take over an enterprise which has a market dominating position in one or several markets in which its aggregate turnover exceeded DM 150 million (Mueller, 1980, pp.87 and 159). Second, where an enterprise with a DM 2 billion turnover attempts to take over an enterprise operating in a market in which small and medium-sized businesses together hold a two-thirds share of the market, and the merging enterprises would subsequently control a 5 per cent share of that market. Third, where large enterprises with a collective turnover of DM 12 billion, at least two of which each have a turnover of DM 1 billion, propose to merge.

These *size* criteria were added to the *market-share* criteria of the 1973 amendment. These latter criteria had defined market domination as, first, a single enterprise having a market share of one-third (Mueller, 1981, p.145). Secondly, in the case of three or fewer enterprises, the share is 50 per cent, while for five or fewer the share is two-thirds. The cartel authorities do not have the power to dissolve market-dominating enterprises; they simply use the criteria to prohibit abuses and, in some cases, mergers (*ibid.*, p.47). A legal presumption in no way proves that a position of market dominance in fact exists (Baur, p.453).

Although merger control dates only from the 1973 amendments of the GWB, it soon became evident that the minimum size threshold for exemption from merger control (DM 50 million turnover) was pitched on the high side. In consequence, large enterprises found that it was possible to avoid reporting certain mergers by acquiring small firms in markets formerly dominated by small and medium-sized enterprises (Mueller, 1981, p.85). This led to a severe deterioration in the competitive structure of these markets, since between 1973 and 1979, 1,390 out of a total of 3,388 notified mergers were covered by this exemption. Hence the 1980 amendments included a rider to the DM 50 million exemption. This was to the effect that control could be exercised if an enterprise with a turnover of more than DM 4 million is taken over by an enterprise having a turnover greater than DM 1 billion.

Other provisions aimed at preventing circumvention were also included in the 1980 amendments to the

GWB. For example, the acquisition of shares in another enterprise is now held to constitute a merger if the acquired shares, together with the shares already held, equal *either* 25 per cent *or* 50 per cent of the voting capital. In other words, there are now two separate share thresholds which could conceivably apply to a company acquiring first 25 per cent and then later up to 50 per cent of another company. Further, even if the acquired shares do not reach 25 per cent of voting rights, but the acquiring enterprise is granted an agreement effectively giving it such control, then a merger is considered to have taken place. Similar provisions apply to interlocking directorates. However, the acquisition of shares by a bank does not constitute a merger if the bank acquires the shares with the intention of selling the shares in the market, does not exercise any voting rights with respect to the shares, and sells them within one year of the acquisition (Mueller, 1981, p.76). In fact, because of explicit exemptions in the GWB, its provisions apply mainly to manufacturing industry and mining (Cable, 1979, p.23).

A lot of what has been said tends to imply that intervention by the authorities, particularly in the merger field, came too late to prevent a re-emergence of concentration. Quite apart from the large number (1,390) of notified mergers exempt from control, a further 1,741 mergers out of the total of 3,388 notified between 1973 and 1979 were permitted. In several important cases the Federal Minister of Economics over-ruled the other authorities and permitted mergers. But it is now time to look at trends in business concentration throughout the period 1950-1980.


FACTORS CONDUCIVE TO GROWTH AND CONCENTRATION

Diversification
In considering the process of diversification (1950-1970) among the top 100 enterprises in West German industry, Dyas and Thanheiser (ch.7) distinguish three groups of companies. First, there was a somewhat surprisingly large group of low diversifiers. Secondly, there was a group of post-war diversifiers. Thirdly, there was a group of companies which were traditionally diversified.

A great majority of the low diversifiers were in industries where the conditions for diversification were generally unfavourable. By far the largest number of enterprises (23 out of 39) in this group were in capital-intensive areas such as steel, oil and

motor vehicles.  Also included here was Ruhrkohle
which was formed in 1968 from 20 coal mining companies because of the critical state of the coal industry.  This problem of over-production in coal plagued
most major steel companies since they had vertically
integrated coal mining into their company structure.
On the other hand, some of the industries in this
group experienced very fast growth - motor vehicles,
electrical engineering and household appliances, for
example.  In the case of the latter two industries
there were also apparently good opportunities for
diversification.  In size, the enterprises in this
group ranged from some of the very largest of the top
100 industrial concerns (VW, Daimler-Benz and Thyssen)
to the smallest.

The post-war diversifiers represented the smallest of the three groups at 29 companies of the top
100.  Although differing somewhat from the previous
group, there was some overlap: half of them were in
either the heavy industries, or those with limited
possibilities for technological transfers.  The other
half were in electrical, mechanical and chemical engineering.  A dozen West German-owned companies diversified into technologically-related fields.  Among
them were three major steel producers - Mannesmann,
Rheinstahl and Hoesch.  Mannesmann's post-war history
is typical of many West German companies: the imposition of Allied deconcentration; the reconstruction
of former links and scopes, followed by horizontal
expansion by merger or joint ventures with (or ac-
quisitions of) competitors.  One such joint venture
by the Mannesmann group was with Thyssen, its major
competitor in steel tubes.  Another enterprise of
particular interest in this group of post-war diversifiers is the family-owned Oetker concern.  This
enterprise diversified into both industry and brewing
during the post-war era.  Bosch also diversified.

A number of features of these post-war diversifiers should be emphasised.  Above all, the post-war
diversification strategies of West German companies
in this group, while obviously broadening the scope
of the enterprise concerned, rarely fundamentally
changed their characteristic features.  Technological
relatedness was the predominant factor.  Diversification, it is important to add, was accompanied by
horizontal and vertical integration.  The most prominent examples of this were the big steel companies,
which had been forcibly deconcentrated after the
Second World War.  Diversification did not become an
important strategic priority to most of them until
well after a decade of efforts to re-establish

vertical links and horizontal scope.

An outstanding feature of the third group (traditionally diversified enterprises) is that it includes many of the world-famous names of West German industry. Companies such as Krupp, Siemens, Bayer and Zeiss all enter the analysis.

Bayer is, of course, one of the big three chemical groups - the others being BASF and Hoechst. Although deconcentrated by the Allies, all three companies have displayed a process of forward integration. By the end of the 1970s, however, these three international giants were to be plagued by over-capacity, falling demand and oil price rises - something they had in common with the rest of the world's chemical industry. Their joint market shares are quite sizeable.

Similarly, in electrical engineering Siemens shared a market leadership with AEG for most of the period under review. Both companies originally had the major part of their capacity in Berlin. During the 1950s AEG concentrated on re-building its capacity within West Germany, whereas Siemens was already expanding its international and technological strength. AEG, as already shown in Chapter 8, was rather heavily orientated towards the production of consumer goods which was to contribute to its deteriorating financial position at the end of the period under review. This was because of intensifying Japanese competition. Siemens grew almost entirely from internal expansion, while AEG considered both acquisition (latterly abroad as well as at home), and collaborative ventures of equal strategic value (also see Vogl, p.239). Ironically enough, AEG's venture into nuclear power with Siemens was also a loss-making operation. In 1978 Siemens bought out AEG's stake (and losses) in Kraftwerk-Union, the nuclear company in question. Hence, at the end of the review period Siemens was a multi-national, relatively profitable giant, while AEG was a loss-making albatross with holdings all over the world. However, even Siemens announced redundancies and slightly smaller profits in 1981.

A slight digression on AEG's economic problems is in order at this stage. This is because of the insights it provides into the possible future adjustment strategies of West German industry. Another company facing adjustment difficulties - significantly in the entertainment electronics business - was that of Grundig. Although this latter company fits into the Dyas and Thanheiser 'low diversifier' category, it will be well worth contrasting its problems with

those of AEG at this juncture. The reason is that
Max Grundig also felt beleaguered by Japanese competition. Indeed, as Dyas and Thanheiser point out
(pp.79-80), declining margins in entertainment electronics may have contributed to Grundig's decision
to abandon his diversification programme as early as
the 1960s.

One of the major economic preoccupations in the
1980s was bound to be a search for a solution to
AEG's problems. In Chapter 8 it was seen that the
banks became large creditors. The Dresdner faced the
largest losses, but the Deutsche Bank, Commerzbank,
together with the Westdeutsche and Hessische Landesbanken, had all made large loans to AEG. As will be
expected from what was said in Chapter 7, there have
been three chief executives since the early 1970s
and the Dresdner Bank's chief executive was the chairman of AEG's supervisory board. The government granted emergency financial aid in 1982 and further help
was requested. Other companies were considering take-
overs of wholly-owned AEG subsidiaries, or existing
partners were invited to extend their holdings. For
example, Grundig, along with a bank consortium, were
considering the purchase of AEG's television and radio
company; similarly, the British company GEC, and later
United Technologies of the USA, were at one time seen
as possible partners in the electronics components
division; Electrolux of Sweden considered the possi-
bility of acquiring AEG's household appliances company; the AEG Communications systems division was
expected to become part of new telecommunications
grouping owned by Robert Bosch and Mannesmann. In
other words, the strategy was to hive off loss-making
consumer goods divisions, and then become a smaller
and more specialised undertaking based on the apparently more viable capital goods business. New capital
would have to be attracted and this would in turn require the confidence of new investors. But in the
early 1980s the holding company (AEG-Telefunken AG) -
which was the main financing vehicle for the group -
had debts to West German banks of DM 3 billion, un-
funded pension liabilities of DM 2.6 billion and trade
creditors of DM 1.7 billion. Application had been
made to the courts to write down unsecured claims by
60 per cent.

It was also intensifying Japanese competition in
the consumer goods field which ultimately forced Max
Grundig to sell a 75 per cent share in his company to
the French electrical goods manufacturer Thomson
Brandt (*Der Spiegel*, 48/82, p.118). Thomson Brandt
was the second largest European company in the field.

The largest company - Phillips Eindhoven - already
held an 18.7 per cent stake in Grundig (MK IV, para.
438). Significantly, Thomson Brandt lay not only behind Phillips but, at an international level, behind
the world's two largest electrical concerns: Japan's
Matsushita and Hitachi. Of equal significance is
the fact that Max Grundig himself was reported as
saying that his company, with a turnover of DM 3.5
billion, was far too small to withstand Japanese competition (*Die Zeit*, 48/82, p.23). Further, both the
French company and Grundig had been making losses,
and only the fact that Thomson Brandt is state-owned
enabled this French giant to find sufficient funds to
purchase Grundig (*Der Spiegel*, 48/82, p.121; *Die Zeit*,
48/82, p.23). Whether the authorities will eventually
approve the merger is going to prove another interesting feature of the 1980s.

Having examined the nature of both AEG's and
Grundig's problems, it is now possible to return to
the Dyas and Thanheiser 'traditional diversifiers'
category.

Also among the traditional diversifiers were
family enterprises of the Ruhr. They can be divided
into two groups. One pattern consisted of iron and
steel manufacture as the point of departure, followed
by backward vertical integration into coal mining and
forward integration into mechanical engineering.
Krupp, Thyssen and Haniel more or less followed this
route. It was seen in the last section that this process also culminated with two massive mergers in the
early 1970s, both of which involved the post-war diversifiers of Mannesmann and Rheinstahl. When steel
output slumped at the end of the 1970s it was significantly the companies which had diversified most
(Thyssen and Mannesmann) which avoided heavy losses.
Krupp and Hoesch were obliged to merge their loss-
making crude-steel capacity into a new company (Ruhr-
stahl AG), although the newly-founded company may
have been undermined by proposals to merge the high-
grade steel making interests of Krupp and Thyssen.
Ironically, at the end of the 1960s, Thyssen had made
counter-proposals which prevented the merging of the
steel interests of Hoesch and Mannesmann (*Die Zeit*,
36/82, p.40). As a result Hoesch spent a period in
the 1970s in an unsuccessful venture with the Dutch
steel firm Hoogovens. Klöckner - the least diversi-
field of West Germany's steel companies - had not
paid a dividend since 1974, although at the beginning
of the 1980s it was trying its utmost to diversify
out of steel making. Finally, Salzgitter was also
involved in loss-making shipbuilding. Hence this

state-owned enterprise had also to contend with its
uneconomic home-ore based plant on the frontier-
corridor.
The other pattern of development began in the
iron and steel trade. It involved Klöckner and Otto
Wolff. Klöckner was broken up during the post-war
deconcentration process, and was reformed by the
family. As already seen, however, Klöckner remained
heavily dependent on steel production. By 1970, however, it far exceeded its pre-war size in manufacturing as well as trading activities. Wolff is not
quite so important in absolute size. One family that
did not fare so well was the Stimnes. Their mining
and trading operations were taken over by VEBA, the
rapidly expanding state-owned group.

Mergers
If investigations into the trend in mergers since the
enactment of the GWB in 1958 are based on the statistics issued by the Cartel Office, there will be a
number of reasons for treating the findings with
caution. First, reporting requirements were fairly
precisely defined only after the 1965 amendment.
This effectively meant that before 1967 the series
is seriously imcomplete. Second, legal and procedural changes in the 1973 and 1976 amendments make
the preceding data not strictly comparable. After
1973 in particular the coverage was extended (Cable,
1980a, p.101).
Nevertheless, it is clear even from these data
that there has been a significant rise in merger
activity since 1958. This statement is substantiated
by Table 9.1, in which the Cartel Office data is re-
produced. Table 9.1 also indicates that there was an
increase in merger activity in 1969-1972. Such a
surge was more or less contemporaneous with merger
booms in the USA, Britain and elsewhere, which is
suggestive of common underlying causal factors promp-
ting mergers rather than the vagaries of statistical
reporting (Bannock, p.56; Cable, 1980a, p.101). This
cyclical tendency is also supported by the insolvencies reported in Table 9.1. Finally, Table 9.1
confirms the further increase in merger activity leading up to the 1980 amendments. It was shown in the
last section that this latter increase was brought
about mainly by large firms acquiring small firms in
markets previously dominated by the latter. Again,
this level of merger activity was not disproporation-
ate by international standards (Cable, 1979, p.10).
There were, then, cyclical tendencies in both
merger activity and insolvencies (Table 9.1). Before

Table 9.1:   Insolvencies and Mergers, 1958-1980

| Year | Annual number of insolvencies | Percentage change over previous year | Annual number of mergers | Percentage change over previous year |
|------|------|------|------|------|
| 1958 | 3,535 | – | 15 | – |
| 1959 | 3,025 | -14.4 | 15 | 0.0 |
| 1960 | 2,958 | -2.2 | 22 | 46.7 |
| 1961 | 2,823 | -4.6 | 26 | 18.2 |
| 1962 | 2,786 | -1.3 | 38 | 46.2 |
| 1963 | 3,132 | 12.4 | 29 | -23.7 |
| 1964 | 3,281 | 4.8 | 36 | 24.1 |
| 1965 | 3,157 | -3.8 | 50 | 38.9 |
| 1966 | 3,615 | 14.5 | 43 | -14.0 |
| 1967 | 4,337 | 20.0 | 65 | 51.2 |
| 1968 | 3,827 | -11.8 | 65 | 0.0 |
| 1969 | 3,809 | -0.5 | 168 | 158.5 |
| 1970 | 4,201 | 10.3 | 305 | 81.5 |
| 1971 | 4,437 | 5.6 | 220 | -27.9 |
| 1972 | 4,575 | 3.1 | 269 | 22.3 |
| 1973 | 5,515 | 20.5 | 242 | -10.0 |
| 1974 | 7,722 | 40.0 | 318 | 31.4 |
| 1975 | 9,195 | 19.1 | 448 | 40.9 |
| 1976 | 9,362 | 1.8 | 453 | 1.1 |
| 1977 | 9,562 | 2.1 | 554 | 22.3 |
| 1978 | 8,722 | -8.8 | 558 | 0.7 |
| 1979 | 8,319 | -4.6 | 602 | 7.8 |
| 1980 | 9,140 | 9.9 | 635 | 5.5 |
| (1981 | 11,653 | 27.5 | 618 | -2.7) |

Sources:   IdDW, Table 77; *Jahresberichte des Bundes-
kartellamtes*; Jordan, p.72; *Statistisches Jahrbuch
für die BRD*, 1981, Table 7.19.1 (writer's translation and calculations).

passing on to the industrial incidence of this merger
activity, however, it should perhaps be briefly noted
that cyclical fluctuations in output varied by industry.  Predictably, oscillations in the iron and steel
industry were the most marked.  Between 1950 and 1980,
there were a dozen falls in this industry's production index, including one of -22.5 per cent in
1975.  Motor vehicles displayed three absolute falls
of -15.0 per cent (1967), -12.7 per cent (1974) and
-4.6 per cent (1980).  In percentage terms, however,
there were even larger booms during the 1950s and
1960s.  Production fluctuations in chemicals,

electrical and mechanical engineering, in that order,
lay much closer to the total industrial production
index. Again, output in all three of these industries
fell absolutely during the 1975 recession. Significantly, this was the first major recession in chemicals. Further analyses of trends in industrial production follow below, but for now the discussion of
mergers continues.
   Cable (1979, pp.13-14) found that during the
period 1958-1977 there had been an increase in the
proportion of mergers taking place outside the industrial sector. Within the industrial sector, however,
mergers were heavily concentrated in a small number
of industries. In descending order of merger incidence the top six industries for the period as a whole
were chemical products, electrical engineering, machine tools, iron and steel, mineral oil products and
food processing. These findings coincide with those
of Dyas and Thanheiser, the Monopolies Commission
(both quoted above) and Kaufer (pp.81-82). Cable *et
al.* (1980a, pp.110-112) also confirm other aspects of
earlier findings. In both the industrial and non-
industrial sectors the majority of mergers were horizontal - that is between firms in the same industrial
category. However, mineral oil showed an outstanding
tendency towards forward vertical integration into
commercial activities, while, to a lesser extent, the
iron and steel industry was also involved in this
activity. These industries were followed, at some
distance, by motor vehicles, electrical goods and
chemicals. But the results of statistical testings
for alternative merger causes and effects in West
Germany do not suggest significant community gains
(Cable, 1980b, p.245).

Concentration
Summarising, then, it is possible to say that industrial concentration and growth went hand in hand during the period under review. For example, mergers
between 1952 and 1968 reduced the number of coal mining companies from 71 to 31, while in steel (the major
acquirers of coal mining companies) the number fell
from 34 to 28 (Owen Smith, 1981, p.202). When the
coal industry was faced with over-production in 1968,
94 per cent of the productive capacity in coal mining
was rationalised into Ruhrkohle. More generally, it
has been shown that the process of diversification
and mergers which preceded the 1973 amendments to the
GWB resulted in a high degree of concentration. In
fact, before the GWB came into force in 1958, many of
the pre-war enterprises were again as concentrated as

they had ever been. These trends in concentration were accompanied by a phenomenal growth in output. Hence, overall industrial concentration undoubtedly rose during the period under review. Between 1950 and 1970 the top 100 enterprises' share of total industrial turnover increased from about one-third to over one-half (Dyas and Thanheiser, p.101). In view of what has been said about the high number of mergers in the 1970s, it will not be surprising to learn that concentration continued to increase. Hence, Table 9.2 demonstrates that by 1980 the top 50 enterprises' share of total industrial turnover was almost a half.

Table 9.2:  The Trend in Industrial Concentration, 1960-1980

| Year | All industrial enterprises | | Top 50 enterprises | Col. (3) as percentage of col. (2) |
|---|---|---|---|---|
| | Number[a] | Turnover[b] (DM billion) | Turnover (DM billion) | |
| | (1) | (2) | (3) | (4) |
| 1960 | 49,600 | 266.4 | 92.3 | 34.6 |
| 1972 | 44,246 | 657.2 | 281.5 | 42.8 |
| 1980 | 39,011[c] | 1208.0[c] | 598.5 | 49.5 |

Notes:
(a) 1960 and 1972 with 10 or more employees
    1980 with 20 or more employees
(b) 1960 incl. turnover tax
    1972 and 1980 excl. value-added tax
(c) 7.6 million employees; total wage and salary costs = DM 259.5 billion

Sources:  Jordan, p.75; *Statisches Jahrbuch für die BRD*, 1981, Table 9.3; calculations from the *Die Zeit* 'Top 100', 36/81, p.16.

Whether a simple merger count (Table 9.1) or turnover (Table 9.2) series best captures the impact of mergers on competition depends not just on the absolute size of the merging firms, but also on size relative to the market. It has already been shown, however, that much of West German industry is dominated by firms with large market shares. The analysis will also return to this topic.

Hence, the rapid economic expansion in the 1950s
and, to a lesser extent, the 1960s was conducive to
both industrial growth and concentration. The growth
path of the economy was traced in Chapter 4, but
Diagram 9.1 shows how rapidly industrial production
rose in the 1950s. Again the growth trend slowed
down in the 1960s, and there were cyclical fluctuations in the 1970s. This chapter therefore continues
with an examination of how the main industrial enterprises fared against such a backcloth.

OTHER SALIENT INDUSTRIAL FEATURES

The Main Industrial Enterprises
From the above analysis, it is possible to conclude
that West Germany is a country of large industrial
enterprises. Bannock (p.56), however, reported that
Germany had many more small businesses than the UK
and their share of output and employment was much
higher. Concentration in both countries was increasing, but the decline of the small firm sector appeared
to be somewhat faster and certainly more widespread
among branches of the economy in Britain. However,
small and medium-sized business account for a smaller
share of *industrial* employment (12 per cent) and
*industrial* production (10 per cent) in West Germany
than in any other OECD country (Peacock, para.4.25 -
emphasis added). Moreover, the number of programmes
assisting such business enterprises in general have
increased considerably in the FRG, as has the amount
of government expenditure for such purposes (*ibid.*,
para.4.26). Hence, as a general principle, the obser-
vation that West German industrial enterprises are
large and important can be supported in several
respects.

First, the large and important industrial concerns in West Germany are often dependent on one large
company. Krupp of Essen is probably the best known
example, but there are others. The Wolfsburg plant
of VW is situation in what was a purpose-built 'new
town' during the Nazi era. Opel of Rüsselheim - a
subsidiary of General Motors - is also the only major
employer in that area. In the chemical industry,
Bayer is synonymous with Leverkusen and BASF with
Ludwigshafen. The traditional association of the
electrical engineering industry (Siemens and AEG) with
Berlin has already been mentioned, although this industry has tended to relocate in centres like Munich
and Wilhelmshafen (ICI is also located here). Dunlop
is in Hanau and Procter and Gamble in Schwalbach am

Diagram 9.1:   Industrial Production, 1950-1980

(a)

Index of industrial
production
(1970=100)

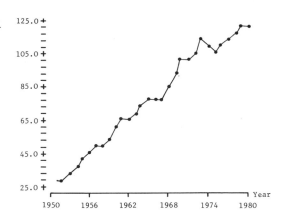

(b)

Index of industrial
production
(1970=100)
$\text{Log}_e$

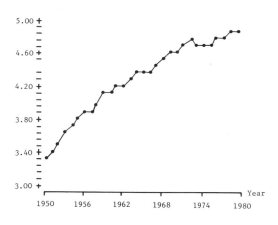

Source:   Plotted from Dresdner Bank, *Statische Reihen*, p.2.

Tanus.

Although these locations display a high regional diversity, both the differing prosperity of the industries concerned, and what was said about the general location of the industrial base in the labour market chapter, mean that industrial turnover is of differing proportionate significance. Table 9.3 gives an unweighted breakdown of general industrial turnover by Länder, together with an indication of recent growth and exports.

Table 9.3: Industrial Turnover and Exports by Länder, 1980

|  | Industrial turnover (DM billion) | Percentage increase 1980/1979 | Percentage of turnover earned from exports |
|---|---|---|---|
| Baden-Württemberg | 186.9 | 8.0 | 26.5 |
| Bavaria | 171.7 | 7.7 | 26.1 |
| Berlin (West) | 21.4 | 8.1 | 12.8 |
| Bremen | 16.6 | 10.7 | 20.6 |
| Hamburg | 35.8 | 10.2 | 18.0 |
| Hesse | 80.2 | 5.4 | 27.9 |
| Lower Saxony | 107.3 | 7.1 | 25.0 |
| North Rhine-Westphalia | 327.8 | 5.7 | 25.0 |
| Rhineland Palatinate | 64.6 | 10.1 | 29.9 |
| Saarland | 18.7 | 1.6 | 32.8 |
| Schleswig Holstein | 29.0 | 9.4 | 17.0 |
| Federal totals | 1061.2 | 7.2 | 25.3 |

Source: Dresdner Bank, *Wirtschaftsberichte, 33*(2), 1981, p.1 (writer's translation).

As a further measure of export strength, Table 9.4 analyses exports on the same basis as Table 9.3, but this time by individual enterprise. The top 30 enterprises of 1973 (before the crude oil price increases and floating exchange rate) included all the various companies discussed in Chapters 7, 8 and the present analysis. Evidence of the almost universal dominance of West Germany in electrical and mechanical engineering exports, when compared to Britain and France, is also given by Saunders (pp.11 and 81-83). Some wider industrial evidence of the growth to this position of dominance may be gauged from the fact

Table 9.4:   Exports of the Top 30 Industrial Enterprises, 1973

| Company | Sector | Exports and foreign transactions as a percentage of total turnover |
|---|---|---|
| Volkswagen | Motor vehicles | 68.4 |
| BASF | Chemicals | 48.7 |
| Siemens | Electrical engineering | 43.0 |
| Farbwerke Hoechst | Chemicals | 58.0 |
| Daimler-Benz | Motor vehicles | 36.7 |
| Bayer | Chemicals | 57.8 |
| Veba | Energy/Chemicals | 5.5 |
| Thyssen | Steel | 30.0 |
| AEG-Telefunken | Electrical engineering | 32.8 |
| Mannesmann | Steel and mechanical engineering | 50.0 |
| Fried. Krupp | Steel and mechanical engineering | 24.7 |
| Gutehoffnungshütte | Mechanical engineering | 42.4 |
| Ruhrkohle | Coal mining | 23.4 |
| Esso | Mineral oil | 4.4 |
| RWE | Energy | 2.8 |
| Deutsche Shell | Mineral oil | 2.0 |
| Rheinstahl | Steel and mechanical engineering | 27.2 |
| Flick-Gruppe | Holding | 21.6 |
| Robert-Bosch-Gruppe | Electrical engineering | 48.0 |
| Opel | Motor vehicles | 51.9 |
| Hoesch | Steel | 30.0 |
| Ford-Werke | Motor vehicles | 64.3 |
| Reemtsma-Cigaretten-fabr. | Cigarettes/Cereals | - |
| Gelsenberg | Mineral oil/Chemicals | - |
| Deutsche Unilver | Food | 16.0 |
| Salzgitter-Peine | Steel and mechanical engineering | 30.5 |
| Neue Heimat | Construction and property developer | - |
| Metallgesellschaft | Chemicals | 28.0 |
| BP | Mineral oil | 2.6 |
| Quandt-Gruppe | Holding | n.a. |

Source:   *Die Zeit*, 2/8/74 (writer's translation).

that in 1954 the export ratios of manufacturing industry in the UK and FRG stood at 13.6 and 14.3 per cent respectively (Panić, p.118). By 1972, the respective ratios were 15.2 and 24.3 per cent. A corollary of this is that the leading sectors of German industry remain highly export orientated. This dependence is brought out if a particular aspect of the overall 25.3 per cent average export ratio in Table 9.3 is examined sectorally. Above all, the top four industries in 1980 had total sales of over DM 100 billion. Of these industries, mechanical engineering had an export ratio of 43.7 per cent, motor vehicles 41.0 per cent, chemicals 38.4 per cent and electrical engineering 29.8 per cent (Dresdner Bank, *Economic Quarterly*, July 1981).

It will also be noted from Table 9.3 that on average over a quarter of industrial turnover is absorbed by exports. This leads to another measure of the size of industrial enterprises, namely the relative international size of West German companies. Table 9.5 shows that 7 West German enterprises were in the world's top 50.

Table 9.5: Rank of West German Companies in World's 50 Largest Industrial Companies (ranked by sales in US$ 1977-1980)

| Rank | | | | Company | Sales (1980) (US$ 000) | Net Income (1980) (US$ 000) |
|---|---|---|---|---|---|---|
| 1977 | 1978 | 1979 | 1980 | | | |
| 21 | 19 | 19 | 24 | Volkswagenwerk | 18,339,046 | 170,964 |
| 20 | 18 | 23 | 26 | Siemens | 17,950,253 | 332,434 |
| 34 | 25 | 24 | 27 | Daimler-Benz | 17,108,100 | 605,149 |
| 24 | 26 | 25 | 29 | Hoechst | 16,480,551 | 251,605 |
| 30 | 27 | 27 | 30 | Bayer | 15,880,596 | 356,342 |
| 31 | 31 | 28 | 31 | BASF | 15,277,348 | 197,641 |
| 37 | 40 | 31 | 32 | Thyssen | 15,235,998 | 61,611 |

Note:
British readers may be disappointed to learn that Britain had only four companies in this top 50, two of which were joint Dutch-British companies and two of which were in oil. The four were: Shell (ranked no.2 in 1980); BP (6); Unilever (17) and ICI (40).

Source: *Fortune Magazine*, 13 August 1979, p.208, and 10 August 1981, p.205.

Not surprisingly, the industries in which a high
degree of concentration has been found to exist -
motor vehicles, chemicals, electrical and mechanical
engineering (including iron and steel), are all represented in the world's top 50.
Another indication of relative international
size is given in Table 9.6. This time the high proportion of German companies in the top 100 is brought
out by a comparison with Britain, France and Japan.
Relative growth rates from such a sizeable base have
also been respectable, even during the relatively
depressed 1970s (also see Chapter 4). In order to
illustrate this, some international comparisons of
industrial growth are presented in Table 9.7.

Table 9.6: Size Distribution of the 500 Largest
Industrial Companies Outside the USA (ranked by sales
in US$, 1980)

| Country | No. of companies in top 500 by class interval | | | | | |
|---------|-------|---------|---------|---------|---------|-------|
|         | 1-100 | 101-200 | 201-300 | 301-400 | 401-500 | Total |
| Britain | 14 | 22 | 19 | 19 | 14 | 88 |
| France | 14 | 8 | 8 | 4 | 8 | 42 |
| Japan | 17 | 22 | 31 | 25 | 26 | 121 |
| W.Germany | 21 | 10 | 7 | 15 | 9 | 62 |

Source: *Fortune Magazine*, 10 August 1981, p.218.

Some Financial and Employment Aspects
Having established the relative size of West German
industrial enterprises, it is possible to proceed to
a comparison of their financial performance at the
end of the period under review. This is principally
achieved by means of Tables 9.8 and 9.9. These
tables confirm much of the analysis thus far. For
example, the serious losses of AEG, but the high
profitability of Daimler-Benz. The profits of
Daimler-Benz are, in turn, in contrast to the losses
of Ford and Opel. Also in the motor industry, the
deteriorating financial situation of VW is noticeable.
Several of the companies just mentioned, along with
Ruhrkohle, Salzgitter, Saarbergwerke, VIAG and
Klöckner, have also been unable to pay dividends.
The state, it will be recalled, has substantial

Table 9.7: The Index of Industrial Production$^a$ in Various Countries (1970=100)

| Year | EEC | | | | | | | | | | USA | USSR |
|------|---------|--------|-------|----------------|---------|-----------------|------------------|---------|---------|---------|-----|------|
| | Germany | France | Italy | Nether-lands | Belgium | Luxem-bourg | Great Britain | Ireland | Denmark | Average | | |
| 1970 | 100 | 100 | 100 | 100 | 100 | 100 | 100 | 100 | 100 | 100 | 100 | 100 |
| 1975 | 102 | 115 | 109 | 117 | 109 | 93 | 103 | 114 | 104 | 108 | 110 | 143 |
| 1976 | 110 | 124 | 122 | 126 | 118 | 99 | 106 | 125 | 114 | 115 | 122 | 150 |
| 1977 | 112 | 126 | 123 | 127 | 118 | 99 | 111 | 135 | 115 | 118 | 130 | 159 |
| 1978 | 114 | 129 | 126 | 128 | 120 | 100 | 114 | 147 | 117 | 120 | 137 | 167 |
| 1979 | 120 | 133 | 134 | 131 | 126 | 104 | 119 | 157 | 121 | 125 | 143 | 174 |
| 1980 | 120 | 133 | 142 | 131 | 126 | 100 | 111 | 157 | 121 | 125 | 138 | 180 |

Notes:
(a) excl. construction.

Source: BMWi, 1980, Table 6.3 (writer's translation).

holdings in many of these companies (also see Owen
Smith, 1979; Vogl, Appx.2).
As a result of their deteriorating financial
positions, some of the companies mentioned in the
last paragraph reduced the size of their labour forces. This is again shown in Table 9.8. Nevertheless,
many of them remain significant employers, which is
yet another indication of the importance of industry
to the West German economy. In fact, seven of the
top ten employers are industrial giants. Ruhrkohle
is also in the top ten. (During the later 1970s the
energy crisis resulted in a resurgence of investment
in the coal industry.) However, it was the Federal
Post Office and Federal Railways which occupied the
two top positions. Absolute numbers are given in
Table 9.10, from which the international nature of
many companies may also be seen.
It will be recalled - Chapter 4 above - that
direct overseas investment became a particularly important item in West Germany's balance of payments.
On the other hand, it will also be recalled - Chapter
6 above - that the proportion of the labour force in
manufacturing decreased after 1960. This longer-term
trend is not, of course, untypical. Moreover, capital
substitution usually means that industrial output continues to expand. Again, some data on this were given
in Chapter 4, but the falling trend in employment,
accompanied by a rising one in output, are both apparent from Table 9.11. However, in the case of West
Germany there also appears to have been a somewhat
greater movement away from the lower-value added
product groups to the higher ones (NEDO, 1981b,
para.14; Saunders, p.83).

### The Efficiency of Industry

Just as West German manufacturing industry, when compared to Britain's, surged ahead and captured valuable
export markets in the period 1954-1972, so she also
made other significant gains. Once again, however,
this period precedes the tangible emergence of the
various economic problems for West Germany which were
isolated in Chapters 4, 5 and 6. It will be recalled
that these problems included relative high labour
costs, stagnating and even falling capital investment,
increasing crude-oil prices, an appreciating exchange
rate, a secularly worsening invisible balance, and
direct capital outflows. Nevertheless, the economic
gains made by West German industry in the majority
of the years under review remain relevant.
Panić (chs 1 and 2) reports that between 1954
and 1972 West Germany's industrial performance

Table 9.8:  The 30 Biggest Industrial Enterprises

| Rank | | Company | Sector |
|---|---|---|---|
| 1980 | 1979 | | |
| 1 | 1 | VEBA | Energy/Oil/Chemicals |
| 2 | 2 | VW | Motor vehicles |
| 3 | 3 | Siemens | Electrical engineering |
| 4 | 4 | Daimler-Benz | Motor vehicles |
| 5 | 6 | Hoechst | Chemicals |
| 6 | 5 | BASF | Chemicals |
| 7 | 7 | Bayer | Chemicals |
| 8 | 8 | Thyssen | Steel |
| 9 | 10 | RWE | Energy |
| 10 | 9 | Ruhrkohle | Coal mining |
| 11 | 12 | Gutehoffnungshütte | Mechanical engineering |
| 12 | 15 | Deutsche BP | Mineral oil |
| 13 | 11 | AEG | Electrical engineering |
| 14 | 13 | Krupp | Steel and mechanical engineering |
| 15 | 16 | Deutsche Shell | Mineral oil |
| 16 | 20 | Esso | Mineral oil |
| 17 | 14 | Mannesmann | Steel and mechanical engineering |
| 18 | 19 | Bosch | Electrical engineering |
| 19 | 46 | Preussag | Energy/Oil |
| 20 | 17 | Opel | Motor vehicles |
| 21 | 28 | Ruhrgas | Energy |
| 22 | 22 | Metallgesellschaft | Mechanical engineering |
| 23 | 18 | Ford | Motor vehicles |
| 24 | 30 | Degussa | Chemicals and precious metals |
| 25 | 26 | Salzgitter | Steel and ship building |
| 26 | 21 | Flick | Holding |
| 27 | 25 | BMW | Motor vehicles |
| 28 | 24 | Deutsche Unilever | Food |
| 29 | 23 | Hoesch | Steel |
| 30 | 32 | Deutsche Texaco | Mineral oil |

Source:  *Die Zeit*, 36/81, p.16 (writer's translation).

| Turnover 1980 | | Profits (-losses) DM million | | Employees | |
|---|---|---|---|---|---|
| DM million | Percentage change over 1979 | 1980 | 1979 | End 1980 | Percentage change over 1979 |
| 39,970 | 15.5 | 479 | 554 | 83,936 | 3.1 |
| 33,288 | 8.4 | 302 | 465 | 257,930 | 7.6 |
| 31,960 | 14.1 | 487 | 522 | 344,000 | 3.0 |
| 31,054 | 13.5 | 961 | 540 | 183,392 | 5.1 |
| 29,915 | 10.5 | 381 | 368 | 186,850 | 2.3 |
| 29,171 | 7.2 | 478 | 534 | 116,518 | -0.5 |
| 28,825 | 10.9 | 331 | 389 | 181,639 | 0.3 |
| 27,128 | 7.0 | 144 | 130 | 152,089 | -3.3 |
| 16,262 | 11.7 | 489 | 570 | 68,007 | 3.9 |
| 16,422 | 1.2 | 32 | 11 | 136,816 | 1.9 |
| 15,417 | 13.2 | 121 | 121 | 86,018 | 1.7 |
| 15,201 | 23.1 | 13 | 198 | 4,340 | 1.2 |
| 15,141 | 7.0 | -278 | -968 | 145,200 | -6.0 |
| 13,919 | 8.9 | 38 | 64 | 85,706 | 0.5 |
| | | | | | |
| 13,899 | 18.6 | 246 | 263 | 4,878 | 1.7 |
| 13,150 | 23.5 | 430 | 408 | 4,567 | 2.9 |
| 13,110 | 4.9 | 147 | 146 | 103,491 | -2.2 |
| | | | | | |
| 11,809 | 9.3 | 117 | 151 | 120,020 | -1.1 |
| 9,412 | 15.3 | 89 | 52 | 21,283 | 1.5 |
| 9,224 | -15.3 | -411 | 253 | 59,876 | -11.3 |
| 9,122 | 46.1 | 207 | 133 | 2,938 | 1.8 |
| 9,047 | 14.6 | 42 | 20 | 27,220 | -0.2 |
| 8,692 | -20.4 | -463 | 483 | 49,767 | -13.9 |
| 8,649 | 42.8 | 55 | 46 | 20,569 | 0.5 |
| 8,578 | 19.2 | -85 | -5 | 56,574 | 1.8 |
| 8,427 | -3.6 | 77 | 82 | 46,891 | -0.1 |
| 8,117 | 9.6 | 160 | 175 | 43,241 | 3.1 |
| 8,095 | 6.3 | 137 | 116 | 35,334 | 0.9 |
| 7,992 | 4.4 | n.a. | 0 | 46,600 | -5.1 |
| 7,554 | 31.4 | 208 | 171 | 4,827 | 0.0 |

Table 9.9: Value Added in the Top 30 Industrial
(DM million)

| Rank | | Company | Value Added |
|------|------|---------|-------------|
| Value Added | Turnover | | |
| 1 | 4 | Daimler-Benz | 11,112 |
| 2 | 3 | Siemens | 10,757 |
| 3 | 2 | VW | 9,933 |
| 4 | 10 | Ruhrkohle | 7,597 |
| 5 | 8 | Thyssen | 6,675 |
| 6 | 1 | VEBA | 6,444 |
| 7 | 7 | Bayer | 6,330 |
| 8 | 9 | RWE | 6,182 |
| 9 | 6 | BASF | 5,969 |
| 10 | 5 | Hoechst | 5,667 |
| 11 | 13 | AEG | 4,937 |
| 12 | 17 | Mannesmann | 4,265 |
| 13 | 14 | Krupp | 4,074 |
| 14 | 31 | IBM | 3,703 |
| 15 | 11 | Gutehoffnungshütte | 3,515 |
| 16 | 18 | Bosch | 3,460 |
| 17 | 25 | Salzgitter | 2,897 |
| 18 | 29 | Hoesch | 2,637[a] |
| 19 | 23 | Ford | 2,584 |
| 20 | 20 | Opel | 2,542 |
| 21 | 26 | Flick | 2,538 |
| 22 | 27 | BMW | 2,297 |
| 23 | 28 | Deutsche Unilever | 2,021 |
| 24 | 45 | BBC | 1,853 |
| 25 | 37 | Saarbergwerke | 1,788 |
| 26 | 39 | VIAG | 1,718 |
| 27 | 36 | Klöckner-Werke | 1,618 |
| 28 | 47 | SEL | 1,599 |
| 29 | 22 | Metallgesellschaft | 1,577 |
| 30 | 48 | MBB | 1,566 |

Notes:
(a) Estimated.
(b) No information on profit distribution.

Source: *Die Zeit*, 36/81, p.16 (writer's translation).

Enterprises, Accounting Year 1980, Domestic

| Paid to: | | | | Retained Profits |
|---|---|---|---|---|
| Employees | State | Debt servicing | Shareholders | |
| 8,705 | 1,393 | 53 | 297 | 664 |
| 9,394 | 454 | 422 | 306 | 181 |
| 8,203 | 1,325 | 103 | 192 | 110 |
| 7,221 | 129 | 215 | – | 32 |
| 5,805 | 307 | 419 | 104 | 40 |
| 4,189 | 1,118 | 658 | 253 | 226 |
| 5,215 | 533 | 251 | 298 | 33 |
| 3,805 | 1,534 | 354 | 288 | 201 |
| 4,740 | 620 | 131 | 280 | 198 |
| 4,401 | 611 | 274 | 359 | 22 |
| 4,849 | 53 | 313 | – | -278 |
| 3,735 | 205 | 178 | 106 | 41 |
| 3,694 | 111 | 231 | 25 | 13 |
| 2,527 | 584 | 2 | 590[b] | – |
| 2,991 | 188 | 215 | 68 | 53 |
| 2,947 | 312 | 84 | 27 | 90 |
| 2,676 | 97 | 209 | – | -85 |
| n.a. | n.a. | n.a. | n.a. | n.a. |
| 2,910 | 41 | 96 | – | -463 |
| 2,885 | 46 | 22 | – | -411 |
| 2,161 | 134 | 166 | 77[b] | |
| 1,781 | 301 | 55 | 100 | 60 |
| 1,683 | 145 | 56 | 137[b] | |
| 1,699 | 77 | 42 | 25 | 10 |
| 1,628 | 36 | 119 | – | 5 |
| 1,222 | 191 | 180 | – | 125 |
| 1,307 | 64 | 258 | – | -11 |
| 1,438 | 62 | 56 | 44 | -1 |
| 1,343 | 113 | 79 | 29 | 13 |
| 1,407 | 75 | 34 | 20 | 30 |

Table 9.10: The Top 10 Employers, 1980 and 1981

| Rank | | Employer | Total number of employees | | Percentage change | | Employees in the Federal Republic | | Percentage change | |
|---|---|---|---|---|---|---|---|---|---|---|
| 1980 | 1981 | | 1980 | 1981 | 1980/1979 | 1981/1980 | 1980 | 1981 | 1980/1979 | 1981/1980 |
| 1 | 1 | Federal Post Office | 532,455 | 542,457 | 10.3 | 1.9 | 532,455 | 542,457 | 10.3 | 1.9 |
| 2 | 2 | Federal Railways | 344,686 | 341,285 | -0.3 | -1.0 | 344,656 | 341,255 | -0.3 | -1.0 |
| 3 | 3 | Siemens | 344,000 | 338,000 | 3.0 | -1.7 | 235,000 | 230,000 | 2.6 | -2.1 |
| 4 | 4 | VW | 257,930 | 246,906 | 7.6 | -4.3 | 156,831 | 160,286 | 0.2 | 0.9 |
| 6 | 5 | Daimler-Benz | 183,392 | 187,961 | 5.1 | 2.5 | 146,323 | 149,096 | 2.9 | 1.9 |
| 5 | 6 | Hoechst | 186,850 | 184,722 | 2.3 | -1.1 | 101,734 | 101,245 | 1.4 | -0.5 |
| 7 | 7 | Bayer | 181,639 | 180,906 | 0.3 | -0.4 | 101,400 | 101,100 | -0.6 | -0.3 |
| 8 | 8 | Thyssen | 152,089 | 149,786 | -3.3 | -1.5 | 127,700 | 125,694 | -0.7 | -1.6 |
| 9 | 9 | Ruhrkohle | 136,816 | 136,552 | 1.9 | -0.2 | 136,816 | 136,552 | 1.9 | -0.2 |
| 10 | 10 | AEG | 145,200 | 123,700 | -6.0 | -14.8 | 116,000 | 99,400 | -7.2 | -8.2 |

Source: *Die Zeit*, 36/81, p.17, and 34/82, p.17 (writer's translation).

*The Industrial Sector*

Table 9.11:  (i) Percentage of Employees in Manu-
             facturing Industry, 1950-1980
        (ii) Index of Total Industrial Production,
             1950-1980 (1970=100)

|      | (i)  | (ii)  |
|------|------|-------|
| 1950 | 35.5 | 28.3  |
| 1955 | 37.8 | 42.4  |
| 1960 | 40.0 | 59.7  |
| 1965 | 39.0 | 77.7  |
| 1970 | 38.7 | 100.0 |
| 1975 | 36.9 | 103.6 |
| 1980 | 34.5 | 122.8 |

Notes:
(i) Incl. mining but excl. construction and enterprises with less than 10 employees (1950-1970) and
less than 20 (1975 and 1980).
(i) For annual data: ungrouped mean = 37.7; ungrouped
median = 38.1; mid-point of modal group (8 obs from
31) = 38.5.
(ii) 1975 was a recession year - see Table 4.7
(i) and (ii) also indicate the roles of capital substitution and investment - see Tables 4.2 and 4.4.

Source:  Calculated from Dresdner Bank, *Statische
Reihen*, pp.2 and 3.

outstripped that of Britain's in terms of the growth
in net output, capital stock, employment, labour
productivity and prices.  Net output in manufacturing
industry in this period increased at an annual average
rate of 6.6 per cent in West Germany compared to 2.7
per cent in Britain.  Moreover, this growth was more
uniformly spread: the coefficient of variation across
the various industries in West Germany was half that
of Britain's.  Similarly, the capital stock grew at
an annual average rate of 7.4 per cent in West Germany compared to 3.9 per cent in the UK.  However, in
both cases capital growth outstripped output growth.
As a result, there was an annual average decline of
capital productivity of -1.1 per cent in the UK and
-0.8 per cent in the FRG.  Since the inverse of this
ratio is the capital/output ratio, therefore, this
latter ratio was increasing (also see MRDB, January
1980, p.13).
    Turning to the labour indicators, Panić first
reports that the annual average increase in

employment in manufacturing industry was 1.9 per cent
in the FRG. In the UK this statistic declined by
-0.1 per cent. However, it will be recalled from
Tables 6.6 and 9.11 that absolute employment in manufacturing in the FRG has fallen since 1970 and the
participation rates peaked in 1960. Nevertheless,
labour productivity in the FRG increased at an annual
average rate of 4.6 per cent compared to 2.9 per cent
in the UK. This productivity differential is attributed by Pratten (p.61) to both economic and 'behav-
ioural' causes. The latter group of causes includes
'manning and efficiency'. Finally, the rate of
annual average price increases in the FRG was 1.6 per
cent. In the UK it was 3.2 per cent.


CONCLUSION

Although the West German anti-trust law evolved in a
fundamentally different manner during the Social
Market era, its impact was somewhat muted. This was
because the law evolved too slowly to prevent the
process of horizontal and vertical integration which
brought about a degree of concentration analogous to
the pre-Second World War period.
    But the rapid recovery of West German industry
during the 1950s was not only accompanied by a process of diversification: this period of unprecedented
growth also resulted in a period of high profits.
Although the 1960s brought slower economic growth,
German exporters continued to expand their share of
world trade. Hence the spectacular recovery of the
1950s, combined with growing domestic prosperity
during most of the 1960s, were in the last analysis
attributable to the resurgence of German industry.
Such a resurgence was due to the *widespread
policy and public support* which industry received.
In a nutshell, most of this book has been either
directly or indirectly concerned with the significance and revival of West German industry. By the
end of the 1970s, however, steel, motor vehicles and
chemicals were running into difficulties. The notable
exception in the motor vehicle industry was Daimler-
Benz. In electrical engineering, AEG's position continued to deteriorate, and the banks were indicating
that some support from the State may be necessary.
    Once again, then, it is the *contrasts* during the
three decades under review which strike the observer.
Indeed, since these contrasts have been the main
theme of this book, they constitute an appropriate
concluding note.

BIBLIOGRAPHY

Adam, H., *Die Einkommensverteilung in der BRD* (Bund-
    Verlag, Köln, 1979)
Adenauer, K., *Memoirs, 1945-53* (Weidenfeld and Nicol-
    son, London, 1966)
Anthes, J. *et al.*, *Mitbestimmung: Ausweg oder
    Illusion?* (Ro Ro Ro Tele) (Rowohlt Taschenbuch
    Verlag, Reinbek bei Hamburg, 1972)
Atkinson, A.B., *The Economics of Inequality* (Oxford
    UP, 1975)
Backer, J.H., *Priming the German Economy* (American
    Occupational Policies 1945-1948) (Duke UP,
    Durham NC, 1971)
Ball, J.M. and Skeoch, N.K., 'Inter-plant Comparisons
    of Productivity and Earnings', *Government Econ-
    omic Service Working Paper* (No.38 - *Department
    of Employment Working Paper* No.3, Unit for Man-
    power Studies, Department of Employment, May
    1981)
Bannock, G., *The Smaller Business in Britain and Ger-
    many* (Wilton House Publications, London, 1976)
Barker, J.E., *Modern Germany* (John Murray, London,
    1919)
Baur, J.F., 'The Control of Mergers Between Large,
    Financially Strong Firms in West Germany',
    *Zeitschrift für die gesamte Staatswissenschaft,
    136* (3) (September 1980), pp.444-464
BBk (Deutsche Bundesbank), *Instruments of Monetary
    Policy in the Federal Republic of Germany*
    (Frankfurt a.M., 1971)
BBR, *Barclays Bank Review* (various)
BdB (Bundesverband deutscher Banken), *Mitglieds-
    verbände und angeschlossene Institute* (1981)
Bendix, D.W.F., *Industrial Democracy in the Federal
    Republic of Germany* (Institute of Labour
    Relations, University of South Africa, Pretoria,
    1978)

*Bibliography*

Bennecke, H., *Wirtschaftliche Depression und politischer Radikalismus: die Lehre von Weimar* (Günter Olzog Verlag, München-Wien, 1968)

Berger, J. and Mohr, J., *A Seventh Man* (Pelican Original, Penguin Books, Harmondsworth, 1975)

Blackaby, F. (ed.), *The Future of Pay Bargaining* (Heinemann Educational Books, London, 1980)

Blitz, R.C., 'A Benefit-Cost Analysis of Foreign Workers in West Germany, 1957-1973', *Kyklos*, *30* (3) (1977), pp.479-502

Blyton, P., 'The Industrial Relations of Work-sharing', *Industrial Relations Journal*, *13* (3) (Autumn 1982), pp.6-12

Blyton, P. and Hill, S., 'The Economics of Work-sharing', *National Westminster Bank Quarterly Review* (November 1981), pp.37-45

BMA (Bundesministerium für Arbeit und Sozialordnung), *Statisches Taschenbuch* (various) (Bonn)

BMF (Bundesministerium der Finanzen, *Beteiligungen des Bundes* (various) (Bonn)

BMWi (Bundesministerium für Wirtschaft), *Leistung in Zahlen* (various) (Bonn)

Board of Inland Revenue, *Income Taxes Outside of the United Kingdom (Federal Republic of Germany, 1976 to 1979)* (HMSO, London, Second Editon, 1980)

Böhning, W.R., 'Some Thoughts on Emigration from the Mediterranean Basin', *International Labour Review*, *111* (3) (1975), pp.251-277

Boléat, M.J., *An International Comparison of Housing Finance Systems* (The Building Societies Association, mimeographed, London, 1978)

Bradley, J., 'Building Societies Would Find West Germany a Tough Market to Enter', *The Building Societies Gazette* (August 1979)

Braun, H., 'Soziale Sicherung in Deutschland', *Der Bürger im Staat*, *29* (4) (1979), pp.211-217

Bresciani-Turroni, C., *The Economics of Inflation* (Augustus M. Kelley, London, Third Impression, 1968)

Brockhaus Encyklopädie (F.A. Brockhaus, Wiesbaden, 1966-1976)

BSA (Building Societies Association), 'Building Societies and the European Community', *Report* of Working Group B: West Germany (mineographed, London, 1978)

Burtenshaw, D., *Economic Geography of West Germany* (Macmillan, London, 1974)

BVR, (Bundesverband der Deutschen Volksbanken und Raiffeisenbanken), *Bericht '80*
—— *Zahlen '80*

Cable, J., 'Merger Development and Policy in West

Germany since 1958', *Warwick Economic Research Papers* (No.150, Department of Economics, University of Warwick, 1979)

Cable, J.R., Palfrey, J.P.R. and Runge, J.W., 'Federal Republic of Germany 1962-1974' in D.C. Mueller (ed.), *The Determinants and Effects of Mergers: An International Comparison* (Oelgeschlager, Gunn & Hain, London, 1980a)

—— 'Economic Determinants and Effects of Mergers in West Germany 1964-74', *Zeitschrift für die gesamte Staatswissenschaft*, *136* (2) (June 1980b), pp.226-248

Cassell, D. *et al.* (eds), *25 Jahre Marktwirtschaft in der Bundesrepublik Deutschland* (Gustav Fisher Verlag, Stuttgart, 1972)

Chester, T.E., 'West Germany - A Social Market Economy', *Three Banks Review* (December 1971)

Chipman, J.S., 'Internal-External Price Relationships in the West German Economy, 1958-1979', *Zeitschrift für die gesamte Staatswissenschaft*, *137* (3) (September 1981), pp.612-637

Commerzbank, *100 Jahre Commerzbank* (Düsseldorf, 1970)

—— *Worldwide Activities* (Frankfurt a.M., 1980)

Commission of the European Communities, 'Action Programme in Favour of Migrant Workers and their Families', *Bulletin*, Supplement 3/76 (Office for Official Publications, Luxembourg, 1976)

Copeman, G., *The Chief Executive: and Business Growth* (Leviathan House, London and New York, 1971)

Dennis, G.E.J., *Monetary Economics* (Longman, London and New York, 1981)

Denton, G., Forsyth, M. and MacLennon, M., *Economic Planning and Policies: Britain, France and Germany* (Allen & Unwin, London, 1968)

*Der Spiegel* (various) (Hamburg)

Deutsche Bank, *100 Years of the Deutsche Bank* (Frankfurt a.M.?, 1970?)

DGB, *Geschäftsberichte* (various) (Bundesvorstand des Deutschen Gewerkschaftsbundes, Düsseldorf)

DG Bank (Deutsche Genossenschaftsbank), *DG Bank and its System: A Brief History* (Frankfurt a.M., 1981)

*Die Zeit* (various) (Hamburg)

Donges, J.B., 'Industrial Policies in West Germany's not so Market-Oriented Economy', *World Economy*, *3* (2) (September 1980), pp.185-204

Donovan, M.H., *Official Grants and Financial Aids to Business in Western Europe: West Germany* (Graham A. Trotman, London, 1977 (basic volume); 1978 and 1979 (supplements)

Dresdner Bank, *Economic Quarterly* (various) (Trans-

lation of principal *Wirtschaftsberichte* articles)
Dresdner Bank, *Statische Reihen* (supplement to *Wirt-schaftsberichte,* June 1981). (Also available in English.)
—— *Wirtschaftsberichte* (various)
Dyas, G.P. and Thanheiser, H.T., *The Emerging European Enterprise* (Macmillan, London, 1976)
Eckstein, W., 'The Role of the Banks in Corporate Concentration in West Germany', *Zeitschrift für die gesamte Staatswissenschaft, 136* (3) (September 1980), pp.465-482
*The Economist* (various) (London)
EEC (European Economic Community), *Reports on Competition Policy* (various)
Eglau, H.O., *Erste Garnitur: Die Mächtigen der Deutschen Wirtschaft* (Econ Verlag, Düsseldorf und Wien, 1980)
*Employment Gazette,* Department of Employment (various) (HMSO, London)
Engelmann, B., *Meine Freunde - die Manager* (Deutscher Taschenbuch Verlag, München, 6. Auflage, 1978). (One of several books by Englemann (same publisher). There is one on millionaires with a very similar title.)
Ergun, T., *Some Economic Implications of Migration to Western Europe since 1945 with Special Reference to Turkey* (M.Sc. Thesis, Loughborough University of Technology, 1975)
Erhard, L., *Prosperity Through Competition* (Thames & Hudson, London, Third Edition, 1962)
Federal Employment Institute of the FRG (undated - several editions) (Nuremberg)
Federal Labour Office (Bericht der Bundesanstalt für Arbeit), *Ausländische Arbeitnehmer 1972/73* (Bundesanstalt für Arbeit, Nürnberg, 1974)
Feix, N., *Integration oder Rotation?* (Institut für Empirische Soziologie, Saarbrücken, 1973)
Fest, J.C., *Hitler* (Pelican Books, Harmondsworth, London, 1977)
*Financial Times* (various) (London and Frankfurt a.M.)
—— Banking, 'Banking in West Germany', *Financial Times Survey* (annually) (various)
—— West Germany, 'West Germany', *Financial Times Survey* (annually - usually October) (various)
Flink, S., *The German Reichsbank and Economic Germany* (Greenwood Press, New York, 1930 (reprinted in 1969)
Ford, A.G., *Income Spending and the Price Level* (Fontana/Collins, London, 1971)
*Fortune Magazine* (various) (Time Inc., Los Angeles, USA)

*Bibliography*

*Frankfurter Allgemeine Zeitung* (various) (Frankfurt
   a.m.)
Franz, W., 'Employment Policy and Labor Supply of
   Foreign Workers in the Federal Republic of Ger-
   many: A Theoretical and Empirical Analysis',
   *Zeitschrift für die gesamte Staatswissenschaft,
   137* (3) (September 1981), pp.590-611
Garlich, D., *Steuerungsprobleme Zentralstaatlicher
   Planung in der Bundesrepublik* (International
   Institute of Management, Discussion Paper 77-17,
   Berlin, 1977)
Garlich, D. and Hull, C., *Central Control and Infor-
   mation Dependence in a Federal System* (Inter-
   national Institute of Management, Discussion
   Paper 77-102, Berlin, 1977)
Gaugler, E., 'Mitarbeiter-Kapital im Arbeitgebenden
   Unternehmen', *Finnish Journal of Business Econ-
   omics,* 4-1979 (Special Edition)
Gaugler, E. *et al.*, *Ausländer in deutschen Industrie-
   betrieben: Ergebnisse einer empirischen Unter-
   suchung* (Peter Hanstein Verlag, Köningstein/Ts,
   1978). (Part of a wide-ranging series of
   empirical studies, all of which are published
   by Hanstein - see both the Introduction to this
   Gaugler volume and Kremer and Spangenberg below.)
Geimer, R. and H., *Science in the FRG: Organisation
   and Promotion,* Fourth Edition (Deutscher
   Akademischer Austauschdienst, Bonn, 1978)
Geiselberger, S., *Schwarzbuch: Ausländische Arbeiter*
   (Fischer Taschenbuch Verlag, Frankfurt a.M.,
   1972)
Gennard, J., *Job Security and Industrial Relations*
   (OECD, Paris, 1979)
Gessler Commission (Bericht der Studienkommission),
   'Grundsatzfragen der Kreditwirtschaft', *Schriften-
   reihe des Bundesministeriums der Finanzen, 28*
   (Fritz Knapp Verlag, Frankfurt a.M., 1979)
Giersch, H., *Growth, Cycles and Exchange Rates - the
   Experience of West Germany* (Almqvist & Wiksell,
   Stockholm, 1970). (Republished (in German) in:
   *Kroverse Fragen der Wirtschaftspolitik* (R. Piper
   & Co. Verlag, München, 1971).) [Page references
   in this book are to the German edition.]
Gordon, A.P.L., *The Problem of Trust and Monopoly
   Control* (George Routledge & Sons, London, 1928)
Gossweiler, K., *Grossbanken, Industriemonopole, Staat*
   (Verlag das Europäische Buch, West Berlin, 1975)
Graham, F.D., *Exchange, Prices and Production in
   Hyperinflation: Germany 1920-1923* (Russell &
   Russell, New York, 1967 (re-issued)
Greza, G., *Sozial - Report* (Inter Nationes, Bonn,

1975)

Greza, G., *Sozial - Report* (Inter Nationes, Bonn, 1978)

Grosser, A., *Germany in Our Time* (Pelican Books, Harmondsworth, 1974)

Gruhler, W., 'Rationalisierungs-investitionen und Beschäftigung', *Beiträge zur Wirtschafts - und Sozialpolitik*, 52, 1/1978 (Deutscher Instituts-Verlag, Köln, 1978)

Guillebaud, C.W., *The Economic Recovery of Germany (1933-1938)* (Macmillan, London, 1939)
—— *The Social Policy of Nazi Germany* (republished by Howard Fertig, New York, 1971)

Hallet, G., *The Social Economy of West Germany* (Macmillan, London, 1973)

Hanby, V.J. and Jackson, M.P., 'An Evaluation of Job Creation in Germany', *International Journal of Social Economics*, 6 (2) (1979), pp.79-117

Hardach, K., *The Political Economy of Germany in the Twientieth Century* (California UP, Berkeley/Los Angeles/London, 1980)

Hardes, H.-D., *Einkommenspolitik in der BRD*, Herder + Herder (Campus: Studien, Frankfurt a.M., 1974)

Hartrich, E., *The Fourth and Richest Reich* (Collier Macmillan, London, 1980)

Henderson, W.O., *The Rise of German Industrial Power 1834-1914* (Temple Smith, London, 1975)

Henning, F.W., *Das industrialisierte Deutschland 1914-1972* (Ferdinand Schöningh, Paderborn, 1974)

Hennings, K.H., *The West German Economy 1945-1979* - Diskussionspapiere, Fachbereich Wirtschafts-wissenschaften, Universität Hannover (Serie C, Volkswirtschaftslehre, Nr.43, Mai 1981). (Manuscript of a chapter contributed to a book on the Economic Development of Europe since 1950, edited by C. Allsop and A. Boltho, to be published by Oxford UP.)

Hesselbach, W., *Public, Trade Union and Co-operative Enterprise in Germany* (Frank Cass, London, 1976)

Hirsch-Weber, W., *Gewerkschaften in der Politik* (Westdeutscher Verlag, Köln und Opladen, 1959)

Hoffman, W.G., *Das Wachstum der Deutschen Wirtschaft seit der Mitte des 19. Jahrhunderts* (Springer-Verlag, Berlin, Heidelberg, New York, 1965)

Homze, E.L., *Foreign Labor in Nazi Germany* (Princeton UP, New Jersey, 1967)
—— *Arming the Luftwaffe: the Reich Air Ministry and the German Aircraft Industry 1919-1939* (University of Nabraska Press, 1976)

Hood, N. and Young, S., *The Economics of Multinational Enterprises* (Longman, London and New York, 1979)

*Bibliography*

Horn, E-J., 'Management of Industrial Change in Germany', *Sussex European Papers* (No.13, Sussex European Research Centre, University of Sussex, 1982)

Huber, P. und Wiegert, R., 'Der künftige Arbeitsmarkt', *Der Bürger im Staat*, *28* (3) (September 1978, pp.183-188

Hutchinson, T.W., 'Notes on the Effects of Economic Ideas on Policy: The example of the German Social Market Economy', *Zeitschrfit für die gesamte Staatswissenschaft*, *135* (3) (September 1979), pp.426-441

Hutton, S. and Lawrence, P., *German Engineers: the Anatomy of a Profession* (Oxford UP, 1981)

Hutton, S.D., Lawrence, P.A. and Smith, M.H., 'The Recruitment, Deployment and Status of the Mechanical Engineer in the German Federal Republic', *Report* to the Department of Industry, London, 1977, Parts I and II (Part I, pp.1-94, contains a general introduction; Part II, p.95 onwards, contains the results of a survey)

IdDW (Institut der Deutschen Wirtschaft),*Zahlen* (various) (Köln)

IDS (Incomes Data Services Limited), *International Reports* (various) (London)

IG Chemie, *Projekt Schichtarbeit - Gesamtergebnis der Problemanalyse*, (i) Langfassung, (ii) Kurzfassung, (iii) Tabellenband (Hauptvorstand, Hannover, 1981)

ILO (International Labour Office), *The Exploitation of Foreign Labour by Germany* (ILO, Montreal, 1945)

Institute of Economic Affairs, *Job 'Creation' - or Destruction?* (London, 1976)

Jacobi, O. et al., *Gewerkschaften und Klassenkampf: Kritisches Jahrbuch, 1974* (Fischer Taschenbuch Verlag, Frankfurt a.M., 1974)

Johnson, N., *Government in the Federal Republic of Germany* (Pergamon Press, Oxford, 1973)

Johnson, N. and Cochrane, A., *Economic Policy-making by Local Authorities in Britain and Western Germany* (George Allen & Unwin, London, 1981)

Jordan, R., 'Entwicklung und Stand der wirtschaftlichen Konzentration in der Bundesrepublik Deutschland - Ein empirischer Uberblich', *WSI-Mitteilungen*, *29* (August 1976), pp.71-77

Kaufer, E., *Konzentration und Fusionskontrolle* (J.C.B. Mohr (Paul Siebeck), Tübingen, 1977)

Kaufmann, G., 'Banken in der BRD', *Der Bürger im Staat*, *23* (4) (1973), pp.256-264

*Keesing's Contemporary Archives* (now Longmans,

London) (various)

Kindleberger, C.P., *Europe's Postwar Growth: the Role of Labor Supply* (Harvard UP, Cambridge, Mass., 1967)

Kliemann, H.G. and Taylor, S.B., *Who's Who in Germany* (International Book and Publishing, Munich, Third Edition, 1964 - 2 vols A-N and M-Z)

Koch, U.E., *Angriff auf ein Monopol* (Deutscher Instituts Verlag, Köln, 1981)

Knapp, M., 'Reconstruction and West-Integration: The impact of the Marshall Plan on Germany', *Zeitschrift für die gesamte Staatswissenschaft, 137* (3) (September 1981), pp.415-433

Krautkrämer, U., 'Arbeitslosenversicherung', *Der Bürger im Staat, 29* (4) (1979), pp.239-242

Kremer, M. and Spangenberg, H., *Assimilation ausländischer Arbeitnehmer in der Bundesrepublik Deutschland* (Peter Hanstein Verlag, Königstein/Ts, 1980)

Kühlewind, G., 'The Employment of Foreign Workers in the Federal Republic of Germany and their Family and Living Conditions', *The German Economic Review, 12* (4) (1974), pp.356-364

Labour and Social Affairs, *Reports* (various) (FRG Embassy, London)

Lambsdorff, O. von, 'Goals for the 1980s - Competition, Price Stability and Adjustment', *World Economy, 2* (4) (February 1980), pp.415-425

Laursen, K. and Pedersen, J., *The German Inflation 1918-1923* (North-Holland Publishing Company, Amsterdam, 1964)

Lawrence, P., *Managers and Management in West Germany* (Croom Helm, London, 1980)

Lembruch, G. and Lang, W., 'Die Konzertierte Aktion', *Der Bürger im Staat, 27* (3) (1977), pp.202-208

Leptin, G. and Melzer, M., *Economic Reform in East German Industry* (Oxford UP, 1978)

Lydall, H., *The Structure of Earnings* (Oxford UP, 1968)

Maldonado, Rita M., 'Why Puerto Ricans Migrated to the United States', *Monthly Labor Review, 99* (9) (1976), pp.7-18

────── 'Analyzing Puerto Rican Migration - A Reply', *Monthly Labor Review, 100* (8) (1977), pp.34-35

Manchester, W., *The Arms of Krupp* (Michael Joseph, London, 1969)

Mann, G., *The History of Germany Since 1789* (Pelican Books, Harmondsworth, 1974)

Marburg, T.F., 'Government and Business in Germany: Public Policy Toward Cartels', *Business History Review, 38* (1) (1964), pp.78-101)

Markert, K., 'Merger Control in Western Europe:

National and International Aspects' in
O. Schachter and R. Hellawell (eds), *Competition
in International Business* (Columbia UP, New York,
1981)
Markmann, H., 'Incomes Policy in Germany: A Trade
Union View', *British Journal of Industrial
Relations*, 2 (3) (1964), pp.322-339
Marsden, D., 'Vive la différence: Pay Differentials
in Britain, West Germany, France and Italy',
*Employment Gazette* (Department of Employment,
HMSO, London), *89* (7) (July 1981), pp.309-318
and p.324
Marshall, A., *Industry and Trade* (Macmillan, London,
Third Edition, reprinted 1932)
Martin, P.L., 'Germany's Guestworkers', *Challange*
(July-August 1981), pp.34-42
Martin, P.L. and Miller, M.J., 'Guestworkers: Lessons
from Western Europe', *Industrial and Labor
Relations Review*, *33* (3) (1980), pp.315-330
Masur, G., *Imperial Berlin* (Routledge & Kegan Paul,
London, 1971)
MBR, 'The German Inflation of 1923', *Midland Bank
Review* (November 1975), pp.20-29
Mellor, R.E.H., *The Two Germanies* (a modern geography)
(Harper & Row, London and New York, 1978)
Mendershausen, H., *Two Postwar Recoveries of the
German Economy* (reprinted by Greenwood Press,
Westport, Connecticut, 1974)
Mestmäcker, E-J., 'Competition Policy and Antitrust:
Some Comparative Observations', *Zeitschrift für
die gesamte Staatswissenschaft*, *136* (3)
(September 1980), pp.387-407
Mierheim, H. und Wicke, L., *Die personelle Vermögens-
verteilung in der BRD* (JCB Mohr, Tübingen, 1978)
Milward, A.S., *The German Economy at War* (Athlone
Press, University of London, 1965)
MK I (Monopolkommission), *Mehr Wettbewerb ist möglich*,
Hauptgutachten I, 2. Auflage (Nomos Verlag,
Baden-Baden, 1977)
MK II (Monopolkommission), *Fortschreitende Konzen-
tration bei Großunternehmen*, Hauptgutachten II
(Nomos Verlag, Baden-Baden, 1978)
MK III (Monopolkommission), *Fusionskontrolle bleibt
vorrangig*, Hauptgutachten III (Nomos Verlag,
Baden-Baden, 1980)
MK IV (Monopolkommission), *Fortschritte bei der
Konzentrationserfassung*, Hauptgutachten IV
(Nomos Verlag, Baden-Baden, 1982)
Morris, M., *The General Strike* (Penguin Books, Har-
mondsworth, 1976)
MRDB, *Monthly Report of the Deutsche Bundesbank*

(various)
Mueller, R., Heidenhain, M. and Schneider, H., *Das Recht gegen Wettbewerbsbeschränkungen/German Antitrust Law* (Fritz Knapp Verlag, Frankfurt a.M., 1981)

Mueller, R., Stiefel, E. and Brücher, H. (for the Dresdner Bank), *Doing Business in Germany: A Legal Manual* (Fritz Knapp Verlag, Frankfurt a.M., Eighth Edition, 1978)

Müller-Armack, A., 'The Social Market Economy as an Economic and Social Order', *Review of Social Economy*, *36* (5) (1978), pp.325-331

Muir, R., *A Brief History of Our Own Times* (George Philip & Son, London, Second Edition, 1935)

Mukherjee, S., *Governments and Labour Markets* (Political and Economic Planning, London, 1976)

NEDO (National Economic Development Office), *Iron and Steel SWP: Progress Report 1980* (London, 1980)

―― *Toolmaking: A Comparison of UK and West German Companies* (London, 1981a)

―― *British Industrial Performance* (London, 1981b)

Newton, K., *Balancing the Books* (SAGE Publications, London, 1980)

Nikolinakos, M., *Politische Ökonomie der Gastarbeiterfrage* (Rowohlt Taschenbuch Verlag, Reinbek bei Hamburg, 1973)

Oberhauser, A., 'Death duties and property taxation as a means of a more even distribution of the stock of wealth', *The German Economic Review*, *13* (1) (1975), pp.1-15

OECD (Organisation for Economic Co-operation and Development), *Economic Outlook* (Paris, bi-annual, various)

―― *Economic Surveys* (Germany) (Paris, annually, various)

―― *Guide to Legislation on Restrictive Business Practices* (Seventh supplement to fourth edition, Vol.1 (Germany), Paris, 1981)

―― *Reviews of National Policies for Education (Germany)* (Paris, 1972). (A classification of educational systems, including Germany, was published by OECD in the same year.)

―― *Unemployment Compensation and Related Employment Policy Measures* (Paris, 1979)

OEEC (Organisation for European Economic Co-operation), *Industrial Statistics 1900-1959* (Paris, 1960)

Opie, R., 'West Germany's Economic Miracle', *Three Banks Review* (March, 1962)

Ott, A.E., 'Arbeitszeitverkürzung als Mittel zur Bekämpfung der Arbeitslosigkeit?', *Der Bürger im*

*Staat*, *28* (3) (1978), pp.218-221

Owen Smith, E., 'The Federal Republic of Germany' in
P. Maunder (ed.), *Government Intervention in the
Developed Economy* (Croom Helm, London, 1979)
—— (ed.), *Trade Unions in the Developed Economies*
(Croom Helm, London, 1981)

Paine, S.H. in R.T. Griffiths (ed.), *Government,
Business and Labour in European Capitalism*
(Europotentials Press, London, 1977)

Panić, M. (ed.), *The UK and West German Manufacturing
Industry 1954-72* (NEDO Monograph 5, National
Economic Development Office, London, 1976)

Peacock, A. (in collaboration with R. Grant,
M. Ricketts, G.K. Shaw and E. Wagner), *Struc-
tural Economic Policies in West Germany and the
United Kingdon* (Anglo-German Foundation for the
Study of Industrial Society, London, 1980)

Peltzer, M. and Nebendorf, K., *Banking in Germany*
(Fritz Knapp Verlag, Frankfurt a.M., 1973)

Pen, J., *Income Distribution* (Pelican Books, Harmondsworth, 1974)

Pettman, B.O. and Fyfe, J. (eds), *Youth Unemployment
in Great Britain and the Federal Republic of
Germany* (MCB Publications, Bradford, 1977)

Petzina, D., *Die Deutsche Wirtschaft in der Zwischen-
kriegszeit* (Franz Steiner, Wiesbaden, 1977)

Phelps Brown, H., *The Inequality of Pay* (Oxford UP,
1977)

Ponto, J., 'Die Macht der Banken', *Schriftenreihe
Rechts- und Staatswissenschaftliche Vereingigung
Frankfurter Juristische Gesellschaft*, 8 (1971)
—— *Die Chance der Freiheit* (Vorlesung vor dem
Tabak-Kollegium im Alten Rathaus zu Bremen aus
Anlaß des 200-jahrigen Bestehens der Vereinigten
Staaten von Amerika, 1976)

Pounds, N.J.G., *The Economic Pattern of Modern Germany*
(John Murray, London, Second Edition, 1966)

Power, J. (with A. Hardman), *Western Europe's Migrant
Workers* (Minority Rights Group, London, Report
No.28, 1976)

Prais, S.J., 'Vocational Qualifications of the Labour
Force in Britain and Germany', *National Institute
Economic Review*, Number 98 (November 1981),
pp.47-59

Pratten, C.F., 'Labour Productivity Differentials
within International Companies', *Occasional
Papers* (No.50, Department of Applied Economics,
University of Cambridge, Cambridge UP, 1976)

Prittie, T., *The Velvet Chancellors: A history of
post-war Germany* (Frederick Muller, London,
1979)

*Bibliography*

Ray, G.F., 'The Size of Plant: A Comparison',
   *National Institute Economic Review*, No.38
   (November 1966), pp.63-66
—— 'Labour Costs and International Competitiveness'.
   *National Institute Economic Review*, No.61
   (August 1972), pp.53-58
Reuss, F.G., *Fiscal Policy for Growth without
   Inflation* (John Hopkins Press, Baltimore Mary-
   land, 1963)
Roll, E. in H. Marquand (ed.), *Organised Labour in
   Four Continents* (Longmans Green, London, 1939)
Rutherford, M. in A. Rowley (ed.), *The Barons of
   European Industry* (Croom Helm, London, 1974)
Š - Deutscher Sparkassen Verlag, *A Versatile Partner
   in all Money Matters* (Stuttgart, 1979)
Sadowski, D., 'Finance and Governance of the German
   Apprenticeship System', *Zeitschrift für die
   gesamte Staatswissenschaft, 137* (2) (June 1981),
   pp.234-251
Sauer, W., 'The Contribution of Small Units of Enter-
   prise to the German Economic Miracle',
   *Occasional Papers* (Siena Series No.13, Acton
   Society Trust, 1978/79)
Saunders, C., 'Engineering in Britain, West Germany
   and France: Some Statistical Comparisons of
   Structure and Competitiveness', *Sussex European
   Papers* (No.3, Sussex European Research Centre,
   University of Sussex, 1978)
Saunders, C. and Marsden, D., *Pay Inequalities in the
   European Communities* (Butterworths, London,
   1981)
Schiller, G., 'Channelling Migration: A Review of
   Policy with Special Reference to the Federal
   Republic of Germany', *International Labour
   Review, 111* (4) (1975), pp.335-355
Schmid, G. and Peters, A.B., 'The German Federal
   Employment Program for Regions with Special
   Employment Problems', *Regional Science and Urban
   Economics, 12* (1) (1982), pp.99-119
Schneider, H., Hellwig, H-J. and Kingsman, D.J., *Das
   Bankwesen in Deutschland/The German Banking
   System* (Fritz Knapp Verlag, Frankfurt a.M., 1978)
Schöller, P., Puls, W.W. and Buchholz, H.J., *Federal
   Republic of Germany: Spatial Development and
   Problems* (Schöningh, Paderborn, 1980)
Schuster, D., *Die deutschen Gewerkschaften seit 1945*
   (Verlag W. Kohlhammer, Stuttgart, 1973)
Shonfield, A., *Modern Capitalism* (Oxford UP, 1965)
Smith, P. and Swann, D., *Protecting the Consumer: An
   Economic and Legal Analysis* (Martin Robertson,
   Oxford, 1979)

Sonderdrucke der Deutschen Bundesbank, *Jahr-esabschlüsse der Unternehmen in der Bundes-republik Deutschland 1965 bis 1976*, Nr.5 (up-dated in 1977: Nr.6)

*Sozialberichte* (various) (Der Bundesminister für Arbeit und Sozialordnung, Bonn)

*Sozialpolitische Informationen* (various) (Der Bundes-minister für Arbeit und Sozialordnung, Bonn)

Spahn, P.B. (ed.), *Principles of Federal Policy Co-ordination in the Federal Republic of Germany: Basic Issues and Annotated Legislation* (Research Monograph No.25, Centre for Research on Federal Financial Relations, The Australian National University, Canberra, 1978)

Statistical Supplements to the Monthly Report of the Deutsche Bundesbank (various)

*Statistisches Jahrbuch für die Bundesrepublik Deutsch-land* (various) Statistisches Bundesamt (Wies-baden Verlag, W. Kohlhammer, Stuttgart und Mainz)

Stein, J., *The Banking System of the Federal Republic of Germany* (Bundesverband deutscher Banken, Cologne, Tenth Edition, 1977)

—— *Das Bankwesen in der Bundesrepublik Deutschland* (Bundesverband deutscher Banken, Köln, Twelth Edition, 1979)

Stephen, D., 'Immigrant Workers and Low Pay' in F. Field (ed.), *Low Pay* (Arrow Books, London, 1973)

Stewart, S., *The Significance of the German Case* (mimeographed, 1980)

Stingl, J., 'Role and Structure of the German Federal Employment Institution', *International Labour Review*, *116* (2) (1977), pp.197-207

Stolper, G., Häuser, K. and Borchardt, K., *The German Economy, 1870 to the Present* (Weidenfeld & Nicolson, London, 1967). (Contains biblio-graphical history of previous German and English editions - page references are to the first joint German edition.)

Stolper, W.F. and Roskamp, K.W., 'Planning in a Free Economy: Germany 1945-1960', *Zeitschrift für die gesamte Staatswissenschaft*, *135* (3) (September 1979), pp.374-404

Subsidy Reports (various), Bundesministerium der Finanzen, *Subventionsberichte* (Bonn)

Swann, D., *Competition and Consumer Protection* (Penguin Books, Harmondsworth, 1979)

Tillotson, J., 'The *GKN-Sachs* Affair: A Case Study in Economic Law', *Journal of World Trade Law*, *14* (1) (1980), pp.39-67

*The Times* (various) (London)

Turner, H.A. and Jackson, D.A.S., 'On the Stability
of Wage Differences and Productivity-Based Wage
Policies: An International Analysis', *British
Journal of Industrial Relations*, *6* (3) (1968),
pp.322-329

UNESCO (United Nations Educational, Scientific and
Cultural Organisation), 'Science Policy and the
Organisation of Research in the FRG', *Science
Policy Studies and Documents*, No.12 (Paris,
1969)

VÖB (Verband Öffentlicher Banken), *Wir die
Öffentlicher Banken* (Bonn, 1981)

Völker, G.E., 'Impact of Turkish Labour Migration on
the Economy of the Federal Republic of Germany',
*German Economic Review*, *11* (1) (1973), pp.61-77

Vogl, F., *German Business After the Economic Miracle*
(Macmillan, London, 1973)

Vollmer, R., 'The Structure of West German Foreign
Trade', *Zeitschrift für die gesamte Staatswissenschaft*, *137* (3) (September 1981), pp.575-589

Wallich, H.C., *Mainsprings of the German Revival*
(Yale UP, New Haven, 1955). (German version:
*Triebkräfte des deutschen Wiederaufstiegs* (Fritz
Knapp Verlag, Frankfurt a.M., 1955). All un-
dated references in the text are to this work
and the pages cited are to the edition in
English.)

——— 'The American Council of Economic Advisers and
the German *Sachverständigenrat*: A Study in the
Economics of Advice', *Quarterly Journal of
Economics*, *82* (3) (August 1968), pp.349-379

Watrin, C., 'The Principles of the Social Market
Economy: its Origins and Early History', *Zeitschrift für die gesamte Staatswissenschaft*, *135*
(3) (September 1979), pp.405-425

Westaway, A.J. and Weyman-Jones, T.G., *Macroeconomics*
(Longman, London and New York, 1977)

*Westdeutschlands Weg zur Bundesrepublik 1945-49*
(symposium) (Verlag C.H. Beck, München, 1976)

Winterhager, W.D. *et al.*, *Comparative Study of the
Financial, Legislative and Regulatory Structure
of Vocational Training Systems: Federal Republic
of Germany, France, Italy, United Kingdom*
(European Centre for the Development of
Vocational Training, Berlin, 1980)

*Wirtschaft und Statistik* (various) Statistisches
Bundesamt (Wiesbaden Verlag, W. Kohlhammer,
Stuttgart und Mainz)

WSI (Wirtschafts- und Sozialwissenschaftliches
Institut des Deutschen Gewerkschaftsbundes),
*Pressedienst* (various) (Düsseldorf)

Wunden, W., *Die Testilindustrie der Bundesrepublik Deutschland im Strukturwandel* (Kyklos-Verlag, Basel/J.C.B. Mohr (Paul Siebeck), Tübingen, 1969)

Zell, S.P., 'Analysing Puerto Rican Migration: Problems with the Data and the Model', *Monthly Labor Review*, *100* (8) (1977), pp.29-34